THE COMPANION GUIDE TO
Umbria

THE COMPANION GUIDES

GENERAL EDITOR: VINCENT CRONIN

*It is the aim of these Guides to provide a
Companion, in the person of the author,
who knows intimately the places and
people of whom he writes, and is able to
communicate this knowledge and affection
to his readers. It is hoped that the text
and pictures will aid them in their
preparations and in their travels and will
help them to remember on their return.*

THE GREEK ISLANDS

PARIS

THE SOUTH OF FRANCE

ROME

VENICE

LONDON

FLORENCE

JUGOSLAVIA

TUSCANY

THE WEST HIGHLANDS OF SCOTLAND

EAST ANGLIA

In preparation

SOUTHERN ITALY

TURKEY

GREECE

SOUTH-WESTERN FRANCE

SOUTHERN SPAIN

THE COMPANION GUIDE TO

UMBRIA

MAURICE ROWDON

Collins
ST JAMES'S PLACE, LONDON
1969

Maps by Charles Green
© *by Maurice Rowdon, 1969*
Printed in Great Britain
Collins Clear-Type Press
London and Glasgow

To my daughter

chiara di nome,
più chiara per vita,
chiarissima per virtù

Contents

Contents

Illustrations

MAPS AND PLANS

Introduction

Umbria has been called the heart of Italy: it has no sea-coast, nor does it lie on the border of a foreign country, which makes it unique among Italian provinces. It is enclosed on one side by the Tiber valley, on the other by steep hills along the western edge of the Marche: a spacious, sweet, slumbering, and above all intimate region where people take visitors seriously; very much its own world, comparable to nothing else in the peninsula; jealously loved by the inhabitants, even when they hate each other; a little continent of its own that arouses strange nostalgias, even apparently after a lifetime spent there.

It is very little known. Yet it has some of the brightest treasures in the Christian world. Its museums and picture galleries are carelessly guarded, and there are two or three thefts a year: but strict supervision would be against the province's character. Perhaps Umbria never will be known, however many people go there, because of the strange carelessness it likes to preserve, and its detached intimacy, with something mystical about it, a strong sense that *tutto passa*, everything fades away, even if it fades away into the hands of a robber—like the landscape itself that seems to dream and merge into low, smooth hills which quickly become bleak and savage as they get higher, a seal of melancholy on the sweetness below. In the summer the wide fields lie brown and parched, mists hide the distances; the whole of the valley of the Topino river below Assisi can be filled with brilliant white mist on a spring or autumn day, like a vast sea of foam stretching to the hills beyond the Tiber, westwards. And in the winter the air is crisp and light, relayed from the hills to the plains and back again according to the time of day.

The Umbrians were a great religious people in ancient times. The name Gubbio may come from the god Jove, who was always worshipped on a height. His name was invoked in the protection of the sacred woods of Spoleto. A mediaeval town actually called Giove lies on the southern tip of the province, and its name may have an ancient reason. The Flaminian Way that cut through Umbria and passed close to Gubbio may have been designed for pilgrims as well as armies: at least it may have grown out of the paths used by pilgrims since Etruscan times. The bronze tablets at Gubbio called the Eugubine Tables describing rites and prayers, written partly in Latin characters and partly in Etruscan, show that there was a common worship between all three peoples, the Etruscans, the Romans and the Umbrians. Spello was an important religious centre too, and the springs sacred to the god Clitumnus, on the way to Spoleto, belonged to Spello in Roman times.

Originally the Umbrians occupied a vast zone—they may have been part of one of the Indo-European shifts south that happened about a thousand years before Christ. At first their region stretched as far north as the mouth of the Po and included the whole breadth of the peninsula, all of what we call the Marche and Tuscany today. The Etruscans then pushed them across to the eastern side of the Tiber from the coast and brought Tuscany into being, absorbing Orvieto in the south and Perugia in the north. The Gauls then pushed the Etruscans inland, and Umbria came to be formed out of the central, rather mountainous region, leaving the sea-coast to the latest invaders. So Umbria is really a marriage between the Umbrians and the Etruscans, combining a certain light intimacy with something mystical and sad.

It was a marriage of necessity: the peoples had to combine against the Romans. Perugia on its fine strategic hill, commanding the southern approaches, put up the longest and fiercest defence. But in 295 B.C. the whole of central Italy became Roman, and slowly Umbria grew into one of Rome's most loyal provinces.

Every Umbrian town that we shall see had much the same history, beginning either with Umbrian or Etruscan settlement (according to its place on the map), then enjoying greater or lesser prominence under Roman rule (as a military camp like Todi, a stopping-place along the Flaminian Way like Carsulae, an agricultural market like Mevania, a religious centre like Gubbio, or a favoured imperial city like Spello), before it fell victim to barbarian invasions which swept all the temples and forums and country villas away during the bitterly slow fall of the Roman empire. The Goths, the Lombards, the

Introduction

Byzantines, the new imperial troops (partly composed of Saracen mercenaries), all had a share in the pillage between the first centuries of Christianity and the dawn of the independent townships or communes in the eleventh and twelfth centuries.

The province had great strategic importance for Rome, for its valleys led to the northern coasts of the Adriatic—and in early Christian times to Ravenna, where a Byzantine court administered Italy. So barbarian armies were drawn again and again to her hilltop towns: apart from Foligno and Bevagna and Terni almost none of the Umbrian towns lies in the plain, for sound strategical reasons (and sometimes because of malaria). But almost everywhere Christianity was helped by these barbarian attacks: Bishop Herculanus in Perugia led the defence of the city against the dreadful Totila in the sixth century, Bishop Fortunatus in Todi and Bishop John in Spoleto did much the same at other times. There again the Flaminian Way served a purpose, similar to what might have been its original one, as a path of pilgrimage: the first Christian settlements sprang up all along it. People began to cling to the new warm glow of the Christian story that seemed to summarize, in the Passion, all the suffering there had been since ancient times, and for the first time to give it form. It made it possible for Rome to renew her power, this time through the Church; the Christian empire shifted its seat from Byzantium to Rome, and the Frankish invasions under Charlemagne brought an end to barbarian rule by bringing down the Lombardian duchies; that was the beginning of the Holy Roman Empire. It made a period of reconstruction possible, and the independent communes which Frederick I encouraged began to flourish all over Umbria. But now that there was little danger of foreign invasion these towns started quarrelling among themselves, and the Church began to corrupt from inside.

It was this that made the impact of St Francis so great. He took the last traces of paganism out of the new empire, in a deliberate revival of the story of Christ through his own life. He was the real shift from Byzantium to Rome. His work was really to end a numbed state of mind based on the implacable fact of original sin, and on the hope of a Second Coming that would remove this implacable fact: in effect, the mind was still a slave, waiting; that is, it was still pagan. Above all, daily life had hardly changed since ancient times. The new Christian world wanted new habits and forms, and lacked them. *'Noi troppo odiammo e sofferimmo. Amate. Il mondo è bello e santo è*

13

Introduction

l'avvenir,' he said in his *Canticle of Love*—'We hate too much and suffer. Love. The world is good and the future sacred.' When he said 'hate' he meant civil war, because this was what governed Umbrian life virtually between the tenth and fourteenth centuries, long after he died. The Umbrians were a ferocious and bloodthirsty people: they produced the fiercest *condottieri* or mercenary knights—Fortebraccio, Piccinino, Brancaleone da Norcia. The old noble families, running feudal estates, were now challenged by the commercial middle class (St Francis was born into it) that began to rise in the eleventh century: that too was part of the hatred—a social one. And St Francis preached against feudalism.

But whatever the violence after his death, there was a quite new kind of Christianity. St Francis humanized the story of Christ again, he brought the New Testament to light as if it had never before really existed as a book to be read by simple people. The new attitude was called humanism and it was the seed of what came to be the Renascence in art: it said that all life was radiant—the human creature especially so—with the eternal elements which had brought it all into being and were filling it every moment. All over Umbria painters began to slip—always drowsily and often unwillingly—from the Byzantine style, and to come under the influence of Sienese and Florentine masters who were provoked to new work by St Francis's life. A distinct Umbrian painting slowly came into being, beginning with Oderisi (a friend of Giotto's) in Gubbio, through Palmerucci and Ottaviano Nelli to Nicolò Alunno and Mezzastris and Melanzio, until it reached a climax of individual feeling in Perugino and Pintoricchio at the end of the fifteenth century. That disturbing movement really began in Assisi, with the work of Cimabue and the Roman painters on the Basilica of St Francis; and it went on in Giotto, who told a story clearly and plainly, in direct human terms, so that poor people could understand it for the first time. That was how humanism connected with the Renascence, and why they were basically the same thing, and derived from St Francis.

Yet while all these painters were working, Umbrian towns were governed by one private family after another, much of the time tyrannically, or were fighting other towns, or were gripped by internal factions fighting each other. The greatest division of all, which cut through all politics and all religion and even family life, a ferment of evil that looked as if it would never end, was that between the Guelfs and the Ghibellines. They came in with the new Christian empire

14

and were really an aspect of it. They were a source of division by which the empire was administered safely from outside. Frederick I (called Barbarossa, perhaps because he had a red beard, perhaps because it seemed stained with blood) nearly always left his Italian enemies to divide among themselves and quarrel, once he had beaten them. And the Guelf-Ghibelline struggle was no more Italian than he was: it originated in Germany—from two factions called 'Waiblingen' and 'Welf'. In fact, Barbarossa (a very clever Bavarian) was elected emperor because he had good connections with both. In Italy the names lost their German meaning entirely and married Italian themes—the Guelfs were those who supported the pope, the Ghibellines supported the emperor. And between these two every town in the province was torn.

It was only after first the imperial administration, then the rule of the private families (the Oddi and Baglioni in Perugia, the Trinci in Foligno, the Vitelli in Città di Castello, the Montefeltri in Gubbio), began to collapse that the Church increased its authority over the separate Italian states and became the one arbiter and diplomat of them all. The fifteenth century in Italy was a time of visible civilization, when town life began to bustle with a new pride, as if French chivalry (basically an expression of the Christian concept of love) had been absorbed into civil life, again through its first Italian exponent, St Francis.

By the sixteenth century the Church had laid its drowsy but seldom ineffective hold on Umbrian life: it brought peace; it became the owner of fortresses. Pope Paul III built one fortress smack on top of a house belonging to the Baglioni family, whom he had just brought to their knees. Cardinal dell' Albornoz is a name we meet with all over Umbria for the frowning battlements he left behind. So the Church was the new tyrant, though its sternness was always mitigated by the poor man's story that lay underneath all its claims (often so deeply as to be hidden). And perhaps for that reason its administration was the most successful there had ever been: it was no less hated, but it survived. Not until Napoleon's troops came into the country were the friars and priests challenged. Napoleon ordered them out of their monasteries and brought in new laws, such as the one that forbade cemeteries within the confines of a town. He ended the tradition of hired murder that had prevailed everywhere since ancient times. The Church returned after he left but not as securely. The nineteenth century was a bad time for the Church in Italy;

papal troops were eventually driven out of all Umbrian towns—in Spoleto we see a reference on one of the city gates to the 'sad rule of the popes' that had been ended. Italy was unified into one country (1859-66).

Umbria then became a vast province together with the Sabine hills in the south. These, with their capital Rieti, now part of the Lazio, were separated in 1923 from Umbria. And Umbria was divided into two provinces (properly speaking we should call Umbria a region), one under Perugia and the other under Terni: and this is how it remains, administratively, today.

Only six per cent of Umbria is plain; over forty per cent is hilly, over half mountainous, which explains why the density of population is the lowest in central Italy, because of the poor opportunities for development and communications. And it explains the relative poverty. Umbria had little or no part in the industrial revolution that took place in the north of Italy after the last war; it remained as always detached and sadly traditional, with its rural basis undisturbed, and therefore staunchly communist. But Umbria's future development on industrial lines (communism is only an aspect of the yearning for this) may be surer for being slow.

It is quite a homogeneous region, much more so than Tuscany which is divided by one hill after another, with narrow plains and many small valleys (a geographical fact which made Siena and Florence different worlds). That same difference does not exist in Umbria. Terni (her most industrial town) in the extreme south, and Perugia, a university town in the extreme north, are distinctly and intimately Umbrian.

Umbria's form—long plains bordered by easy hills—and the fact that she has always been important strategically for Rome, and close to Rome and therefore so often its favourite, mean that she has some of the finest roads in the peninsula. The Flaminian Way is alive again in the form of the superstrada (a four-laned highway not under toll control) that joins Perugia to Terni (through Foligno and Spoleto), giving the driver easy access to the Autostrada del Sole to Rome. In two years or so Umbria's network of superstrade will be complete: the one from Perugia to Todi already runs half way; there is one joining Chiusi (the exit station on the Autostrada del Sole that serves Umbria) to Siena, and its completion as far as Perugia is planned. It will then be possible to drive from Siena or Florence straight through Umbria by superstrada alone.

A book of this size cannot hope to cover the whole of crowded Umbria. I have omitted as little as possible, but the towns of Cascia and Norcia, in the hills behind Spoleto, and Gualdo Tadino and Nocera Umbra, in the hills behind Assisi, have had to go, together with Cannara, Bettona, Deruta (the home of Italy's ceramic industry) and Umbértide. Each of these places, with the exception of Umbértide, is worth a short visit, and the hill-towns make an excellent day trip (special trains leave from Spoleto for Cascia and Norcia) : and in both there is in fact much to see. Urbinum Hortense, near Cannara, is a wonderful ancient Roman site for its position, but with little by way of ruins to see. Norcia is the birthplace of St Benedict, who saved Christianity by founding the first monastic order just as, centuries later, another Umbrian saved the Church by founding his.

Transport is slow in Umbria—inevitably, with so many small towns to serve, some of them locked deep in the hills. Timetables are available at the tourist offices (see maps and Appendix 2), but since these change we should always take the trouble to ask as well. The tourist office should be our first port of call on arrival at any town. They will be able to tell us (in our own language if necessary) not only the times of trains and buses, and the likely connections, but where to eat and what local events are afoot, as well as providing detailed information on hotels. They will make appointments for us (to see a special museum collection, or even to hire—as we can in Assisi—a group of minstrels) : they will arrange for seats at festivals and concerts, and tell us about any special tourist buses we may need to spots in mid-country, such as the delightful Fonti di Clitunno or the waterfalls near Terni. The tourist office on the main square of Assisi is a mine of help and advice for the whole province. Without the friendship of Mr Carlo Ronci and his assistants there I could not have written this book. But then, Umbria is an experience that begins and ends with its people, as we soon find out.

CHAPTER 1

Perugia I

Perugia, though the capital of the province and its largest city, is crammed together on the top of a steep hill, just as if history had made a plan for it not to spread beyond its powers. And this has, in fact, been its history: the commercial possibilities of the town have been much greater than its achievements, so that its prosperity now is not of the unstable kind, here today and gone tomorrow; it has industries, but not a great many more than before the war, when its famous Perugina chocolate factory started; the city's leading commercial family today owns not only this but the Buitoni interests (spaghetti and cereals of all kinds) and the fashion store that has its best-known branch in Florence, Luisa Spagnoli.

What factories there are lie necessarily below the town: and the intimacy of the Perugian streets, together with a certain sweet, easy-going and voluptuously hedonist element in the Perugian character (they call it degeneracy themselves), remains. The original walls hold the same city in their crumbling grasp, almost. And we see the city nearly from above if we approach it from the Autostrada del Sole—a great splash of red across the top of a hill, not attractive at all, rather bleak in its suggestion of a Victorian biscuit factory, and giving no sign of its treasures. The red is from the local stone.

Until Perugia solves her grotesque traffic problems (cars may even cross the pavement of the main street at one point) the best way to visit the town is from somewhere else—Assisi or the lake district. The fine hotels of Perugia—wherever they are—are inevitably close to the grinding of uphill traffic along cavernous lanes. If we come by car we should leave it at the large car park below the main town just short of the Stazione S. Anna. Coming in from Florence on one side or from Assisi on the other we shall reach this park by the same road, as it runs along the southern edge of the city. Walking into the town

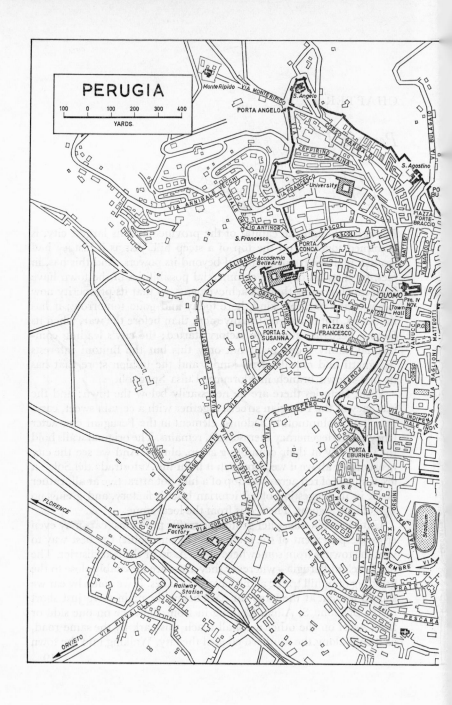

PERUGIA

100   0   100   200   300   400
YARDS.

Enlargement of City centre

from this park we take the Via Marconi, turn left at the Corso Cavour and take the staircase lane which will lead us to the Via Oberdan and Piazza Matteotti: just before the end of the traffic-less Via Oberdan we should notice the Ristorante del Sole on the right where we can eat well, either sitting inside by a Roman wall, under low Gothic vaults, or on the terrace with a view across to Assisi.

The itineraries I give here are of course made nervous by the traffic, as the streets besides being narrow are mostly without pavements. Those on holiday to escape traffic will choose the most important things to see (they are indicated in bold type) and go straight there, without following the routes religiously. The town promises traffic reform soon. One day is too little for even a quick look at Perugia; two are a minimum and three adequate. If time is very short there are three places of major interest which we shall not want to miss: the National Gallery of Umbria, with twenty or so rooms which offer virtually a history of Umbrian painting from the fourteenth century on, and the Collegio del Cambio where Perugino painted the walls; both are close to the main square (Piazza IV Novembre) down the Corso Vannucci. The third must is the Arch-aeological Museum of Umbria with its Etruscan and Roman exhibits, in the tiny Piazza Giordano Bruno, off the Corso Cavour, on the south-western edge of the city. We should remember, by the way, that all national museums and galleries in Italy are closed on Monday.

Perugia began as an Umbrian town and became Etruscan at a rather late date. Of the bronze pieces found on the outskirts few are earlier than the fourth century B.C. Its first strong walls were put there at that time and it was an important *lucumonia*, that is, the seat of the supreme magistrature of a tribe (the word is Etruscan in origin). There were many gates, with roads leading to other important centres like Cortona and Arezzo. At first Perugia was the centre of fierce resistance to Rome—the Umbrians and Etruscans found a common enemy here: its hill, commanding approaches from both the south and the west, made it a hard nut for the Romans to crack. But this happened: in 295 B.C. the whole of central Italy succumbed to Roman rule and from that time on Perugia was one of Rome's most loyal allies. This wasn't all plain sailing: after Caesar's murder, during the civil war between Mark Antony and Octavian, the latter's troops besieged it and then prepared to sack it; one of the citizens, Cetius Macedonicus, was so outraged that he roused every-one to revolt and set fire to Octavian's house and destroyed half the city with it, rather than give in. Perugia always had this tremendous ferocity of spirit, until it settled down under the Church. When Octavian became the Emperor Augustus times were better, and the city received the name *Augusta Perusia* which we shall see on some of the city gates. Little is heard of it in the time of the empire —a good sign, meaning serenity. We do know that the Emperor V. Tibius Trebonianus Gallus (A.D. 251-3) referred to Perugia as a *ius coloniae*, and after this the city took the official name of *Colonia Vibia Augusta Perusia*, sharing full rights with Rome in its status as a colony. This has made some people wonder why there are so few Roman monuments in the city: until now no amphitheatre or even theatre has been found. But if the Etruscan civilization remained intact there, which it probably did due to the superb hilltop position, later Roman building was probably unnecessary, and the original Etruscan town continued to serve its inhabitants longer than in most other places. There is a second reason in that to stay perched on its good defensive hill the city always had to use old buildings as the foundations of new, so that only a few arches and town gates and stretches of wall remain from ancient times.

Perugia suffered like all other towns in Umbria from the various barbarian invasions, and Totila destroyed it in 547 or thereabouts, after a siege of seven years and some very bitter fighting. It was one of Umbria's first bishops, Herculanus, who stirred the people to this resistance: he became Perugia's patron saint (Bonfigli has painted the story—see Room 22 at the National Gallery of Umbria). The struggles between the Goths and the Byzantines, of which Totila's siege of the city was part, brought great trouble to the whole province (the Byzantine general Narses finally killed Totila in the hills behind Assisi): the Christian empire was administered—from Italy's point of view—from Ravenna, where there was a court, and Belisarius, the first of Justinian's generals to tackle the Goths, operated mainly from there, the northern terminus of the Flaminian Way. The fact that the Flaminian Way went smack through Umbria, and had some of its best strategic positions there, inevitably brought continual alarms and outrages. A period of peace and heavy taxation followed the defeat of the Gothic armies (553), with some very necessary reconstruction. But then more barbarians flowed down, this time the Lombards, who made the Goths look like gentlemen. In 592 Perugia became part of the Lombardian duchy established at Spoleto, for— unlike the Goths—the Lombards were slowly absorbed by the Italians

23

and became a definite influence on civil life, as the number of Christian conversions among them grew from the year 600 onwards. They divided Italy into two duchies: Spoleto, and Benevento in the south.

Gradually the emphasis of government began to shift from Constantinople and Ravenna to Rome, in the person of the pope: he was the one element of possible agreement between enemies. He even allied himself with the Lombardian duke of Spoleto against Ravenna, so confused was the situation. And Perugia still had not lost her sense of independence or her natural sympathy with Rome: in 726 she also supported the pope against Ravenna, over some new rule forbidding images in churches. When, eighteen years later, the Lombards laid siege to her in a local struggle the pope, in return for her good services, implored them not to sack the city (the Lombard king is said to have become a monk as a result, and to have retired to Cassino). During the Frankish invasions, which were Italy's liberation from the Lombards, Perugia was kept as a possession of the pope's, by way of a gift from the Frankish king, Charlemagne. And of course the founding of the idea of a new western—this time Christian—empire based once more on Rome (such was the continuity of the tolerant Roman genius) could only bring stability: by a neat trick the pope made Charlemagne the first emperor, and tradition says that Charlemagne didn't like it at all. It was this new stability—the Gothic, Lombard, Byzantine and Frankish, not to say Saracen, invasions now over—that made it possible for the towns of Umbria to develop again, this time in the form of independent and self-protecting communities or *comuni*. Partly that was necessity too, after so many centuries of uncertain life. And Perugia gradually became the most important town in the province.

In the Middle Ages the city was nearly always in the hands of the Guelfs: that would be natural after her long association with Rome. She accepted, if not always the dominion of the pope (he often fled there when things got too hot in Rome), at least his protection. No fewer than five conclaves were held in the duomo. And the fact that Perugia was predominantly Guelf, coupled with her fierce expansionism, meant that neighbouring towns like Assisi were Ghibelline by reaction. The Guelf and Ghibelline division went so deep that it embraced every habit—clothes, architecture, forms of address; the Guelfs designed their battlements with square crenellations, the Ghibellines with the pointed swallow's tail. The loyalties became quite lost in venomous hatred and far surpassed politics let alone religion, just as if the Umbrian people had a dreadful historical destiny towards violence—a need for it even, at least in her noble and powerful classes. Pope Martin IV (1261-5) excommunicated Perugia for her cruel devastation of Foligno: for the next two or three centuries the city was continually at war with her neighbours, as if security from foreign invasion had left a gap in bloody acts which had to be filled. Assisi, Siena, Arezzo, Città di Castello, Gubbio, Foligno, Spoleto—all struggled with her. And Perugia always imposed severe penalties on the defeated: Foligno must not rebuild her defensive wall, Arezzo had to provide marble to decorate Perugia's duomo, Città della Pieve must send material to pave her streets.

And then—it was bound to happen—war broke out between Perugia and the pope (1369), and ended in the city's defeat. The pope was determined to bring her to heel this time and a papal legate was installed in Perugia (1370) to govern it directly. There was a rising against this: the tyrannical French abbot of Monmaggiore was removed and his fortress at one of the city gates destroyed (1375), but the days of Perugian democracy were over. This time the Perugians turned against one another. Even among themselves they were ferocious and bloodthirsty, with a vicious habit of stone-fighting when there were no other weapons about. This was what limited the city's power in the end, and burned out her energies—a ferocity so passionate that it was suicidal.

The suicide was realized in the mad hatred between private families in their struggles for the virtual dictatorship of the city during the epoch of the signoria, or personal lordship. There were wild street-fights, sudden murders, though naturally the alarms were not continual: we are talking of more than a century in time. The signoria of Biondo Michelotti brought peace for a little while, but he was murdered in 1389 and authority went to the Visconti family, then was wrested from them and returned to the pope. Ladislao of Naples took over between 1408 and 1414, and again under Braccio di Fortebraccio da Montone (though he himself was no less expansionist and bloodthirsty than the others) there was a period of government with justice—though only eight years of it, until 1424. Then there was a climax of hatred between the Oddi and Baglioni families which went on for generations: their names are still famous in Perugia today for the arts of bloody vendetta. When finally the

Oddi family was more or less wiped out, the Baglioni turned on one another.

The brothers Guido and Rodolfo Baglioni chased the Oddi family out of the city in 1488. A few years later groups of Oddi outlaws tried to re-enter but were massacred. Then there was a terrible mutiny on July 14th, 1500, when in a fit of barbarous indignation the Baglioni brothers were cut down in the streets together with most of their family. From this time on their authority decreased, and the hold of the Church grew: when another Baglioni murdered the papal legate in 1535 Paul III began to take over the city; three years later he imposed a salt tax and the people rebelled against it ('the war of the salt') but he broke them a second time. He took the city by force and built the famous Rocca Paolina or Pauline Fortress on the ruins of the Baglioni houses: we can see it today—and the houses underneath.

After that Perugia lay under the sleepy hand of the Church—for two centuries, until she was occupied by French troops in 1798: but the Napoleonic dominion was brief, and the city returned—less happily and less sleepily now—to the Church. When the 1848 republic was briefly declared in Rome the Perugians seized their chance and tore down the hated Pauline Rock, or part of it; but it was rebuilt almost at once. Eleven years later another chance came and the papal legate was chased out of town: this time the pope sent up two thousand Swiss troops and they committed a terrific carnage (still almost personally remembered today) on June 20th, 1859. But in the following year the Perugians reversed this when the *bersaglieri*, the picked troops of the new national movement, entered the city, and the Pauline Rock was demolished once and for all.

Fontana Maggiore—The Duomo—National Gallery of Umbria—Sala del Collegio della Mercanzia—Collegio del Cambio

The natural centre of the town, to which all roads will take us, is its highest point, with the duomo above and the side of the Palazzo dei Priori below, and a fountain which will immediately take our attention in the middle—or rather to one side of the middle. This square is the Piazza IV Novembre (November 4th was the date of Italy's armistice with the Austrians in 1918). And it seems right to take the fountain as our introduction to the city because of its grace, craftsmanship and intimacy, its air of having seen many baking suns and bloody arguments, and its seeming to fit the square better than anything else in it, for this is an awkward square, unequally shaped and sloping, not at all serene. But the **Fontana Maggiore** is serene: it is in two tiers—round, elegant and undemonstrative, with four steps leading up to it all round; the first tier has twining pillars of marble with bas-relief panels between them, and the higher tier has panels of high-relief figures against a background of pink marble. It is all surmounted by a basin and three nymphs in bronze. The whole thing was designed by Fra' Bevignate (1257-77), a citizen of Perugia, while the sculptured figures are by the Pisano brothers, Nicola and Giovanni, perhaps helped by Arnolfo di Cambio. There was an earthquake in 1348 and the fountain had to be rebuilt: and of course time and troubles have altered it. A chalky deposit slowly formed on its marble. There was an accurate restoration in 1948 which did away with certain additions made in earlier restorations—among them little columns and also a bronze group of griffins and lions (the griffin was always Perugia's symbol) that had been put there in the fourteenth century—above the three nymphs, of all places. Thus what we see is nearer the original than anything since the day it was unveiled.

The lower basin has twenty-four compartments divided by pillars in sets of three, and each compartment is divided into two panels with bas-relief pictures in each. Therefore we have forty-eight pictures in all. If we walk round the fountain until we reach the panel of *two eagles* (almost facing the duomo) we shall be able to follow the series from the beginning: *Adam and Eve, the Expulsion from Paradise, two stories of Samson*; two panels showing the *allegory of the lion and the little dog*; two *stories of David*, followed by *Romulus and Remus*; then *the wolf that gave milk to the twins*; the *vestal virgin* with a cage in her hand (perhaps the symbol of virginity); two Aesop fables (*the crane and the wolf, the wolf and the lamb*); followed by twenty-four panels showing *the months of the year*, with the agricultural work proper to each—the grape harvest, sowing of crops, tilling, hunting and so on, after which there are panels of *the Guelf lion and the Perugian griffin* (now we see why bronze lions and griffins were once put at the crown of the fountain), with seven panels of the liberal arts—*Grammar, Dialectic, Rhetoric, Arithmetic, Geometry, Music, Astronomy*, followed by a panel depicting *Philosophy*.

The upper basin rests on little columns that are actually placed

27

into the lower basin, if we look carefully: it has an inscription describing the 1322 restoration, in Gothic characters. Here there are twenty-four statues, with pink marble panels separating them. We begin with *Salome,* who faces the entrance of the duomo: we recognize her by the head she carries. Then there is *Moses,* followed by *Matteo da Correggio* (the podestà or ruler of that time), the *Archangel Michael, Euliste,* who was the mythical founder of Perugia, *Melchisedec, Ermanno da Sassoferrato* (a Captain of the People), *Victory, St Peter* with his key, a figure of the *Roman Church, Rome* (a 1949 copy), *Theology, the cleric of St Laurence* (bishop of Spoleto), *St Laurence* himself, the *nymph* of the land round Chiusi (on the edge of Umbria), *Perugia, the nymph of Lake Trasimene, St Herculanus* (bishop of Perugia), *the priestly traitor, St Benedict* and *St Maurus, St John the Baptist, Solomon, David.* The bronze group of three nymphs crowning the fountain is also by Giovanni Pisano, and was cast in 1277. The nymphs carry an amphora from which water can flow.

To see the **Duomo** to its best advantage we should walk across the square and climb the outer staircase of the Palazzo dei Priori: this will take us away from the traffic, too. We are looking at the cathedral's dark, sprawling, gloomy side, not the front, and the tall arches we see on the left of its wide steps are the **Loggia di Braccio Fortebraccio,** of later date than the church and built at the express order of Fortebraccio himself in 1423. He was the signore of Perugia at that time, and the Loggia formed part of his house (destroyed in the sixteenth century). A long stone bench under it usually supports old men spitting and gossiping, with pigeon-droppings all round them. There are four arches mounted on stout octagonal pillars (restored in 1928). When we walk across the square again we should remember to look at the so-called *stone of justice* attached to the wall under these arches: it was put there in 1233 to commemorate the extinction of Perugia's public debt. And we should peep up at the arches while standing directly under them: we shall see that they have an emphatic outward lean.

The duomo is called S. Lorenzo and is an untidy Gothic construction: the wall we are looking at is unfinished, its brickwork gaping. The church was planned in 1300 and started fifteen years later, and the last touches were put about a century afterwards. There is marble facing only on the lower part, a chequered design of pink and white. The bronze *seated statue* at the top of the steps on a pedestal is Pope Julius III, who restored to Perugia the magistrature

28

which Paul III (builder of the hated Rock) had taken away from her: it is a sixteenth-century piece, the work of Vincenzo Danti.

The church itself will offer us little else than craftsmanship of this kind; Perugia suffered greatly from the baroque period—she was rich enough to dismantle her churches and replace early works of devotion with works of craft, and the vast bronze statue we see here is one of them. The doorway too is baroque: imposing and grave, the work of Galeazzo Alessi (1568), with two heads providing bas-relief capitals for the inset pillars on either side. Above the door, behind glass, in a little compartment which is lit up at night, we see a crucifix put there in 1539 to commemorate 'the war of the salt' which was such a triumph for the Church: the story goes that a soldier shot his cannon into the wall by mistake and was so sorry about it that he had this crucifix installed in the hole. On the right of the doorway we see *a pulpit* built in 1425 in homage to St Bernardine of Siena, who preached from it: it is made of older fragments —shining, delicate, golden mosaics. St Bernardine, a Franciscan, travelled everywhere to preach peace: from these steps he watched citizens burn their books and finery at his request. Farther along the wall there are two niches set one above the other: the upper one was an addition of 1467 and is empty, while the lower one was filled with its present *Madonna and Child* in 1954. If we walk round the right-hand corner of the church we shall see its actual façade in the adjacent Piazza Danti, with an ugly and massive door from the baroque period which is rightly not used as the usual entrance.

Inside the duomo we find a tall, airy church of three naves divided by stupendous octagonal pillars which make a doubly ugly effect because they are painted to imitate marble. They have gilt capitals high above from which radiate the crossing arms of the vaults. The whole thing is designed to look as big as possible, which is the smallest intention an artist can have. The ceiling has been frescoed in slight colours, making a not unpleasant overall effect so long as we don't look too hard. This church lacks intimacy: but its airiness gives a little repose. Above the main entrance there is a fantastically ornate gilt frame round a *Madonna and Child with SS. Laurence, Constantius and Herculanus* (the patron saints of Perugia) by Luigi Scaramucci (1650), which is for devotees of the baroque only. To the right of this doorway there is—again for devotees—the tomb of Bishop Giovanni Andrea of the famous and terrible Baglioni family, who died in 1451. Going down the church from the back we find on the first pillar on the left a fresco of the local fifteenth-century school, showing St Bernadine of Feltre, which is now almost entirely faded. At the third column down on the right the fresco of the *Madonna delle Grazie* (the Madonna of the Graces) has been framed and turned into an altar where communion is regularly given: the candles usually burning there make it the heart of the church, and it is the most serious work in the place, though a little insipid— by Giannicola di Paolo (1460-1544). This artist was born, like Perugino, in Città della Pieve (see p. 242).

Beginning our tour of the church in the left nave, we find at the very back of the church the **Cappella del S. Anello** (Holy Ring), where the legendary nuptial ring of the Madonna is kept: it was stolen by the friar Winter di Magonza from a church in Chiusi in 1473 and brought here. The loot is kept above the altar inside an elaborate curtained tabernacle of beaten copper, gilded and silvered and embossed by local artists at the end of the fifteenth century. A picture by Perugino used to be at this altar but it was taken by Napoleonic troops to the cathedral of Caen. In this chapel there are splendidly carved wooden seats with inlaid backs rising to a vast bas-relief cornice of wood that holds a gallery above— the work of a local artist who took nine years to do it; the gallery itself is the work of Ercole di Tomaso del Riccio (1565). We should peep at the first chapel down this nave for its *Mary imploring Jesus to halt the plague*, which has a hint of reality and is not grandiose.

In the right nave, again at the back of the church, we find a chapel that matches that of the Holy Ring opposite: this one is the **Chapel of St Bernardine** and has a wrought-iron gate from the fifteenth century. The carved wooden seats along the wall are interesting, with a careful design of leaves and rams' heads above, and putti and bas-relief panels of the most painstaking thoroughness, the work again of Ercole di Tomaso del Riccio, together with his brother Iacopo (1567). The windows too are pleasant, showing *a sermon by St Bernardine*. There is a massive altar of shining pillars crowned with gilt. The next chapel down is the **Cappella del Battistero** (Baptistery), which we must enter with our courage in our hands because of an appalling fresco from 1876 and a vulgar and heavy seventeenth-century crucifix on the left, in order to see another work of excellent craftsmanship by Pietro Paolo di Andrea (1477), this time in stone, a square façade with a delicate floral bas-relief design. The next chapel down we shall like better if we just hurry past.

At the main altar we should have a close look at the wooden choir round the apse for its pleasant inlaid wood and its bold carving in two tiers, a fifteenth-century work and therefore earlier than the other woodwork of the church. Before leaving the chancel we should glance up at the superb vivid windows behind the altar: we are likely to think them the most ancient in the church but in fact they are the work of two sisters (Moretti-Caselli) alive today in Perugia. Their father did the stained-glass rose window over the main door but this is less harmonious and in the grandiose style.

The cathedral museum (***Museo dell' opera del duomo***) holds the real treasures of the church. We reach it through the right arm of the transept, where we find a door leading to the sacristy: the museum attendant is often to be found here. For the price of a ticket (L.100) he will lead us first to the cloister of the presbytery (*chiostro della canonica*), where conclaves were held for the election of five popes—Honorius III (1216), Clement IV (1265), Honorius IV (1285), Celestine V (1294) and Clement V (1305). Only the four-teenth-century well in the middle with its pink marble panels between little pillars, a delicate reminder of the Fontana Maggiore outside, remains from the time of the conclaves. Otherwise it has all been redesigned in the Renascence style. Under the arches we see fragments of wall from the earlier cloisters, and capitals and bas-reliefs.

The museum is on the left side of this cloister as we enter it from the church. Following the exhibits anti-clockwise, we find (1) above the door itself a picture only interesting because it is done on hide, of *St Laurence*. Richer things await us. The big fresco by the door (2) is a *Madonna and Child with saints*, a graceful work of civilization by the school of Perugino: in the Madonna's tender, dreaming expression and the youth watching her with the delicacy of a girl you have all Perugino's happiness, as we shall see it later in other places. At its side (4) there is a *Pietà* which is simple and stiff—its stiffness an effect of devotion—by Bartolomeo Caporali (1486). There is then (5) a *Madonna enthroned between SS. John the Baptist, Onuphrius and Laurence, with a bishop*, which is said to be Luca Signorelli's first great work (1484): here we see the Italian obsession with striking a figure suggested for the first time, so that real feeling is crushed in a superb design, painted with a dazzling professional eye

31

for composition. The faces bear the first hint of that defensive, provincial haughtiness that had its climax in fascism: yet it was painted only two years before the picture at its side, the *Pietà*; they are different worlds.

Farther along we find a triptych (7), *Madonna and Child between St John the Baptist and St John the Evangelist*, a warm, pleasing, sincere work that doesn't attempt much depth by Meo da Siena (1345-70). The *Madonna and Child* below (8) is a fourteenth-century fragment in the Umbrian-Sienese style. Above it another *Madonna and Child* (9) of the fourteenth century is by Andrea Vanni: a sombrely rich piece, gilded and ornate. The small framed pictures we see above (including also 12 and 15) show *St Peter, St Paul* and *the martyrdom of St Laurence* all by Giannicola di Paolo (1460-1544). *The death of the Virgin* (11) is a mute, unruffled, closely designed work that shows the heavy and warm presence of the Byzantine tradition, by an Umbrian artist (1432). *The Madonna enthroned between SS. Nicholas of Bari and Laurence* (13) by Pompeo Cocchi retains a certain richness and feeling—from the twilight of the Renascence. In the corner (14) there is a tabernacle with a *Madonna and Child* in bas-relief stucco, with *St Laurence and St Jerome* in the leaves of the cupboard. This is dated 1480 and is by a pupil of Pintoricchio called Nicolò del Priore. The next triptych (16) is a soft and strangely dreamlike *Madonna and Child with saints*, attributed to Starnina of Florence, who died in 1409 or 1413: the colours have an enchantment as if they came into being only for this picture and had never existed before. The canvas (18) by Ludovico di Angelo (1484), *Christ between SS. Anthony the Abbot, Martha, Jerome and Francis*, is a rustic high Renascence piece. The wooden processional tablet (19) at its side, in bas-relief, shows *Christ and the Virgin enthroned*: one can pull it out and see the other side, a water-paint *Redeemer* from the fifteenth century. A summery, russet, fading *Madonna and Child* (21) is by the Lo Spagna school (1515).

In the exact centre of the room there are *manuscripts* under glass, one of them (1) a fragment of the scripture according to St Luke from the sixth century. At the end of this centre case, farthest from the door, there is an illuminated copy of the Apostles (2) which is open at the beginning of St Mark (we see the words above a rough picture, '*Marcus leonus gerit figurus*—this lion represents St Mark'), from the eighth century. Then there is (3) a Genesis of the ninth century with a more elaborate painting. We see also a small

Startled pigeons and a helicopter above the Piazza IV Novembre,
Perugia. Julius III shelters under the Loggia of Braccio Fortebraccio
against the unfinished side-wall of the duomo.

Above left: Detail of the Fontana
Maggiore in the Piazza IV Novembre.
Above right: The Volte della Pace, or
'vaults of peace', so called because
peace was discussed here with enemy
factions and neighbouring towns.
Right: The Palazzo del Capitano
del Popolo, built by Lombard
masons (1472–81). In the lunette a
statue of Justice, flanked by
Perugia's griffins. The balcony was
used by the town crier and has iron
clasps for torches.

breviary from the twelfth century (4), and two missals (5 and 6) of
perhaps the same period, where a growing sense of form is apparent:
they are like a miniature history of the first painting in our modern
world, the Madonna's head inclined in the Byzantine manner but
with something more casual and natural about it, like a hint of the
Sienese school; we know the date of these missals because of the
lack of St Francis's Mass in them, which puts them most probably
before the end of the twelfth century. On the other side of the
case there are antiphonaries (books of psalm-verses sung in the form
of responses by alternating choirs) from the thirteenth and fourteenth centuries (15, 16, 17). These are large enough to be seen by
singers in a group, reading from the one copy. There are richly
painted chapter deeds from the seventeenth century (18). In closed
cupboards there are the *Codes of Justinian* from the eleventh century:
if we are studious the attendant will show them to us. In another
cupboard—the same applies here—there are *Lives of the Saints* from
the eleventh and twelfth centuries.

In a second room across the corridor we find various exhibits of
less interest. In a cupboard by the window in the right-hand corner
we shall find a bishop's stool from the twelfth or thirteenth century
which bears no mark of time: the wood can only be found in
southern India and is called 'wood of iron' by the French. At its
side there is a missal case of wood covered with silver, from the
twelfth century, and there are chalices, tabernacles, vestments of
various epochs.

If when we leave the museum we go to the far left of the cloister
we shall find a long slope leading to the second cloister of the presbytery, which is in a state of abandonment: the fifteenth-century
porches round it are now incorporated into houses. This takes us
into the Piazza Cavallotti, and we should trace our way back to the
central square, as there is no more to examine there. This will mean
going up the Via delle Volte (or 'Street of the Vaults'), which passes
under vast, smoke-blackened arches. These belong to the original
Palazzo del Podestà, which we should nowadays call the town hall.
It was burned down in 1543, and the smoke has penetrated the stone
permanently: the little area is forbidding, as if too much power
had been wielded (and challenged) there. The road we walk on was
cut through the burned ruins of the palace, to join the lower part of
the town to the cathedral square. The little church we see on our
right just before we turn into the square is the Maestà delle Volte,

C.G.U —C

33

which has a sixteenth-century front. This is now closed (its name is derived from a fresco once inside). At its side, under an arch of the old palace, we shall see a small doorway now standing in the open, a mere frame of red and white stone serving no purpose, with leafy capitals set into its pillars and an iron grille across its arch. This once formed part of the church. If we enter this yawning doorway we shall see a house made out of a tower, supported by three massive arches flung over to the next building, dating from the thirteenth or fourteenth centuries when the original palace was still there. Other houses of mediaeval origin surround the little courtyard.

Again in the central piazza, with our backs to the Loggia and the duomo, we have a good command of the *Palazzo dei Priori* (otherwise known as the town hall or Palazzo Comunale), a powerful, harmonious, forbidding building like most of those which bear the same name in Umbria, places where violence has been hatched. But this is one of the most superb examples, with its semi-circular outer staircase that narrows to a balcony with a great door behind it. The palace was started in 1293, and the part we are facing now is the earliest wing. If we look along the main side of the building—that is, along the busy Corso Vannucci—and count ten windows down from the corner we shall see that the wall curves slightly, where a further wing was added.

The balcony leads to a higher terrace suspended on three tall arches of red and white stone: before 1328 a church stood here, and the pulpit we now see jutting between the first and second arches belonged to it. In that year the palace was enlarged to absorb the church, while a century later, between 1429 and 1443, it was extended down the Corso Vannucci, beyond the curve. The building didn't get its crenellation (Guelf, of course) until it was under papal rule, nor its present windows in sets of three. It was restored in the nineteenth century. The materials that went into building it are part travertine, part limestone and part the red and white stone of nearby Bettona.

The arched doorway at the top of the staircase leads to the *Sala dei Notari* (Hall of the Notaries). Above the door there are two stone sills, from which usually hang chains and a long bar with the padlocks and keys of the gates of Siena, to commemorate Perugia's victory over that city at Torrita in 1358. There were also until recently a bronze griffin and a lion, cast in the thirteenth century: the chain and bar and animals are all at present under restoration.

If this entrance to the Sala is closed we shall find another door inside the Palazzo (Corso Vannucci entrance), on the first floor. At one time the Sala dei Notari was the Grand Council Chamber: it has a series of eight wide and sweeping Romanesque arches which support a roof of wooden beams with painted compartments: and most of the wall space is covered with designs and frescoes. The frescoes were begun in 1297 and are attributed to the Roman master Cavallini, who also worked in the Upper Church of St Francis in Assisi, as we shall see: at least, his pupils certainly worked here. The frescoes deal with lay subjects—legends and fables—alternating with stories from the Old and New Testaments. The arms seen everywhere are those of the various Captains of the People and the Podestà up to the year 1499. Braccio Fortebraccio's arms can be seen crowning all the others arrogantly on the end-wall at the top. The wooden seats that skirt the walls are from the sixteenth century. It was in 1582 that the hall came to be the meeting-place of the town's notaries, whom we would now call solicitors.

Those who wish to visit the Biblioteca Augusta on the second floor with its manuscripts and books (about two hundred thousand of them) should note that it is closed annually between October 3rd and 15th.

We should now walk down the **Corso Vannucci,** Perugia's best-loved walking place where friends go arm in arm in the evening and tiny transactions—the yeast of Italian economic life—are made in the morning. This really quite short stretch of road has many secrets, among them Sandri's coffee-bar, almost opposite the entrance of the town hall (National Gallery of Umbria, Sala dei Notari, etc.): savoury snacks can be had there, and fresh cakes arrive about eleven on most mornings. The best coffee in town can be had farther along in the Piazza della Repubblica (no more than a widening of the Corso) at the Medio Evo café, on the left as we walk from the duomo.

The name of the Corso is taken from that of Pietro Vannucci, whom we know better as the painter Perugino (that is, 'of Perugia'). We shall notice as we walk along how its pavements are polished bright by the loitering of thousands upon thousands of feet through the centuries.

The entrance to the Palazzo dei Priori a few yards down is un-mistakable because of its splendour. The arched stone frame is minutely and extravagantly carved with twirling pillars and designs of leaves and tiny panels with allegorical figures, the work of artists

35

from northern Italy. In the lunette of the arch we see statues of Perugia's three patron saints, though people disagree not only about who these carved saints are, but who the patron saints are. While there are three principal patron saints (Laurence, Constantius and Herculanus), the three over the door are Laurence, Louis of Toulouse (whose brother, king of Naples, beat the Ghibellines at Genoa) and Herculanus, though some put Constantius instead of Laurence.

If we look up we shall see that the first storey has eighteen triple windows side by side, and the second storey one more.

This is the entrance to the **National Gallery of Umbria,** where we shall see the province's finest collection of paintings. We enter a tall stone foyer of Gothic vaults and arches, with an immense fifteenth-century chest facing us. On our left we see the arms (a ram rampant) of Braccio Fortebraccio. A staircase on the right takes us up to the gallery, or a lift if an attendant is there. In summer the hours are 9.0 a.m.-1.0 p.m. and 3.0-5.30 p.m. Winter times differ in the afternoon only—2.0-4.0 p.m. On holidays and Sundays the Gallery is open only in the morning and entrance is free. A catalogue in English can be had at the entrance upstairs for L.500.

The entrance room, still called the Sala del Consiglio Generale or General Council Chamber, contains frescoes taken from various churches, and the work of Umbrian artists painting in the Sienese style from the thirteenth and fourteenth centuries. We should remember here that the Byzantine tradition of painting lingered much longer in Umbria than in Tuscany, was clung to with love, perhaps because of the province's detachment and long mystical history, which made the first warm faith of Christianity valid long after it had been disturbed elsewhere. The influence of the Sienese schools, more open and casual, sweet and personally intimate, was slow: but it made a good marriage in what the textbooks call the Umbro-Sienese school—not fine, but sincere and truthful.

The oldest work in the gallery is the wooden *crucifix* in this room (with lowered arms), numbered 925 in the catalogue. There is a Latin inscription underneath which mentions the date 1236. This crucifix came from Roncione di Deruta, east of Assisi. There is a pleasant and mellow *martyrdom of St Julian* by the door (48), some say by Andrea da Firenze from the end of the thirteenth century. *The dormition of the Virgin* (1001) has clear and sombre tones, the work of a local fourteenth-century artist. There is a warm, stirring

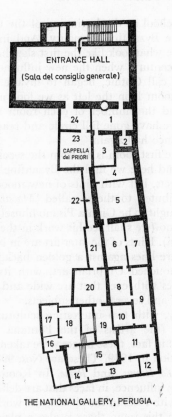

ENTRANCE HALL
(Sala del consiglio generale)

24 | 1

23

2

CAPPELLA
dei PRIORI

3

4

22

5

21 | 6 | 7

20 | 8

9

10

17 | 18 | 19

16

11

15

12

14 | 13

THE NATIONAL GALLERY, PERUGIA.

Assumption by a follower of Fra' Angelico (56), a marvellous dream with two figures sitting on the grass, and Christ and the Madonna above. *The adoration of the Magi*, a fragment (994), has glowing yellows and oranges, where we recognize the influence of Simone Martini. In the *Nativity* (52) we have an example of where a Sienese sweetness joins the Umbrian melancholy and darkness, with its Byzantine undertone. The local Perugian school of the late fourteenth century painted the *St Julian* picture (53), with its bright and vivid design and striking reds: the Madonna's cloak here hangs out over two groups of praying nuns. *The crucifixion of St Peter*—he was crucified upside-down—is by the same local school a century or so before (718). *St John the Evangelist* (20) gives us a glimpse of the work

37

of the Spoletan school at the beginning of the thirteenth century, still locked in the Byzantine formality. And in the rough *human figures* (9) we have what look like the first sketches of Christian art, from the twelfth century, when the new influences of the northern world, which we call Gothic, began to invade Italy.

We begin at Room 1 on the left as we look across the entrance hall: we shall find the number of each room marked above the doorways, until we have gone full circle and reached number 24— back to the entrance hall again.

The work in the first room is all from the second half of the thirteenth century, and here we find the Byzantine tradition intact in its choice of subjects, but with hints of new moods. The vast *Crucifixion* (26) is attributed to the so-called '*Maestro di San Francesco*', who was once thought to be Giunta Pisano himself, but is now called a follower of Pisano (we shall see his work in the Lower Church of St Francis of Assisi). Hints of the later art are in No. 877, in its stark and absolutely sure lines against a golden background. In No. 31 we have the untouched Umbrian art, with its sombre dimness, its long, dark faces with eyes that are wide and black and still—a *Madonna and Child* and several other subjects.

Room 2 is tiny, with two interesting sculptures by Nicola and Giovanni Pisano (the artists of the Fontana Maggiore in the cathedral square): in fact, these pieces were taken from the fountain during its restoration in 1949. These are Nos. 998 and 999, *the wolf suckling Romulus and Remus*, and *Rome*. In Room 3 we see the beginnings of Sienese influence, in faces that are delicate and reflective, their skin sallow with roses in the cheeks, the work of Meo da Siena and his school. In this room there is also a pleasant wooden *Madonna and Child*.

In Room 4 we follow the Sienese influence through a local pupil of Meo da Siena (Nos. 76-81). There is an interesting wooden *Crowned Madonna* from the beginning of the fourteenth century (944). In 981 we see the beginnings of a distinctive Perugian art, in a certain graceful reflectiveness. And No. 69 is a longing glance back to the Byzantine by a Sienese artist: a small piece in which the Child is looking up at his mother, bending back his head and touching her delicately on the chin.

Room 5 is devoted to the Sienese artists proper, with a Bartolo di Fredi triptych (58) and one of his finest works (88), a large triptych where there is a wonderfully somnolent beauty in the

Madonna's eyes. We also see a splendid Taddeo di Bartolo (66), *Madonna and Child enthroned with saints*, a rich red and golden composition where the Madonna has real human beauty and a delicate flush.

In Room 6 we shall find a strange Gothic statue of wood (960) from the beginning of the fifteenth century, *St Catherine of Alexandria*, minus her usual wheel and palm branch. It is painted blue and has the style of lay-art. There is also a small wooden *Pietà* of the kind we shall see in other Umbrian churches, with Christ stretched out across the Madonna's lap (854). Another *St Catherine of Alexandria* in marble (745) is in the Rhenish style, from the end of the fourteenth century. In the triptychs (for example, 84, which is by a painter from Montepulciano, near Siena) the humanity of the relationship between the Madonna and the Child is very striking: in this one the mother's lips touch him ever so lightly. There is no formality, no deliberately divine representation as in the Byzantine art. Intimacy—the family—is now rendered sacred.

In this room we shall also find the earliest Ottaviano Nelli in existence: it is a *polittico* (1004), dated ten years before his *Madonna del Belvedere* in Gubbio. Before leaving this room we should look at the stiff, gaudy, striking *adoration of the Magi* (134) by a painter with Gothic tendencies from the beginning of the fifteenth century. By this time 'Gothic' has lost its general meaning of life-influence as in the eleventh century, and denotes something rustic and devout and German, where the mediaeval simplicity remains.

We shall probably want to sit and study the glories of Room 7, and there are comfortable seats. In the triptych by Piero della Francesca (111-114) we have reached a culmination of Renascence art, with every detail clear, the buildings in the clean symmetry that Giotto was the first to give them, but now there is a deliberate, relaxed composition too, where the clarity—almost but never quite a fixity—does not make the figures less natural or easy. The Benozzo Gozzoli *Madonna and Child with saints* (124) is not one of his best; it has little feeling. But the Fra' Angelico (91-108) has a bright golden splendour that crowns the room, and it is amazing how few people even look at it. The Child's body, perfectly formed, with a delicate, smooth, healthy skin, captures all the fineness of the subject: the picture has an extraordinary fitness and unity, as if nothing could possibly be added. The bright blues are like those of Duccio 'the Greek'. And in fact here is a splendid realization of that Greek sense

39

of the divinity of the human person, shining in health and natural virtue, which—far more than 'classical' symmetry of line—was the basis of humanism and therefore of this art: everything is laid open and bare, in a new spaciousness like the smell of spring flowers, with a light joy rarely seen in Italian life or Italian art of any epoch. When we see the sheer happiness in the triptych we realize how little happiness there really is in the greatest Italian masters: we find humanity, intimacy, sweetness, drama, but happiness was not a legacy of Rome.

In Room 8 the wooden nuptial chest (729) from fifteenth-century Florence with its bas-relief gowned figures and men in stockings—the story of Lucretia Borgia—reminds us suddenly of the civilization that flowed from Italy to the rest of Europe after the thirteenth century: suddenly the Dark Ages are far away. It is like a visit to Florence on a sparkling morning. The chest hints at full homes, music, ringing streets, the rustle of dresses and hours of talk. If that is civilization it may make us feel we haven't got it any more: 'the wine of life is drawn.' Perhaps that is why we look at the past so much.

Room 9 brings us to the time when religion begins to fade and its subjects have a trivial, though still graceful, look. The colours and designs begin to fascinate us at the expense of everything else. A dazzling craftsmanship begins, though it is still not quite shorn of its artistic objectives. Here is mostly work by Benedetto Bonfigli, a local artist who died in 1496; the major influences of his style were Fra' Angelico and Gozzoli, and of course the Sienese school. In Nos. 142-6 he collaborates with Bartolomeo Caporali, another citizen of Perugia. And in Room 10 we find the element of triviality growing still, in various minor artists of the fifteenth century.

Room 11 has more work by Bartolomeo Caporali, and in the *Madonna della Misericordia* (432) by Fiorenzo di Lorenzo (he died in the second decade of the sixteenth century) we have a first glimpse of baroque art. The next two rooms, 12 and 13, are devoted entirely to this artist, and here we see how something morally slack comes to be hidden under craftsmanship: and we may wonder if this is not the key to all baroque art. Since the collapse of humanism, due to the violent Lutheran revolution in Germany, there has been this theme in Italian life, a forced outer discipline combined with the collapse of values inside, which reached its culmination in the fascist movement.

In this room (13) there is also a Perugino (180) where infinite care has been practised, and where the grace of movement and design take away from the theme of the *Nativity*. He has a simpler and graver *Pietà* (220).

In Room 14 we find in the small panels (227, etc.) of Benedetto Bonfigli the full, civilized splendour of Perugia's last great school, in vivid and spacious lay scenes where the Florentine sparkle is hinted a little awkwardly. In the Perugino series (223-6) there is a climax of harmonious and intricate design. Nos. 225 and 224 are two paintings by Pintoricchio and Perugino in collaboration. Umbrian painting really reaches its height in these two men, though there is an uncertainty in Pintoricchio, not in the painting but in the feeling, so that he is sometimes satisfied with a chronicling of events (we see this unevenness of mood in his Baglioni chapel at Spello). But he is never formal or posed in the least. He was the pupil of Fiorenzo di Lorenzo, while Perugino went to school under Verrocchio in Florence and seems closest to Piero della Francesca in his marvellous sense of space, which is always summery and veiled with a warm yellow tone. Pintoricchio's colours have terrific variety, and are surprisingly close to Perugino's. The two men were contemporaries, Pintoricchio 1454-1513 and Perugino 1445-1523. Pintoricchio has a splendidly designed landscape while Perugino's is spacious, rather bare, truthful, warm, like Umbria.

Room 15 is devoted largely to Perugino, 238-243-5 to 247-9 to 261 are fragments from the main altar of Perugia's church of S. Agostino: originally these were an altar-piece, or *ancona* as it is called, of thirty panels, painted by Perugino between 1512 and 1523, with the help of other artists. There is a wonderful sweetness in the blond Christ and the Baptist: for Perugino the countryside is present all the time, dominating, yet the landscape is hardly depicted in his work—only a distant line of Umbrian hills; other artists who have a carefully designed countryside give no breath of it compared with this man. He has a way of seeming to paint the air: as if he knew what the air felt like, how hot and how heavy, and what colour. The vast and glorious Pintoricchio (274), heavily framed, a triptych that takes up most of the wall, conveys a jewel-like intimacy, where the tiniest gilt and threaded designs are followed through with a peculiar autonomy of form, keeping to their own rich world; yet it is not a glowing world—we are closer to Duccio than to Fra' Angelico.

Rooms 16 and 17 show all the falsity of the Signorelli school (203). Bernardino di Mariotto, a local artist who died in 1566, has sharp lines and designs with a striking vigour, in 156, 155, 175. Room 18 is devoted to members of the Perugino school (these are called *peruginesco* in Italian, while *perugina* is the word used for schools prevalent in the town without particular reference to this artist). Room 19 has a striking *adoration of the Magi* (287) by one of the artists who helped Perugino, called Eusebio da S. Giorgio: the tones are dark and thick, done with full realism, so that we feel right there, but without losing a sense of the theme and without the posturing of the baroque. Berto di Giovanni, also in the Perugino workshop, is awkward and sincere, and has a splendid *Madonna and Child* (356): he worked in collaboration with Sinibaldo Ibi, another follower of Perugino.

In Room 20 we are let loose in the baroque. The next room offers no escape either, except in the *adoration of the Magi* (477) by Arrigo Fiammingo, a Flemish artist named originally Heinrich van den Broeck, who united Flemish styles with the Italian. He died in Rome in 1597.

Room 22 consists of thirteenth- and fourteenth-century objects of bronze and ivory and gold—chalices, mitres, plates from the Abruzzi, Siena, France. There is the work of a Foligno artist, usually called Roscetto, who ran the most important workshop in precious metals known in Umbria during the fifteenth century. Room 23 used to be the chapel of the old Palazzo dei Priori and was used for private worship by the magistrate himself. Benedetto Bonfigli did the frescoes round the walls on a commission of 1454, but the work was hardly finished forty years later (story of the lives of St Herculanus and St Louis of Toulouse). Arrigo Fiammingo was given the job of restoring the walls in 1564, and he repainted the *Crucifixion*. The ceiling was done in 1954. There are fifteenth-century ballot boxes (720 and 721) for the election of the magistrate and the town officials. The last room (24) has sculpture by Agostino di Duccio, a Florentine artist who died about 1481, to be distinguished from the thirteenth-century painter Duccio di Buoninsegna or 'the Greek'. Here we see fragments (882 to 891, 988 to 993): these were once part of a façade for the church of the Maestà delle Volte which we have seen (it was demolished in the middle of the sixteenth century). And with that we are back in the gallery's entrance hall.

After this survey of over two hundred years of painting we shall probably need a rest, or at least a visit to Sandri's across the road, before we look at the **Sala del Collegio della Mercanzia** (emphasis on the 'i' in the last word), that is, the hall of the mercantile college, which was given by the town to the merchants' corporation in 1390. This is two doors down from the entrance to the National Gallery as we walk towards the duomo. There is no entrance fee and hours are 9.0 a.m.-1.0 p.m. and 3.0-6.0 p.m. (5.30 p.m. in the winter). On holidays it is closed in the afternoon.

The corporation commissioned the decoration of this hall in its present late-Gothic style at the beginning of the fifteenth century. The whole thing is a dazzling display of intricately carved wood, covering every inch of the walls and ceiling, and forming vaults with numberless designed panels. In the left wall as we enter there is a superbly inlaid and carved *pulpit* with four sets of twirling pillars, each in clusters of three: above, there are the gilded figures of *Strength, Justice, Prudence* and *Temperance* in very slight bas-relief; here we have the puritan virtues of a trading middle class in its heyday, which we shall find repeated as a motif in the Collegio del Cambio when we visit it farther down the road. On the right as we come in there is a more richly carved *tribunale* or long desk, where the merchants sat: the lunette above has the gilded griffin of Perugia standing on a bale bound round with rope—the arms of this corporation. Underneath a cornice there is a row of arches with twirling columns that half emerge from the wall. And there are two levels of benches for the 'consuls of the mercantile college'. The desk has five richly carved panels by Costanzo di Mattiolo, who did them in 1462. At the end of the room we see a mediaeval safe.

Outside again, we turn right and after passing the entrance to the National Gallery come to the **Collegio del Cambio** (hours 9.0 a.m.-12.30 p.m. and 2.30-5.0 p.m.), which was the seat of the town's money-changers, built at about the same period as the mercantile hall, between 1452 and 1457. The best visiting time, for the light, is late morning.

We enter a dark vestibule with wooden benches whose backs are carved (this is all a seventeenth-century addition), and at the end-wall—the room is quite windowless—we see the actual counter of the so-called 'college of the jurists of the exchange'. But it is the second room we have come for, where Perugino frescoed the walls and where we pay an entrance fee of L.100. This is the *Sala dell'*

43

Udienza del Cambio, the room where the exchange officials held audience. The ceiling is in two shallow Gothic vaults, their spines meeting in rosettes, their sections decorated. Round all four walls there is a quietly rich wooden bench with inlaid backs of floral design (also from the sixteenth century), and behind the highest seats of the *tribunale* we see a cornice of carved wood surmounted by two bas-relief lunettes containing griffins, with a niche between them holding a terra-cotta seated statue of *Justice.* The two levels of seats were for the *uditori* (auditors) and the *notari* (public notaries). The vast desk was carved by a Florentine artist in 1492. On the left wall as we go in there is a small pulpit called the *ringhiera* or balcony which was added in 1562 in the bleaker Renascence style.

And then there are the frescoes by Perugino, considered by some his major work. On January 26th, 1496, the Exchange College gave him this commission and he worked on it for two years. Andrea d'Assisi, a member of his workshop, was his main helper, and perhaps also Raphael. These frescoes were restored in 1949. They were to demonstrate that human perfectibility could be attained by the human example of Christ, and that harmony could be obtained by the fusing of ancient culture with Christian feeling. This was proposed by the humanist Francesco Maturanzio (1443-1518).

We are provided with a standing lamp that can be swung round to illuminate the frescoes when little outside light is available. In the ceiling, among vivid grotesque figures reminiscent of Roman wall-paintings, we see medallions enclosing the principal gods of the classical world: *Apollo* in the centre riding a chariot, and by the window *Mercury, Venus* and *Diana* or the Moon, while on the other side are *Saturn, Jupiter* and *Mars.* The women here—Venus and Diana—are of particular natural beauty.

On the wall right of the large window as we face it is the single figure of *Cato,* symbol of wisdom: next to him and above we see the seated figures of *Prudence* and *Justice,* while under these from left to right there are *Fabius Maximus, Socrates* (looking not at all ugly), *Numa Pompilius, Camillus, Pittacus* and *Trajan,* with the dark, bare, spacious Umbrian hills far behind them as they stand in reflective attitudes. In the mock-pillar between this and the next panel there is a self-portrait of Perugino, made to look as if it is a canvas bag hanging on the pillar. In the next panel above there are two seated figures again—*Strength* and *Temperance,* and underneath *Gaius Licinius, Leonidas, Horatius Cocles, Publius Scipio, Pericles, Cincinnatus,*

44

standing in the same style as the other figures, with the same Umbrian landscape behind them. Venturi the art-historian claimed that he saw the hand of seventeen-year-old Raphael in the figure of Strength.

In the next panel, on the end-wall, the *Transfiguration* has that characteristic warm spaciousness of Perugino: Christ is opening his hands, framed in a light that surrounds him like a shell. At its side there is a *Nativity*, with a Madonna of great natural dignity. We see how the religious subject at once stirs Perugino to real painting, whereas the other 'classical' panels remain posed and rather rhetorical and flat: the fusing of 'ancient culture with Christian feeling' was easier said than done—provincial humanists found it a safe cliché.

The last panel, on the right-hand wall, shows *the Eternal Father among angels and cherubim*, with two groups underneath, one of men and the other of women, the men being the prophets *Isaiah*, *Moses* and *Daniel* (this last is supposed to be a portrait of Raphael), *David*, *Jeremiah* and *Solomon*, while the women are sybils—the *Erythrean*, *Persian*, *Cumaean*, *Libyan*, *Tiburtine*, *Delphic*. This panel is perhaps the loveliest in design, movement and human feature: the heart of the humanist teaching—where it is no longer academic—is realized.

In the corner we pass into a second, smaller room (a light is available here also) finely decorated with gilt framework, while gilt spines divide the pictures in the roof. This is the Chapel of St John the Baptist, painted by a pupil of Perugino, Giannicola di Paolo, whose work we have seen in the duomo museum and the National Gallery. He is said by the art historians to have been influenced by Raphael. In the roof, which was painted between 1515 and 1518, we have an *Eternal Father* in the middle, and *apostles, evangelists, doctors of the Church, patrons of Perugia* all round. At the altar there is *the baptism of Christ* (a tavola framed in gilt designs and pillars) and at each side of it, in smaller framed panels, the Angel and the Virgin of an *Annunciation*. On the walls on either side, which are of a cruder order, there is *the life of the Baptist* in four parts, with sybils at the edge of the arches over these panels. In a medallion at the altar there is a *St John the Baptist* by another artist. The inlaid wooden benches date from 1509. In the fourteenth century this was a chapel in its own right, and was then bought by the college to become an annex of the other room.

Piazza d'Italia—Palazzo dell'Università Vecchia—Palazzo del Capitano del Popolo—Volte della Pace

If we turn right when we come out of the Collegio del Cambio we shall find ourselves after a short walk in the Piazza della Repubblica, where the road simply widens and the pavements become spacious enough to be taken over by cars.

Continuing along the Corso Vannucci we come to a further square, this time with trees and flower borders and gravel paths that make the encroachment of cars impossible. This is the Piazza d'Italia. The vast palazzo on the left (No. 2) with tall pillars supporting an elaborate balcony, and the canopy of that supporting a further smaller balcony above, is the seat of the National Institute of Assurance: like a lot of nineteenth-century palaces that look fit for captains and kings (this is called **Palazzo Cesaroni**), it fell into the hands of money-makers instead. It is a pleasant example of Italian banking architecture, sharing the grand aspirations of the Victorian style without its suffocating, restless proportions. Opposite it, with a long porch under great arches, lies a sterner and more ordered building with simple, narrow windows, called the **Palazzo del Governo** (the Prefecture): it seems (but isn't) earlier, because of its sober neo-classical lines, and we must remember that Italy had no Enlightenment, no 'Augustan' period in the eighteenth century, so that whatever we see of last-century architecture comes straight from the Renascence through the baroque, without an intervening period of encyclopedias, Utopian thinking and belief in intellect.

The Perugians like to walk here at sunset in the hot months, and two large, cool-looking hotels have chosen this square as the most fashionable site in town. We should go to the small **public garden** by the Palazzo del Governo for its terrace that commands the 'heart of Umbria' across the roof-tops. To the right we look towards Lake Trasimene, and sometimes the towers of Città della Pieve can be seen: to the left is Todi and the depression of the Tiber, then Montefalco and Bettona, the Clitunno valley and Trevi, Foligno, Spello and the cupola of S. Maria degli Angeli under the pink and sometimes dazzling white cloud of Assisi. There are binoculars mounted on the terrace.

If we go to the left corner of this garden and cross the road we

46

find another terrace built out on a spur of the famous Pauline Rock, whose stupendous sloping wall we can see below us.

Returning to the Piazza d'Italia we should take the right side of the Assurance building (No. 2) along the Via Baglioni, and we shall come out into the Piazza Matteotti, a straggling square made fascinating by the low, grey building on the right, the **Palazzo dell' Università Vecchia** (the original university building). This square, by the way, was formerly called the Piazza del Sopramuro because it is built on the city's Etruscan wall: in a moment we shall see that it sits on a kind of cliff, commanding another view of the country beyond.

The ground floor of the old university consists of wide Gothic arches which now enclose shop-windows: these date from 1453. The upper part of the building has two storeys with square windows (a Guelf design), the lower ones (of the *piano nobile* or noble floor, so called because that was where the reception rooms were) being crossed with stone bars. This whole upper part was built in 1483 at the order of Pope Sixtus IV, who made it the seat of the university, which it remained until 1811.

Extending from this palazzo farther into the square we see the **Palazzo del Capitano del Popolo** (we can look at this from the steps of the Post Office opposite). It is an intimate, jumbled, mysterious building which reminds us at once of mediaeval architecture north of the Alps: and in fact the palazzo was put up by masons from Lombardy between 1472 and 1481. It has an elaborate arched entrance of carved stone, rather like that of the Palazzo dei Priori, with a statue of Justice in the lunette and two Perugian griffins on either side. The palazzo curves slightly. On the right there is a balcony used by the town-criers, with iron clasps for torches. This building and that of the former university next door now comprise the city's Palace of Justice. If we cross over to its No. 18A, between the shops, we shall find an archway that takes us down to an indoor market entirely perched on a great terrace, from which we have another vast view across to Assisi. From the right of this terrace we can look at the arches holding up the former university: their height is over forty-five feet and they have been filled in for extra safety.

Turning right after returning to the square we reach a church (chiesa del Gesù) just where the square begins to narrow. This is sixteenth-century: inside, we see a richly carved ceiling in bas-relief and gilt, with deep compartments. For students of the baroque, the apse is a dazzling example of extravagant craftsmanship. Leaving the church and looking towards our right we see a narrow staircase-lane rising darkly under the buildings on the other side of the road, called **Volte della Pace**—the 'Vaults of Peace', because peace between the factions, or between Perugia and neighbouring towns, was always made here. It came into existence in the fourteenth century and of course the 'vaults' refer to the tall arches that make a ceiling for the lane, blocking out light.

S. Severo and Raphael's first fresco

Here is a short and pleasant walk for a cool, sunny morning. Piazza Danti is adjacent to the central square and has the proper though less attractive of the duomo's two façades dominating it: keeping to the extreme right of this crowded little square we shall find almost at once the Piazza Piccinino, which is one sea of parked cars so crammed together that exit seems impossible (and often is). The name of this square refers not to the fact that it is very small, which it isn't, but to Niccolò Piccinino (1388-1444), who was one of the most brutal mercenary soldiers of his time. These *condottieri* were captains who hired out their services to the *comune* or the *signore* of the town: the *condotta* was the contract made between them, when the number of soldiers to serve and the price were agreed. These knights were mostly of noble origin—the commercial people were too busy with their deals to find time for even their own battles.

The road on the right leading out of this square is the Via Bontempi, and if we turn left from this along the Via Raffaello we shall come to a tiny piazza of that name where we see the little church of **S. Severo.** It is at the top of a hill, cool and enclosed, quite hidden from the rest of the city, shaded with trees, served only by narrow lanes which make it unprofitable for the car. A view from its little terrace shows us once again the country round Assisi. No surprise, then, that there was an ancient 'Temple of the Sun' where the church is now: this is an eighteenth-century building, on another one of 1007, while the temple lies under both. The form of the temple is kept, square outside, with a small cupola. In the adjacent chapel (we ring at No. 11 for the attendant if necessary) there is a fresco by

Magnificent fifteenth-century windows and Guelf crenellations, legacy of papal rule, adorn Perugia's Palazzo dei Priori, now the National Gallery of Umbria.

No one seems quite agreed on the identity of Perugia's three patron
saints in the lunette of the extravagantly carved entrance to the
National Gallery.

Raphael. We have a chance to sit down here: facing us is a fresco in every way inferior to what we have seen before, and not even in a good state of preservation. The fuss is due to the fact that this is Raphael's first complete work. Only the upper half is by him (1505): on the left, *SS. Maurus, Placid* and *Benedict the Abbot*: on the right, *SS. Romuald, Benedict the Martyr* and *John the Monk. The Eternal Father, an angel* and a head of *St John* can no longer be seen above. The art historians often describe this work as marrying Umbrian styles with Florentine: the artist went to Florence the year before he painted it, and is said to have been impressed by *the Last Judgment* of Fra' Bartolommeo. These figures are also described as 'sweet' and a departure from Perugino on the one hand and the Umbrian schools on the other.

The lower half consists of *six saints* painted after Raphael's death (1520) by Perugino in his old age (he died three years later). To my mind they have far greater ease than Raphael's work, though people usually say that Raphael broke free from Perugino's 'static' lines. The *Madonna and Child* in the niche is a terra-cotta piece from the fifteenth century.

When we come out of the chapel we turn right into the Via dell' Aquila and climb the staircase-lane on the left that brings us to the Piazza Biondo Michelotti, the highest point of the city (1,500 ft) and another glorified car-park. The centre of the Etruscan and Roman city perhaps lay here, and it was the site of a castle (Rocca di Monmaggiore, under a French abbot) until 1375, when the people destroyed it. We cross to the right-hand corner of this square and take a ramp leading straight into the Piazza G. B. Rossi Scotti (he was a miniaturist who died in 1926), usually known as **Porta Sole,** 'the Sun Gate' (we are on the east of the city), and shaded by trees: if we look down over the balustrade we find that the square is supported by a series of vast arches with cypresses and a vineyard before them, the work of Matteo Gattaponi in 1374. Again we look out across country, this time towards the north. Far to the right there is the beginning of the Apennines. On the left of the terrace we find the little church of *S. Angelo della Pace,* built in the six-teenth century on the order of Pope Paul III, perhaps to celebrate peace between Perugia and the Vatican. And on the right of this church we have a wide staircase-lane so steep that no car will risk it, though there is probably no law to stop it trying: so we have an unhindered walk which will bring us out—passing on the left a piece of the old city wall, its base Etruscan—to the Piazza Fortebraccio, and we can return to the main square by turning left under the vast arch of the Gate of Augustus, which we shall see later.

S. Agata—Oratorio di S. Bernardino—S. Agostino—Convent of the Blessed Dove—S. Angelo—S. Agnese

In the main square again we should take the narrow lane on the right of the Palazzo dei Priori as we look at it from the duomo: that is, the Via della Gabbia or Cage Street, where the criminals used to hang in cages from the roof of the palazzo. At the end of this lane we turn right into the Via dei Priori, downhill, and continue along it until we come to the first turning on the left, Via S. Agata, too tiny to be seen on the map. It has a church of the same name, built at the end of the fourteenth century, with an unusual doorway, its arch framed in a cusp on two slender pillars like a tiny roof. Inside (if it is closed we should ring at No. 4), the original skeleton of the church has been kept despite restoration, with three massive pillars set in the walls on either side, from which the crossing arms of two vaults emerge, pleasantly decorated. On the left wall we see a fourteenth-century fresco, *the legends of St Severus*, in large panels which fill the wall to the top: they are faint, with the Umbrian stillness like a last suggestion. Behind the altar there is a *Crucifixion* of the Sienese school, a fragment: and below this is a *pentittico* (a word rarely found even in Italian dictionaries, but it means an altar-piece with five panels), painted in the first half of the fifteenth century, as we see from the brightness of the gold: the artist was Lello da Velletri.

Farther downhill on the left there is the church of *S. Filippo Neri,* which was built between 1627 and 1649, its vast baroque front dominating the Piazza Baldassare Ferri. Inside we find another extravagant riot of gilt and pillar, and bad painting fills every inch of the roof.

On the left of this church through an archway we see the Via della Cupa which leads us to the Via Deliziosa, a lane that we should visit if we wish to see the house of Perugino, at No. 17: there is a plaque. Continuing along the Via della Cupa we come to an opening from which we may look across a valley west of the town called the Valletta del rio La Cupa (the stream is called *la cupa,* perhaps from the Latin word for barrel, perhaps meaning 'dark, melancholy'), and we have another glimpse of the city-wall. The oldest gate, in Etruscan times, was here. On the left we see (white stone dotted with red blocks) the church of S. Maria della Valle, which has been restored but is of thirteenth-century origin.

After our view across the valley we should return to the Via dei Priori and turn left along it, downhill, until we reach a small square where we see the apse and bell-tower of the mediaeval church of *SS. Stefano e Valentino:* beyond it, where the road narrows on the left, there is a house with a vast tower mounted above it—the seat of the Sciri family, probably of twelfth-century origin, and one of the few towers to survive in Perugia. Like Siena and San Gimignano in Tuscany, this city once had many towers, symbols of prestige and arrogance, from which boiling oil could be poured on to fellow tower-owners below. The road (Via del Poggio) continues under an arch here and immediately afterwards there is the little square of the *Madonna della Luce,* with the sixteenth-century church of that name before us: this has an unusual rose window set into the wall above the porch, its slanting edge decorated with *festoni*, friezes of flowers and leaves—a 'festoon'. To the right of this as we face it—a strange idea to put two churches side by side—is *S. Luca* or St Luke's, which belonged to the Knights of Malta and was built a little later than the church at its side, as we see from its having less sobriety. On the left of the coupled churches we look down steps to the pointed **arch of St Luke,** which is clearly ancient with its great blocks of stone and in fact was the Etruscan gate of the city, in Roman times the 'Trasimene Gate', leading towards the lake.

We now bear right from this narrow square into the Via S. Francesco, passing on the left—just after the church of St Luke— the house of the Knights of Malta with its crossed Guelf windows.

Then we see below us the lovely, spacious square of *S. Francesco al prato* with its lawns and row of pines on one side, the tall church of St Francis radiant with white, shining stone amid traces of pink. And, hugging close to its left transept, there is the brilliant little **Oratory of S. Bernardino.** This was once an open field, becoming a Franciscan site through their tradition of open-air preaching: hence the name of the square '*al prato*' or 'in the field'. The church of St Francis is actually a roofless shell, its windows empty frames, as we shall see if we approach it closer. The roof was demolished about fifty years ago because the earth started slipping. It was built in 1230 and restored many times since: we can peep through holes in the door to see the wreckage.

So it is the intricate façade of the oratory on its left that will draw us. This was built between 1457 and 1461, the work of Agostino di Duccio, whose sculptures we have seen in the National Gallery of Umbria. Every part of this façade is a carefully carved bas-relief of figures and designs, and the colour of the marble used is delicate and rosy, with green paint above, in a delicious harmony. The oratory was built in honour of St Bernardine's visits to this city: he always stayed in the Franciscan monastery near by, and preached in this field.

The façade consists of a Romanesque arch high over two doors, skirted on either side by tabernacles that enclose figures between twirling pillars, one on top of the other. The upper tabernacles enclose *Gabriel* (left) and the *Virgin of the Annunciation* (right): the lower consist of two saints, *Herculanus* and *Constantius*. The central arch has a large lunette set back into the wall with bas-relief figures—*St Bernardine* mounting to heaven in a shell of flame, with angels, cherubim and heavenly musicians all round him, floating half-horizontal. Above this part of the façade, closing it from the roof, are the words *Augusta Perusia MC CCC LXI* (the date of its completion, 1461). In the angle of the roof are high-relief figures of *Jesus blessing* between an angel and a seraph. Above the two doorways, in tiny, delicately carved panels, we see *five stories of the life of the Saint*, with *six Virtues* in the lower arms or jambs of the arch on either side, and *six angelic musicians* at their sides so that they face us.

Inside the oratory we shall find as the altar-stone a fourth-century *sarcophagus* with superbly preserved figures in togas standing between fluted columns and holding scrolls: the lid is thick and elaborately carved. On the right we see Jonah being eaten by the whale, on the left Jonah after he has been spewed out, resting on the shore. The seated figure below, among the figures in togas, is said to be Jesus in the Temple, but there is no evidence for this. This tomb belonged originally to a Roman of the empire: only in 1260 did it become the tomb of the Blessed Egidio of Assisi, after it had been found in the St Francis church next door. On the right of the altar there is a baroque chapel where three years ago the gilt panels of the ceiling fell in—another effect of the earth-slip.

We should now walk round to the façade of the wrecked church (rebuilt in 1927 according to a model of the original) : and a strange hotch-potch of designs it is, fascinating for that reason, more like a mosque than a Christian church, a series of abstract geometrical patterns of pink and white stone, while the rose window is filled with a continuation of these themes in a way we have probably not seen before in Italy.

With this façade on our left we now walk downhill along the Via Alessandro Pascoli, a line of trees on our left and a view across the hills outside the city. Where this road bends round on itself we leave it and continue uphill, with a small strip of Roman wall on our left, at the base of a modern block of flats. At the top of the hill we pass under one of the arches of the city's aqueduct, put there about 1277 and providing the Fontana Maggiore in the main square with water, among other services. There is a further arch to walk under, and then we mount a staircase to the Piazza Forte-braccio—our second visit, and this time we can take a closer look. The vast palazzo on our left as we enter the square dominates it all, a baroque splendour of the eighteenth century, built on a drawing by a Roman architect: and its grand, sweeping authority, never devoid of warmth, does remind us of Rome, though it has an ugly pillared entrance. Goldoni is supposed to have acted in its little theatre. This is the **Palazzo Gallenga Stuart** (formerly Antinori), and today the seat of the University for Foreigners (*Università per Stranieri*) : there are always six to seven thousand foreign students in Perugia, and the university derives from a 1926 foundation, established to spread knowledge of Italy—a fascist idea that survived and even thrived. Students come here mostly to learn Italian.

On our left if we face this palazzo we shall see the immense **Arch of Augustus,** and realize that it dominates the square after all, being set so high above it that we miss it at first. It is some-times called 'the Etruscan arch', but has had other names—'the Old Gate', the 'Triumphal Arch' and so on. It was the principal gate of Perugia in Etruscan times: a glance at it tells us of great martial powers. The huge blocks of stone are simply placed together, without cement of any kind, to form an immovable, tall arch. If we walk through it to the other side we shall see that the highest blocks simply lean on one another like boulders, cut into the necessary shapes. The lower part, including the arch and the internal roof, are Etruscan, like the two towers on either side (300-200 B.C.). The upper part with its smaller, walled-in arch is Roman and belongs to the time

53

when the gate was restored (40 B.C.): the words *Augusta Perusia* were written inside the arch then. The delicate loggia on the left tower and the fountain at the base are sixteenth-century additions.

On the right side of the Palazzo Gallenga Stuart as we face it the Via Ariodante Fabretti takes us to the Piazza dell' Università, an ugly square overseered by the pink brick face of an eighteenth-century church—the Chiesa degli Olivetani (the Olivetans were members of a Benedictine congregation formed in 1313 by Bernardo Tolomei at Monte Oliveto, near Siena): the church-front is not pretty either, but thick-pillared and bleak. On the left of it is the *Palazzo dell' Università,* which used to be the Olivetan monastery attached to the church, and this is the present university, moved here in 1811 from its old quarters in the Piazza Matteotti: it was made a *studio generale*—the mediaeval term for university—by Pope Clement V in 1307, and in 1886 became independent of the Church, though in 1925 it lost its independence to the State. The subjects read here include surgery, medicine, commerce, economics, pharmacy, jurisprudence, farming. Down its long corridor, attached to the walls on either side, are Etruscan inscriptions found on the tombs and in various parts of the city. Like most Etruscan funereal inscriptions they can be read, and refer to the deceased, his immediate forbears, his age and so on. The difficulty of the Etruscan language is that the inscriptions found say the same kind of thing over and over again, and therefore provide a tiny vocabulary. Even the word for 'father' is not known, in spite of these numberless inscriptions. The prayers found in Gubbio (which we shall see later) have been a great help, comparable with the famous Zagreb mummy, in that they provide a parallel text in another language, but here again there are repetitions and the number of different words is small. Etruscan has an alphabet very close to the Greek but no similarity to Greek as a language. In fact all the attempts to compare it to other languages have failed. Perhaps it died out as dialects do—absorbed by the new Roman power but not protracted in official forms or in literature.

We return to the Piazza Fortebraccio and take the uphill lane going sharp left immediately as we re-enter the square—the Corso Garibaldi, narrow and busy with shops, that rises into the mediaeval quarter. On the right we come to the Piazza Domenico Lupatelli (Lupatelli was a popular patriot who died in the Risorgimento in 1844), with the Gothic **S. Agostino** of the thirteenth century along

54

one side. The lower part of its front has a design of pink and white stone, while above there is bare unfinished brick: happily its very ugly doorway is being broken down to reveal the original form (the movement among Italian restorers at the moment is to get buildings back to their first shape where possible). Inside this church we see one nave altered in the eighteenth century to a bare and cold frame, but fourteenth-century frescoes have recently been brought to light behind the baroque structure. At the first altar on the left as we go down the church there is a *Crucifixion* that takes up the whole altar-wall, where the angels cup Christ's blood from his wrists and the Madonna weeps, her long blonde hair loose. This is by Pellino di Vannuccio and was painted in 1387. There is a *Nativity* on the right of it and at the second altar down an *Immaculate Virgin* (note the white rabbit at her feet).

The apse of this church has a splendid choir of inlaid wood (1502) with panels of subtle designs—urns in tiers and garlands and putti, alternately inlaid and in bas-relief. This choir is supposed to have been carved on the basis of a drawing by Perugino, and the whole thing was completed in 1532, a work of three decades. If we wish to see more of the Flemish painter Arrigo Fiammingo there are two canvases at the next-to-last chapel on our left as we go out: these are *Jesus and St Andrew* and *the martyrdom of St Catherine*, but they are dark with dirt and in any case mannered. But at the last altar (still on the left) we have a *Madonna of the Graces*, against a rich back-ground, by Giannicola di Paolo (1460-1544), whose work we have seen before.

Outside again, we find on our left the **Oratorio della Con-fraternita di S. Agostino,** a fifteenth-century building with a ceiling of stupendous richness and craftsmanship: I know nothing else in Umbria like it. The ceiling simply cascades with carved gilt putti and angels and floral designs, falling to meet the frames of the bad pictures below. It will silence the enemies of the baroque for as long as they spend looking at it. The whole thing embodies the triumph of craftsmanship over art: it is the work of a Frenchman, Charles d'Amuelle, in 1695.

We continue up the Corso Garibaldi, passing at No. 86 on the left an ex-church of the fifteenth century which now houses the local Communist Party. At the top of the hill at No. 191, in a flat-walled building with bare windows like a prison is the **Monastero della Beata Colomba**—the convent of the Blessed Dove, which belongs to the second order of the Dominicans. A plaque over the doorway commemorates the legendary meeting between St Francis and St Dominic (they were contemporaries), and there is a bas-relief of the 'blessed dove' with the olive branch of peace above it. We push open the door and find on the right the 'cell of the blessed dove'— wondering by now who the blessed dove is. If we ask at the enclosure-grille (*parlatorio*) a nun will escort us inside. It is a tiny room with an altar, its window giving on to the street. We learn that the Blessed Dove was a nun of the third, or lay, order of the Dominicans: at the moment of her baptism a dove appeared, which resulted in her name. But she was known for more serious things—outside the city —and is said to have made peace between the Baglioni and the Oddi families during their terrible feuds, a work of heroism in itself, considering their passion for blood. She died in 1601. There is the usual humbug about relics: at the altar we see some bones from her skull, and more mouldy things in the cupboard. There is a picture of her in the cell, and the canvas of *Christ bearing the Cross* is attributed (by the nuns) to Lo Spagna, though it probably isn't: it was once a curtain, they say, and stood before the Blessed Dove's bed; at that time there was no painting on it, but she saw a vision of Christ which miraculously 'remained imprinted' on the curtain (which proves it wasn't by Lo Spagna).

We go on uphill and after passing under an arch we take the Via del Tempio on the right: crowning this little road is the squat round church of **S. Angelo**, which some say was once a pagan temple dedicated to the Christian rites in the fifth or sixth centuries, but in fact it is an entirely Christian building from the end of the fifth century, built on the shell of another which may well have been a pagan temple. Its tiled cupola is in two parts, the upper one rising to a white cross. Originally it may not have been circular in this way, but in the Greek-cross form. The Gothic door has inset twirling pillars from the fourteenth century. It is a restful spot, with thick lawns on either side of the path and young cypresses bordering it, remote from the city, while the massive crenellated brick towers of the Porta S. Angelo appear over to the left at about the same height.

Inside (if it is closed we must ring at No. 16 in the wall), we have a circular church with an inner ring of sixteen ancient Corinthian pillars, with all their bases different, their capitals delicately carved. Like other round churches we may have seen (S. Stefano Rotondo in Rome, for example), its roof is visible and rests on the inner ring of columns. Here each pillar is made of a different material—granite, black marble and *cipollino* (a white-grey marble called 'little onion' because of its greenish markings). Brick spines rise from these to the centre of the roof or dome, with twelve simple arched windows filled with alabaster to admit the light (these, and the whole dome, were a fourteenth-century addition). When the church had the form of a Greek cross there were four chapels, of which only one remains today. Walking round the church anti-clockwise we see on the right-hand wall a fragment from a fourteenth-century fresco, then we look into a little chapel with one alabaster window and a pleasant fresco, slight but sincere, from the beginning of the fifteenth century—a *Madonna and Child*. Next we have the only chapel that remains from the former church, in the form of an apse; a little hole in the wall left of its entrance contains a round, polished, deep-red, nearly black stone like a vast egg, which we shall see again in the Archaeological Museum, among the Etruscan finds: these may have been used on the tombs to designate the sex of the deceased, or perhaps to demarcate one tomb-area from the next. It is evidence here of Etruscan occupation.

We return to the Corso Garibaldi and take the tiny street of Via S. Agnese facing us. At the top of this is a courtyard with the entrance to the **Convent of S. Agnese** in the left corner. These nuns are Poor Clares and the convent was established in the fourteenth century. We ring the bell and a nun will take us to the chapel, where we find at the altar a fresco by Perugino painted two years before his death, the *Madonna of the Graces between two saints* (1522). The two nuns praying on either side of the Madonna are portraits of cousins of Perugino (they were nuns at this convent). The Madonna has a sweet, placid, gracious look, her hands open in an act of receiving and accepting. We may peep into a nice courtyard with a deep well in the middle, across which the nun will take us, if we are interested in a further fresco, by Eusebio da S. Giorgio (1519).

On the Corso Garibaldi again, we finish it by going to the ***Porta S. Angelo,*** one of the city-gates with open country beyond, unmarred by suburbs or factories. This gate was rebuilt by Lorenzo Maitani (see Orvieto chapter) in 1326, then again under the signoria of Fortebraccio. And it was restored in 1931, which accounts for its neatness.

57

The Companion Guide to Umbria

S. Maria Nuova—il colle di Porta Sole—S. Maria di Monteluce

Piazza Fortebraccio is again our starting-point: going left from the Arch of Augustus as we face it is the Via Pintoricchio, which takes us round the north-eastern edge of the city, where the hill drops abruptly and we are close to the city-wall: it is a narrow, noisy road, reminding us suddenly that we are in the capital of a province; and it has a pavement.

We should glance across the road at No. 1, where the fragment of an Etruscan urn is stuck to the wall: and this irrelevance, with its intimate touch, sets the tone for the walk we are about to take. Farther along at No. 7 we have the home of Pintoricchio, but the town does not prize him enough to give him a plaque, though it names the street after him. At the bottom of the road, up some steps on the right, there is the church of **S. Maria Nuova** whose side-wall with its two Gothic arches (in Via Roscetto) is almost the only thing left of it from the thirteenth century when it was built. Like the other churches of Perugia, it has been restored many times. But we should give it a quick visit, if only for the diagonal spines of the apse which remain from the original design. At the second altar on the right there is a banner by Bonfigli painted in 1472 showing *Jesus hurling thunderbolts on Perugia* and *the Madonna with SS. Benedict and Scholastica* (she was St Benedict's sister) *and the Blessed Paolo Bigazzini*, who are trying to placate the divine wrath. Yet there is no commotion in the picture: it is still and stylized. In the apse we find a very fine wooden choir with infinitesimal floral designs and twirling imitation columns (1456). In the left transept, facing us as we enter it, a much damaged *Crucifixion with SS. Francis and Laurence* can be seen, from the fourteenth century, and there are further more vivid remains on the other walls. The clean and spacious *Madonna and Child with SS. Jerome and Francis* on the left of the side-entrance in this nave is a copy done in 1822 of a sixteenth-century work: the original may have been taken to France, though Napoleonic troops are blamed for too much in Umbria; there were always plenty of local art-robbers, and they persist in Umbria today (see Spello). At the very back of this nave there is a splendidly simple *Madonna adored by two angels*, rustic and a little stiff, from as late as the sixteenth century.

Immediately after passing under the sharp-pointed Arco dei Tei

58

we turn left along the Corso Bersaglieri, which takes us uphill to the dwarfed gate of the **Porta S. Antonio** (1374): from here we have a command of open country, this time to the north of the city, with part of Perugia jutting out on our left like a mediaeval town on its own hill, separate and just discovered. The tall arches which we see on the extreme left are those supporting the terraced Via delle Prome leading down from the 'Piazza del Sole', as it is popularly called: in fact, we are looking at the 'hill of the sun-gate'—*il colle di Porta Sole*. A few roofs to the right of these arches there is the delicate loggia of the Arch of Augustus, and to the right of that the front of the Palazzo Gallenga Stuart, followed by the S. Angelo quarter which was in our last itinerary.

If we take the Via Enrico Cialdini on the right of the gate (noticing a plaque on the arch that commemorates the city's brave resistance to the Vatican's mercenaries and the end of the 'sad rule of popes' in the last century) we pass under the city-wall and come down by means of a staircase to the large, open and bustling Piazza Monteluce, which at midday swarms with schoolchildren (always a happy presence in Italy) and at other times with visitors to the hospital, which together with a church called **S. Maria di Monteluce** blocks the other side of the square as we face it coming down the steps. The hospital was once, by the way, a monastery attached to the church. S. Maria and was built in 1219 and enlarged in 1284, then entirely rebuilt after a fire at the beginning of the fourteenth century. It was given its geometric pattern of pink and white squares in 1451, though the double doors with their Romanesque arches date from two hundred years before that, together with the rose window. The interior is a one-naved hall with much gilt in the chancel. The altar, of thin Gothic arches supporting an altar-table in fourteenth-century red stone, is a graceful relief from the blaring baroque. Behind the altar, in a magnificent gilt frame, with vast pillars on either side (a priest will draw up the curtain if it is closed) there is a sixteenth-century *coronation of the Virgin* with a *Resurrection* underneath which the priests are proud of, and which conveys neither a crowning nor, of all things, a resurrection. In the sacristy behind there are fragments of Sienese work, or rather frescoes by Umbrian artists in the Sienese style: but these are hardly visible under the ghastly sixteenth-century depredations. There is, in much better condition, a *Crucifixion with SS. Clare and Francis* by Fiorenzo di Lorenzo (Pintoricchio's teacher), painted in 1491.

59

This is the end of our walk and we can return to the centre of town by the Via Alinda Bonnacci Brunamonti (she was a nineteenth-century poetess) which takes us to the Porta Pesa: if we here take the uphill lane facing us on the other side of the road we shall quickly find Via Roscetto, and then Via Bontempi again.

CHAPTER 2

Perugia II

We have now covered the whole upper or northern part of the city and our next walk will begin from the Piazza d'Italia, that is at the southern end of Corso Vannucci. This is perhaps the happiest quarter of the town, straggling and noisy with shops and stalls, part of it already by birth inaccessible to traffic, swarming with people at every hour of the day: an excellent area for bread, cheese, pizza and for standing and staring.

As this walk is long and includes the important Archaeological Museum and S. Pietro (a very large and tiring church), we shall probably want to do it in several excursions.

Porta Marzia and the Rocca Paolina—S. Ercolano—S. Domenico—the Archaeological Museum

We cross to the left of the Piazza d'Italia and on the other side of Via Baglioni find a narrow lane sunk under the level of the road called Via Marzia. This passes below the massive outworks of the **Pauline Rock,** which supports the Piazza d'Italia we have just come from: and as soon as we turn the corner we see on our right, embedded as it were in the brickwork of the wall, the Etruscan **Porta Marzia**—the Gate of Mars. This dates from the third or second century B.C., but only its arch and the crown remain, as the gate was demolished by Sangallo the architect to make way for Paul III's vast defensive rock; thus the arch became actually part of the defensive wall. Its serenity—the fact that it once belonged to the countryside—remains, and defies the cars that are parked here or churn their way uphill as if the basic pedestrian rights to air and movement no longer existed. On either side of the arch there are stone heads, one of them broken, and on either side of these two Corinthian pillars, their capitals closing a kind of loggia of four Ionic columns, making five compartments: and in these compartments are three human busts with a horse-bust at each end—a warm, rustic medley. There are Roman inscriptions above and below: COLONIA VIBIA ('the Vibian Colony', from the middle name of the emperor who endowed the city with colonial rights) above; AUGUSTA PERUSIA below. The latter perhaps derives from the time of the reconstruction of the city after the great fire of 40 B.C., while the one above is naturally dated somewhere between A.D. 251 and 253 when the emperor gave the *ius coloniae*. And some people say that both were put there at this later time. A door in the archway (visiting hours 9.0 a.m.-12.30 p.m. and 4.0-7.0 p.m. in the summer, closing an hour earlier in the winter) leads us to the subterranean Via Bagliona, which used to run through this part of the city before Paul III built his fortress slap on the Baglioni family house and even the local churches where they worshipped. This was a revenge of fate, as Malatesta Baglioni had built his house on the ruins of another one belonging to the Guidalotti family, whom he crushed in 1389. It is strange to walk into a mediaeval street, underground and no longer used, and stare up at the clean towers and arches, with floodlights on them, and at terraces where no one sits now. The road is only open because it served Paul III a good defensive purpose—it led to the artillery stores.

If we walk on down the Via Marzia and turn sharp left where the fortress-wall ends we shall find ourselves in the Viale Indipendenza, with trees on either side. Before this bends sharply to the right we pass a fountain and benches—we may need them by now—and a little further on the steps (put there as an addition in 1607) of the church of *S. Ercolano* which is set inside the city-wall, on the actual site where this saint was martyred. The front consists mostly of a massive, lightly Gothic arch acting as a cover for the main door, with a line of closed arches above, and the whole façade is unusual for being divided into three huge blocks, each with its single inset arch. The church was started towards the end of the thirteenth century, in the form of a temple, with a central cupola, as we shall see if we step inside: but it is now covered almost everywhere with seventeenth-century stucco work and gilt and bad frescoes, which again we owe to Perugia's prosperity; what a mercy that during this period Assisi couldn't afford to overhaul her churches, though it was often suggested. The main altar here is formed out of a Roman sarcophagus of the fourth century A.D., containing the body of the martyred saint. It has a simple design of curved lines, a reminder that the baroque began from a classical model. The bas-relief on this sarcophagus shows lions savagely devouring horses: we rarely see such intact pieces of Roman realism.

If we descend the steps going left from the entrance we shall find ourselves looking up the fascinating staircase-lane of Via S. Ercolano, which rises with shops and stalls on its right side to the narrow arch of S. Ercolano, or the **Porta Cornea** as it is otherwise called —one of the gates in the city's Etruscan wall, modified in the thirteenth century. We see a stone Romanesque lion from that time at the tip of the arch.

But we go downhill along the Corso Cavour and cross straight over the Via XIV Septembre (on September 14th, 1860, the *bersaglieri* entered Perugia in the name of King Vittorio Emanuele and a united Italy), walking on until we reach, on the left, the Piazza Giordano Bruno with its round fifteenth-century fountain carved with the city's griffin, and beyond it, towering above us, the immense naked brick front of **S. Domenico,** spoiled not by being incomplete but by a tall stone frame round the door put there in 1596. The church was started in 1305 on a drawing by Giovanni Pisano, then rebuilt in the early sixteenth century after the collapse of one nave, so that it lost its original form. A double ramp of steps leads up to the entrance, another peculiarity, taking up so much room that the square's curious irregularity loses appeal.

Inside we have a tall and rather bare three-naved church whose vastness has survived baroque fuss: we are struck most by the great stained-glass window behind the altar, which pours a kindly light into the white bareness of the naves on a sunlit day. Beginning in the right nave, at the fourth chapel down, called the **Cappella del Rosario** (the Chapel of the Rosary), we find a confusing heap of baroque prettiness with something serious underneath: and we soon see that this is due to the unusual altar-wall with its sculptures and stucco-work inside a design of arches and niches, the work of Agostino di Duccio (1459). Above the arch in which the altar is set there is a pleasantly decorated cornice and a lunette where figures are set on pedestals; these issue from the frescoed wall in an unusual way —a *Madonna and Child* with an angel kneeling on either side, and putti and musicians painted behind. The stone arch round this lunette has a further painted rim of flowers and foliage, while the arch itself is mounted on a set of two pillars at each end. The whole thing gives an impression of classical serenity and assurance, as if we were looking at an original Roman work: yet there is Christian intimacy added. In this artist, perhaps because he is a sculptor, we have the ancient art most completely and undeliberately absorbed, without the slightest desire for effect. He really achieves in this little altar-wall what the Collegio del Cambio, with its written humanist intention, tried hard for. In the niches below, on either side of the tall arch surrounding the altar, there are figures of *Gabriel* (top left), the *Virgin Annunciate* (top right), *St John the Baptist* (lower left) and *St Laurence*. It was in 1869 that the disturbing prettiness came in, with a fearful fresco in the baroque tradition round a glass-encased *Madonna* by Domenico Bruschi, a local artist: his picture shows saints and Pope Benedict XI (died 1304), and unfortunately it dominates everything, hiding the little pictures round the inside of the archway (1532) by the Florentine artist Bernardo di Girolamo, which describe *nine miracles connected with the rosary*. The same artist painted the two medallions above, *Isaiah* and *David*. The Madonna and Child in their case are hideous enough, being dolls, but they are mitigated by sweet clothes. This chapel survives from the original church.

In the right-hand transept there is another chapel with several excellently preserved votive frescoes (those painted for private families as a thank-offering) from the fourteenth century. There are several Madonnas, rapt and still, and the fragile *Madonna and Child* closest to the chapel altar is especially lovely. The next chapel towards the main altar has a grand stone tabernacle, a monument to the Blessed Benedict XI which was brought from the former church of S. Stefano in 1700, and placed in this chapel with the remains of the pope in 1959. This monument is often said to be the most complete example we have of Italian Gothic art, by followers of Arnolfo di Cambio or perhaps Lorenzo Maitani (the architect of Orvieto cathedral). The pope lies behind curtains which are being drawn aside from his body by figures, and above there is a *Madonna and Child* in Gothic style with *St Benedict* and *St Dominic*, who are presenting the kneeling pope to her.

At the high altar we enter the light of the vast stained-glass window we noticed on coming into the church: this is in the form of a Gothic arch, 70 ft by 30 ft, the largest in Italy apart from that of

Milan cathedral. It shows *twenty-four saints*, each in his own section, the lower (and brighter) parts having been taken from an earlier window (1411), while the others were made after 1459. The wooden choir behind the altar was carved by an artist from Bettona, and above it we see fragments of frescoes from the earlier church. On the left of the high altar there is a further chapel, where Fra' Angelico painted a *polittico* in 1437 which we have already seen in the National Gallery of Umbria. In the chapel immediately left of this (*Cappella degli Angeli*) we find further fragments of fourteenth-century frescoes by the same hand that painted the apse, showing (above, right) a simple and moving *Epiphany*, with other scenes. If we walk back down the church on this side we pass a stupendous gilt, blue and green organ with pillars, one of a number of extravagant and joyful wooden organ-lofts in Umbria. In the first chapel we come to, still in the earlier Gothic form, with a spined and arched ceiling, there are more frescoes by fourteenth-century Umbrian artists working in the Sienese style, and on the right wall as we enter there are *figures of saints*, while on the wall facing us we see *St Peter preaching* (left, above) and *being martyred* (right, above); on the left wall there are *scenes from the life of St Catherine*. Walking on, we find that the third chapel from the exit has a dark, still, well-composed banner, perhaps by Giannicola di Paolo, 1494.

On our right as we leave the church there is the entrance of the **Civic or Archaeological Museums,** which consist of an Etruscan and Roman part on the one hand and a Prehistoric part on the other. Originally this collection was in the Palazzo dell' Università near Piazza Fortebraccio (where only Etruscan inscriptions remain on the corridor walls) and was finally set up in this building (the former monastery of S. Domenico, whose church we have just seen) in 1946. The hours of visiting are 9.0 a.m.-1.0 p.m.: it is closed every afternoon and of course all day Monday. There are outdoor exhibits (round the cloister), apart from the museum upstairs.

The Etruscan-Roman museum was founded in 1790 in the private collection of Francesco Friggeri, and grew later from the many near-by excavations until it was one of the most important collections in existence.

We enter a large cloister with lawns and hedges in the middle, and small Etruscan sarcophagi and fragments from walls and friezes lining the arched walk all round. This cloister is called *Chiostro maggiore*—in other words, the main cloister of the Dominican

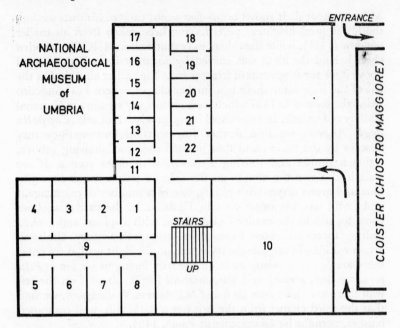

NATIONAL
ARCHAEOLOGICAL
MUSEUM
of
UMBRIA

CLOISTER (CHIOSTRO MAGGIORE)

STAIRS

UP

fathers—and was built between 1455 and 1579. We should stroll round the cloister first, passing one urn and Roman tablet after another. Nearly every urn is carved with a legend: it would take us hours to decipher each one, and many would be left uninterpreted. There are sacrifices, battles, rites. In the middle of the far wall, that is, exactly half way round the cloister, a round well-head shows *the battle of the Greeks against the Amazons*; then a sarcophagus shows *the myth of Meleager.* In the next corner we see the striped pink and white wall of what was formerly the façade of this church, before the great alterations: St Elizabeth of Hungary and St Peter Martyr were canonized here in the thirteenth century.

In a corner of the cloister nearest the present church a staircase will lead us up to the Museum on the first floor. We turn left at the entrance and once more follow the cloister round in a clockwise direction. There are more urns, all of them taken from tombs near Perugia: the first ones on the left are unusual in that they bear a design, perhaps a large rosette or a bull's head, and not an intricate legend with many carved figures or plain unadorned sides such as we have seen downstairs. At the first corner there is the *ipogeo della famiglia Paniatia*, the tomb of the Paniatia family (literally *ipogeo* means 'underground'): this urn has the most lifelike figures in proportion, and we see at once where the Renascence started; these carvers followed styles imported from Greece. The most interesting piece here is perhaps the 'cinerary group' from Chiusi, showing the deceased with winged female demons, but at the moment its place is empty, due to restoration. In a glass case near by is a most elaborate urn with a married couple in the style of the large and famous terra-cotta sarcophagus in the Villa Giulia at Rome (the authenticity of which is often doubted). In the next corner we see on the floor large black egg-shaped stones like the one we found in the round church of S. Angelo, perhaps used by the Etruscans to divide the land into funeral plots, perhaps a symbol of sex, age, position. There is one battle-scene after another on the next urns, before we come to a glass case containing the skeleton of an Etruscan girl, certainly a princess or noblewoman. A few yards farther on we find a small case containing the bones of another woman with earrings, an example of what Etruscan scholars call 'second burial', where the remains were transferred to make room for another body.

We now turn into a wide corridor which will take us to the major exhibits, passing cases of small bone fragments used for the decoration of furniture, found at Carsulae. At the end, on either side of a window (Room 11 in diagram), there are terra-cotta friezes and decorative heads and flowers which have survived from Etruscan roofs: these were to hold the tiles in place, and if we look carefully we shall see how they were inserted under the tiles at the base of the roof; they were found at San Faustino, near the Carsulae site.

We turn to the rooms on the left, beginning in Room 1 with the earliest traces of man: there are almond-shaped stones from a hundred thousand years ago, taken from the Tiber and its tributaries; hoes and points of instruments; the teeth of sheep, stags, goats, pigs, rhinoceros, birds, wolves, lynx, hares, tortoises, bears, leopards, foxes, oxen, all found in the mountains of Cetona in 1940. Room 2 has Palaeolithic finds from the Abruzzi mountains: there are larger stones, also from Tuscany and Cetona. In Room 3 we see the first signs of agriculture—wheat, barley, beans, meal, from the Neolithic age, and fine-edged tools, scalpels, burnished objects, bracelets. In Room 4 we find the points of lances and spears; stone-tools are more developed than before (the holes in them are for wooden handles), and there are knives and articles for personal care. We now cross over the corridor to Room 5, where we find more delicate articles still, and points of arrows from the Neolithic period. Room 7 has the first pots: and we see pins for the first time. In the corridor again (9) the glass cases on either side contain prehistoric material from other countries.

We now mount the staircase to the large hall (10) where we find, beginning on the right, material from the Bronze Age—needles, razors, hat-pins, daggers, axes of copper and bronze in the form still used by peasants today, two-edged axes, bronze spearheads. We see the idea of a spring—metal in tension—first developed. Towards the end of the right wall we find a large case of pots which typify the Bronze civilization in central Italy, sometimes called the 'civilization of Belvedere' because so many of the finds came from there. If we return down the other wall we find, first, human skulls from Belvedere (we should note the excellent teeth, a lesson for our civilization) and more pots. There are small primitive compasses from the same area, and spindles. We are now coming into the Iron Age, which makes a bridge to our civilization: we see the crescent-shaped razors which figure a lot among the Etruscan exhibits, and the use of which is much discussed; some say they were to wipe sweat off the body, others say they were to wipe off oil, others suggest that they contained brushes; in this earlier epoch they were of more angular shape. There are belts, safety-pins, fully developed springs, and in one case (No. 104, *necropoli di Colfiorito*) a pot reminiscent of the Etruscan *bucchero*, while in case 106 (*necropoli di Cancelli*) we see small scent-pots and tiny vases identical with late-Etruscan ones found in tombs.

Returning down the staircase and turning right into another corridor, we shall find the Etruscan rooms, beginning with Room 12. Here we find a tall *stele* (a slab or pillar often used as a tombstone) with two warriors etched lightly on it, fighting with spears (sixth century B.C.), found near Lake Trasimene. At the exit there is a fascinating sphinx about three feet high found near Chiusi, also from the sixth century. Room 13: a sandstone sarcophagus at the end-wall, from the sixth century, will remind us, like the sphinx we have just seen, of Egyptian civilization; to some it will confirm that the Etruscans were an Egyptian race. The carving on it represents a return from the war, with banqueting scenes on both sides. Also in this room are some *cippi* (the truncated columns sometimes inscribed to commemorate a person or event) of unknown origin, in the same so-called Chiusi style as the sarcophagus.

In Rooms 14 and 15 there are bronzes found near Perugia, with figures traced on them in what the scholars call the Ionic-Etruscan style, where the Greek influence is evident: we see tiny bronze statuettes, and reliefs hammered out of thin bronze sheets. These are from the second half of the sixth century, and were used to decorate carriages or furniture. On these hammered bronzes we see horses, bearded heads in the Egyptian style with the faint characteristic smile, the trace of a man on horseback, serpents. There are single bronze statuettes of a sea-nymph, a four-winged deity, a sphinx, as if they were used for chair-ends or door handles. In beaten bronze there are also griffins, hunters with bows and arrows, a lion attacking a calf, a woman holding a cup or vase, her skirt down to her feet.

Room 16 consists of finds from tombs at Monteluce. The case on the right has vases of Greek manufacture—imported by the Etruscans. On the lower right-hand shelf of this case there is a figure of Hercules strangling a serpent in his cradle. In the left case we see helmets, lances, bronze vases, mirrors, carved bone, jewels and again those comb-like objects in crescent-moon shapes. And there are *kottaboi*, the tall bronze poles sometimes elaborately decorated with discs and figures, sometimes not: the *kottabos* was a wine-throwing game of Greek origin, possibly used for omens and prophecies (see Chapter 3). In Room 17 the case on the right contains the complete contents of a tomb—a helmet, shin-pads, spearheads, a tall widemouthed Attic vase with a bronze lid showing the legend of Triptolemus (sent by Demeter the Greek corn-goddess to teach the Eleusinian mysteries to mankind), and another *kottabos*. In Room 18 there is a mirror with the figures of Helen together with her father Tyndareus and her brothers the Dioscuri traced subtly on it. There is a precious and lovely ear-ring of gold, longer and fatter than a finger, with a curved beaten crown from which a tiny gold head hangs, itself ear-ringed. And there is a bronze pot with a tiny man-bird figure in the centre. At the exit of this room we find the so-called Perugian *cippo*, one of the longest Etruscan inscriptions ever found. In Room 19 the case on the right has more helmets, shin-pads and arms, while that on the left contains small pots and mirrors of the late-Etruscan epochs. A small urn in the corner has a head of

Medusa on the front between two griffins, with a figure of the deceased half-leaning on the lid.

Room 20 has material from other tombs opened near Perugia, including gold rings with inset stones (shaped like tiny heads, some of them), bracelets, gold necklaces and more armaments, with an outsize shield. Room 21: in the case on the right a helmet of bronze is called 'the helmet of Paciano' because of the area of Castiglione del Lago where it was found; it is unusual in being highly decorated with a sort of crest, and may have belonged to a king or general. In the left-hand case there are finds from tombs near Orvieto: a plate with a handle in the form of a winged figure, bronze, another intricately traced mirror, and a candle-holder with three legs. In the corridor outside there is a terra-cotta statuette of a male divinity, found in 1773. In Room 21 we see objects taken from Etruscan votive boxes, from various parts of Umbria: tiny simplified bronze figures, some of them seated, a few coins, warriors with spears, a very strange symbolized figure (in the right-hand case) with a kind of wreath on his head, one strip of bronze for his body and two arms reaching endlessly down to his feet, one of them holding a disc or plate (perhaps a perfume-burner or a simplified *kottabos*).

The Archives are on the first floor, through another and smaller cloister, and contain manuscripts, papal bulls, city records, letters, miniatures, dating from 991 to 1851. There are precious collections, such as the annals of the city's decemvir from the thirteenth century to the nineteenth (the decemvir was a ruling body of ten men, a survival of Roman practice). The library also contains information about the English condottiere John Hawkwood, and other mercenary captains.

Porta S. Pietro—the Church of S. Pietro—S. Giuliana and the Maestro di S. Francesco

Turning left out of the little square when we leave the museum we continue along the Corso Cavour, and notice at No. 130 on the left, now a carpenter's, a mediaeval house with pink and white squares of stone for a front, suggesting a tiny church: in fact, this was once (1333) a hostel for pilgrims and an annexe to the Dominican monastery we have just left. We then reach the **Porta S. Pietro** with its double arch, beyond which lies a pleasant curving road with trees and once again that greatest rarity, a pavement. This gate is known also as the 'Roman' or 'double-doored' gate. What we see before us is from the fourteenth century: but when we pass through and look back there is a magnificent surprise for us—intended for travellers into the city—in the form of a great classical, or rather neo-classical (but the imitation is nearly perfect), gate by the same artist whose work we saw a little while ago in the Chapel of the Rosary at S. Domenico—Agostino di Duccio: and here again he achieves something so serene, so close to the countryside, to that sense of its commanding presence which the Romans had, that it is like the perfect reproduction of an ancient gate, without the crumbling hand of time on it. At least, it would be perfect if it were complete, which it is not, above. It was started in 1447 by an earlier artist, and taken over by Agostino in 1475: he was inspired for his design, apparently, by the Malatestiano temple at Rimini. The central archway broods with a simple splendour, and round the rim there is a motif of round shields reminiscent of the Arch of Augustus, with two fluted columns on either side set into the wall and sustaining the cornice under their capitals.

We are now in the Borgo XX Giugno (June 20th, 1859, is a bitter date in Perugian memories—papal troops re-occupied the city, and the marks of their bullets can still be seen on the houses) which takes us to the church of **S. Pietro**, filling the road before us with its tall spire, pointed and fat like a drawing pencil, and not quite right: but it lies in an unusually restful square—divided in the middle by a road—amid rows of pine trees, with the public gardens stretching away from it with their gravelled walks. This church was built on the site of the city's former cathedral at the end of the tenth century, and has kept the same skeletal form since then. In 1966 it celebrated its thousandth anniversary. The tower has a girdle of supports under a little jutting gallery, half way up, with a Renascence addition above of a cornice and frieze, and the spire stuck pointlessly on that: mostly the work of Florentine artists between 1463 and 1468.

A ramp lined with peaceful trees leads us up to an elegantly cobbled courtyard: we look for a church and fail to find it. This courtyard too is clearly Renascence. And then in the far left corner we see a carved wooden doorway in a stone frame, from the sixteenth century: and this is our unobtrusive entrance. On the left of the doorway we have a glimpse of the original church-wall before the Renascence got to work: these are frescoes preserved behind glass; a *Deposition*, a kneeling woman, a knight on horseback—faded fragments. The church, by the way, closes at noon sharp but is normally open again at 2.0 p.m.

Inside we have a strangely ornate church—vast and not graceful, yet harmonious, perhaps because of its shape: but not only that— the sheer plenty of its decorations, the frescoes, the crowded side-walls, the sumptuous altar, are an element of the harmony; there has been no struggle for size or spectacle for their own sake, and this means that the harmony of the primitive church has survived the enormous decorative weight of later years. A tour of its pleasures and treasures makes a very tiring business if we do it conscientiously. At the end we find that the treasures are really very few, and the tiring thing is looking for them. And the church is dark. We should stroll through, and look closely at a few particulars: complicated maps of the interior should be avoided.

There are three naves, and we are struck first by the ceiling of carved panels, and the series of pillars on either side—nine Ionic pillars with half-arches between them, most of them ancient, of grey marble and oriental granite: the first one on the left is Roman-esque, and that nearest the chancel on the left, like the pillar oppo-site it, is Corinthian of Renascence origin. The second column on the left is called 'the miraculous column' (it has a holy-water font under it) because, according to tradition, the saint who founded this church (S. Pietro Vincioli), by the simple act of blessing the column, made it stay in place after it had begun to topple during construction. A painting of the saint is attached to it.

The rich gilt ceiling is by Benedetto di Giovanni, an artist from Montepulciano. Above the arches on either side of the nave there are vast canvases (ten of them in all) and a vaster one on the back wall, all work of the sixteenth century by a disciple of Tintoretto called *l'Aliense* ('the foreigner') from Greece. The series describes Biblical scenes beginning with the *Nativity* on the right of the en-trance: these canvases are dark and not easily seen, and their style is the opposite of the clarity and economy of Giotto. But we can ask for a light to be shone on to the enormous canvas at the back (*the genealogical tree of the Benedictine order*). While offering no offence, these pictures offer no enlightenment either: it was a bad idea to put them here, though their vastness is thereby lost.

In the right nave, at the corner by the back wall, we shall find a

72

Above: The strange, mosque-like façade of S. Francesco al Prato still drowses in the sun, though land shifts have reduced the building to a shell. To the left, Agostino di Duccio's Oratory of S. Bernardino keeps watch over the square where Franciscans used to preach in the open air. *Right:* The squat round church of S. Angelo on Perugia's outskirts dates from the fifth century.

Above: Perugia's board of trade commissioned the Sala del Collegio della Mercanzia in the fifteenth century — a dazzling display of intricately carved wood. Right: the merchants' tribunal. Left: a superbly inlaid pulpit.

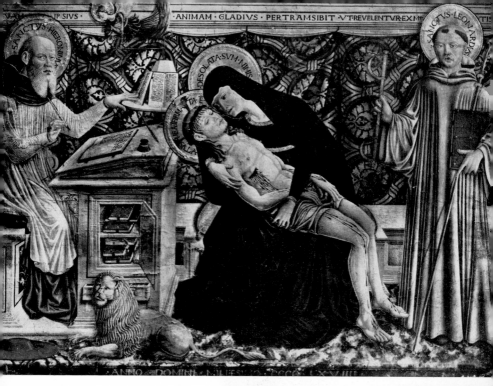

Above: *Pietà* by Benedetto Bonfigli in the church of S. Pietro.

Right: What the Stars Foretell: he will cast your horoscope for fifty lire.

Left: Remains of the Etruscan Porta Marzia, or Gate of Mars, date from the second or third century BC. The Gate was demolished to make way for papal fortifications when the Church took Perugia by force.

Winged Furies like Michelangelo statues support the figure of a
magistrate on this urn from the Ipogeo dei Volumni, an Etruscan-Roman
tomb in a suburb of Perugia.

Madonna and Child by Eusebio da S. Giorgio, whose work we already know, a pleasure to see after the dark heaviness of the overhead canvases: the Madonna is between Mary Magdalen and St Sebastian; the mood is simple, easy, mellow, reflective, in a yellowish, warm light.

We then pass—walking down the right nave—several mediocre pictures until we reach the third altar down, where we see *St Benedict between SS. Placid and Maurus*, giving the Order to the Benedictine monks: this also is attributed—but unconvincingly —to Eusebio da S. Giorgio; only the predella with its scenes of *the martyrdom of St Christine* (we see her being boiled and roasted) may be by him. We then come to the little chapel of S. Giuseppe (there is a light-switch on the left of the door), which has a *Madonna and Child and four saints* by local artists of the sixteenth century. At the altar, *the Holy Family* is a copy of the original Raphael painting. At the end of this nave we shall find a door leading into the sacristy, with three small pictures above the doorway before we actually go in: the *two saints* on the right in this series are copies of Perugino.

We may have to ask one of the fathers to let us into the sacristy if the door is locked. The walls are heavily and crudely painted by Girolamo Danti (1574). A strip of floor (farthest from the entrance) contains some of the famous Deruta tiles, put there in 1563. There are some very pleasant and quietly designed cupboards of inlaid wood from 1472. On the wall by which we entered we see five tiny pictures of *saints* which are attributed—again wrongly—to Perugino: the most authentic is the centre one, but the others have clearly been touched up, and again are probably copies. There used to be seventeen, and at one time they surrounded Perugino's *Ascension* at the main altar: Napoleonic troops took this picture and some of the little ones; they are now in the museum at Lyons. Then others of the little pictures were stolen in 1916. Above these we see, framed, *St Frances the Roman and an angel* of the Caravaggio school. The other framed canvas on the wall right of the entrance is a *Holy Family* of the Parmigianino (1503-40) school. Right of this in the corner there is a small *Christ*, delicate and clear, by Dosso Dossi. At the end of the right wall, also in the corner, we find a picture of *the Child Jesus and infant St John*, which is mellow and graceful: attributed to Perugino's school, and by tradition to Raphael. Near this is an English grandfather clock from the seventeenth century.

73

The altar has intricate gilt stucco-work round it (1487). Above the two doorways on either side of the altar, the *David* and *Isaiah* are again copies of Perugino. In the corner left of the altar a tiny *Madonna and Child*, which has a stark power, is attributed to Garofalo, an artist from Ferrara (1481-1559). In the corner of the left wall *the Flagellation* is painted on copper by an artist of the Caravaggio school, and according to the scholars it could be the first sketch of an original painting by the master himself.

We leave the sacristy and enter the chancel: at each foot of the triumphal arch there is a pulpit of carved stone with bas-relief gilded figures and leaves (1592). The main altar is a vast marble block with an inlaid marble decoration of bright sea-blues and yellows and mottled reds, also of 1592, a work of dazzling sumptuousness. The tomb of the Saint himself is inside the great columned tabernacle. Above, there is a ciborium—a kind of canopied shrine—also made of marble, from 1627. A magnificent choir in two tiers surrounds the apse, carved and inlaid, with a delicious canopy over it all the way round, marked with rosettes, flames and the Perugian griffin repeated over and over again: it is considered the finest choir in Italy and was started in 1526 by Bernardino Antonibi da Perugia, then taken on by an artist from Bergamo in 1535, with helpers. We should also notice at the entrance to the chancel, on either side, beautiful carved wooden thrones with steps leading up to them, splendidly and minutely carved in nut by Benedetto di Giovanni from Montepulciano and an artist from Brescia called Benvenuto: it took them only a year—1555-6. At the back of the apse a door leads out on to a narrow balcony. This door has works of extraordinary craftsmanship on its two leaves; on the left leaf an *Annunciation*, and *the head of St Peter* in the lowest panel; the right leaf shows *Moses saved from the waters*, with *the head of St Paul* underneath. These are inlaid wood pictures by Fra' Damiano, also from Bergamo (1536). The little balcony gets the sun in the morning and will give us a few minutes' natural splendour (we look down across sloping olive groves towards the east) before we plunge into darkness again.

Coming back into the chancel we pass a massive lectern of wood with bas-relief figures and an inlaid bookrest above by Battista Bolognese (1535-7) with the help of a French artist, Monsieur Ambrogio, as the Italians called him. There is terrific craftsmanship everywhere here, but the chancel as a whole is a massive decorative ensemble with no mystery.

74

We now go back along the left nave. At the beginning, close to the chancel, there is perhaps the loveliest thing in the church, which makes our visit not just worthwhile but a must. This is a *Pietà*, where Christ lies stiffly across the Madonna's lap in the culmination of agony which has passed into a gradual dying state like a dream, as if death itself was a dream. It is attributed to Benedetto Bonfigli and dated 1469. On either side of the couple there are SS. Jerome and Leonard.

The chapel by which we are standing has at the altar a marble tabernacle with a bas-relief, the *Child Jesus blessing among angels*, quite harmonious. At the top window of the altar-wall, or rather on either side of it, there are the two parts of an *Annunciation* by Caporali, dated 1521 (a light-switch on the left of the entrance-arch). The decorations are by the same artist. On the right wall, above, there is a pleasant *Madonna and Child and two angels* by Giannicola da Paolo, and underneath it a framed copy of a Lo Spagna *Madonna and Child*.

On the wall between this and the next chapel we have a copy of Raphael's *Deposition*, and in the next chapel, called Ranieri, we find a Guido Reni on the left wall—*Jesus in the orchard*, a very theatrical piece. On the wall between this chapel and the next there is a framed picture by Sassoferrato (the man who did the Raphael copies we have just seen) which is gracefully unassuming.

The next chapel down is the **Cappella del Sacramento.** The canvases here are very ugly. One (*St Benedict sends St Maurus to France*) is such an inept and insipid piece of work, it so crawls with respect for hierarchy, that we should force ourselves to take a long look at it; it shows what natural taste the Italian painters have— the work of Giovanni Fiammingo (active 1579-93), a Belgian. Between this chapel and the next there is an energetic and splendidly designed *Three Magi* by Eusebio da S. Giorgio (1508).

After we have passed down the church a few more yards we come on a heavily framed *Annunciation*, another copy of Raphael, quiet and still, by Sassoferrato again. At the next altar there is a tall wooden *Crucifixion* of 1478: this is behind a curtain and we should ask a priest to draw it for us. And next to that is a late Perugino, a *Pietà* which used to be in the church of S. Agostino, not deeply felt but covered as always with his suave warmth of colour.

If when we come out of S. Pietro we cross the Borgo XX Giugno (the gate we see at the end of this road is the Porta S. Costanzo) we shall find ourselves in the *public gardens,* after passing an awful war memorial dated 1859. These were planted at the order of Braccio Fortebraccio and called 'del Frontone', meaning the triangular section crowning a Greek temple. There is a gravel walk with rows of holm oaks, and at the end—at the parapet—we find the 'amphitheatre' (it is no more than a clearing with arch and pillars) put there by the so-called Arcadians in the eighteenth century and designed by Baldassare Orsini. The Arcadians were the literary people of that time, and they dealt in a kind of dandified humanism, minus the faith. From the rounded parapet we have an almost complete view of the country south of the city.

We should now walk down to the *Porta S. Costanzo* and once outside turn to the right along the Viale Roma in the direction of the town-centre again: at our side we have a row of cypresses on a grassy bank, the lower reaches of the public gardens, more inviting than the planned gravel walks above. Below us on the left there is the new residential quarter, and we look down on TV aerials, tiny balconies with clothes hanging out to dry, water-tanks on flat roofs and pillbox apartment houses on which too little money and imagination have been spent. After about two hundred yards we pass on our left a girls' school (S. Anna) with a fifteenth-century cloister so restful on a sunny day that we should try to look like visiting parents and walk inside. And before us when we come out, like a toy railway station at our feet, is the *stazione Perugia S. Anna,* the terminus of a peaceful local line which serves central Umbria: the trains used to be slow little chug-chug affairs with iron railings which you could lean on, gazing out at the hot countryside, plucking off leaves now and then; but now they've electrified it.

The road bends round the back of this station and ends in the Largo Cacciatori delle Alpi, a modern square. We cross this (passing a Parisian-like café on the corner) along the Via dei Cacciatori delle Alpi, and pass the city's sports stadium on our right, once a big square. The road bends round this with young trees on either side, until we turn right along the Via Baldassare Orsini. At the top we come to the entrance of a military hospital behind a narrow gravel forecourt, the one-time monastery of *S. Giuliana.* If we wish to see the cloisters inside we should ask the sentry: it is worth it because we shall find one of the loveliest cloisters in Umbria, with clipped bushes in the middle, locked in its own world. It is supposed to have been the work of Gattaponi, the architect of Pope Paul III's

76

hated fortress, but this is not certain. At any rate, it came into being towards the end of the fourteenth century with octagonal pilasters in pink and white stone and a closed loggia above which has small slender pillars in sets of two. The well in the middle is from 1466. If we walk round to the farther side of the cloister we shall see the tower of the church next door, crowned with a stone pyramid. As we leave we should notice in the corridor on the right the remains of an earlier thirteenth-century cloister—two pillars and a fragment of Gothic ceiling.

The church of S. Giuliana next door was founded in 1253: the façade we see is a simple structure of pink and white squares added a hundred years later. The chancel has one nave, with a very open Gothic triumphal arch dividing the chancel from the congregation. On the left wall as we enter, high up, there is a large fragment of a *Last Supper*, where we see the influence of Cavallini (one of the Roman mosaic artists responsible for some of the Old Testament scenes in the Upper Church of St Francis at Assisi, and one of the fathers of Giotto's style) and Cimabue. Farther down, on the right wall, there is another detached fresco, a *Crucifixion* in a stiff version of the Byzantine manner, from the fourteenth century, where the later art that came with Cimabue and Giotto has been learned and observed but not appreciated: the old, rapt style, gleaming with faith, is preferred. Round the triumphal arch there are thirteenth- and fourteenth-century frescoes where only the design is vaguely visible, with faint figures. On the wall behind the main altar, above, we see *Christ and the Virgin* in a conch held by angels, by the same hand as the *Last Supper* which we have just seen and in the same grave and assured manner, before the world had to be observed in clear detail in order to be explained to other men: here it is all understood, a shared, glowing world, that seems enclosed in a wonderful hot sleep. Under it is a framed picture from the fourteenth century where the design of the Madonna's cloak, which she holds over the heads of her nuns, is the only motive the painting has: a kind of school painting. Lower down on the right there are the faint remains of a *Madonna del Latte* (the Virgin giving milk) with St John the Baptist at her side, from the same period.

And this is a very good end to our tour of Perugia, as it shows us some of the oldest frescoes in the town—besides one of the most precious cloisters in the world—and in the names of Cavallini and Cimabue it takes us a step nearer that centre of pilgrimage from which the whole province derives its sense of safety and isolation, and its mystical tone: Assisi. But first we shall want to look at something on the road, from the epoch when Umbria's importance as a religious centre began, in Etruscan times.

CHAPTER 3

On the Way to Assisi

Ipogeo dei Volumni

The important Etruscan tomb called the **Ipogeo dei Volumni** (the tomb of the Volumnius family) really completes our visit to the Archaeological Museum in Perugia. It remains on its own site, silent, with that speechless and inscrutable look of a past few of whose signs we understand, dug deep underground in the form of a great room with cubicles leading off, while the traffic bumps over a level-crossing a few yards from the entrance on its way to the Perugia–Spoleto superstrada. It can be combined with our journey to Assisi, as it lies on that road about a kilometre before the untidy Perugian suburb of Ponte S. Giovanni (where a bitter battle was once fought between Perugia and Assisi and St Francis was taken prisoner).

We shall find the *ipogeo* immediately before the first level-crossing we come to, after we have begun the descent from Perugia, housed in an unobtrusive nineteenth-century stone hut; there are narrow spaces on either side where cars may park. It is open 9.0 a.m.-1.0 p.m. every morning: in the winter the afternoons are 2.0-4.0 p.m., in summer 3.0-5.30 p.m. On holidays it is closed in the afternoon.

The tomb belonged to an aristocratic Etruscan family and is dated towards the end of the second century B.C. The hut we enter, besides being the tomb entrance, houses many Etruscan urns ranged in tiers, most of them made of travertine, some terra-cotta and some marble, and one sandstone, found in thirty-eight different tombs. Nearly all of them show traces of colour which has since faded, and most of them are what the scholars call 'architectonic', that is, in the shape of little houses, sometimes with triangular façades, sometimes complete with roof, sometimes crowned with a half-lying figure meant to be the deceased. We shall find more of these downstairs when we visit the actual tomb, belonging to the Volumnius family,

79

and to some of us it will be a surprise to find urns that architectur-
ally imitate full-size tombs while being in full-size tombs themselves.
Why were the dead not simply laid on the beds in each cubicle?
Why are the urns gathered, in this underground tomb, in a small
group? The scholars are little help in these things, perhaps because
the questions are simple. But it seems clear that while the bodies
were laid on the stone or earthen beds at the time of the highest
Etruscan civilization, they were cremated in the later epochs (as
perhaps their slaves had always been) like the Romans, and their
bones or ashes placed in these tiny imitation tombs: so we have,
in a tomb that combines the Etruscan and Roman worlds, both
usages—the full-length beds used for corpses, and the urns.

Generally these little urns we see ranged before us in tiers have
two round shields reversed decorating their fronts, as if their
occupants were military. A few urns have the deceased represented
on the lid with the *patera* in his hands, that is, the large shallow
cup used by the Greeks and later the Etruscans and Romans for
their libations to the gods: we shall remember these from other urns
at the cloister of the Archaeological Museum. And the façades of
these urns show various scenes. On the left we find at the lowest
tier (No. 122) *an episode of the Trojan cycle* in which Telephus threatens
to sacrifice Orestes in the presence of Clytemnestra, so as to be
cured by Achilles, who wounded him, and on the same tier (118)
we see *the Furies*. On the second tier (20) *the blessed life of the Elysian
fields*. Two urns (102) show *the Persian Wars*. On the third tier up
(156 and 157) there is *the head of the Gorgon-Medusa*, and we see many
other examples of this. To the left of these (21, 27 and 98) there is
horse-racing and *men riding sea-horses*. Immediately under the window
on this (left) side, No. 87, we see *the hunting of the Caledonian boar*.

If we now cross to the right side of the room we shall see on the
second tier up (13 and 152) *men playing the flute*. On the third tier up
(91, 107, 105, 19) Perugia's *griffin*. Behind us (55) there is *another
story of the Trojan cycle*, in which Iphigenia is sacrificed, with Aga-
memnon at the altar while a slave brings the ram substituted
by Artemis for the intended victim. On our right under the window
(150) there is *an erotic scene*, with suitable vague movements. On the
first tier in front of us again (18) there is a story from *the Theban
cycle*, and the same on the extreme left of this tier (78), in which we
see the murder of someone at the altar by Penelope, while Ippoda-
mia snatches away the wheel, symbol of his betrayal. At the second

tier on the extreme left of the row (114) we see *the blessed life of the Elysian fields* again, and on the same tier (141) *a demon announcing death*. Behind us (66) is *Scylla brandishing an oar*.

The Trojan and Theban cycles, the Persian wars, the hunting of the Caledonian boar and the erotic scene are all Greek subjects, while the Furies, the demon announcing death, the blessed life of the Elysian fields, the flute-players, the griffins, the horse-racing and the sea-horse riding, and the Gorgon-Medusa heads, are all Etruscan choices. Some people find the Etruscans a joyful and untamed people, others an anguished people given to great morbid terror of death: it depends which of the urns you look at, and both are probably true. Perhaps they inherited the anguish from the Greeks together with their gods and their radiance. Or perhaps anguish grew on the Etruscans late in their civilization, just as it did on the Greeks. But just because tombs are the only evidence we have of them we mustn't think they had nothing else to do but build them and paint them and brood on them.

On the right of the entrance we shall find a small room with glass cases full of objects found in the near-by tombs. The small case against the far left wall (objects actually from the *ipogeo dei Volumni*) has a bronze rod mounted with discs and figures. This is another *kottabos*, the Greek wine-throwing game, of the kind we have seen in the Etruscan rooms of the Archaeological Museum, but much more sumptuous. The base is sustained on three lion's paws each bearing the bust of a Fury, while each bust bears a sphinx on either side. The discs begin half-way up and are of diminishing size the higher they go, with two figures skirting them which were once winged: I imagine these two figures were used to set the apparatus in motion. There also used to be a plate under all these, exactly half-way up: there remains one above, balanced on the head of the uppermost figure, supposed to be the deified soul of the deceased, or the spirits of the dead in general, the *manes*: at least, that is a suggestion. This *kottabos* is even less complete now, due to a theft in 1966. Some say it was a game of skill, others for omens and others for a 'she-loves-me-she-loves-me-not' test. Its presence in the tombs has led people to say that it might have been used to predict death: but its connection with tombs is probably no greater than that of any other household utensil found in them. The scholars say that wine was thrown on to it (presumably from above) while it was in motion (the hanging baubles we see under the top figure made a tinkling noise), and the highest plate, on which it was thrown, then toppled off. But this does not seem much of a game, let alone a skilful one: and it remains one of those confident possessions of scholarship about which almost nothing sensible can be said.

In the same glass case there is the fragment of a shield, a helmet and two shin-pads, indicating the military status of the family: perhaps the head of the family was a general. In the longer case on the left there are vases of various kinds, glass phials, tiny terra-cotta jugs. In the centre of the room one of the cases contains a large *cratere* (from the Greek *krater*), a tall vase with a wide mouth and handles used by the Greeks, Etruscans and Romans for mixing wine and water during their banquets. In another case of its own there is a painted *cratere* of local make, from the third century B.C.: it shows *Hercules about to free Hesione,* and *Hercules with Hesione freed.*

And now to the tomb itself—with perhaps the loveliest urns we shall ever set eyes on. A dark ramp leads down to the entrance: a great slab of stone that was once the door lies on one side. This is an imitation of a Roman house almost to size: we have no bending and squeezing to do, as in most of the underground Etruscan tombs. It is all excavated out of tufo rock, which is relatively soft. And the interior remains just as it was found, apart from the pottery, bronze and jewellery in it. We pass through the square entrance and notice on its right jamb some Etruscan writing, carved into the stone: all we know is that it is 'vertical' writing, which may have signified something different from the horizontal (the Etruscans, by the way, read from right to left).

The rectangular room we enter first, the *atrium* or central court of a Roman house, is empty save for three short corridors on either side—that is, six in all—leading to the cubicles or *cubicula*, meaning bedrooms. And straight ahead of us, containing seven urns grouped in a strange intimacy, not symmetrically, is the *tablinum* or re-ception-room which always lay beyond the central court and was used both to receive guests and to store the family archives. We should glance at the ceiling of the *atrium* which is a mock roof. If we look back we shall see over the entrance in bas-relief a shield con-taining the face of Gorgon (the creature who turned men to stone with a look, her hair a coil of snakes) with a dolphin on either side. Over the entrance of the *tablinum* (designed like the pediment of a Greek façade) we see a more elaborately carved shield with another Gorgon's head and this time a sword or scimitar on either side and a bird perched on its handle (perhaps representing the spirit over-coming love of war), and male heads (the left one now missing) on either side of these. On the left of the *tablinum* entrance there is a terra-cotta snake's head curling out of the wall, a feature we see in every part of the tomb, some of them now missing though the hole remains visible, being the serpent of the underworld. Serpents always accompanied heroes, and were their genius. This at least is what the scholars say, but we should remember that in ancient Egypt the serpent represented the passions or sexuality, and was always shown in the clutches of the bird or spirit. In the entrance-arch of the *tablinum* hangs a little terra-cotta statue representing the tutelary genius of the place, with a lamp hanging from it which is an imitation of the original bronze one now destroyed. And the ceiling has another Gorgon's head.

The seven urns inside the *tablinum* remain in the same position as they were found in 1840, without any pattern, as a family itself would stand. The head of the family was a magistrate and his urn, the largest and most elaborate, is in the centre, a tall monument in two parts. The deceased rests on an elbow on a couch above, with cushions at either end, and the couch-legs are draped all round. The base, that is the lower half, has two carved figures with wings, the Furies, one of them carrying a torch, their faces remarkably reminiscent of Michelangelo: every guide will mention Michelangelo here and for once it isn't an academic comparison; it strikes you with an extraordinary vividness, you feel that Michelangelo must have had these figures as models, but of course they were brought to light centuries after his death. It shows what a thorough and deliberately backward glance the Renascence was. These two figures have an extraordinary calm nobility: between them are the traces of a fresco, which may have referred to the entry of the soul into the underworld. The deceased leaning on one elbow is Arunte Volumnius the son of Aulus (*Arnth Velimnas Aules*, in the Etruscan writing).

On the right are four urns of less importance, belonging to other members of the family, three of them with Gorgons' heads on the front, carved as finely as the two Furies on the main urn. On the left there are two urns, one of them with a woman on a throne—Velia Volumnia, daughter of Arunte (in Etruscan *Veilia Velimnei Arnthial*). The other urn is of a later date—the first century A.D.—and is a replica of a little temple in marble, without figures or base (the roof is detachable) and so ordered and symmetrical that we are clearly in the Roman, and no longer the Etruscan, world. The writing here is both Roman and Etruscan, unlike that on the other tombs: *Publius Volumnius Auli Filius Violens Cafatia Natus,* that is to say, Publius Volumnius the son of Aulus and a member of the Cafatia or Cafazia family, the grandson of a former more famous Publius Volumnius who had been a friend of Cicero's and a wealthy man. The Etruscan is written at the top and the Latin on the pediment of the façade.

This tomb should lay the ghost of the 'problem' of Etruscan-Roman origins which the scholars find difficult. In fact, the scholars may have invented the problem by dividing the Etruscans and the Romans for study purposes, when these peoples were not in practice divided at all. They simply melted one into the other. The Etruscans settled—started—Rome, therefore they were the first Romans. In the *ipogeo dei Volumni* we see perfectly the transition from one phase of Etruscan life to the next. The last occupant, a Roman from imperial times, returned to his Etruscan roots. It solves half the mystery of the Etruscan people once we consider that we have the climax or debasement of their civilization (depending on which way we look at it) spread before us in the form of ancient Rome, which is not a mystery to us at all.

CHAPTER 4

Assisi I

Assisi stretches across one of the slopes of Monte Subasio like a great wide staircase, built in the red and white stone of the hill itself, on some days pink, on others vague like a cloud, sometimes brilliantly white. The approach from the small town of S. Maria degli Angeli in the plain is that traditionally used by travellers (Goethe left his coach here and walked the rest), and today it is Assisi's only railway station (a fifteen-minute bus-ride away). It gives a sudden, shining view of Assisi from below, spread brightly across its hill from left to right in a series of parallel roads, high and exhilarating and for-bidding at the same time. The other approach, which leaves the Perugia-Spoleto superstrada some kilometres before S. Maria degli Angeli, and convenient only for car drivers, shows it to us more gradually: the town appears slowly out of the mist (that of heat or winter), like a sheet draped on the hill, a little menacing, ghostly as Cassino used to be.

Both approaches reveal the gaping foundations of the Basilica of St Francis on the extreme left of the town, tunnelled arrogantly into the hill, all the more precipitous and towering as we draw nearer (the bus will take us close to it, one stop before we enter town). The Church clearly spared no cost here. And this approach gives the right idea, because St Francis the Basilica does dominate the rest of the town—detached, hardly noticed by the inhabitants ('such a long way,' they say in the main square), but with a brooding sense of its own power because it holds the key to the town as a centre of pil-grimage, which is Assisi's all. Two million people are said to visit it every year. And the church is the only papal see outside St Peter's in Rome, with a papal throne and papal apartments inside the monastery's enclosure.

And the soul of the place is St Francis himself, not at all detached

85

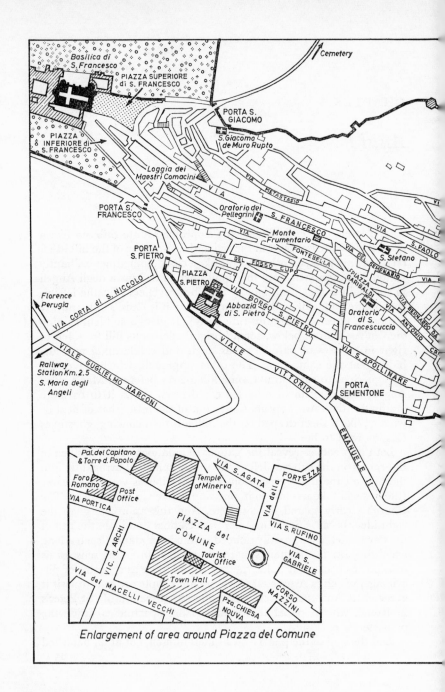

Enlargement of area around Piazza del Comune

from the town but still as strong as a living memory. I heard an inhabitant say in a puzzled way once, 'You see, he was a little mad—inspired—he used to coo to the pigeons and baa at the sheep' (taking animals seriously is still mainly a joke in Italy). And because of this memory dominating the town, and the church that guards it, Assisi has survived as an intact mediaeval city more perhaps than any in the world, its tiny lanes and outdoor staircases (many of them curling between the houses, unnavigable by even the smallest car) barely altered since five hundred years ago. Assisi is controlled rigidly from this point of view: not a stone may be altered without local permission, and factories are kept at a distance, beyond the town boundaries, mostly at Bastìa.

Assisi began as an Umbrian settlement, in fact one of the region's centres of religious worship, like Gubbio. There are some Etruscan influences but few, and the rule holds that the Etruscans (perhaps fearing the sharp winds and bleak hills and the lack of access to the sea) did not penetrate these eastern regions of Umbria in great number. In the year 309 B.C. there was a battle between the Romans and the Umbro-Etruscan confederation at the foot of Monte Subasio, and after this the hill became known as 'the mount of Minerva Asisia'—we shall see the town's famous Temple of Minerva later. Then the town became Asisium under the Romans, dedicated to the Sergia tribe. About the origin of the name little is known but there are theories. An old legend says that Asio, brother of Hecuba, Queen of Troy, founded the town after the fall of Ilium, and gave it his own name. But other scholars say that the name comes from Acu, meaning the Levant, because it was east of Perugia: though this too seems a tall story.

The people were converted to Christianity by St Rufinus (the duomo is dedicated to him): he was martyred here in A.D. 238. The town suffered the usual spoliation under Totila and, like Perugia, came under the powerful Lombardian duchy of Spoleto. And then, again like Perugia, it achieved a sturdy independence after the danger of foreign invasion had passed for a time. Its traditional enemy was naturally—they are so close, after all—Perugia, now its master administration-wise. Assisi was Ghibelline, mostly because Perugia was Guelf, but it had Guelf factions. Barbarossa returned the town to the Duke of Spoleto after its period of independence: Assisi rose against this rule at the end of the twelfth century, during the life of St Francis, when a middle class was already powerful enough to challenge the old patrician families (St Francis belonged to a new commercial family, and St Clare to a patrician). Then there came the rule of private families, including the Sforza and the Montefeltri, after which, like all other Umbrian towns, Assisi passed into the hands of the Church—though not without some trouble at the beginning: fighting went on between rival factions, especially between the Nepis and Fiume families (both exist today), whose quarrels over many generations terrorized the town and divided it into 'upper' and 'lower' parts, a division that still holds (not entirely as a pleasant joke) and figures in the astonishing May Day celebrations.

Sixteenth-century Assisi was more pleasant than mediaeval Assisi, but only because it was a backwater under the bland and sleepy protection of priests and directed, like the ancient empire, from Rome, where blandness had been an art of government since Etruscan times. This period more than any other gave the town its present atmosphere, a little apart, a little drowsy, and still a little burning with the old fires of hatred that St Francis tried to quench.

It was only recently that what the Church calls its spiritual awakening happened: it became a centre of vast pilgrimage. That was the result of the seventh centenary of St Francis's death, in 1926: during the celebrations a total of two million pilgrims (the sum of two million figures a lot in local Franciscan calculations) came from every part of the world. In 1939 Pope Pius XII put the seal of authority on it by proclaiming St Francis a patron saint of Italy, together with Catherine of Siena (St Clare was made the patron saint of television, of all idiocies). It was not the first time the pope had given his seal of approval to the memory of St Francis, for a much earlier pope laid the first stone of the Basilica we see today: the memory of St Francis was a great power over the imagination, and perhaps like Christ's (St Francis intended the analogy), a danger to sober government.

Assisi really was at one time a city of silence, as d'Annunzio called all the towns of Umbria. Until very recently its dominant sounds were the trickle of fountains and the plod of feet, and church bells, and the faint rush of a warm breeze from the valley. Cars have robbed it of a lot. On a hot day when nothing moved in the fields it seemed to lie separate in its own time, belonging only to the sky, while the bare hills brooded at the back like silent guards. It still is detached, to the irritation of a lot of the inhabitants (though not the brightest): the age-old Italian sadness—the sense of a helpless, priest-ridden life—survives here more than anywhere else in central Italy, partly because the priest remains an influence if not really a power. So the roar of the car is cherished as at least one thing not five or so centuries old, and not produced by the Church.

At the same time the town enjoys her detachment as few others in Italy can afford to. It remains more or less one family. People born here find themselves yearning for its special tedium when they are away; and its importance in the history of ecclesiastical power rescues it from provinciality too; it is never a backwater. It has far more tourism for its size than any town in the world. So many languages are spoken in its streets, there are so many convents and monasteries of every nationality, that the tedium is never quite complete, always bearable and sometimes sweet. The processions and feasts are shared by everybody, unless they are very much church affairs, which are shared less. A certain sweetness and lightness remain intact between people, the origin of which is certainly St Francis: not the wildest enemy of the Church, even of Christianity, could doubt that. But the poor feel, 'What a pity his power came down to us by courtesy of the priests' (*forchettoni*, as they are called in Italy, meaning 'a big fork-full'—of other people's property and labours). St Francis will never be quite a priest or even monk for them, but a living person. It is difficult to doubt a man who deliberately became poor from being rich: he knew exactly what he was doing; he knew that power and influence, although the words are usually run together, are basically incompatible.

Anyone visiting Assisi for the first time comes away with an amazing sense of that saint, though he may not visit a church or know more than a few facts about him, such as that he loved animals.

St Francis—'the little Frenchman' and 'a fool of God'—twelve companions— the Rule of Poverty and the Basilica

St Francis was born in 1181 or 1182, the son of a cloth-merchant who was rich by local standards. Giovanni Bernardone was his real name, and the name '*il Francesco*'—the little Frenchman—came to him perhaps because his father had just taken a trading journey to France at the time of his birth, or because the child was half-French anyway (his mother came from Provence); or it may have come about gradually because he spoke fluent French and liked the songs and tales of chivalry that were coming from France at this time, brought by minstrels and troubadours. These songs were perhaps the greatest external influence on his life—the seed of his gaiety as a playboy and of his gaiety as 'a fool of God' later on.

There was every reason to call him 'the little Frenchman'. Chivalry was not just a fashion, though this was how it seemed to people yearning for fashions, but a new concept of love, the fulfilment of a Christian concept in daily life, mostly in the life between men and women. Neither the world Christ grew up in nor the Roman world—much less its Greek predecessor—gave women much of a sacred position in life: but this is precisely what the new chivalry did. 'Falling in love' really came into being for the first time—a love not strictly for the act of sex, or for producing children, or even quite for pleasure. It carried something moral with it too, the connection of women with a certain kind of vision. It endowed women with a new place in life—Christ was the first to suggest it in his (socially outrageous) treatment of whores and heathen women; every creature was God's, he said, and in that godlike. It was a new radiance in the darkness of family and racial and class interest— the idea that a human creature could be beyond all these, his own possession, because he was the possession of God, however foolish he was, however bad. It was the beginning of freedom in our sense. It was love as free choice, not interest or appetite: and chivalry—its songs and adventures devoted to women—was exactly this. Never before had the relation between men and women been an act of light and freedom, never before an adventure, much less an adventure of ideas. And naturally the love extended, by inference, to wherever a creature of God was found: it came to cover all life, because love is a state and not a decision; it was a certain form of gaiety. If grasped properly in youth it could lead to self-abnegation in age; and this is what happened to St Francis.

It was either an illness or his imprisonment as a twenty-year-old soldier that changed him from the first gaiety to the second. The events are mixed up at this distance of time: and a lot of legend has been piled on. But the skeleton of his life is clear. He wanted to fight again after his release from prison—some say in the Crusades, some say in Apulia against Frederick II the Hohenstaufen. He set out: he wanted to return a real knight; he already had the horse, that first social mark of the gentleman. But he suddenly turned back and never thought of soldiering again: some say because of a dream. He put the horse back in its stable and started behaving oddly, at least in the eyes of the townsfolk. But then he'd been very wild before. He had dressed in a sort of harlequin's coat, with one colour down one side and another down the other. But there was something different now. He paid no further attention to clothes, for one thing. He told his old friends that he'd fallen in love, but didn't specify with whom; that he would soon be marrying the most marvellous bride in the world, but she never appeared; yet it was all in the wild style of his old language. He said he'd become a man of great wealth, but there was no sign of money. And he disappeared for long periods. He said he was going into the country to speak to his bride, then hid himself in a cave for an hour. As his bride was invisible and his wealth was invisible, he had clearly fallen in love with the invisible: which for most of the people round him meant that he was off his head.

This was supported by the way he behaved. He did unpredictable things, like visiting caves. And people began to discount him, which seemed to be exactly what he wanted. Gradually he came to be despised. The shame of having given up a knight's career without explanation—which meant on the face of it cowardice—was enough to bring him contempt.

A family crisis was started when his father sent him to Foligno to sell some cloth and he sold not only the cloth but the horse as well and then tried to convince the frightened priest of the little church of S. Damiano to take the money for church repairs. The priest refused: naturally he didn't want to get on the wrong side of a powerful local family. And St Francis is said to have thrown the money in at the window (we can see the window today), where it lay untouched. Probably his father took it as another wild game and rode to S. Damiano to fetch him back home: after all, from being wild his son had become criminal—not an unlikely step. Perhaps it was only the last straw in a long list of deliberate disgraces. They were certainly deliberate: Francis knew what he was doing and was out to provoke a definite public action. In front of the bishop—in front of the bishop's palace, in a little square we can visit today, not much changed from what it was then—his father invited him to stop playing the fool: and there was quite a crowd of onlookers. Francis's answer was to play the fool even more: he took all his clothes off.

The bishop was probably as frightened as the priest of S. Damiano had been and he hurried to put something round him. The meaning of the act was clear: Francis was renouncing everything; he didn't give a damn for the family inheritance. It was the last act of shame his father could tolerate, and he publicly, at this moment, gave him up and stripped him of his inheritance.

From that moment on Francis began curing lepers, restored the churches of Porziuncola, S. Damiano and S. Pietro, and above all he begged. It was the beginning of a begging order. There again the act was deliberate: and in its deliberateness his life was a reflection of Christ's, who also premeditated every step he took, so that the events would later read like a continuous and simple story, leading clearly to a foreseen climax. The point of being a beggar was that you had nothing further to lose: you were free to love everyone. If you threw yourself on the mercy of other people you saw the truth about them. As no one was lower than the beggar, no one was beneath his intimate consideration, or above it. His intimacy with the world grew; he was alive to the most trivial frets. He became available for other men's misery.

People in Assisi still talk today about the special quality of St Francis's eyes as he passed you in the street: as if he had a secret personal knowledge of you, was almost part of you. It made you feel extraordinarily significant. His gaze made you good, peaceful. He was now dressed in the tunic of the simplest Umbrian peasant, with a *funicella* or rope-belt with three knots tied in it, which remains the Franciscan habit today.

He became aware of nature in a new, intimate way: the sun became 'brother sun', the moon was 'sister moon'; his *laudi* or written praises, which became the habit of his life, were the seeds of literature in the Christian sense. It was like suddenly waking up to the throbbing life in everything: the radiance of things was that they had been created. And this is what he brought out in people, the part that was radiant in them, belonging to them as none of the facts *about* them did. This is why animals felt confident with him. People said he could even stop the birds singing if he wanted to.

All this, again, was deliberate. The old pagan fears—of a sky that avenged itself on you for a word spoken in jest, of animals that were really demons, of woods that were full of evil spirits—were as strong as they had always been (and indeed they persist in Italy today). In fact Christian habits had not yet entered the fabric

93

of daily life. The first Christianity had been practised in Constanti-nople, and Italy had been administered from Byzantine Ravenna. Now Rome was alone. And it could not support the dead weight of what it called heresy (really the collapse of bad belief) that was growing every day. It was on its last legs: there were now all kinds of sects and occult groups, as in the last days of the empire. And the point about Francis's practical life was that he kept the Church from falling completely. He again addressed the poor—with a poor man's story. And he did it by making nature—every animal, plant and element—the radiant possession of a sound and perfect God who answered grace with grace and was not vengeful or indeed a person at all. He made nature a place where we belong, not a fearful bog of unpredictable and mainly malevolent tricks. It really meant re-capturing the west for Christianity: it meant *creating* Rome. We may even say that St Francis brought Christianity into being as far as the western organization of it was concerned. He altered people's minds: he captured the human imagination in precisely the same way as Christ, whose story had gone through the ruined Roman empire like magic, had captured it a thousand years before. It was why Francis's first act was to become a poor man himself.

There has always been a lot of talk about whether or not the Church squashed his teaching after his death. The fact is that it couldn't have done this if it had tried. His teaching—which was really that of joy—had already been translated into too many things by the time of his death for that to be possible: he had created so many living memories—like Christ again—that they had melted into daily life without people knowing it. And we know this to be the case because of the frescoes of Cimabue and Giotto, and the work of Dante: the beginning of a definite Christian art and poetry quoted him as their beginning, as the source of their feeling. If the Church had really obliterated his memory and power of influence you would not see any frescoes in any churches, let alone Cimabue and Giotto frescoes in the Basilica of Assisi. The unbelievable array of art in Italy in the centuries immediately following St Francis's death will never be understood without referring to this astonishing life-discovery, open to any and every person.

The Church did reverse St Francis on his home ground, in Italy. It brought back the Middle Ages, once its power was assured again. It did cauterize the imagination—a faculty he had done everything to stir: the history of the Counter-Reformation and the Jesuit movement are a testimony of that. But it could not stop the influence spreading abroad and culminating in movements of reform, in the belief that each man should have his own conscience and act on it— a belief as foreign to the earlier church as bigamy. St Francis would have been horrified by most of the reformers, especially Luther, but his life laid the seeds of reform just the same, in its first soil which we call humanism. Had the Church reacted to his teaching better it would have saved the world from Reformation: it would have reformed itself.

St Francis's first two companions were Bernardino da Quintavalle, another wealthy citizen of Assisi (his house is still standing), and someone called Pietro Cattani, who seems to have been a canon. The third was a poor man named Egidio: and with him something like an order of monks began. When Francis had twelve companions— a deliberate reflection of the twelve disciples—he went to Rome (1209 or 1210) and obtained from the very enlightened and magnanimous pope of that time, Innocent III, approval for his Rule, a list of recommendations based on the principles of poverty, chastity and obedience. The Church didn't mind the chastity, much less the obedience, but it wondered where the poverty would lead: you couldn't run a church-empire on a shoestring; and without an empire there wouldn't have been a Europe.

The stupendous basilica built after St Francis's death was the Church's answer: it simply ruled the rule of poverty out of court— so much so that the Franciscans today are one of the richest orders in existence. St Francis was aware of the danger—the moment he formed the Order: but without an Order his work would have remained that of a sect, and in the end—after his death—perhaps an heretical sect, which would finally have been forgotten.

After his visit to Rome he returned to Assisi and began preaching peace and the end of feudal rights. He went to Perugia, Cortona, Arezzo, Florence, Pisa and did penance on an island in Lake Trasimene. In 1212 he received Clare. She is said to have watched him from the crowd when he threw his clothes off outside the bishop's palace. That was the beginning of the second Franciscan order—the installation of the 'poor Clares', the young 'brides of Christ' (he performed the symbolic act of cutting Clare's hair) at the little church of S. Damiano. Later a third order was created for lay Franciscans (Dante, Giotto, Leonardo da Vinci, Michelangelo, Gutenberg, Velazquez, Rubens and Cervantes were members).

And then, after his foreign travels, began the period of his life—the last—which few people have understood because it seems to reverse all the radiance of his former self. He retired (1224) to Mount Averna, a high, bare hill near Arezzo where he had already founded a monastery, and more or less fasted himself to death there, nearly blind, exposing himself to the savage cold of that height. When the body reaches a certain stage of submission to the will it can take extraordinary exposures, as we know from the voluntary ascetics of every religion. The word ascetic meant in its original Greek form the régime of training necessary for an athlete: in the genuine mystics like St Francis it meant precisely the same thing—and not less joy, only invisible joy, that burst into moments of ecstasy.

The following year he was treated in Rieti and then Siena for a disease of the eyes called glaucoma and not long afterwards he died in Assisi, at the bishop's palace again (1226). He asked to be taken down to Porziuncola when he felt death coming on, and there he recommended to his companions 'the dearest Lady, Poverty', as if he knew that the Order might fall down on this one principle. He was canonized only two years later. His first biographer was Tomaso da Celano (1229), one of his own companions, so that we have a reliable key to his life.

The Basilica of St Francis

After he died one of his followers, Brother Elias, whom he had elected Vicar-General of the order, thought of raising a church in his name, where his body would be housed. And the Church, in the person of Cardinal Ugolino del Conti, protector of the Order, agreed. In fact, the cardinal became pope a little later and as Gregory IX gave an official order to Brother Elias to build a new church on an immense scale and in three parts—a basilica, a monastery and a palace for the Vicar-General: he ordered the provincials of the Franciscan order to help.

The most zealous of St Francis's followers were against the magnificence of the project. But the Vatican never really dealt with the argument: the pope simply laid the foundation stone on July 17th, 1228, the very next day after Francis was canonized. It seemed like a hurried job: as if the rule of poverty was being buried with the saint.

The **Basilica of St Francis** was planned as two separate

Above: The gaping foundations of the basilica of St Francis seen from outside Assisi. *Below:* The Lower Church of St Francis. The frescoed arch on the left leads to the Simone Martini chapel. St Francis's tomb is in the crypt below.

Above: Pietro Lorenzetti's miraculous *Madonna dei Tramonti* in the Lower Church. *Below:* St Francis renounces his inheritance — the fifth fresco from Giotto's *Life of St Francis* in the Upper Church.

churches, one on top of the other, from the very beginning. The lower part constituted the crypt, and was completed in 1230: the building of the upper church went on while the crypt was still being tunnelled out of the hill below. St Francis's body was brought there at once, and until the fifteenth century could be seen, like that of St Clare today: but its place underneath the high altar was sealed up, due to continued threats from Perugians (any enemy of Assisi at that epoch would have been called Perugian) to remove it.

No one is quite sure who the architect of the church was, but people say that Brother Elias himself made the first drawing of the whole complex of buildings. During his period of generalship building went on fast, but after he was excommunicated in 1239 (see p. 131) it slackened: not until 1253 was the church consecrated (by another pope, Innocent IV) and even then it lacked the side-chapels. The painters started their work about 1236, and at the end of that century the Lower Church was enlarged with the entrance we see today, and the side-chapels were built. With the completion of the chapel of St Catherine in 1367 the church became what we see today.

The Lower Church of St Francis

The church will have been obvious to the visitor by its arched foundations rising tier on tier up the hillside, so that wherever he is staying in the town he will know what direction to take. And to help him, all the roads of Assisi lead to it and are parallel to one another. We are clearly meant to go to the **Lower Church** first, though a glimpse of the upper one will try to draw us in, especially if we already know that the Giotto frescoes are there.

The Piazza Inferiore di S. Francesco or Lower Square lies framed in an arched porch from the fifteenth century, under which pilgrims used to rest from the sun: today the car-park attendants use it. We should notice the little iron rings in the wall every yard or so for tying up animals. When deserted, especially on a still summer day, this square belongs to the countryside below, refers to it in a strange way, in a dialogue that even now hasn't quite been broken. This presence of the countryside, immediately under the city walls, is what gives Assisi its mediaeval character more than its actual stones.

C.G.U.—G

The town has kept a sanity rare in Italy today, where ragged suburbs built in the last ten or fifteen years suffocate approaches and hide the fields.

As we face the Lower Church entrance we have behind us the little **Oratory of St Bernardine of Siena** with its double doors under one archway, added by the Third or Lay Order in the fifteenth century: the stone bas-relief shows *St Bernardine between two saints.* This is a delicate little corner after the massive, towering glimpse we have had of the Basilica from the square. And on our left, in this little introductory courtyard, with squat posts bordering it formerly used for horses, we have the gateway of the monastery itself, under a high and wide archway once open to the public: the brief stretch of road behind it, leading to the door of the Enclosure, has a fountain and what used to be a hostel for pilgrims. Over this archway we see *the arms of St Francis,* two hands crossed over the other, one representing Christ's, the other a man's.

And now the entrance of the Lower Church itself, grand and hushed—warning us of a certain rare solemnity inside. At one time its two tall wooden doors, under a single archway like the little Oratory opposite (which imitates it), were exposed to the weather: the protective arch and canopy on robust (perhaps ancient Roman) pillars were added in the fifteenth century by Francesco da Pietrasanta. It frames the entrance with a very open Roman arch, and the inscription running along the top refers to the Minor Friars of the Franciscan Order (the *minors* and *majors* of the town were the people and the noble classes: hence the monks called themselves *minori*). The portal sheltered underneath is actually later than the church inside, from the fourteenth century, with slender pillars rising together to a Gothic point, under a rose window with intricately carved radial arms: and under this, in a small triangle, its gilt shining no more, there is a figure of *St Francis blessing,* in mosaic. The two tall carved doors are later still, from the middle of the sixteenth century.

We enter the dimness of the church—and find ourselves in perhaps the most elaborate crypt ever conceived, in which Mass and other offices are continually celebrated and where not one inch of wall or arch is untouched by the painter. Everything is shrouded for the act of prayer or self-examination, and it is a favourite place for confession. This is the home of St Francis's tomb. As we shall see later, it is in extraordinary contrast to the church above, and intentionally. The idea of public worship—the crowds, impatient children and pews—belongs upstairs.

We shall see the chapels grouped near the entrance (including the Chapel of St Martin where the Simone Martini frescoes are) best by strong morning sunlight, while the area round the main altar is best seen in the afternoon, though most parts of the church will need the help of electric light, for which we may ask any of the friars not taking confession. They are not always gracious, unless we show that we are anything but poor. Determined humble persistence helps.

The first impression is of a strange, dark, vivid grotto tunnelled under the earth, its low Roman arches alternating—never at the cost of harmony—with Gothic ones. The lowness and roundness of the Roman arches one after the other make a grave effect, unmarred by the crossing Gothic lines, which seem perfectly uncalculated; though this is the first appearance in Italy of that new style from France. We peer into the darkness down to the high altar, which lurks there like a light in a cave. So carefully was the Lower Church planned that its floor slopes gently down towards the altar from the back—a descent of over three feet, to give those at the back a better view.

This Lower Church is one simple nave—we turn left into it from the entrance—unencumbered by open chapels or side-naves: this is, in fact, the original form; the side-chapels were added later because a one-naved basilica was simply not big enough for the great number of pilgrims who came to Assisi. We must imagine the church ending where the first pillars of the nave stand, at the level of the holy water font. The side-chapels are hardly apparent at first: this is why our first impression is a simple and direct one; we have an impression only of arches; even the steps leading up to the side-chapels are invisible to us from the back.

The ceiling is divided into five *campate* or vaults made out of crossing arches, and in the main part of the nave each of these contains a chapel on either side. Only the ceilings remained untouched by frescoes, except for the one over the chancel: they are simply painted, with the arches minutely and colourfully decorated. This divergence of one pattern from another, in arch after arch, should disturb the harmony but again does not: over the whole Lower Church there is an atmosphere of clustered and bursting growth—not an inch fails to offer a pattern of circles or squares or intertwining lines or leaves or cubes, no space is without the aspiring Gothic

99

point or the sweeping, stern Roman arch, and this is not to mention the blazing colour or, when our eyes are used to the dark, the frescoes that have captured every wall, each telling a different story not only by virtue of its subject but by its style and tones. Most visitors hurry in and hurry out again, with hardly more than a glance. But we should spend at least half a day going slowly from one discovery to the next. The numbered plan opposite will help us. People who believe that the Upper Church with the St Francis series is the real point of any visit will find themselves reluctant to leave the Lower Church after all, once they have penetrated its darkness. Guidebooks often advise a pair of binoculars and a torch, but the walls were painted with the poor natural light in mind, the colours were pitched according to it, they were meant, like stained glass (stained to restrain and not enhance the natural light), to be seen from below by the unaided human eye.

Immediately on our left after entering (1 on the numbered plan), before we reach the holy water fount, we shall see beyond an iron gateway the little **Chapel of St Sebastian,** with a fresco (1646) behind the altar which would be pleasant to look at if we had nothing of an earlier period to see. We are lucky, by the way, not to have the whole of the Basilica, including the Giotto series upstairs, painted over in this style: it was often suggested in the seventeenth and later centuries but never done. Beyond this little chapel is the first fresco—actually on the wall—that gives a sign of the earlier world: a *Madonna and Child enthroned with SS. Francis, Anthony the Abbot and Rufinus* (Francis carries no staff and bears the stigmata), the only known work of Ceccolo di Giovanni, who seems to have been a pupil or helper of Ottaviano Nelli. The Madonna has a sad, reminiscent gaze: here and there on her cloak we catch a glimpse of the original colour before it faded, green and purple, so that we can imagine the lively splendour these frescoes had at the beginning. Otherwise it is a gauche little piece: the hand of the Madonna is strangely bent, and the statuettes round the throne look academic and stiff. It lingers between the early seriousness of the Cimabue, Giotto and Lorenzetti periods and the picturesqueness of the Renascence at its climax: a work of the fifteenth century. Opposite this—that is, on the right wall (2) as we enter the church— we see a tall stone sepulchre high up with a canopy and a massive urn placed on its shelf: this was erected for the Cerchi family in the fourteenth century, and the urn came from a Queen of Cyprus, its

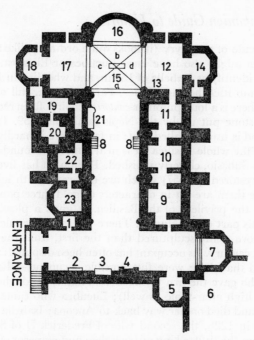

LOWER CHURCH of S. FRANCIS

handles made of porphyry (it looks quite ordinary, like a clay pot). This queen might also have been Eucubea or Elisabea, whom the historians identify as Isabella of Ibelin, and who died in 1267. Some say the tomb itself belongs to her. Farther down, still on the right wall (3), there is a long pulpit or *cantoria* (choir-loft) in red and white Subasian stone put up by the Nepis family in 1459. It looks like marble and is usually called that: in fact, there is hardly a piece of marble in the whole Basilica; it is nearly all from round the corner, on Monte Subasio, cleverly polished. The pulpit has five panels on the face (restored in 1657) which are decorated with inlaid stones, and above them are set in characters of gold three papal bulls referring to the privilege of the Basilica. It gives a pleasant hidden glow to this part of the church. There is another sepulchre farther on (4), more richly sculptured than the first, from the end of the thirteenth century. Its occupant has often been disputed: at one time it was said that there were five possible occupants—the Queen of Cyprus who gave the urn to the Cerchi family (and who may have given the high altar-table as well); Eucubea who came to Assisi as a pilgrim and died on her way back to Ancona; Isabella of Brienne who died in 1228, the second wife of Frederick II of Swabia; her father John, the titular king of Jerusalem and emperor of Constantinople, who died in 1237; and his successor as emperor of Constantinople, Philip I of Courtenay, who died in 1283. Now only the two males are considered, the figures on the tomb not being female at all as was hitherto thought (they show bare feet, which female figures never did), and of these two men John is preferred, as he ended his life a Minor Friar.

Continuing along the same wall we come (5) to the **Chapel of St Anthony the Abbot** which contains the tomb of a Duke of Spoleto, Blasco Fernandez, together with that of his son: they were both murdered in 1367. (At Christmas a great spreading crib covers this chapel, with a trickling fountain, flocks of sheep and castles on the hill.) Access to the **cloister** is through the chapel. This (6) used to be the monastery's cemetery, until the Napoleonic order of 1804 (the Order of St Cloud) insisted on burial-places being outside towns. The arches are on two storeys, the lower from the fifteenth century, the higher from the sixteenth. The oldest date among the tombstones round the cloister is 1295, belonging to the first construction. Here doves are caged in the winter, fondly fed and watered by the friars, and among the cypresses in the middle of the cloisters there is a modern statue of the saint which is not too insipid. We shall find in this cloister a large sarcophagus from the second century B.C. of the same type as that used for the burial of St Francis: but this one has clearly been used as a water-trough. There are pipes of stone made by the first builders of the Basilica: they carried out a clever operation of drilling massive blocks of stone with an iron spike turned by asses, on the same principle as a mill; they were called to Perugia to do the same work, and their pipes were mostly used for conducting water. On the right side of the cloister as we enter it there is a Latin inscription with an interesting mistake, doubling the 's' in nearly every word: '*Isstud Esst Sepulcrum Francissci*—This is the Franciscan cemetery', due to the hard *s* used in local speech and heard most clearly in the word *Assisi*. Looking through the cloister gate at the side of the church we see bulky pieces of white pillar (often thought to be marble but again Sub-asian stone) which were taken from the tomb of St Francis in the Lower Church because they were thought too grand and luxurious. We should note the vast pillars, or rather towers, of red stone that flank the church and are its mainstays. There are twelve of them, and like everything else in the design of the Basilica they have a symbolic meaning—the twelve disciples, whether of Christ or St Francis. Even the colour of the stone used was intentional: while the Lower Church was built in red, to denote the darkness of the tomb, the death of the flesh, the Upper is in white, to represent the immaculate Christ and his public or evangelical mission. Looking from the cloister gate we can also see the white walls of the Upper Church, between the red of the towers: and the boundary line between the two colours can be seen in parts of the church, exactly where the Lower Church ends and the Upper begins. The red cylindrical pillars or towers are, of course, planted right down to the base of the Lower Church, so that they grip the whole construction: they sprout out of the Lower Church because they are part of the *inside* walls of the side-chapels there, while their upper halves are part of the *outside* walls of the Upper Church (which consists of one nave without side-chapels).

We should now return to the Lower Church and begin again at the entrance with a clearer idea of how the whole two-basilica construction was conceived. If we turn into the nave and face the main altar we shall see on the first pillars of either side, at the mouth of the nave, the signs of an earlier wall that was once fixed into them: this was the back of the first Lower Church, before the side-chapels or the transept of the entrance were added. The entrance to the church before these were added would have been roughly where the choir-loft or *cantoria* is now. And of course these first pillars are the roots of those red-stoned towers we saw from outside, and now we can see how they also form the base of each arch belonging to the side-chapels.

Before turning into the main nave we should notice, exactly facing the entrance, across the first transept, the ***Chapel of St Catherine or the Crucifix*** (7), built by Matteo Gattaponi (from Gubbio) on the order of a Spanish cardinal who was buried there for a time: it has a simple polygonal design in red and white stone in squares, the frescoes barely visible, though they are a little more so in the afternoon; these are *scenes from the life of St Catherine of Alexandria* by Andrea da Bologna (1368). On the left wall there is a portrait of the Spanish cardinal by the same painter. Andrea da Bologna was also responsible for the *eighteen saints* depicted on the three stained-glass windows of this chapel, which for quiet sombre light and elaborate simplicity seem to summarize the whole Lower Church.

Now the main nave. The frescoes on the wall to the left and right —between the arches that form the entrances to the first side-chapels—are always described as by the '*Maestro di S. Francesco*': that is, no one knows who he was. For a long time they were ascribed to Giunta Pisano (1202-56) but this is now rejected. We know that the painting of the St Francis Basilica started in 1236, the lower basilica having been finished in its primitive form six years before, and that these walls were the first to be done, or are the oldest to survive. And they are the first sign of the new so-called Gothic art. The word Gothic here means the whole period of art which coincided with the replacement of the rounded Romanesque arch with the pointed one, and the building of churches not by masses placed squarely on each wall and rising solidly to sustain a roof but by a sort of skeleton of pillars, ribs and buttresses which held the walls and vaults together like a thin shell. It began towards the end of the twelfth century in the north of France and spread slowly across the rest of Europe. And in the Basilica we have not a clean, much less startling, manifestation of this new style as in Orvieto cathedral, but a mixture, a perfect compromise, which confronts us in the conflicting arches of the Lower Church as soon as we step inside. Only in the Upper Church is the Gothic fully released—where it belongs.

When we come to use the word Gothic about frescoes it is harder
to say what we mean. There is no clear distinction of ribs and vaults
and arches. But the feeling is new. There is a new approach to the
human face, to movement and the shape of hands, to the whole
purpose of decorating walls and altars at all. The subjects change—
not at first but slowly. The New Testament begins to displace the
Old. And then even living people, like St Francis or St Martin, are
described in their daily lives. And from that the life of Christ is
described, in daily terms, with living gestures: his pain is shown on
the cross, vividly as the pain would be for us; his mother weeps like
any mother; the faces watching are individual, each with its special
alertness to the scene, and its own story too. If we look back at the
previous art we see that the faces tend to have the same set eyes, are
rapt in the same way, and the shape of the bodies is uniform, as if
only a sort of representation was necessary to these painters, not an
actual depiction of live events. The Byzantine art lay in a stillness
which never appeared again: it had no shadows, no dimensions,
no movement, and always shone with gilt; it was warm, belonging
to an earlier, less fragile and troubled dawn. In that art the pain of
the cross is seen no less, but for us it is 'formal' or 'stylized', that is to
say, we no longer share the signs by which their pity and grief were
shown. We see the warmth and know that the stillness belongs to an
unbroken world: but we, broken from a real communal life for
generations past, look for the individual face, marked with its own
story, because that is ourselves.

This new 'Gothic' style came from France, and so in an indirect
but unmistakable way did everything we see in the Basilica, even to
the life of St Francis himself, which brought it all into being. In a
word, it was a new sense of the divinity and radiance of the human
creature that spread through Europe and destroyed eventually what
we call the Middle Ages, though in fact it was the light discovered
by them. Christ's reply to the accusation that he had blasphemed by
calling himself the Son of God was, 'Is it not written, ye are gods?'
And just as Christ himself had been influenced by Greek thinking,
so the new 'humanism', as it came to be called, found its expression
through a study of Latin and Greek texts. The divinity of the human
person had been suggested in the art of ancient Greece: the exact
image of a man or woman in the fullness of youth was a god—
Apollo or Venus.

The means by which that Greek awareness came into our lives was humanism: just as its climax in art was called the Renascence. Literally speaking, humanism was the study of two things, Greece and Rome on the one hand, and the New Testament on the other, that is to say a joint illumination of the radiant human creature considered as a god. An effect of this was the later translation of the New Testament into the vernacular. The Old Testament gradually ceased to dominate—in word and art. Classical art was studied—really the art of the body—and it brought into being for the first time in Christian art those easy and natural figures we see in Cimabue and Giotto, replacing the awkward and shortened figures of the earlier epoch.

But this study of classical art, far from being in isolation from the story of Christ, was an illumination of it. Otherwise it would not have been thought necessary or worthwhile: more, it would have been thought pagan; in fact, that was the main axe of the opponents of humanism; they said it was just an excuse for pagan feeling.

The Basilica in Assisi came to be built and, above all, painted in a new way because St Francis had revived the sense of Christ as a living man. And in depicting the life of the Saint himself in terms of the clothes and buildings and faces seen every day at his time the new artists were depicting no less than a revived Christianity, or a Christianity of the New Testament. The pain on the cross was shown vividly: the Madonna flinging up her arms as we see her in the Upper Basilica (the Cimabue *Crucifixion*) was the first clear sign of a total revolution of thought, a miniature of what Christ had achieved in his day. Compared with that, what is usually (and quite wrongly) called a Renascence was an exercise, finally losing all religious anxiety, and paving the way for art-for-art's-sake.

But these frescoes of the Maestro di S. Francesco, hardly visible in the dimness, still glow with the old Byzantine splendour: it is little wonder that the Umbrian painters clung to this style longer than others, because it seems to fit the parched earth and bare hills of the province so well. And here in the gloom of a crypt they suggest a hot, still day. But they are *stories from the life of Christ* and we see in their faded remains, restored to a little more definition recently, the traces of real faces, turning this way and that: on the right wall *appearance of the cross*, *the Crucifixion* (we see one arm of the cross over Mary's head), *the descent from the Cross*, *the deposition*, *Grief over the Body of the Redeemer*, and lastly *Madonna with Child and angel*. On the left wall opposite these we see *the story of St Francis*, told for the first time but without the clear and careful exposition we shall find upstairs by later hands. These panels show him *giving up his worldly goods* (the bishop hastily covering his nakedness), then *Innocent III dreaming of him holding up the Lateran in Rome*, then at the next arch *St Francis talking to the birds*; the next panel shows *the Saint receiving the stigmata*, and the last—just before we reach the papal throne—*his death*.

We should note when passing it that the **papal throne** may only be used by a pope, unless express papal permission is given to a cardinal or bishop. In fact, this half of the Lower Church can be closed off by its railings to form a 'papal chapel' when the pope is present. This close relation with the Vatican has given the Basilica and monastery their special tone from the beginning: it is the 'privilege' extended to St Francis. The Concordat between the Church and Mussolini, by the way, was prepared in Assisi during the centenary celebrations in 1926. The last pope to come to Assisi was John XXIII, for the opening of the Ecumenical Council.

Half way down the nave there are staircases (8) on either side leading us to the crypt where **St Francis's tomb** lies. For centuries it was sealed up under the earth to prevent robbery, but at the end of 1818 a large tunnelling operation was started, until after fifty-two nights (work could only be done at night) the tomb was found exactly as it had been depicted in frescoes, bound round with iron grilles above and below. The 1818 tunnel became what is now the crypt, erected this century in a classical style with Romanesque arches which preserve the gravity of the Lower Church. The tomb is at the altar, raised above it, with a hole roughly made to expose it to the light. And here the Saint still lies. At the four corners of the little apse his most faithful followers are buried, and if we walk round the sides and back of the altar we can read their names behind iron grilles—Fra' Leone, Fra' Rufino, Fra' Masseo and Fra' Angelo. As we leave the crypt there is a tomb—facing us just before we go up the stairs—belonging to the Blessed Giacoma dei Settesoli, a Roman noblewoman, one of the Saint's great benefactresses, whom he called by the name 'Fra' Giacomina', as if she were one of the Order despite her sex. The hideous 'votive lamp' we pass under on the way out was given by all the town councils of Italy in collusion.

Returning to the Lower Church we should go back to the entrance and this time walk down the church through the side-chapels on the right. The first chapel (9) contains *scenes from the lives of St Stephen and St Louis* painted in the late sixteenth century and nothing to remark, but the windows are like those in the St Catherine of Alexandria chapel, remarkable for their harmony in intricate and vivid design, with an overall sweetness that reminds us of the Sienese masters: and in fact they were probably designed by a pupil of Simone Martini, perhaps by the artist himself. In the next chapel facing us as we enter, actually on the tower on our left, is *the martyrdom of St Laurence*; on the wall before us, *Jesus praying in the garden*, and behind us a fragment, *the arrest of Jesus*. These frescoes are probably by Andrea da Bologna, who worked in Assisi after the death of Giotto. The **St Anthony of Padua chapel** (10) contains frescoes by Cesare Sermei da Orvieto, a seventeenth-century painter. On one of the walls St Anthony preaches before the pope and makes a mule kneel before the Holy Sacrament, which looks what it is—a silly thing to do.

But these first chapels are only a little gauntlet before we reach the serenity of the third chapel down (11), the **Chapel of St Mary Magdalen,** painted in the fourteenth century on a commission by the bishop of Assisi (Tebaldo Pontano from Todi, who died in 1329). Various hands are responsible for the work, among them—where it is better—Giotto himself, or perhaps a good pupil. But there are disagreements about this.

We shall almost certainly recognize these frescoes from reproductions, which show us more detail than we can see with the naked eye. We should ask for electric light here on almost any day, as the sun rises and turns on the other side of the church. On the wall behind us as we come in there is the marvellous *Noli me tangere* with its lovely gesture of almost touching, and the sweet refusal as Christ turns, in a kind of radiance. Next to it we see *Mary Magdalen at the port of Marseilles and the princess dead on the rock, with the Saint talking to the angels above.* Under the *Noli me tangere* there is the gentle, rapt, reflective *Mary Magdalen with Tebaldo Pontano*, its soft reds fading; she gazes down (not really at him) and holds him by the hand; he is dressed in monk's habit. On the wall opposite there is the fading but still solemnly ceremonious movements of *the dinner at the house of the Pharisee*, with a wonderfully suitable element of falsity in the ceremony; at its side, *the resurrection of Lazarus*. Under these on the left is what some claim to be the first portrait ever made (also attributed to Giotto)—*Tebaldo Pontano protected by St Rufinus*. But there are disagreements about this too: we should take it as part of the whole new approach embodied by most of the frescoes in the Basilica, that is the depiction of daily life. Above these there is *Mary Magdalen receiving communion from St Maximinus*.

The *Noli me tangere* and the *Resurrection* panels have such a resemblance to the walls in the Scrovegni chapel in Padua, in their tones and style of gesture, and the sallow faces with their deeply marked features, that it is difficult not to think of Giotto. Before leaving this chapel we should look at the inner arch of the window, where every care has been bestowed on the *saints*, which some people take as the clearest evidence of Giotto's presence here. In the archway over the steps leading back into the nave there are life-size panels of more saints—Catherine, Agatha, Andrew, George, Peter, Matthew, Agnes, Rose, Nicholas, Paul the Anchorite, Paul the Apostle and Anthony the Abbot. High above, over the arch, there is a *St Zosimus carrying clothes to Mary Magdalen*, who is in a cave. The windows are by a master of the fourteenth century—*scenes from the life of Mary Magdalen and the saints*. We should also note the arms of Bishop Pontano (four sets) on either side of the two smaller arches of the chapel. If we look up at the ceiling we shall see the figures of *Jesus*, *Mary Magdalen*, *Martha* and *Lazarus*, and here we shall recognize the heavy lines and sallow complexion of the Giotto face. Some say they are his without possibility of doubt: but I see no reason why a bold pupil should not have done them.

Continuing down the right of the church we come out into the transept (12), with the main altar before us towards the left. And here we are at once surrounded by frescoes attributed to the Giotto workshop, except for one panel which we should look at first, by Cimabue. This is in the right transept and we should take a seat with our backs to the high altar, so as to accustom our eyes to the light: in any case this is a good idea when surrounded by so much colour by so many hands. Cimabue is on our immediate right (13), *Madonna and Child enthroned with four angels and St Francis* (he is standing on the right of the picture). This still has the swelling glow of the old art, something grand about it that later becomes inhibited to serve detail and story: the panel even swells out of its proper size, as if to suggest the earlier dawn which could never be captured again. Formality is there too, as a last gesture. The St Francis here is the most famous image of the Saint we have, and that most used. There is something about this panel that baptizes the whole enterprise of the Basilica, as if it was really Cimabue's spirit that pervaded the work and kept it going after his death.

Just above this we see *the presentation in the Temple* by the Giotto workshop, and a *Nativity* higher still. Turning round to the wall on our left we have at the top the famous *flight into Egypt* (left-hand panel) and *Jesus disputing in the Temple* under it. Below this there is the first panel of the St Francis miracles—*the Sperelli child falls from an upper storey and remains unhurt* (in this picture we are supposed to see Dante—he is the kneeling figure on the right of the picture, and some say that the figure standing by him is Giotto). We turn back to the wall on our right for the second series of frescoes which begins lower down (left-hand panel, next to the Cimabue *Madonna and Child*) with a *Crucifixion* (the now almost invisible figure on the right of the picture was probably intended to be the counterpart of the St Francis figure in the Cimabue *Madonna and Child*, and could be St Anthony of Padua). The *Epiphany* is just above this, while farther up still there is the *Visitation*. Again, still in the second series, we turn to the left wall and continue with *the massacre of the Innocents* at the top right-hand panel, and below it, straddling the arch, *the Holy Family returns to Nazareth from Jerusalem*, with a narrow fresco underneath, *St Francis holding a skeleton* (*sister Death*).

If we now face the chapel before us without moving from our seat we shall see above the chapel's arch an *Annunciation*, with the angel on one side of the apex and the Virgin on the other, while in the panel on the left of the arch we see *the girl of Suessa being dug out of the ruins of a house*. We can walk up the little staircase that rises to this panel and have a closer look: the figure with a hand touching his chin, the last on the right, is said to be Giotto; and some say that Dante is next to him. We can also look more closely at St Francis and the skeleton.

And now for the panels at eye-level, which are clearly not part of the two series above. On the right wall there is the tomb of five companions of St Francis (behind the iron grille) with their portraits. On the left of the doorway to one side of this there is a *Madonna and Child between two saints* which is said to be by a pupil of Simone Martini, with a background like a tapestry, in a drowsy, glowing warmth that we shall see realized again in the chapel by Simone Martini himself when we come to it. On the left there are *five saints* also attributed to him or a pupil, with the lovely portrait of St Clare by which that saint is usually represented (it cannot be taken as a portrait, though).

The chapel towards which we have been looking so long (14) is dedicated to S. Nicolò or—as he is usually called to distinguish him from another St Nicholas—*S. Nicola di Bari.* This chapel was built at the order of Napoleone Orsini at the end of the thirteenth century, and the tomb is Giovanni Orsini's, with angels bending over the figure of the deceased (he died in 1292). And on the walls there are frescoes where an extraordinary clarity and economy of detail, working towards one dramatic and basically mystical end, reveals the Giotto school. They were done about 1342. As in the Simone Martini chapel which we shall see later, there are *saints* round the inside of the arch, twelve in all. If we go into the chapel and stand with our backs to the altar (again we must ask for light) we shall see (with the light shining straight into our eyes in a subtle revenge for the trouble we have given the friars) *St Francis and St Nicholas recommending Napoleone and Gian Gaetano Orsini to Christ.* Below on the left *the Baptist and Mary Magdalen* (hair covering her nakedness). The rest of the walls are taken up with *the story of St Nicholas.* On the right wall high up under the arch—we now turn to face the chapel-altar—we see (top right) *the Saint furnishing a dowry to three girls,* and lower down a panel almost entirely lost to the damp, *rescue from shipwreck.* Lower still, *the Saint blesses a kneeling penitent* (who has a rope around his neck), and below this *two saints* not belonging to the series. To the left of these on the same wall we see (higher panel), almost invisible for being so close to the roof, *the Saint revives a child*: lower down *he frees a slave* (we see him coming from the sky and plucking the slave away as he serves at table), and lower down still *he restores the slave to his parents* (they are astonished and overjoyed). Turning to the other wall (that is, facing the chapel-altar, on our left) we see in the highest panel *a Jew beating the Saint* and below that *the Saint appearing in a dream to Constantine,* and *the Saint saving three innocent men condemned to death.* The windows are original and have a simplicity we rarely see intact nowadays, especially in a set of three: they are from the fourteenth century and show *sixteen saints.*

We now go to the high altar (15) where we stand in a bewildering mass of dark colour, with the vault above completely frescoed (we catch a hungry glimpse of the left arm of the transept where the Lorenzetti panels have been restored to something like their first splendour). But before looking upwards or left we should rest our eyes on the altar itself, though again we shall not see it properly unless the light is turned on for us. It lies long and fairly low at the top of several steps, a Gothic piece with gracefully carved floral columns forming little three-leafed archways, and decorated with tiny mosaic stones. There is no need to be inhibited by the friars singing in the stalls behind the altar if they happen to be there; just as there is no fear that they will be inhibited by us. The altar slab, which is one enormous piece of stone, is said to have been the gift of a Byzantine emperor, or perhaps of that Queen of Cyprus whose urn we saw in the entrance: but I have heard a friar say that this too comes from Monte Subasio up the hill. If we stand exactly facing the altar and look at the steps before us we shall see a hole which burrows under the earth to the tomb of St Francis, where a light is shining: the metal grille has been pulled to one side to allow coins to be thrown down.

And now, looking up at the vault above the high altar, we see the work of one who is now called the '*Maestro delle Vele*' (literally 'Master of the Sails', that is, the four sections of the vault) but who was once known as 'Giotto and/or his school'. These frescoes are the *Allegories*, based on the Rule of the Franciscan Order, strangely and oppressively raw and yet colourful too, as if to dwarf us down below and haunt us at the same time; this double impression is perhaps due to their being so austerely logical and clear, yet contained in a completely effortless intimacy. Their importance (for the painters themselves and the Basilica) lay in their gazing down on to the tomb of St Francis himself: therefore they must capture mystically his life and mission. In a strange way the feeling in them triumphs over the actual work done. The first compartment we should look at is the *Allegory of Poverty*, in that part of the vault that faces the nave (*a*): here we have a reminder of the troubadour-theme, so close to St Francis, in the figure of Lady Poverty who stands on a rock in a great rosy mist, her hand being joined in marriage to that of St Francis by Christ, who stands between them; St Francis, his stigmata clearly seen, holds out the ring, while on the other side Hope stands next to Charity (offering her heart to the married couple). Poverty hands the ring to Hope. At each side there is a group of angels: on the right three young men (symbolizing Pride, Envy and Avarice) show contempt for Poverty; on the left a young man offers his cloak to a poor man. At the feet of the bride and

St Clare (*left*) by Simone Martini, and St Francis (*right*) by
Cimabue, both in the Lower Church.

Right: The Upper Church
of St Francis, with steps
leading to its lawned piazza.
The basilica, like Rome, is
a Holy See and the pope
has his own apartments
here.

Above: The twelfth-century façade of the duomo reflected in the basin of an equally venerable fountain.

Left: The Easter procession of the dead Christ leaving the duomo for the basilica of St Francis at the other end of the town.

bridegroom we should notice the tiny barking dog, the boy throwing a stone, another trying to reach Poverty with a stick. Above, one angel offers God a splendid cloak while another offers him a great building, symbolizing possessions.

To the right of this (*b*) there is the *Allegory of Chastity*, another crowded fresco: in a tower with battlements, itself part of a great castle, we see Chastity in a window, with two angels flying towards her with a diadem and palm; a white standard flying above the tower represents Cleanliness, while Purity and Strength lean out of a hole in the wall to offer a shield and a white flag to a youth who, helped by two angels, is being purified in a bath in order to gain admittance to the castle. Soldiers keep watch, with shields. On the far left St Francis with two angels behind him is inviting three others to enter, a member of the Third or Lay Order of Franciscans, a Minor Friar and a Poor Clare; the member of the Third Order here is Dante. In the right corner Penitence and three angels are putting Love to flight with sticks (an odd thing for a Christian, let alone an angel, to do), and Love here is accompanied by Concupiscence and Filth, odd companions again.

The fresco to the left (*c*) is the *Allegory of Obedience*, where Obedience sits in a lodge holding up his hand for silence, while a friar kneels before him submitting to the yoke: at the sides we see Prudence with a compass, mirror and an astrolabe (an instrument for watching the heavens), and Humility with a taper. An angel is stopping a centaur from entering (under Humility): the centaur symbolizes Violence; near Prudence a man and a woman guided by an angel are asking to be put under the yoke (of obedience). At the sides of the lodge there are groups of angels, some of whom are holding horns of sacred oil with which to anoint kings, meaning that whoever accepts the yoke has the right to enter the kingdom of heaven, is the king of his own life. On the roof of the lodge we see St Francis between two angels: the yoke he carries on his shoulders is tied with a rope which is held above by the hands of God.

In the last section of the vault (*d*) we see the *Apotheosis* or *Gloriosus Franciscus*: St Francis, splendidly clothed, is seated on a throne among angels singing hymns of praise, and above there is an altar cloth symbolizing Victory. Before we lower our eyes we should note the bright and elaborate decorations that divide these frescoes along the ribs of the vault.

The apse (16) has three squat windows which shed a subdued

light over the wooden choir round the back of the church: this is marvellously carved and inlaid in three tiers (1471). A *Last Judgment* in the vault over the choir is a mistake from the seventeenth century, though if separated from the other frescoes in the Basilica it would look at least serious (Sermei): it was painted over an earlier work. Michelangelo was unknowingly responsible for this kind of thing: for the artists of his time he had reached the highest possible expression in art, and anything earlier seemed ridiculous next to his fully realized scenes, rather as Beethoven was called the bombshell that ended music. Every artist wanted to imitate him. The feeling was that Cimabue and Giotto and Maso and even Lorenzetti and Simone Martini had not really painted at all: they were 'primitive' and even barbarous.

When we see the frescoes of the Sienese artist Pietro Lorenzetti (1290-1348) in the left arm of the transept (17) we can thank God twice over. Following the series from the right as we enter this part of the transept, we see first *St Francis receiving the stigmata*; then a grim, violent, overbearing scene with spears and symbols of murder behind, *the arrest of Jesus*. Above this, *the Last Supper* shows, with a poignancy that hardly seems possible with paint alone, the last hours before Christ's death, in which his disciples are visibly saying goodbye: some cry and others are simply perplexed, while he is the quiet master of the scene, with his secret plan of self-sacrifice. Now we must turn round to the opposite wall (above, left) to see the *Flagellation*, where—as in all the Lorenzetti panels—solemn and righteous cruelty is contrasted with the patient, mourning face of Christ. The second series begins on the left of the first New Testament panel we looked at (*the arrest of Jesus*): it is *the washing of feet*, and above this is *the entry into Jerusalem*, Christ's hand delicately raised in blessing, while a cloak is laid down for his ass to step on.

Turning to the other wall again, we see *the journey to Calvary*, and here is the glorious climax of the new Giotto art, where all the details are cleanly and minutely given, as firmly and splendidly as they are in the music of Bach's St Matthew Passion. There are sadness, jealousy, vengeance, the most bestial cruelty among the citizens, soldiers, judges, elders and merchants; dogs bark and you can almost hear the clashing of the spears; and then inside it all is the quiet presence of Christ himself.

Under it we see Lorenzetti's large *Crucifixion*, a great part of it damaged: the cross rises above the clanging crowd with their horses and overhead flags; Christ's hair is long and golden, and there are angels in the sky. Underneath it there is the small but miraculous *Madonna and Child between SS. Francis and John the Evangelist*, the so-called '*Madonna dei tramonti*', or Madonna of the sunsets, on a gold background: happily we can approach this piece closely, since it is at eye level; and a natural light comes from one of the doors opposite leading to the Upper Church, which explains the title. The Child Jesus seems to be asking the Madonna something and she points to St Francis. According to mediaeval legend, he is asking her which of the two saints is the more worthy of her blessing, and she is answering, 'St Francis, because he suffers more': and St John, just about to speak, is giving her his agreement to this; he seems actually to solicit the Madonna's blessing for the other man. And underneath this is a tiny *Crucifixion*, also on a gold background, which is over the tomb of Princess Maria of Savoy, the daughter of Carlo Emanuele I, and a Franciscan of the Third Order, called 'the royal pilgrim' (she died in 1656). Turning now to the right we see a dramatic and tender *Deposition*, and above it *the descent into Limbo*. Going over to the other side of the archway we find the *Entombment* below, and *Resurrection* above. Both of these are Lorenzetti too.

In the *Deposition* the subject forms a beautifully rounded ensemble, which leads some people to say that Lorenzetti is too studied. But the care of the form is the care of the feeling: every figure, with the semi-circular ensemble it takes part in, states the same tenderness. Nothing is done for its own sake. Everything is observed with care—the blood that has spilled from the left arm of Christ, the larger pool of blood under his feet, the hammer, the pincers used to take out the nails—and this care is exactly the same as that with which Christ is being taken down from the cross. It is also in the way the Madonna caresses his hair, her eyes closed with grief; in the crouching figure robed in red kissing his feet; in his own spent, thin, pale body with its painful twisting that suggests the utmost point of exhaustion. In the *Entombment* the face of Christ is paler than the rest of the body, as if a terrific shock had been sustained worse than the slow dying that came afterwards, while Mary's face touches his in the most tender, hushed intimacy as he is lowered into the tomb. All Lorenzetti's faces are grave and utterly real; and this is the point about the care he takes—it is always towards a faithful image of whatever he wants to show: even in the face of St Francis receiving the stigmata—a rather frigid and ecclesiastical subject—

St Francis is shown as awed, a little frightened, trying to withdraw almost.

These panels were restored three years ago. They had become covered with spots of black fungus, probably caused by changes of atmosphere from humidity to heat when the church was over-crowded. A fresco is more prone to this than distemper or gold because it does not absorb spots of damp easily. This is not the first time they have been cleaned. Half were done in 1738 and the rest in the last century. The cleaners have left a tiny square patch on each panel to show the previous state.

It is difficult to establish when they were painted, but the his-torians seem agreed on 1320-30 or 1326-30. Not all of what we see is Lorenzetti's own hand, though he supervised everything. He is thought to have worked himself on the lower panels, and supervised the work above.

Beyond the archway, that is in the extreme left of the transept (18), we have the **Chapel of St John the Baptist.** There were once twentieth-century frescoes here but they were later blotted out in sky-blue, in the interests of art. The attraction here is the stained-glass windows, the central one from the fourteenth century; and then, under these windows (easily missed) a triptych by Lorenzetti, full of the melting ease and assurance and delicate brilliance of touch that we have seen in his other work: another *Madonna and Child with SS. Francis and John.*

Leading out of the chapel left is the sacristy (19). Here we usually find a friar who will conduct us through to the **secret or inner sacristy** (20), which is actually in the base of the tower (while the first sacristy was once a courtyard). Before we pass through we shall notice above the doorway a splendid *Madonna and Child, two angels, SS. Francis and Clare* by the so-called '*Maestro di Figline*', looking vivid and self-assured amid the new distemper of the wall. The previous sacristy was burned down in 1952 and was thereby restored to its original form: in the seventeenth century it had been made into two storeys, the floor of which collapsed in the fire, removing a staircase that used to run between the sacristy and the Upper Church. It also removed the ceiling painting by Sermei and Giorgetti (seventeenth century) so that we can now see the *Madonna and Child* clearly, as well as the decorations on part of the ceiling from Giotto's time. The great cupboard of carved wood (1629) in the inner sacristy was saved: this contains the hood of St Francis and a habit; a hair shirt;

a parchment of the Benediction written by him for Fra' Leone; the stone on which his head rested in the tomb; a horn of ivory given to the Saint by the Sultan of Egypt; some chamois leather that covered the wound of the stigmata in his side; felt gloves made by St Clare for the stigmata; a piece of cord from his tunic; a veil of Giacoma dei Settesoli (used for the Saint when he was dying); a cloak used by the Saint in his last illness; a chalice used by him and his companions at Mass: and, most important of all, the Rule of St Francis approved by Innocent III, with this pope's seal underneath.

We should ask the friar to conduct us by a little staircase from the first sacristy to the pulpit or tribune (21) which we have already seen from the central nave: here we can see at close quarters *the coronation of the Virgin*, attributed now to Maso, a pupil of Giotto's, sometimes called Giottino or little Giotto. He is discovered by a sweetness and glowing tender calm that is not always found in Giotto himself, who went straight to the story and drama. Mary in this fresco has the trace of a smile as she watches Jesus; the lower part is damaged by damp, but we see the angels' heads, each an individual portrait, showing a different wonder. The Madonna and Christ have that mystical sweetness we find realized perfectly a century later in Fra' Angelico. Around the arch is *the martyrdom of St Stanislas* and his *miracle*: he was cut into pieces at Cracow, and the martyrdom shows a man carrying the Saint's sawn-off legs aloft. His miracle was reviving a youth to life. There is a stone slab in this pulpit, under the *Crucifixion*: the tiny area was sometimes used for the celebration of Mass among the friars.

We should now return to the main nave: opposite the pulpit we have just visited, on the other side of the nave, and close to the opening of the presbytery, at the height of about twelve feet, there is a piece of column actually set into the wall, distinct from the other material, and above it an iron grille covering what was once a hole. The story goes that this piece of column fell straight on to a woman during the canonization service of St Stanislas, bishop of Cracow, in 1253 (Innocent IV was celebrating it). Miraculously she was un-hurt and—to round off the story nicely—she was cured of an awful disease she had had for years.

From the entrance we now go down the church through the side-chapels on the left, and the first frescoed one we come to—choosing if possible a radiant morning—is the **Chapel of St Martin** (23) painted by Simone Martini. At once we are the in mellow, intimately glowing, restful world of the Sienese artists: as if a special civilization was achieved in them, turning everything real into the gracious without the slightest effort, in a tenderness never quite realized before, the climax of that awed respect between one creature and another which was the theme of chivalry and the French *chansons*. The Chapel of St Peter of Alcantara (22) has a double stained-glass window of thirteenth-century origin.

Inside the arch by which we enter from the nave there are saints in pairs, *Mary Magdalen and SS. Catherine of Alexandria* (holding the wheel), *Clare* (holding the lily) and *Elizabeth of Hungary*, with, above, *SS. Francis and Anthony of Padua, Louis of France and Louis of Anjou*. If we now face this arch with our backs to the chapel altar we see above it *St Martin with Cardinal Gentile Partino da Montefiore kneeling before him* (the Cardinal died in 1312). We see the Cardinal's hat with its strings, left outside the church on the balustrade: the church is depicted simply, by slender pillars, not realistically, just as in Giotto. And the walls, too, are occupied with the story of St Martin. Turning to our right we see *the Saint dividing his cloak with a poor man*, cutting it with his sword as he sits on his horse with wonderfully dignified but intimate poise. Above this, *he revives a child in a crowd*: this is much damaged by damp. And higher still, *the Saint is present at the funeral of St Liborius, Bishop of Tours*. On the same wall, to the right of these, the lower panel shows *the death of the Saint* and his *assumption into heaven*, while above it *the Emperor Valentine renders homage to his goodness*. Turning to the other wall we see, lower panel on the right, *the Saint renouncing arms and going against the enemy with a cross*, a very graceful picture with the military commander sitting before his tent of war, a laurel wreath round his head, showing in a miraculously effortless way his perplexity and his fear for St Martin's safety. Higher, *Christ appears, bringing to him the cloak he had given*: and above that *he takes leave of St Hilary, Bishop of Poitiers*. To the left of this, in the higher panel *the Saint celebrates Mass in Albenga assisted by angels*: and in the panel under this *he is made a knight by the Emperor Constantius*—we see the spurs being placed on his heels, while music is played behind him. In the arches of the windows there are *eighteen saints*, and the stained glass was also designed by Martini.

The Upper Church of St Francis

We reach the **Upper Church** by one of the doors behind the main altar from which daylight is coming, and have a glimpse of the upper cloister on our way there (we shall see it from below if we visit the monastery later). This brings us out into the chancel, so that we at once see the whole length of the Upper Church from behind the altar. We are now in a different world: everything is light and warm, no longer dim and reflective. The contrast is great because it was intended: mellow and happy light here belongs to the celebration of Mass and public gatherings, to evangelism as opposed to meditation. The Lower Church is meant to be Christ crucified, while this is Christ victorious.

And as in the Lower Church, every inch of wall has been painted. The ceiling is composed of five vaults—including that of the chancel —with crossing arms to form Gothic arches. These arms lead down —and are supported by—vast pillars set against the walls, each one a set of five clustered together, giving the impression (especially as the church has one clear nave) of vastness combined with warmth, so that out of the French Gothic model it achieves something distinctly Italian. High up, the walls form an open gallery which circles the whole nave, rising above the main door to the level of the rose window, while at the other end of the church it passes under the three-lobed arches. The whole has a glad harmony blazing with mellowed colour, while the floor (red and white Subasian stone) reflects it perfectly. Here is the home of Giotto's famous series telling the story of St Francis. But first we should take a walk down the church: on a dull day we should ask the attendant—after showing him the colour of our money—to put up all the lights at once; otherwise the sun will do it for us. We should also glance at the fourth window in the right wall, numbering down from the back of the church towards the altar: unlike the others it is by no means flush in the centre of its arch. This was probably done so as not to blind or distract the spectator standing at the back of the church, and to give him the impression of uninterrupted immensity. And for this same reason the frescoes are not the same size, if we look carefully. Nor are the vaults above. This Upper Church is not the same length as the Lower, but longer, and its façade therefore does not sit on the Lower Church's back wall as we would expect. At the back of the church, if we look up, we see a space between the last vault of the ceiling and the façade, and a certain split in the frescoes on either side where perhaps an earlier arch or half-pillar was withdrawn when the present façade was built.

We must begin with the frescoes where the new art was first suggested, that is, with the work of Cimabue, in the transept. Again, we shall need light on a dull day, and the attendant will illuminate whatever part of the church we go to, in turn. We start in the left transept and at once see that these frescoes are in a worse condition than almost any we have seen in Umbria. It is due to the loss of the whites: Cimabue used lead oxide and it eventually turned black. So we have the impression of a negative in these panels. But this may only be part of the explanation. A fresco-painter should make fresh plaster every day and remove what unpainted surfaces there are at the end of that day: if he paints on dry plaster next morning his colours will fade in time. (This is why many of the Giotto colours in the St Francis series have faded too.)

Cimabue and his helpers began work in 1277 in this transept. On the left wall as we enter it we see his *Crucifixion*, and this we may say begins the new art, if a single panel ever did: we see something quite different from the old styles—it must have astonished people at the time; and it still has the power to astonish us if we have been looking at works in the Byzantine tradition rather than the baroque —here the arms of the Madonna are flung into the air with grief for the first time. Only the outlines of this picture can be seen but we can imagine for a moment that when filled it could—almost—look like a baroque piece, for its movement alone: this is the first seed, after all, of something which after centuries declined into melodrama. It is real movement, as opposed to the later posturing. There is nothing stylized here. Christ's body bends with the weight of its suffering, whereas in the old Byzantine representations it seemed to float graciously. Yet the outlines that we see in this work are suave and gentle too. The angels are weeping. The Madonna is like any desperate mother. In the crowd we may even notice Jewish faces. There is a possibility that Giotto worked with Cimabue on this as a pupil: and some say that Duccio of Siena also learned from him. The figure of the monk crouching at the foot of the cross in unbearable grief is St Francis.

The other panels (going right from the *Crucifixion*) describe five apocalyptic scenes, which are now only just recognizable: a *vision of the Throne, with the mystical lamb and the homage of twenty-four elders*; then *Christ in judgment, with angels calling the four corners of the earth*; the vision of the *seven angels of the seven sorrows*—we see them floating round Christ, in outline. On the last wall of the three we see, first, *the vision of the destruction of Babylon*, with houses falling on top of one another, and lastly *the vision of St John in Patmos*. Inside the arches above, and in the open gallery, the frescoes of *angels* are in a better state of preservation. The stained-glass windows show *stories from Genesis* and *saints*, perhaps by a French master of the thirteenth century.

Turning to the apse behind the altar we find more Cimabue frescoes, this time *the life of Mary*, from the *Annunciation* to the *Coronation*, all in the same barely recognizable condition. Under the central window the two large medallions, now almost invisible, contain the faces of Gregory IX and Innocent IV. And underneath these is the papal throne, a simple stone piece of the thirteenth or fourteenth century under a canopy also of stone. The windows show *persons and stories from the Old Testament* and *the life of Jesus*, from the end of the thirteenth century: only the darker of this set of windows is not original. The wooden choir that fills the semi-circle of the apse is a wonderfully elaborate piece of work, each seat with its mock cornice and Gothic-pointed steeples, carved in two tiers, with an inlaid picture behind each seat showing Minor Friars and some notable people, including Sixtus IV. Along the side of the right transept these inlaid pictures show doorways, cages, musical instruments. In this part of the transept the frescoes, still by Cimabue, treat *the life of St Peter*: the centre panel shows his crucifixion upside-down. There is a *Crucifixion* in the same position as on the other side of the transept, but much less visible. The windows are perhaps by the Romans who worked here just before Giotto, and they depict *scenes from the Old Testament* and *the life of Jesus*. They are not all intact.

As we walk towards the high altar we should look up and compare the windows of the whole transept from left to right: that on the left was the work of French artists, the centre German, and the right Roman. The high altar was consecrated in 1253, its table wonderfully worked in a mosaic of white, red, yellow, green, gold and blue stones, a joyful design which deserves a long look, especially as its design is not symmetrical. The mosaic on the other side of the altar facing the church is more severe, in squares.

Now we should look up at the roof of the apse, with its ruined frescoes: but if we look carefully we shall make out the four Evangelists, each in the act of writing, inspired by angels, with a view of the town evangelized in front of each one: *Matthew* in Judah: *John* in Asia: *Luke* in Greece: *Mark* in Italy. In the last we can see Rome —the Pantheon, Hadrian's tomb, the pyramid of C. Cestius, military towers.

Before we examine the other frescoes we should walk down the church and look up at the vaults again: the third from the entrance has four medallions showing half figures of *Jesus*, *Mary*, *St John the Baptist* and *St Francis*. Each has an angel on either side, and these frescoes are attributed to the thirteenth-century Iacopo Torriti (dates unknown). They have the warmth of the old art and seem in close connection with what we have seen downstairs, by the Maestro di San Francesco. Torriti was one of the Roman artists engaged on the Upper Church. His work here is dated 1290, and this is the only date of his we know. He began in Rome as a mosaic artist in the Lateran, and his work makes a clear bridge between the old art and the new, not in subject so much as in approach and materials. The mosaic is now replaced by soluble paints. For the fresco is really the art of the poor. The splendours of the old Byzantine world are replaced by new modest methods.

In the *four doctors of the Church* which we see when we look up at the first vault nearest the entrance Giotto is supposed to have tried his hand alone for the first time. People say that he proved himself capable of the St Francis frescoes by these first trials. But whether they are by Giotto or Filippo Rusuti (one of the Roman artists at work here), they are the first clear indication we have in picture form of humanism. The doctors are not disputing like the figures of a Byzantine mosaic, they are actually wondering and asking questions; their concern is individual for the first time, not schooled; they are anxious for themselves as if grace is now a lonely goal, not won by shared faith as before. Here, in four sections of a vault, are the first clear and economical story-telling pictures too: the towns and buildings behind the doctors are outlined, symbolized; there are the columns and suggested domes that we shall see later in the St Francis scenes. The figures are not as natural as those in the later work: there is the old foreshortening and awkwardness, the bodies

122

are twisted up, lacking dimension. But the human dialogue has begun. Here for the first time are details from daily life—books open on desks, a cloak thrown casually over the back of a chair, tables and stools. In the arch between this vault and the entrance of the church there are *eighteen saints*, which perhaps belong to the same period and author, though they show a greater suavity.

Giotto di Bondone, probably born in Florence (1267-1337), is said to have begun work here when he was about twenty-five. Some say he studied under Cimabue in Florence, and almost certainly he worked under him for some time in the Basilica. Cimabue died ten years after he came. Giotto had already been to Rome and seen Pietro Cavallini (1250-1330) at work on his mosaics in S. Maria in Trastevere (1291), though we are not certain here either. The three Romans, Cavallini, Torriti, Rusuti, did the first work in the Upper Church, together with Cimabue and his school. At the level of the windows, above the Giotto frescoes of St Francis, we see their *stories from the New and Old Testaments*. The style of these panels is not uniform. There is the warmth and stillness of the previous art, where the hands of the Romans are most clearly seen and where the mood is still that of the Byzantine mosaic, and others where Giotto or his school have clearly taken a major part. But these names— even that of Giotto—are no more than a vague indication of different styles: some people deny that Giotto was ever in Assisi; others say that he could not have done the St Francis series because the colours are too brilliant. We should remember that the painting of churches was a collective matter, under one or more *maestri*: the facts about individuals will probably never be clear, in some cases.

The *stories from the Old Testament* are on the right wall as we look towards the altar, beginning at the top and progressing clockwise from the transept: 1. *Separation of light from darkness*; 2. *Creation of Adam* (much damaged); 3. *Creation of Eve*; 4. *Original Sin* (partly damaged); 5. *Expulsion from Paradise*; 6. lost; 7. *Sacrifice of Cain and Abel* (also totally damaged); 8. *Cain murders Abel* (partly damaged). For the next panel we return to the transept on the same wall, and begin again, lower down: 9. *Building of the Ark*; 10. *The Flood*; 11. *Sacrifice of Isaac*; 12. *Abraham visited by the angels* (partly damaged); 13. *The deceit of Jacob*; 14. *Esau before Isaac*; 15. *Joseph sold* (damaged); 16. *The brothers of Joseph in Egypt* (damaged). We should notice the glowing warmth of the earlier art in Nos. 13 and 14: some people, on the other hand, find Giotto's hand here. I think it is only apparent towards the end of the whole series, that is, in Nos. 15 and 16.

The *stories from the New Testament* are on the other wall, that is to say, left as we face the altar, beginning again at the top, from the transept: 1. *Annunciation* (much damaged); 2. *Visitation* (lost); 3. *Nativity*; 4. *Epiphany* (much damaged); 5. *Presentation in the Temple*; 6. *Flight into Egypt*; 7. *Dispute in the Temple* (only Jesus visible here); 8. *Baptism of Jesus*. For the next panel we return to the transept and begin again lower down on the same wall: 9. *The Wedding at Cana*; 10. *Resurrection of Lazarus* (damaged); 11. *Arrest of Jesus*; 12. *Flagellation* (damaged); 13. *Journey to Calvary*; 14. *Crucifixion*; 15. *Deposition*; 16. *Mary at the tomb*. This series, unlike that of the Old Testament, continues on the back wall of the church: 17. *Ascension*; 18. *Pentecost*. And here also are two medallions representing SS. Peter and Paul. The Roman artists are said to be entirely responsible for the very first frescoes—those of the Creation; and the Cimabue school for most of the others, before a new hand—perhaps Giotto's—becomes apparent at the end of both the Old and the New Testament series.

The life of St Francis by Giotto begins on the right side as we face the altar, and close to the transept, continuing right round the church uninterruptedly and including the back wall. There are twenty-eight panels in all. They have been touched up and restored a good deal. All but four or five of them are said to be by Giotto. There are remarkable similarities in tone and line and exposition between these panels and those at the Scrovegni chapel in Padua, which are acknowledged to be his. There is the same pallid, strongly marked face. We must not underestimate the Roman artist Cavallini's influence on him, especially in the matter of depicting a face, the supple hands, and in the laying on of paint: we have only to look at Cavallini's work at S. Cecilia in Trastevere to see that.

Giotto's series was suggested by a reading of the life of St Francis by St Bonaventura. The scenes begin with (1) *The young Saint honoured by a poor man in the main square of Assisi*: we should notice the clean, almost symbolic representation of the Temple of Minerva between St Francis and the poor man, who lays down his cloak for him to step on: Giotto is less known for sweetness and tenderness than his pupil Maso or Giottino, but here in the marvelling expressions of Francis's two companions (they are holding hands,

124

which was customary among Italian menfolk until our epoch) we have all the sweetness that later pervades, and perhaps provokes, the Sienese school. The Temple of Minerva in this panel, by the way, has five columns instead of its actual six: we also see the tower of the Palazzo del Popolo at its side, a shorter version than the one we know today. (2) *The Saint gives his cloak to a poor knight*—three simple facts, Francis's horse (a mark of social position), the thick and sumptuous cloak he is holding out, and the awed bending movement of the poor man as he takes hold of it, gazing into Francis's face; the buildings at the top of the hill on the left are the edge of Assisi with Porta Nuova, and on the other side there is the Benedictine Abbey of Monte Subasio. (3) *He sees in a dream a palace full of arms* (coats of armour, shields, etc. marked with the cross); on the night following his act of charity a heavenly voice tells him that these arms are for him and his 'soldiers'. (4) *Praying at San Damiano, where the voice of Christ exhorts him to restore the church.* (5) *He restores his clothes to his father before the bishop of Assisi*; Francis's face has a youthful and determined seriousness, while his insulted father looks as if about to punish him like a child; friends hold him back, and the bishop —bored and somnolent like the Church herself—simply holds a cloth round Francis to safeguard the proprieties. (6) *Innocent III sees the Saint in a dream holding up the Lateran.* (7) *This pope approves the Rule.* (8) *The Saint appears to his companions on a chariot of fire.* (9) *Fra' Leone sees the throne destined for the Saint in heaven.* (10) *The Saint chases the demons out of Arezzo.* (11) *The Saint, before the sultan, proposes the trial by fire.* (12) *His ecstasy, while four of his companions look on, awed.* (13) *He celebrates Christmas at Greccio.* This last is famous as perhaps the most careful and whole of Giotto's compositions, in which detail and absolute economy are maintained; so much so that a French scholar recently tried to discover the notes being sung by the shape of the singers' mouths, so as to name the music. (14) (this and 15 are on the back wall) *He makes water flow to satisfy the thirst of a sick man*: everything is centred here on the grateful and delighted profile of the drinker as he lowers himself to the water, and the panel is pervaded by dry rock. (15) *He preaches to the birds in Bevagna*, a perfect depiction of country silence, with the minimum of figures; the birds are goldfinches, quails, sparrows and pigeons. (16) (continues from the back of the church) *The death of the knight of Celano, in the presence of the Saint*—another balanced composition in which the left side is dominated by the Saint's grave and almost frightened expression, and the left by the wild grief of the family, the women with their hair down. (17) *The Saint preaches before Honorius III.* (18) *He appears at the chapter of the Minor Friars in Arles.* (19) *He receives the stigmata.* (20) *His death and funeral.* (21) *He appears to Bishop Guido of Assisi and to Frate Agostino.* (22) *The patrician of Assisi, Girolamo, is convinced of the stigmata.* (23) *The grief of the Poor Clares at San Damiano over the body of the Saint*: San Damiano is here represented as a rich and great church, symbolizing its power. (24) *His canonization*, (partly damaged). (25) *The Saint appears to Pope Gregory IX to dissipate the doubt as to his stigmata.* (Here a new hand appears, and the panel is attributed to the so-called '*Maestro di S. Cecilia*' because of its similarities of style to a picture dedicated to S. Cecilia in the Uffizi Gallery of Florence). (26) *The healing of a gentleman of Ilerda from a mortal wound* (also attributed to the Maestro di S. Cecilia). (27) *The Saint revives a gentlewoman in order to confess her and rid her of the devil, before she dies a second time.* And, lastly, (28) *The freeing from prison of Pietro d'Alife, accused of heresy.*

We may want to pay the Upper Church a separate visit to look at the windows. The first windows on the right as we enter the church (from its proper entrance) are from the end of the thirteenth century, designed some say by the Roman school and some say by the Maestro di S. Francesco. They depict *St Francis and St Anthony of Padua and stories from their lives*. The second, third and fourth windows on the right show *apostles and episodes from their lives*, the work of French artists, also from the thirteenth century. The first and second windows on the left, *the Redeemer and the Virgin with angels, prophets and saints*, are again by the Roman school in the same period. The third and fourth windows on the left show *saints and the Madonna*, and these may have been designed by Fiorenzo di Lorenzo (fifteenth century).

On the left of the entrance there is a holy water font which will catch our eye: a tiny and delicately carved stone piece from the thirteenth century. If we walk down the church we shall find a pulpit protruding from the last pillar on the left, a graceful work with twining columns and figures of the saints, from the first half of the thirteenth century. St Bernardine of Siena preached from this pulpit in 1426 and 1427, and St John of Capistrano in 1430. St John, by the way, joined the Franciscans after being governor of Perugia, and after marrying.

Before leaving the Upper Church we should have a look at the *sinopie*. These are to be found in the sacristy, in the left transept. Painting a fresco means applying tempera or soluble paints to a layer of fresh plaster: this plaster is made with lime which, when it penetrates fresh paint, acts as a binding agent. Before the plaster is laid on the wall the area to be painted is marked out and a charcoal drawing made of the outlines of the subject: then with a rose-coloured paint called *sinopia* (from the city of its origin in Turkey— Sinòpe) the whole scene is sketched out. Thus, when frescoes are taken down from the wall for restoration (the whole layer of plaster is removed) the so-called *sinopie* or sketches are found underneath. About five years ago there was restoration work on a few of the Old and New Testament scenes, and the sketches we find in the sacristy are the *sinopie* of these.

At one time we would have gone back to the terrace behind the apse to see the Treasure, but this is temporarily closed for reorganization. It has been raided four times in history, so it is a wonder anything is left: but the store was always vast. We must remember that friars of nearly every order were the purveyors in the past of music, architecture, letters: were islands of learning throughout Europe and Byzantium, and islands of civilization during the barbarian invasions. They therefore amassed great collections. The first to raid this particular treasure-house of paintings, relics and precious metals was Muzio di Francesco, head of the Ghibelline faction in Assisi, in 1320. The Baglioni family did the same in 1492, and the local Fiumi family five years later. The French under Napoleon were the last. It nowadays includes fifty-seven pictures from the fourteenth and fifteenth centuries left to the monastery by an American art historian, with panels by Lorenzetti, Fra' Angelico, Signorelli, Taddeo di Bartolo, Masolino da Panicale, Bicci di Lorenzo, Segna di Bonaventura, Bartolo di Fredi. There are also *sinopie* from the Simone Martini chapel in the Lower Church. A documented history of the Basilica and Monastery will be on show, as before, when it is re-opened.

We shall by now have looked at the façade of the Upper Church many times, with the grass slope before it (Piazza Superiore di San Francesco, or the Upper Square) endowing it with freshness and a look of improvisation. It is divided into three parts, horizontally, the highest one triangular. The lines are simple and grave: two doors under one tall Gothic arch below and a splendidly intricate rose window in a double form, with symbols of the evangelists at each of the four corners, protruding from the wall. On the left of the front we see, just below the level of the rose window, the so-called Loggia delle Benedizioni (gallery of blessings), the work of Valentino Martelli, 1607.

CHAPTER 5

Assisi II

*Town Library—Museum and Roman Forum—Temple of Minerva—
Pintoricchio*

We should begin our first tour of the town at the St Francis Basilica
again, leaving it by the Via S. Francesco, the middle of three roads.
Here we have intact mediaeval houses on either side, and even a
pavement to walk on. We shall notice the so-called 'doors of death',
like those in Gubbio (see p. 201).

Just after a small church on the right we have a break in the
mediaeval fronts: at No. 19A there is something more deliberately
splendid, the Palazzo Bernabei, built in the seventeenth century and
designed by Giacomo Giorgetti. It used to be known as Palazzo
Sperelli (we remember the fresco, in the Lower Church, of the
Sperelli daughter falling from a window) and today is a school. On
the left farther on, at No. 24A, there is a good example of a 'door of
death'. At No. 14 we see the Casa dei Maestri Comacini (architects
from the Lake Como district who undertook commissions all over
Italy in the Middle Ages), which is built in the Lombardian style,
very low, with squat arches: the arms of the *maestri* (an open compass with a flower underneath) are just at the point of the middle
arch; a hammer is represented over another arch above, a square
rule over another. On the right is a large coat of arms dated 1477:
another faded bas-relief on the left, above, may also be a coat of
arms. This house was restored in the fifteenth century. At No. 12
there is the imposing **Palazzo Giacobetti** which was also designed
by Giacomo Giorgetti: it has a balcony with ornate stone supports
underneath and the arms of the family above. And this palace is
imposing inside too, with connecting rooms that run along its street-
side, as in a royal palace. A visit is possible as it houses the ***Biblioteca Comunale,*** or town library, though we should be accompanied by a friar or enquire at the Tourist Office for an appointment.

It also houses the Propertian Academy of Subasio (a cultural society started in 1554), and the International Society of Franciscan Studies.

The Biblioteca Comunale has over fifty thousand volumes and used to be the richest in Europe for its collection of *codici* or statute books alone (more than seven hundred of them). Statute 338 contains St Francis's famous *Cantico delle Creature*, the Hymn of the Creatures, said to have been written when he was dying, at S. Damiano. There are books of Gregorian chant, dating from the thirteenth century, with illuminated letters, and an illuminated Bible of seventeen volumes in lambskin, dated 1280, the gift of St Louis of Anjou. We can see a fifteenth-century copy of the town's statutes bound in a chain, which used to be in the town hall and could be consulted by anyone: it gives the order of procession for the corporations or guilds (merchants had the honour of coming last; surprisingly, shoemakers had a high place while tailors came very near the front); it also shows the places where markets were held, who could wash at which fountains, so that the smallest details of daily life were covered. In this book, too, there is a list of the castles in and near the town, and the payments for *pedaggio* or toll (the tourist still pays this mediaeval tax on all hotel bills).

The library has a room containing eighteen volumes of papal bulls—priceless originals with their seals intact, about a thousand of them. It houses the music composed by Franciscans during six or seven centuries, which in style is close to that of the 'Roman school' of church music: especially the seventeenth century is important in this collection, including the whole work of Father Porta, a contemporary of Palestrina.

Among the papal bulls in this library (*bulla*, from the word to 'stamp' or 'seal') we shall find what we might call the Magna Carta of the St Francis Basilica: Pope Gregory IX's bull of July 22nd, 1230, in which he declares the Basilica to be 'papal'. It bears the signatures of the cardinals, each with his personal cross doodled in with ink, intricately, giving the impression of infinite leisure and repose. These bulls are tied round either with common string or with silk: those tied with silk were nice ones, *bulla favorabilis*, which you untied with pleasure; while those tied with common string, *filo canapis*, involved a punishment or a warning or a statement of displeasure. The bulls in Assisi's library seem to be mostly tied with common string: one of them addressed to the bishops advises them to be nicer to Franciscan friars. The Pardon given by the pope to

Brother Elias (responsible for the building of the Basilica and St Francis's successor as Vicar of the Order) is here: few people realize —and the Church seems none too anxious to point out—that this man was excommunicated for being a close friend and admirer of Barbarossa, emperor and enemy of the popes. He then joined Barbarossa's court and travelled in the East as a guest of the Patriarch of Constantinople. He died at Cortona, and received the Pardon just before his death.

Opposite the Palazzo Giacobetti there is a long hospital which, though restored and changed, gives an impression of great age. Farther along on the right there is at No. 11 the **Oratorio dei Pellegrini,** or Pilgrims' Oratory, which was part of this hospital in the fifteenth century. In the evening when the candles are lit it looks inviting and mysterious: no more than a tiny room. On the crumbling front, under a jutting roof with carved supports, we see a fresco, *the Redeemer in glory between SS. James and Anthony the Abbot,* by Matteo da Gualdo (1462-98), of which a tiny piece of Christ's face remains, and some red and orange blotches. Through a graceful little roseate curtain we pass into a tiny place of prayer, frescoed all round. The *four doctors* in the roof above us is a neutral work by Pier Antonio Mezzastris. But the fresco behind the altar is a delicate and humble piece with especially soft tones by Matteo da Gualdo (1486), *Madonna enthroned with Child between SS. James and Anthony the Abbot and angels,* figures surrounded by a Renascence elegance which has not yet run riot into posture. On the left wall there are two panels, rustically green, *St Anthony the Abbot blesses the camels,* and at its side *he gives alms.* On the right wall there are two panels representing *miracles of the Saint,* both by Mezzastris. On the wall behind us we shall notice *Christ in glory* above the arch of the doorway, with *SS. James and Anthony the Abbot* on either side, together with a figure of *St Ansanus* (the first apostle of Siena) which has been attributed, probably falsely, to the young Perugino on account of a certain spacious delicacy.

Continuing up the Via S. Francesco we pass on the left side two houses of the thirteenth century with arched entrances, and then the **Palazzo Bindangoli,** designed by Giulio Danti (1500-75), today the seat of the Università degli Studi S. Paolo (College of Pauline Studies). Then on the right at No. 3 there is the porch of the **Monte Frumentario** with its seven three-lobed arches, built in 1267 as part of the hospital: now a cinema. On the walls under its porch there are very faint remains of fourteenth-century murals. Immediately after this, still on the right, we come to the *Oliviera fountain,* which was put there at the order of Oliviero Lodovici in 1570 as an ornament: people began washing their clothes there, which resulted in the notice we see above: 'PENA UN SCUDO E PERDITA DE PANNI PER CHI LAVA IN QUESTO FONTE'; that is, 'a fine of one scudo and the loss of his washing for anyone who washes clothes here.' There is a thirteenth-century arch over the road which we now pass under, into the Via del Seminario: the imposing series of arches above us on the left, under a long balcony, with a supporting wall leaning down to the roadway, belongs to the Theological Missionary College of the Franciscan Friars. At No. 7 of this narrow street (the pavement has now deserted us) there is the Seminario Vescovile (Episcopal College) in two parts, one thirteenth- and the other fourteenth-century, which includes the side of what used to be the old monastery of S. Angelo di Panzo.

We continue up this subtly winding lane until we come into Via Giotto at the top of the hill; it goes left towards the main square, still rising. By now we will probably have noticed the fountains at every corner, many no longer used except at Christmas (for the cribs). On all sides, too, we see Subasian stone—walls and pavements: if we look closely we shall see large fossilized snails in almost every block.

As we begin our walk up Via Giotto we should notice on the right at No. 29 a balcony in red Subasian stone with a coat of arms. The road now becomes Via Portica. Before we reach Assisi's main square we see at No. 9 on the right an ornate rectangular doorway decorated with putti, flowers, a fountain, from the fifteenth century. And at No. 2 on the left we have the **Museum and the Roman Forum.** The museum is in what used to be the crypt of a church called S. Nicolò, no longer used; rectangular with two naves, from the eleventh century; Romanesque tunnelled arches form the entrance, and the bases of some of these arches on the left are perhaps Roman. Immediately on the left as we enter we see a Roman sarcophagus etched with the figure of Bacchus, leaning over drunkenly, from the second century A.D. There are memorial stones, and fragments of figures, one of which is almost intact except for the head—perhaps an Apollo, but some say Castor or Pollux, a group known to have stood in the former Roman square: this latter idea is supported by the fact that there is an iron attachment in the figure's chest, which perhaps connected it to the horse in the group. At the end wall facing us there is a memorial stone to Ottidius Attianus of the Ninth Praetorian Cohort, who died at the age of twenty (*'vixit annos XX'*). Next to the Apollo or Castor we see an Etruscan figure of Charon holding a purse to receive money for conducting the dead over the Styx. On the other side of the Apollo there is the lid of a small sarcophagus showing a man lying on his bed, while a woman and—most unusual—a child stand by him: perhaps a representation of the dead man's family. On the left of the Etruscan piece showing Charon stands part of a statue of Minerva, thought (because of the flatness of its back) to have been attached to the Temple of Minerva in the main square, at the pediment: and in fact, as we shall see later, there is space for it. On the left of this we see the markedly phallic top of an Etruscan tomb. On the walls there are fragments, found in various houses of Assisi, of ancient wall-paintings: a complete piece has been preserved under glass—a warrior with a spear, with that natural ease on which the Renascence clearly drew. In this part of the room there is also a gracious wall decoration in a good state of repair, a design of flowers (perhaps poppies) and various fish—dolphins, crabs—found some years ago under the church of S. Maria Maggiore, in an ancient temple.

To the right of the entrance a long and narrow corridor takes us into what was the main square of the town in ancient times, a whole side of it in a remarkably good state of preservation: with a little imagination, and by squinting the eyes, we can see it all as it was. And there is a drawing on the wall to help us, showing the Temple of Minerva raised on its own terrace above the level of the square, and the Castor and Pollux group with horses in the middle. In this picture, two doorways lead from the square beneath the temple's terrace, presumably to a staircase that emerged under the temple's columns: and these two doorways are intact for us to see in this corridor, one a little shorter than the other (probably because of later alterations, to support buildings above). We must imagine that the square extended on in width to the extent of the present square above (forty-five yards). We should note the long gutter near the wall, into which water from the whole square flowed: if we stand at the far end of the corridor and look back we shall see the gentle slope towards the gutter. There are grilles above us, over which cars and pedestrians pass, showing us the depth of this former square, compared with the present level of the Temple of Minerva. Where the

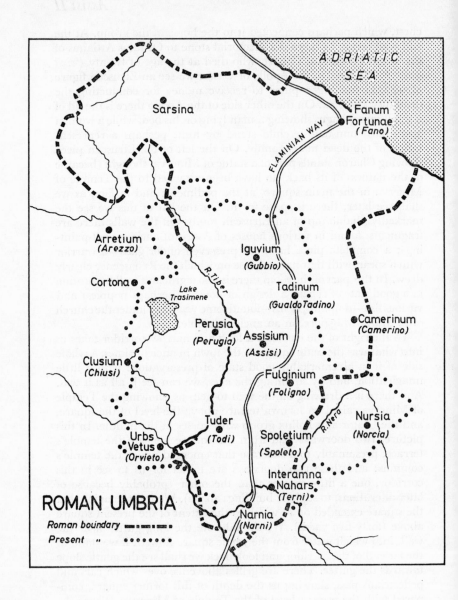

ADRIATIC
SEA

Sarsina

Fanum
Fortunae
(Fano)

FLAMINIAN WAY

Arretium
(Arezzo)

Iguvium
(Gubbio)

Cortona

R. Tiber

Lake
Trasimene

Tadinum
(GualdoTadino)

Perusia
(Perugia)

Camerinum
(Camerino)

Assisium
(Assisi)

Clusium
(Chiusi)

Fulginium
(Foligno)

R. Nera

Nursia
(Norcia)

Tuder
(Todi)

Spoletium
(Spoleto)

Urbs
Vetus
(Orvieto)

Interamna
Nahars
(Terni)

Narnia
(Narni)

ROMAN UMBRIA

Roman boundary ━ ▪ ━ ▪ ━ ▪
Present   ••••••••

corridor widens and there is a long stone platform we have the tribune where the seven magistrates sat (we see fixtures for seven seats): the number of magistrates depended on a town's importance. On the wall behind there are holes running in a straight line—a bronze inscription was once here: the bronze was stolen.

By going down a corridor that faces this platform we can visit the actual site of the Castor and Pollux monument: we find its base with four columns, and an inscription describing how a banquet of dedication was held (the monument was given to the people of Asisium by a private family), and how much money was spent first on the 'decurions', that is the members of the town's senate (an expenditure of fifteen sesterces, equal to between two and four asses in real value), how much on the 'sexvirate' (six governing officials—thirteen sesterces), and how much on the people (eleven sesterces). We walk on past the tribune and come to the latest excavations of all (1959) in the area of the fountains and shops, at the corner of the square. Just before the end of the corridor we should note high up on the wall on our left an inscription referring to the repair of this wall and the columns of the Temple of Minerva. We come to a square fountain or bath below the level of the square, with steps leading down to it, and a perfectly intact arch of travertine above. If we look carefully we shall see that the sides of the bath have been built up ever so slightly at the bottom so as to stop water seeping out between the stones. An enormous thoroughness pervades Roman building. If we care to look back along the Forum wall from this point we shall see that although it supports whole buildings above (and has done for centuries) not one block of stone is out of line, and the wall shows not the slightest slope. A further fountain lies beyond the one we see, so far unexcavated. At the very end the gutter underfoot makes a right turn, denoting the end of the square. Here the shops began; their thresholds are still intact, together with the holes where the shutters were secured, exactly in the way they are in Italy today. Here vases for oil and wine were found: the wine jugs were dug into the sand, and the sand round it was watered to keep the temperature low.

Continuing along the Via Giotto to the main square we find immediately on the left the restored **Fonte Portica,** another porched fountain below the level of the street. If we look up at this point we shall see a tiny pulpit bulging from the wall (1354), from which St Bernardine preached in 1425. This was once the side of the church of S. Nicolò in which St Francis and his companion Bernardo da Quintavalle consulted the Bible for guidance as to the Rule of Perfection. This building is now the Palazzo della Pretura (police courts), with the Post Office on the ground floor. If we like to think of kings—and enjoy pretty houses—we should stand in this corner of the square and look back at the first house facing us in the Via Portica from which we have come, pleasingly shuttered like a French villa, with a balcony: a plaque tells us that Umberto, king of Italy, once stayed here.

We are now in Assisi's main square, the *Piazza del Comune.* Looking across with our backs to the steps of the Post Office we see on our left the thirteenth-century Palazzo del Capitano del Popolo (restored in 1927), with its Guelf crenellation above, and immediately next to it the powerful *Torre del Popolo,* or people's tower, with Ghibelline battlements. This tower was started in 1212 and finished nearly a hundred years later: we should go to its base and have a look at the public measures (1348) for bricks, tiles and slates in the Middle Ages, with an inscription above them. To one side of this there is a pleasantly designed doorway (1504), now the entrance of the traffic-police station.

Farther on we come to the **Temple of Minerva,** built at the time of Augustus, which sets the tone for the square and dominates the other buildings of whatever date or height. It was this temple for which Goethe left his carriage at S. Maria degli Angeli and strode all the way up the hill, past the Basilica of St Francis and the rest of the town which he described in his *Italian Journey* as 'the monstrous bowels of churches on top of each other in a Babylonian pile'. Now that Roman art is no longer the fashion poor Goethe is decried for this: the Middle Ages are in and pagan temples out. But it remains a fact that the underparts of the Basilica of St Francis do look rather like a set of bad teeth sometimes, and they do have a forbidding—'Babylonian' is just the right word—effect on the humble eye that watches from below. Perhaps they were meant to. And the columns of the Temple of Minerva, crumbling and scratched, do suggest a remarkably joyous and sunlit world, with an unstinting dignity and mellow celebration of life. If we look closely we shall see that the grooves in the columns have here and there been filled with a kind of cement or hard plaster; it was done with the perspective from below in mind. In fact, we shall rarely see a fluted column without it. What we see is really the porch or *pronaos*, as it was called, of the

136

temple, a vestibule in front of its entrance: there are six Corinthian columns, fluted all round so that they appear slim and fine. It is a Greek temple exquisitely realized. On a wall under the porch we see the perforations made by the clamps of a former bronze inscription. The architect designed his steps ingeniously, seeing the great space between the temple and the Forum below: a difference of nine feet was too much for an imposingly gradual slope of steps; so he dug steps actually between the columns, and this much space was gained. In 1539 the temple became the church of S. Maria sopra Minerva (St Mary on Minerva). A century after that it was transformed inside to the baroque style by Giacomo Giorgetti, which makes it a gay and cosy drawing-room.

If we walk left as we come out we shall find a fountain whose cheerful presence balances that of the temple and makes the square look like the top of the world on a sunny day. On the left as we walk towards it we notice a little staircase-lane rising up between the buildings, called Via Tiberio d'Assisi (the artist of certain frescoes we shall see at S. Maria degli Angeli): a short walk up this will take us out of the noise of the square at once, between mediaeval houses close on either side, built on ancient Roman stones. The tiny restaurant La Fortezza where Guglielmo cooks excellent and varied dishes every day is in the next staircase-lane towards the fountain. Facing us as we return to the square we see the *Palazzo dei Priori,* from the thirteenth century, now the town hall, consisting of four connected buildings which occupy nearly the whole side of the square. In the restoration of 1927 the crenellation on the earliest of these palazzi was rebuilt. We should notice the magnificent deep arches cut through these buildings in two places to reach the streets behind. And here we shall find the town's *picture gallery,* over the doorway of which five or six coats of arms are clustered.

Like many others in Umbria, Assisi's picture gallery is said to be under restoration but stays the same—rather a mess. It is worth a brief glance if we have time. On the right as we come in there is an unusual thirteenth-century fresco on a lay subject—a splendid *cavalcade.* Among the other exhibits in the first room there is a wooden *crucifix* that shows Giotto's influence, and a *Madonna and Child with St Francis* from the same period and perhaps same hand. There is a *Crucifixion* where the Virgin's robes are strangely and finely decorated—by an artist of local or perhaps Marche origin, and near this there are further examples of the slow and heavy local

137

style that remembers the Byzantine mood and little else. On the wall facing us from the entrance there is a tall panel of clear Giottoesque origin where the only clear remainder is the Child's face and the slenderly framed building behind. Farther along this wall in the next room we come to a really warm work by Ottaviano Nelli which has suffered from its long stay in a country church: a *Madonna and Child with SS. James and Anthony the Abbot*. To the right of this there is a Tiberio d'Assisi—*Madonna and Child*—with a pleasant roseate harmony. The two *angels* (busts) on the other wall are by Matteo da Gualdo. The *Annunciation* is perhaps by Petrucciolo (an Orvieto painter, 1372-94). Opposite this we see something rare in Italy—rustic art with a humble and intimate story to tell, separate from the schools of its time, a fifteenth-century work: it tells the legend of St Julian the Hospitaller, who has just murdered his mother and father in their bed, while his wife stands screaming behind him; the legend says that he mistook his mother for his wife, and his father for a lover. He built a hospital as penance.

In the next room we have more of the graceful and pleasing Tiberio d'Assisi, recognizable by his soft rosy tones. The last room has two gilt doors of the seventeenth century, amid a hotchpotch of objects—ceramics from Deruta, drawings by Giorgetti, Sermei and others of that time, showing the superb craftsmanship of the baroque artists: these splendid rough drawings alone are worth a visit to the gallery.

S. Rufino—Rocca Maggiore—Porta Perlici

If we turn right on coming out of the art gallery and enter the deep archway called Via dell'Arco dei Priori we shall find a little church with a Renascence front behind a piazza, its bricks showing (another luxurious intention never realized). This is the **Chiesa Nuova** (1615), built at the expense of Philip III of Spain and constructed —supposedly—on the foundations of a house belonging to Pietro Bernardone, the father of St Francis. Before going in we should have a look (left) at the ruggedly imposing back wall of the Palazzo dei Priori, which has been restored to its original lines. Inside the church there are five cupolas in the form of a Greek cross, another baroque drawing-room for prayer. A door to the left of the main altar can be opened: this leads us into a narrow closed courtyard where we see two filled-in doorways said to have belonged to the Bernardone house. One of them is a 'door of death' with the steps that once led up to it removed: we see the probably Etruscan foundations of the wall, perhaps once part of the Forum. Dante's lines on Assisi and district are displayed on a plaque attached to the wall (see Appendix 4).

A few steps farther down take us to a tiny chapel supposed to have been the store-room or perhaps stable of the Bernardone house. On going back into the church we might peep into a low doorway on the right as we leave; we see a kneeling statue lit by a candle— conjecture has it that St Francis was imprisoned here by his father after his Foligno escapade (see p. 92).

If we turn right outside the church and take the lane by the church-wall (Vicolo Superiore di S. Antonio) we shall come to a little square with the door of an oratory facing us. There is an iron grille through which at most times of the day we can peer into the tiny room: it is the **Oratorio di S. Francesco Piccolino,** where St Francis is supposed (by a long stretch of imagination) to have been born; we are asked to believe that in the heart of winter his wealthy mother left her comfortable apartments above (for this was the first Bernardone house) to give birth to Francis. A 'mysterious pilgrim' (she figures a lot in these apocryphal tales) told her to.

Steps on our left as we face this oratory will lead us up to the Corso Giuseppe Mazzini, where we cross straight over to a further staircase-lane under arches. We keep on rising (crossing the Via Roma too) until we reach the Via S. Rufino, where we turn right towards the **Duomo** or cathedral of that name. We rise towards it steeply, between mediaeval houses and frequent 'doors of death'. And at the top we come to an unexpectedly splendid and restful square where, withdrawn, the ancient crumbling front of the church stands before us, a strangely final word on the town of Assisi and its baptism into the Christian epoch (it was begun in the ninth century). Today, incongruously, it is the town's most fashionable place for marriages and functions (though all its interior splendours were removed in baroque times).

Its tower is often in the clouds on grey days, while the dark face is clear. Many people think that the St Francis Basilica is the town's cathedral, but a glimpse at this church repudiates the idea serenely. It even makes the Basilica, with its thirteenth-century foundation, look new-fangled. It is clearly from a surer and sounder epoch than St Francis's time: the story of Christ is nursed simply and intimately, still closed in the catacombs, those dark, underground rooms that echoed with chants all day, hidden from the persecuting world. St Rufinus, the first bishop of Assisi, was martyred here in the third century; his body is said to lie under the main altar.

The church was enlarged in the eleventh century by Bishop Ugone, and restored by Giovanni da Gubbio in 1144: a century later it underwent another restoration and was reconsecrated (1228). The façade is in three horizontal parts—the only survivor of the church's many re-births. The lowest part is from the twelfth century, divided into square compartments by stone strips: it has three doors of roughly the same design, with stone lions on each side of the tall centre one (the left-hand lion is eating a man's head). The door itself is framed in a darkly austere design, an arch of square patterns and lilies and bas-relief figures—there are griffins lying prone along the pillars and biting each other, dragons or crocodiles with wings, a king enthroned, angels, couples, and inside the arch itself a bas-relief Christ, tucked into a niche between the sun and the moon, looking primitive and stern, his face masked with a dumb certainty that the later epochs knew nothing about, while the Madonna on the left of his throne gives milk to St Rufinus. The right-hand door has little flowers and animals carved all round it, while in the lunette formed by the arch there is in bas-relief the scene of two birds drinking from a bowl, with griffins standing on either side of the door. The left-hand door corresponds more or less to this, with two lions drinking from a bowl in the lunette. Above the doors we see a horizontal dividing line of carved animals' and men's heads supporting a fine gallery of arches, with slender pillars. Farther above there is a magnificent rose window taking up nearly the whole of the centre compartment of the façade, intricately carved, seeming to rest on three tiny figures which themselves are standing on animals: at the four corners are the symbols of the evangelists. On either side there are smaller rose windows, the left one between two figures and the right one surmounted by two animals, one of which has fallen off. The top and third part of the façade crowns it with simplicity—a lightly Gothic arch closely framed by the triangular roof: these were added in the thirteenth century, so that we must imagine the primitive church as lower and gaunter, in the Romanesque style. The bell-tower also is Romanesque, partly from the eleventh century: it now has a clock protected by a tiny wooden roof.

The inside of the cathedral has three naves divided by rectangular and not at all pretty columns, with high arches that reveal the original form of the building before sixteenth-century artists converted it to the flamboyant. The baroque sacrilege was total here: anything previous to 1571 was swept away. An old baptismal font remains: we see it at the back right-hand corner of the church, girt round with an iron grille; St Francis, St Clare and Frederick II of Swabia (or the Hohenstaufen, king of Sicily and grandson of the Holy Roman Emperor) were baptized here, according to tradition. We see little more of it than a cylinder of stone. There is an insipid fresco above it, dated 1882, which I predict will one day be blotted out. Opposite this font a hole in the wall covered by a tiny iron grille is the source of another tall story about the 'mysterious pilgrim': the hole is said to bear the imprint of her knee, and the custom is for modern pilgrims to touch it; she was present at St Francis's baptism and after speaking to his mother promptly disappeared.

The first chapel down the church on the right is by Giorgetti, a superb café (imagination will provide marble iron-legged tables and soft plush chairs). Anyway, it has nothing to do with prayer (1663), though, like a café, it has nothing against prayer either.

At the last altar on the right going down the church there is a Dono Doni *Christ amid saints* for those who like his work, and a *Crucifixion* behind the main altar. The presbytery is octagonal, under a cupola which we did not see from the square outside, as it is hidden by the tall façade. A glance upwards at its frescoes will make us want to look quickly down again—angels in their nightshirts, with doleful expressions and stars all round. There are hideous nineteenth-century statues of St Francis, St Rufinus and St Clare. To revive, we should go behind the high altar and have a look at the nicely carved wooden choir in two tiers (1520). Going to the left of the high altar as we face it we find the wrought-iron partition of the *Cappella della Madonna del Pianto,* and above its altar the most worthy thing in the whole church, a humble German *Pietà* of terra-cotta in the tradition we have noticed elsewhere in Umbria where Christ lies across the Virgin's lap, almost straight: said to be a work of the fifteenth century. On the right side of the apse we enter the sacristy through which we reach—we should ask an attendant or priest—the oratory where St Francis is said to have been praying when his companions had the vision of the flaming chariot: originally it was separated from the church, and was connected in the sixteenth century.

We enter the **Cathedral Museum** by the same corridor: in this corridor, by the way, there are capitals from ancient columns, and fragments of mediaeval building. The museum is well-lighted, and for once we are able to see frescoes clearly and in pleasant conditions. Facing us is a triptych by Maso, or Giottino (we remember his *coronation of the Virgin* behind the pulpit in the Lower Church), painted in a soft, russet glow, the face of Christ pale and shrunken: it is a *Crucifixion*, with the *Flagellation* on one side and the *Entombment* on the other. On our left there is another magnificent triptych, which stops just short of extravagance, by Nicolò Alunno (1470), surrounded by a rich mass of gilded frame: a *Madonna and Child and four saints*. This painter is sometimes called Nicolò da Foligno: we see the words '*Opus Nicolai de Fulgii*'. In the predella we find a wonderfully graphic *martyrdom of St Rufinus* and a *Deposition*, the whole work glowing and warm. On its left there is a third triptych, this time by Matteo da Gualdo (1462-98): a *Madonna and Child between SS. Bernard and Sebastian*, a rough work compared with the Nicolò Alunno at its side. On the right stands a restored processional banner of the fourteenth century, a *glory of St Francis*, with a *Crucifixion* on its other side. On the wall to the right of the entrance there is a rustic *Nativity*, perhaps from the twelfth century, and next to it a late *Madonna and Child* of unknown origin.

Back in the main church we should visit, before leaving, the **Roman bath** on the right of the exit as we face it: at Christmas this is the site of a vast crib. Above the doorway a Roman inscription mentions the names of the six magistrates of Assisi responsible for it (first century A.D.).

Outside the church we should ask an attendant to show us to the **crypt** through a doorway on the left side of the square. Here we shall find the former church, from the time of Bishop Ugone in the eleventh century: though this was the second church on the present site. We see the base of the present bell-tower, which was constructed actually on top of the Roman bath, so that we are looking also at the outer wall of that too. This church may have been a pagan temple in origin, as it tends to the circular form, with Roman arches making five or six naves. There are bits of frescoes from the eleventh century. And this crypt also contains the first tomb of St Rufinus—a Roman sarcophagus carved with the story of *Diana and Endymion*. Outside the crypt there is a little courtyard with a deep and vast well: it has been closed for a long time, some say after a man disappeared down it. This is the *Pozzo della Mensa*, meaning the well belonging to the bishop or his household: almost ten feet across and seventy feet deep, carefully walled with stones that fit into each other. Near by are the remains of the cloister belonging to this earlier church.

We may already have noticed the lovely fountain in a corner of the square outside, long and simple, cheerful even in dark weather, as if too many generations of sun had bleached it for darkness ever to penetrate. It was put there in the thirteenth century, and restored in 1532. Passing this fountain on our right we enter (uphill) the Via S. Maria delle Rose: after No. 2 we come to the former Palazzo dei Consoli (early thirteenth-century), with its double arched windows and sheer wall with Etruscan and Roman stones at its base.

Farther on, beyond an archway, there is the Convent of St Apollinaris on the right, with its typical little vestibule which we can enter. An iron grille in the wall connects to the Enclosure and there is the usual wooden tray on a swivel, which serves to carry objects into the convent without the receiver being seen: this is said to derive its standard size from the necessity of receiving new-born illegitimate babies, deposited by the mother and swung round to a new life. At the top of this steep and quiet hill we see the thirteenth-century front of S. Maria delle Rose, no longer used as a church, with a short open bell-tower at its side: now the parish cinema, its films approved by the Church. From the parapet we look down on the roofs of Assisi towards the main piazza, with the church of St Clare over to the left.

If we now walk actually under the bell-tower and turn right, we are suddenly in the country, with birds singing close to us and olive groves extending on either side of the narrow walled lane (the Vicolo S. Maria delle Rose).

Then as we look up we see, a little behind us, the stark remains of the castle that the people of Assisi so much hated and which they tore down with their own hands, the **Rocca Maggiore.** For a quiet unmolested walk by day or night this is perfect, with the light roar of the town close by, and the brisk air described by Dante flowing from the Topino valley on the other side. We shall be able to look down into this valley from the castle, by a straight drop. The walled path narrows and we come to the neat and tree-sheltered fourteenth-century church of *S. Lorenzo,* now private property, its gates locked. Steps going left lead up to an ordinary road, with the broken castle-walls crowning it at the top. Beyond us is the Topino valley from which the walls of Assisi have been quarried, and behind us the tower and façade of the cathedral, so that we look down on them from surprisingly close quarters. But a visit to the castle will take us to the highest vantage point of all, from which on a clear day we shall see the town laid out below in a brown cluster of roofs, the Basilica perching on the rib of a hill in a jumble of towers and buttresses and arches far to the right, while the vast plain shimmers beyond. As we draw level to the castle-entrance we can look straight down on the Ghibelline crenellations of the tower next to the Temple of Minerva, in the main square. The hill must have swept up behind this temple in Roman times like a marvellous garden, offering a clear view.

The Rocca Maggiore is a survival of German feudalism, with a massive squat defence-tower at one corner (added by a pope) which seems to direct itself at the town below. The castle was one of the chief fortresses of the duchy of Spoleto in the Lombard empire: in 553 the Goths left Italy once and for all with the defeat of Totila, but they were followed by another barbarian tribe of German stock, called by the Italians 'long beards' or 'Longibardi'. These despised all peoples south of the Alps. The Byzantine empire that administered Italy, or tried to, crumbled under them, apart from Rome and some of the coastal areas. The Lombard kingdom came to stretch from the edge of the Lazio to the Alps, except for the land controlled by Ravenna (the Byzantine court), while the two Lombard dependencies—the duchy of Spoleto and the duchy of Benevento—ruled central and southern Italy. They were defeated finally by Charlemagne the Frank (774) and so much was the Byzantine concept finished by this time that Pope Leo III thrust the crown on him and vested in him the new 'Holy Roman Empire' (A.D. 800). But the defeat of the Lombards was not the end of their existence in Italy. They differed from the Goths not only in their greater barbarity but in their ability to melt into local populations wherever they were. Slowly they were converted. And they left many marks of their own culture on Italian life. The whole idea and practice of the free *comune* derived from them, not to mention much of the art of building in the north of Italy. Even family habits were passed on: when St Francis cut Clare's hair after he had admitted her to the Order he was following the Lombard practice for newly wed women.

Assisi's castle derives from Lombard rule too, though the walls we see are actually from the fourteenth century. After the Lombard defeat it continued under the duchy of Spoleto, still German. Frederick II of Swabia was sent there by his grandfather for his childhood education, and lived at the castle, it is said, under the care of Duke Corrado di Lutzen. When the duke and his court were away at Spoleto in 1198 the anger of the people broke and they demolished the place entirely. This was when St Francis was sixteen or seventeen, a time when Assisi, like many other towns, was struggling for an independence commensurate with the new wealth of its middle class. During the period of independence that followed, the castle went into eclipse, but when the town passed under the administration of the Church its site became useful again: Cardinal dell'Albornoz had it rebuilt in 1367 on a design by Ugolino di Montemarte. From that time it belonged to whatever faction or family governed the town. In 1485 Giacomo Piccinino, the Perugian condottiere, began a polygonal tower at its north-west corner which we can reach today by a long walk inside one of its walls. This was completed by the Church (Pius II): if we walk to the very top of the hill before entering the castle we can see it at the edge of what is now a pleasant field. It was Paul III who between 1535 and 1538 stuck on the vast cylindrical tower that faces not the north but the roofs of the little town itself: he was responsible, we shall remember, for the hated Rocca at Perugia too.

The castle is surrounded by a stout outer wall, with what used to be its living quarters tucked safely inside round a quadrangle. We walk up to it under arches—slabs of the red Subasian stone. No roofs or ceilings have remained, unless we include the very top one of the central tower itself. We enter a closed courtyard after we are within the walls, and here we see an open staircase which presumably once led to the sleeping quarters. It is a place for browsing, since there is no look-out post which we cannot reach by squeezing ourselves along narrow, half-ruined corridors. We shall see holes in the floor which look straight down on to an entrance, through which a man could be halted (for ever if necessary). On the ground floor of this inner castle there were the kitchen, the pantry, the oven and a large hall: we shall also see the cellar, a sea of mud now. A wooden ramp at the top of the outdoor staircase leads us to the rooms of the tower, one on top of the other, except that the ceilings are now missing. The staircase of this tower winds narrowly round one straight column, with room enough for one person only— 103 steps in all, taking us to one of the finest views we shall ever have of the country behind Assisi towards the Marche. We see the Tescio winding like a muddy snake far below among low green hills. Across the outer courtyard we shall find a low entrance conducting us to the tower completed by Pius II, which is like the fist of a long arm stretched out from the castle, facing north-west.

Returning the way we came we find at the side of the little church of S. Lorenzo a long staircase leading right down to the Piazza S. Rufino and the cathedral again. But at the bottom of the staircase we turn left, that is, away from the cathedral, uphill along the Via Porta Perlici, which ends in the town-gate of that name (twelfth century). There are two arches, enclosing a courtyard now tarred over, with a café which we may need by now. At the base of the inner arch there are blocks of stone from the Umbrian and Roman epochs, and we should notice the stone hinges too. An inscription above it tells us that in the year 1199 (when the Rocca Maggiore was sacked and the town's independence achieved) a road to the Marche was opened from this gate.

Wandering back along the road we came by we turn first left into the narrow Via del Comune Vecchio: after passing between intact mediaeval houses we find at No. 6, on the left, a house behind a courtyard said to have once been the Palazzo del Comune or town hall: a modest survival, perhaps, of the time when factions ruled the town and Assisi had little to do with her own destinies. Almost opposite this house, at the corner of an alleyway, there is a splendid and perfectly preserved house of the fourteenth century, so squat and neat and restrained that it seems to be barricading itself against the world outside. Continuing along the road (Via del Comune Vecchio) we come out into the vast Piazza Giacomo Matteotti with a new boarding-school built by the Franciscans in the 'twenties so that they could reoccupy the Basilica (an arrangement with the State). On the left of the square we take the Via del Teatro Romano, which takes us round one side of what was a Roman amphitheatre in the first years of the empire. We shall find no remains: but the houses, built on the bricks and stones of the Roman foundations, follow exactly the oval form of the original, with gardens where the arena once was. We can walk to the top of the hill overlooking this whole group of houses, so that we stand where the highest seats of the amphitheatre used to be. It is difficult not to feel, as we look down on the shell of a theatre once open to the sky, that we have lost something since then. Assisi has no theatre: her concerts are rare. The Roman theatres—even their simple stage presentations —were cruel affairs. But still we have lost something.

Returning to the Piazza Matteotti we should take the road leading out of it on the other side, the Via Galeazzo Alessi, with the **public gardens** on our left as we walk downhill: these offer quiet paths among thick-leafed holm oaks for the foot-weary, and another bar in the summer season. We can then follow the road down to the centre of town again. Alternatively we can return by crossing Piazza Matteotti and following the side of the cathedral (Via del Torrione), with a massive piece of Roman masonry at its edge as our signpost. We see the cathedral's cupola and semi-circular apse-wall. We should look at the base of the cathedral tower as we pass it: it has a block of stone almost eight feet in length; this whole area was clearly given up to temples and theatres and baths in Roman times.

The Basilica of St Clare—S. Maria Maggiore—S. Pietro

The Piazza S. Chiara is virtually a second town-centre—more buses and cars can squeeze into it than into the Piazza del Comune. And above all it has a long parapet where we can sit and take the marvellous air from the Topino valley on a warm day, with the road winding up to Assisi just beneath us and the solemn façade of St Clare's at our side, its convent wall sloping down among olive trees.

St Clare was born eleven or twelve years after Francis, in 1193, and lived nearly thirty years after his death. Chiara Offreduccio was born of a noble family, and their house looked out on the Piazza S. Rufino. From about 1207, when she was fourteen, Assisi began to talk about 'Francis', the son of a local merchant, who had suddenly renounced a military trip to Apulia and was behaving in an odd way. The stories—and perhaps the sight of him in the streets—won Clare's silent attention, and unknown to the rest of her family, they mapped out her future life. But her mother, Ortolana, had something to do with this too. She was a remarkably pious woman and in her youth had gone on dangerous pilgrimages to Rome: from her Clare learned her first habits of fasting and prayer, which became the basic themes of her convent life.

Sixteen years before her birth Barbarossa had installed the Duke Corrado in Assisi's castle to try to protect the old social order— against heavy odds. It was a time of increasing importance for merchants like Francis's father—men who travelled and, in their persons, represented a disruption of the old feudal ties. This first middle class, entirely urban, was bitterly hostile to the traditional landowning nobility. When Clare was five the Rocca Maggiore was sacked by the people, and the noble families—including hers—fled to the country. But they were followed, and then they moved to Assisi's worst enemy, Perugia (1202). At this time, until about 1209, there was constant war between the two towns, but during a brief peace the family moved back to Assisi.

It was now that Clare began consciously to follow Francis. She refused absolutely to marry, though the husband had been chosen, and she told her family that she wanted to serve Christ. The basic Franciscan rule grew clear to her: a person who owns nothing has nothing to defend, and is therefore free (to serve God). This was what Francis preached to a town exhausted by war: only in this way, he said, could real peace be achieved; and the force of his words was in their not sounding theoretical—everyone knew that he himself had thrown up a wealthy life.

In 1210 one of Clare's cousins became a follower of Francis, so that some contact between Francis and herself was possible. She asked to speak to him privately, and convinced him of her vocation: he was apparently unwilling to let her follow him at first, but gave way when he recognized something like his own determination. The Palm Sunday of 1211 was the last time she dressed sumptuously, like a young noblewoman, for the distribution of olive branches in church. That night she left her house secretly and walked to Porziuncola, where Francis and his companions were waiting. As an act of caution—he expected great trouble from her family, and it came—he took her straightway to a Benedictine convent near Bastìa. The family tried to get her away but she claimed the convent's protection: they pleaded with her, and in the end she showed them her head, already shaved. The family left but now the nuns were afraid, or so we may imagine from the fact that Clare left too. This time Francis installed her in a Benedictine convent on the road to Spello, S. Maria di Panzo. But after sixteen days another crisis broke: she was joined by her sister Agnes, and this time the family was determined. Her father, Favarone, sent twelve men to the convent on horseback to bring them back by force. Here the story is vague, perhaps because the Church dislikes admitting that they succeeded (there is a story that Clare's body became miraculously heavy and the men had to drop her).

We only know that a short time afterwards she persuaded her family to let them both remain nuns, and this was accepted graciously, without the kind of reprisals taken against Francis by his father. Now that the family trouble was over, and seeing that Clare was determined not to remain in the scholarly order of the Benedictines, Francis gave her the tiny church of S. Damiano, which was her home until her death: she was behind the Enclosure there for forty-two years. Gradually others joined her, all promising obedience to Francis.

Though she neither preached nor travelled like Francis, Clare's life was remarkably similar to his: the prayer which was her main activity achieved the same personal importance as his *laudi*, and had the same function, of subduing self-interest and partiality by means of praise, in a continual spiritual communion that tried to guide every action and thought. Francis, with the help of the bishop of Assisi, had to insist on her eating a certain amount each week. They also persuaded her to take on the office of abbess, to fill her life with practical duties apart from prayer. After her death her companions said of her that when she prayed she was radiant; an extraordinary sweetness came into the room. '*Chiara di nome, più chiara per vita, chiarissima per virtù*,' Francis's first biographer wrote of her: 'clear by name, clearer by her life, and clearest of all in her spirit.'

After the death of Francis her following grew: her third sister, Beatrice, joined her, then her mother. In 1234 Agnes of Bohemia founded the same Order in Prague. Two years before her death Clare asked the protector of the Franciscan Order, Cardinal Rainaldo Segni, to have the 'privilege of poverty' included in her Rule when it was approved by the pope: the members of her order were to own nothing personally, and even nothing in common; they were always to be 'Poor Clares'. It was perhaps the most important act of her convent life. This rule holds today for most of the Order: a few of the convents have possessions in common, though not the convent of Assisi. The 'privilege' did become inserted into the Rule approved by Pope Innocent IV in the year of Clare's death. It was this that preserved her Order in the strict Franciscan tradition for centuries afterwards. Perhaps she learned from what she saw happen among the male Franciscans.

The **Basilica of St Clare** was started in 1257, four years after her death, in the same red-and-white Subasian stone motif as the Franciscan basilica: and it was consecrated eight years later. The shape of the other basilica is also imitated to a slight extent: if we look at the side-walls we shall see that there are the same number of round towers forming the skeleton of the building, though they are modest in size. The façade, too, is divided into three parts like that of the Upper Church of St Francis (which in turn may have been designed as an imitation of the cathedral).

There is a large rose window mounted over the Romanesque doorway (the Gothic of the St Francis Basilica is not followed here, in what seems a deliberate choosing of modest traditions). Massive arches support the church on the left as we look at it, and beyond them we can see a chapel (red squares of stone with white borders) protruding into the roadway—an addition of the fourteenth century: beyond that is the transept, while the tower remains invisible behind.

The façade is the simplest we shall see in the town, for a big church: an austere repetition of the cathedral's three horizontal divisions without the slightest decoration, apart from the intricate stonework of the rose window. The front entrance is closed except on holidays and Sundays, and the usual one is under the half-arches on the left.

We enter a very dark church, one clear nave that has the appearance of being simply a large vestibule before we enter the chapels beyond, its ceiling divided into four vaults, their ribs leaning on the twelve towers we have glimpsed from outside. The walls are bare, and as in the Upper Church of St Francis there is an open gallery running round them high above. The main altar is enclosed behind a wrought-iron gate of the eighteenth century (though the pillars at its corners are from the fourteenth century). Above the altar there is a tall thirteenth-century crucifix mounted on wood by the so-called '*Maestro di S. Chiara*', who, like the Maestro di S. Francesco, remains unknown. In this at first sight Byzantine crucifix, hanging over the altar, there is a touch of the later art in the way Christ's body bends with the weight of its suffering, which connects the

150

artist with the period a little before Cimabue and Cavallini; and tradition calls him the pupil of Giunta Pisano (1202-55). In the vault over the altar we see in each of the four sections two saints: as we look up with our faces towards the altar we see at the front, *St Agnes the Roman* and (perhaps) *St Agnes the sister of Clare*; right, *St Lucy* and *St Cecilia*, left *St Catherine* and another, unidentified, saint; back, the *Madonna* and *St Clare*. A group of angels in prayer surrounds them: this whole vault was the work of a follower of Giotto, it is thought, at the beginning of the fourteenth century. It is difficult to see more than their delicate tones.

In the left arm of the transept, on the end-wall which we can approach closely, there is a fresco of the *Nativity* of the Umbro-Sienese school, fourteenth century. High up on the three walls of this corner (uncovered and restored in 1927) we have *stories from the Old Testament*, which are often compared to the 'Roman' panels in the Upper Church of St Francis. They were painted at the same time, towards the end of the thirteenth century. We see *the creation of the animals, the construction of the ark*, and on the central wall *Adam and Eve*: on the left *the disobedience of Adam and Eve*. We shall find them more plainly decorative and rougher than what we have seen in the St Francis Basilica. In the right arm of the transept we shall find *stories from the life of St Clare*: these are on the right wall and are attributed to the Maestro di S. Chiara, that is, to the earliest period of the building. On the wall facing us there is *the funeral of St Clare* and, below, *the removal of her body* (that is, from S. Damiano to Assisi): these are attributed to a Giottoesque artist, perhaps the same who did the ceiling over the main altar. Above on the left wall there is *the massacre of the Innocents* and *flight into Egypt*: on the right wall, above, *the dispute in the Temple*, while the one above it is ruined. These are from the same artist. High above on the left wall, in the lunette, there is a *Last Judgment* of the same period.

Just in front of the high altar on the right there is a door leading into the **Cappella del Sacramento,** a wall of which leans on the old church of St George, where St Francis received his first education (now the cloister behind the Enclosure). Here we are in the heart of the church, a pleasant, square, restful chapel without a window. On our right, beyond a glass partition, we see a further chapel. Over the entrance through which we have just come there is a *Nativity* with an *Annunciation* above, both graphic and to the point, like all this church: painted at the end of the fourteenth century in the new 'Gothic' style. On their right is an *Epiphany*. On the left wall there is a triptych perhaps by the Maestro di S. Chiara again, a *Crucifixion* and *four saints*: on the left wall also a *Madonna and Child amid saints* which some people attribute to Maso (Giottino) and which has a certain delicacy. Apart from this, there are a *Deposition, Resurrection* and *Entombment* which some people attribute without much evidence to a follower of Lorenzetti.

We now pass round to the second chapel beyond the glass partition, the **Cappellina delle Suore,** or the Little Chapel of the Nuns. Above its altar, and behind glass, we see the simple pre-Gothic cross which legend says spoke to St Francis in the little church of S. Damiano (the one now at S. Damiano is a copy), from the twelfth century. There is no effort at depicting suffering or an actual moment of life here: it is just a representation of a subject known to everyone, and therefore almost a symbol compared to the later art. Behind us as we face the altar there is a wrought-iron gateway dividing the church from the Enclosure, where a nun will show us various relics of the two saints—St Francis's white deacon's cassock embroidered by St Clare herself; her cloak and waist-cord; a case with a lock of her hair; St Francis's sandals, and a habit: his socks made by St Clare; the tunic which he put on (he is said to have begged it) after he renounced his inheritance; the papal bull which St Clare received before dying, approving the Rule of her Order with its privilege of poverty, signed by Innocent IV (1253).

When we come out of this chapel we turn left to a staircase under the level of the floor which will lead us (another imitation of the St Francis Basilica) to the tomb of St Clare. Like that of the Lower Basilica, this crypt was burrowed under the earth in the nineteenth century (1850-72): its present form is modern, 1935. Over the altar, in an illuminated hole, we see the place where her tomb was found. She was removed from the sarcophagus there (a staircase leads up to it) and placed behind glass in a new position behind the altar. The skeleton has been given simulated skin.

Coming out of the church we cross its square again as if towards the main square but take the lower of the two roads facing us in that direction (Via S. Agnese). After passing under a bridge connecting the houses on either side we notice on the right, where the road widens, the remains of a Roman wall. The narrow road winds to the left, and here begins our first visit to the 'lower town', that is, the half that lies under the level of the main square: the rivalry between 'upper' and 'lower' towns, once bitter hatred, has survived as an amiable and confused grudge.

Where the Via S. Agnese winds left we get a good view of St Clare's convent, and the tower behind its façade. Just before it straightens again, on the left, there is the Oratorio di S. Crispino which we recognize by a fresco in the lunette above its entrance, a *Madonna and Child* by a fourteenth-century Umbrian artist. We then come out into the Piazza del Vescovado, where St Francis renounced his possessions before the bishop. It has a *fontana del lione*, so-called because there is a lion faintly carved on it, misted over by time. This is a restful little square, sloping downhill to the *vescovado* or bishop's palace itself and to the Romanesque church of **S. Maria Maggiore,** which was the town's first cathedral. It is also the oldest church in Assisi, its first known date being 963: after a fire it was rebuilt on a design of Giovanni da Gubbio between 1212 and 1228. Indeed, its simple façade reminds us of Gubbio, in a style that combines the honest and rustic with the prosperous: and again we see the red and white motif in Subasian stone. It is divided into three parts, but vertically this time, with strips of stone, and behind the church we see a stout tower. Inside, there are three naves, rather bare, with vast rectangular pillars dividing them. These are not uniform: two in the left nave have splendid capitals, perhaps taken from the original church. The walls were once bright with frescoes of the fourteenth and fifteenth centuries, but whitewash covers them. Some fragments have been recovered, though the one complete fresco in the apse was ruined by damp in the last century. If we find a priest we should ask him to take us down to the crypt where we shall see the low arches of what was either an earlier church or the crypt of an earlier church. The site has become famous among archaeologists for the fact that excavations there a few years ago revealed an ancient temple with frescoed walls (permanently and quite inexplicably closed to visitors).

On our left as we come out of the church there is the gate of the bishop's palace, and a courtyard which has nothing of the past about it, except perhaps its shape. St Francis lived here in 1226, when he was gravely ill with the dropsy.

If we are tired by this time we can get back to the main square by walking to the upper level of the Piazza del Vescovado and take one of the rising staircase lanes: if we trace our staircase-journey properly, we shall suddenly, and with surprise, emerge into the main piazza from an archway under the Palazzo dei Priori.

Otherwise we continue downhill from the bishop's palace along the Via Giacomo de Martino: when this lane bends downhill we see before us a doorway on our right with a fresco, *Madonna with Child and angels*, from the fifteenth century, which has survived wholly. We continue along the Via S. Apollinare, coming out almost at once in a strange, captivating little corner where the church of **S. Giuseppe** stands on our left, its rose window no more than eighteen feet from the ground, so close to the doorway under it that we have a better view of a rose window's carved stone radial arms than we shall ever have again: we realize the work that must have gone into the vaster windows like those of the cathedral. This corner is all snugly higgledy-piggledy: the entrance is pushed too close to the edge of the wall. The church belongs to the convent of S. Giuseppe now, a school for girls. If we ring the bell where the words *Educatorio Femminile di S. Giuseppe* are written a nun will show us into a sitting-room to see the traces of some Giottoesque frescoes (some people say Maso). There is a *Crucifixion* and an *Annunciation*. Facing us as we go into the second room is a *St Apollinaris* with a *Madonna of the olives* immediately on the right of the entrance, and *St Christopher carrying the Child Jesus* on his shoulder. It is hard to find Maso's gentleness in these frescoes.

We walk on towards the Porta S. Pietro which we see at the bottom of the road (Via Borgo S. Pietro), standing undauntable among the roofs with a great fir-tree at its side, a perfect survival from the twelfth century. We walk past the modern Cittadella Cristiana on our right, recognizable by the vast plate-glass window of its dining-room and its air of a luxury hotel: it is run on private capital, though the president is a priest; the idea is to provide a Catholic meeting-place and lodgings for students, in an effort to revive the idea of a cultural monastery, but as a lay organization. At the bottom of the hill the square of St Peter's spreads to our left, neat and chained off from traffic (an experiment by the local tourist office): there are strips of lawn and cypresses, and a parapet overlooking the valley, with the squat front of the Benedictine **S. Pietro** closing one side. This church was first built in 1029, but its present enlarged form derives from the thirteenth century: it was reconsecrated (1253) under the Cistercians, whose Rule is an austere version of Benedictinism (the Trappists are a branch of them). The

façade came into being in 1268: this time it is divided both vertically and horizontally into six parts, with two tiny doorways on
each side of the main one which are like 'doors of death', perhaps
due to the fact that this church began life outside the city walls in
an exposed position. The main door has a gracefully carved Romanesque arch, and there are three deep-set rose windows which take
up nearly the whole of the upper half of the front, with the flat line
of the roof immediately above them.

The inside is austere and completely undecorated: a strange contrast to the splendour of the St Francis Basilica, which logically
should be the soul of bare simplicity. The three naves are divided
by massive rectangular pillars, and a chancel lies wide and dominating at the top of five steps (these cross the whole width of the
church). The effect is of utter seriousness. The dome over the apse
shows its bare bricks, subtly fitted into each other, probably on a
Provençal design. The roof is vaulted in the Gothic form, with eight
arches supporting it, while the side-naves have curved brick ceilings
like that of the cupola. The apse has two plain windows. If we look
back at the middle entrance we shall see fourteenth-century tombs
on either side of it, with slender pillars and simulated cornices. The
side-walls of the chancel have other tombs of the same period. And
this is all the embellishment the church offers. If we go up the steps
of the chancel we shall see in the side-chapel on the left the clear
remains of frescoes—an *Annunciation* and a *Madonna and Child enthroned*, while on the right wall there is Matteo da Gualdo's triptych
Madonna and Child (centre), and *SS. Peter and Rufinus* on either side.

*The house of Bernardo da Quintavalle—S. Francescuccio—Porta S.
Francesco*

We should begin our next walk from the Piazza del Vescovado again
as there are still undiscovered little glories in that part of town. We
should go to its top—the side opposite the bishop's palace—and take
the Via Bernardo da Quintavalle to the left, a narrow winding
lane with compact mediaeval houses on either side, their stone
darkened and polished with age. We can see the traces of old
Romanesque arches, filled in like the 'doors of death'. Then we shall
come to a tiny church on the right with the remains of a fresco of the
Lorenzetti school on its wall: this is **St Gregory,** built in the second

half of the thirteenth century. Exactly opposite this is the thirteenth-century house of the Blessed Bernardo da Quintavalle (No. 11A): here St Francis dined and Bernardo, his first companion, watched him pray and fall into an ecstasy; there is an inscription in Latin on the wall to this effect. We continue straight on until the Via Giotto takes us, left, down into the Piazzetta Garibaldi, so-called because Garibaldi once stayed in the long house that dominates it (the Palazzo Fiumi Roncalli). If we turn sharply back to the left, along the Via Antonio Cristofani, we shall face after only a few steps a long and magnificent mediaeval house of three floors with small, arched windows (probably restored), a tiny bell-tower and an external staircase with one column supporting a porch over the entrance. There are iron rings for horses at the main entrance below. At the side of this house, close to the square, we see the oratory of S. Leonardo, called *S. Francescuccio,* meaning 'little' or even 'poor little' Francis: this is the seat of the so-called Confraternity of the Stigmata. Above the doorway in a broad niche there is an Umbrian fresco, a simple and gentle reminder of the Byzantine dawn in art, despite its late date at the end of the fifteenth century: its subject is *the institution of the Pardon, with Christ and Mary enthroned and surrounded by angels.* On the right, very faint but still showing its fineness and care, in fact made smoother and more beautifully vague with time, entirely in green distemper, there is a fresco by local artists of the same period, *Works of Mercy.*

Walking downhill again across the Piazzetta Garibaldi we turn left immediately after the house in which Garibaldi stayed: this is the little Via degli Ancaiani (we shall hear of this family in Spoleto). We see far below us the Porta del Sementone, a thirteenth-century gate which has been restored since. There is no need to walk right down to it. Instead, we should return to the Via Fontebella from which we have come and turn left downhill: at No. 12, on the right, we see a tall mediaeval house with a stout roofed tower, its ground-floor arches intact and defence-holes all over its wall; this is the *Monte Frumentario* (the mediaeval hospital), the other side of which we saw in the Via S. Francesco. Immediately after this on the same side there is a fountain called *Marcella,* from which the road derives its name: it was built at the expense of a Marcello Tuto, a Sienese citizen, in 1556; from its cheerful steps we look down on the church of St Peter and its monastery, with open country beyond. Continuing downhill we see on the left at No. 23 a glass-covered fresco in a niche excellently preserved, a *Madonna and Child with two saints* by Lorenzetti pupils, where something of his delicacy is captured. We then reach the **Porta S. Francesco** with its wooden doors still on their hinges: these were closed in the last war when Allied troops reached Assisi, and they had to knock to get in. From here the Piaggia di Porta S. Pietro takes us, as its name shows (*piaggia* means hill or decline), to the other gate of St Peter's, while the Via Frate Elia takes us to the Lower Square of the St Francis Basilica.

S. Paolo—S. Stefano—S. Giacomo de Muro Rupto

There is one other part of the town we have missed so far—that on the left of the main square as we face the Temple of Minerva, but along the upper road, the Via S. Paolo. At No. 5, squeezed into a corner reminiscent of the little convent of S. Giuseppe which we have already seen, there is the little church of S. Paolo, with the remains of *three saints*, a fresco of Dono Doni, above the doorway. Farther on, after we have passed No. 14 on the right, we see a large fragment of Roman wall said to have supported an embankment behind the Temple of Minerva. We can imagine what a vast picture the Forum must have presented. After this we take the first little turning on the left, Vicolo S. Stefano, which leads us to the church of that name if we keep to the higher of the two paths offered us: it will bring us to a tiny square where cars will never penetrate, walled round, silent, remote from the town, closed on one side by the squat thirteenth-century façade of **S. Stefano.** The inside has one simple nave, and a dark chancel lit by a narrow slit of window: the roof is supported by four Gothic arches and one Romanesque arch over the apse, in a form repeated all over Umbria in the tiny churches. There is a mediocre but sincere fresco of the fifteenth or sixteenth century.

We now return to the Via S. Paolo and continue towards the St Francis Basilica along a lane that becomes, with a view over the whole western plain, the Via Metastasio, its name due to the house at No. 14D where Felice Trapassi, the father of Pietro Metastasio, lived: Metastasio was born in 1698 (the name is a Greek rendering of 'Trapassi'), and became famous as a court poet of that time, in the 'Arcadian' or neo-classical tradition; he was one of the originators of the poetic text with musical accompaniment, that is of 'melo-drama', and therefore what became opera.

Just past this house on the right we find a gateway that takes us to the church of *S. Giacomo de Muro Rupto,* at the farther end of a courtyard: the story goes that there was a hole in the city wall here through which people reluctant to pay toll used to climb. This church dates from about 1088. We ring a bell at the door facing the drive and a nun will take us through a cloister of fat pillars and low arches to the church: at one time this was behind the Enclosure and the convent was Benedictine. The church has one nave and there are some remains of frescoes from the fifteenth and sixteenth centuries. The one behind the altar (1536) is a *Madonna and Child with SS. Benedict, Roch and Francis, Rufinus and Scholastica* (the last the originator of the Benedictine Order for women, and sister of St Benedict). The sacristy is now a little chapel.

The road continues winding downhill, its course quite unaltered since mediaeval times, and then we see below us the gate of S. Giacomo, which formed part of the town wall in the twelfth century. Here the road becomes the Via Cardinale Raffaele Merry del Val, famous for his part in the Church's Concordat with fascism, and we find ourselves looking down on the Upper Church of St Francis again.

CHAPTER 6

Assisi District

San Damiano

On a fine day nothing is better than a walk down to St Clare's convent of **San Damiano,** now a small Franciscan monastery. Cars can be driven almost to the door but we can just as easily go on foot, approaching it slowly between the olive groves, with the silence growing round us. The church is open all day: an hour when everybody is eating will show us the convent as it must have been for Clare and her companions; little has changed in the immediate surroundings. But in the last five or so years, since Italy's brief industrial boom, a crop of detached houses has sprouted all over the plain below, which at one time shimmered and slept in the heat with hardly a roof to be seen. We leave Assisi by the Porta Nuova (the Via Borgo Aretino leads us to it from the Piazza S. Chiara), and just outside the gate we find a steep footpath going to the right: this will take us to the Perugia road, where we shall soon see a signpost leading us down to S. Damiano. If we are good walkers we can include S. Maria degli Angeli (seen towards the right as we go down, its tall cupola conspicuous in the plain), reaching it from St Clare's convent by cross-country paths.

In the thirteenth century S. Damiano was just an oratory in the fields. After St Clare died it continued as a convent for a further seven years, when the nuns were transferred to their new church in Assisi (1260). From that time it has been preserved as it was in Clare's life, the friars living in new quarters behind.

We come into a little quadrangle before the church, and pass a small outdoor chapel now dedicated to the victims of Nazi concentration camps, with an awkward fifteenth-century fresco, *Madonna and Child with SS. Francis and Clare.* It is the front of the church that has our attention, with its squat and rustic air, a porch low and sunken before its one door, and a rose window above which the porch

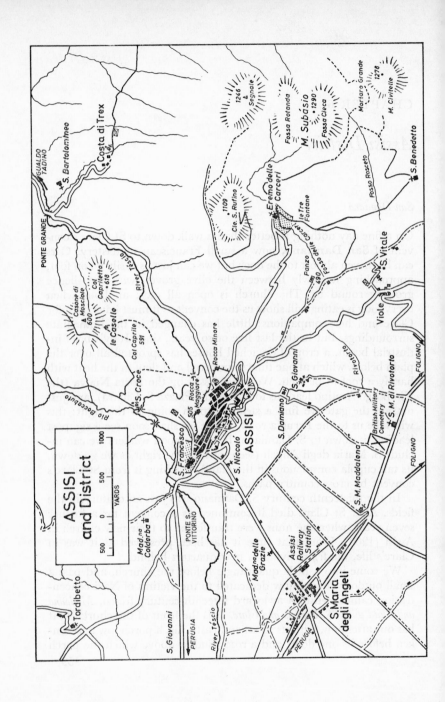

ASSISI
and District

YARDS
500   0   500   1000

interrupts, perhaps due to a rustic oversight in the measurements. To the left of this simple rose window, above, there is a doorway without any balcony, cut straight into the wall, from which it is said that St Clare in 1341 showed herself to the attacking Saracens and Tartars of Frederick II's army, with a monstrance in her hand, and frightened away the troops. But perhaps the soldiers, having been sent to fight Assisi's Guelfs and not to pillage, simply respected churches.

Under the porch, on the right, there is the **Chapel of S. Giro-lamo,** closed by a wooden grille: behind the altar, a *Madonna and Child with SS. Francis, Clare, Bernardine and Jerome.* This is by Tiberio d'Assisi (1517), and, unlike work of his that we shall see at S. Maria degli Angeli, lacks great feeling. On the left wall we see *SS. Roch* (showing the plague-spot in his leg—he is invoked against skin diseases) *and Sebastian,* a fresco of the same school.

The tiny church has one nave, dark and simple like a cave, its ceiling in the form of a Gothic arch, without supports. On the wall immediately on the right of the entrance (we can switch on a light) there is the tiny window, now walled in, where St Francis threw the money he derived from selling not only his father's cloth but his horse as well. Around this are the traces of a fresco, *the Saint offers money, and is followed by his father,* of unknown fourteenth-century origin. Farther down, still on the right, there is a chapel which was added to the church in 1535: in it we find, at the altar, a wooden Christ of real feeling where the facial expression changes as we walk from one side to the other; the work of a Franciscan monk, Inno-cenzo da Palermo, 1637. At the high altar of the church the wooden crucifix is a copy of that now in the church of St Clare, said to have addressed St Francis when he was twenty-three. We pass along the side of the main altar to the apse behind, where we see the tiny wooden choir (1504) with another fresco in the dome above it, *Madonna and Child with SS. Francis and Rufinus* which, though a work of the early fourteenth century, is fully in the Byzantine tradition. The inscription round the top of the choir reads: '*Non vox sed votum, non clamor sed amor, non cordula sed cor, psallit in aure Dei. Lingua con-sonet menti et mens concordet cum Deo*—Not the voice but the vow, not loudness but love, not the chord but the heart, resounds in God's ears. Let the tongue harmonize with the mind, and the mind accord with God.' The window in the back of the apse, partly covered by the choir seats, was the one through which the Poor Clares took communion and before which the body of St Francis was carried after his death, on the way from Porziuncola to Assisi.

On the right of the apse we enter a vestibule, down a slight incline, under the floor of which four Poor Clares, companions of the Saint, are buried: a notice on the wall says that their bodies exhale a gentle fragrance, but this is the pinewood of a throne against the right wall. Down some steps on the left we find the sacristy with a very rough wooden choir and an equally rough lectern, which are those used in the time of St Clare. On the lectern we see a list of the Saint's first companions, on parchment. There is a weak fifteenth-century fresco behind the altar. On the left of the altar as we face it there is a small niche in which St Francis (he was a small man) is supposed to have hidden when his father was searching for him. And there is a small oil painting depicting this.

Returning to the vestibule we walk up the narrow stone staircase and find a low doorway (right) leading into the little garden of St Clare, actually a tiny terrace from which we have a view of the plain below, protected by a wall on each side, where the silence is still untouched: in the fullness of summer this feels as safe as it must have done centuries ago, with a breeze stirring the olive trees below, the whole plain seeming to swell in the heat, its greens lost in the shimmering haze. Here St Francis is said to have written his *Canticle of the Sun*, in which 'brother sun' is praised for his daily illumination, for showing God in his splendour, while 'sister moon' and the stars are formed 'clear and precious and lovely' in the sky. One can imagine St Clare sitting here in the evening, in the first coolness. A fragment of the door she used is on the hinges of the entrance, protected with wire mesh.

We continue up the staircase and reach St Clare's oratory, a room with a tiny apse and altar much like a farmhouse parlour in shape, with rough frescoes on the walls showing *the Madonna and saints*, from the fourteenth century. On the left of the apse there is an opening in the wall where the sacrament was kept in St Clare's time. And there is a cupboard full of relics: a phial containing a drop of St Francis's blood, the bell with which St Clare called her companions in from the fields, a breviary written by Fra' Leone, St Bonaventure's crucifix.

On the right of the cupboard there is another staircase, taking us into the dormitory of the first Poor Clares. The closed doorway at the end is the one we saw from the courtyard, where St Clare appeared before Frederick II's troops. On the left wall close to where we have entered there is a wooden cross attached to the wall, usually with a bowl of fresh flowers before it, showing where St Clare died. Swallows make their nests in the rafters during the summer; they swoop above our heads.

We leave this dormitory by a doorway on the right of the altar, and find our way to a small, peaceful cloister below. In the right-hand corner there are frescoes, *St Francis receives the stigmata* and an *Annunciation* by Eusebio da S. Giorgio (1507), with the signatures of pilgrims scratched all over them, not a great sacrilege. To the left of this we find a door which we can unlatch if we find it closed, re-vealing the refectory hatch; the refectory's low, arched ceiling is grimed with smoke; the wooden leaves of the hatch through which we look are original, by the way. So indeed are the tables and benches we see inside, made of stout oak. It gives us a better idea of how the Poor Clares lived than anything else in the monastery: nothing has changed here since the Saint's time. On a sunlit morning, with the light pouring in thinly from the windows, we can sense the life of the country, with the nuns returning from a day's work in the fields. A bowl of flowers marks St Clare's own place; during a visit by Pope Gregory she is said to have blessed the bread and left the im-print of a cross on it (loaves were almost certainly marked with a cross before baking). On the same end-wall we see very dimly two frescoes, *the crucifix that talked to St Francis* and *St Clare, to obey the pope, blesses the bread, leaving an impression of the cross on it,* by Dono Doni, now much ruined. The tiny staircase behind us once led to the cells and a further dormitory, but these are now behind the Enclosure.

S. Maria degli Angeli

A different experience awaits us at **S. Maria degli Angeli,** where a vast church hovers over a straggling village of the same name. This is the unsightly dome we have seen from Assisi—though an excellent landmark. And S. Maria degli Angeli is Assisi's railway station.

It is also the centre of Franciscan superstition and tall stories, though the tiny chapel enclosed inside the church was the birth-place of the Franciscan Order. We approach a hotchpotch of buildings round a spacious square, clearly designed to feed and provide stamps and postcards for thousands of pilgrims of every nationality, every year. Along the brick side-wall of the church we notice a fountain which served earlier pilgrims and their horses— the *fontana delle* 26 *cannelle* (taps), decorated with the arms of the Medici family who ordered it to be placed there in 1610. The one pleasant building in the square is on the right, a porch with twelve pillars and a closed terrace above, reminiscent of the cloth-drying building we shall see in Gubbio: a former Franciscan lodging-house, built (surprisingly) in the sixteenth century, on a drawing by Galeazzo Alessi, and now the Post Office.

The church of S. Maria degli Angeli which rears up opposite it was started in 1569, at a time when there was nothing here but huts surrounded by dense woods. St Francis's chapel, called the Chapel of Porziuncola (emphasis on the *un*, and meaning 'a little piece of earth'), and the infirmary close to it where St Francis died (now called the Cappella del Transito or 'Chapel of Passing') and the Cappella del Roseto, all of which we shall see, were the only buildings. The idea when the church was projected at the end of the sixteenth century was to house these three chapels in a building which would be both sacred and big enough to hold the thousands of pilgrims who came annually for the Celebration of the Pardon (August 1st and 2nd). The whole thing was designed in the first place by Galeazzo Alessi, but Giorgetti, Martelli and perhaps Giulio Danti (like Alessi, from Perugia) also worked on it. It was finished one hundred and ten years after it was started, with only one of its towers built. And the earthquake of 1832 brought the whole lot down again—apart from the façade, which is hidden from us today by one of the most swaggeringly vulgar pieces of 'Roman' baroque ever conceived, an addition of 1928, intended as a climax to the Franciscan centenary celebrations. This towering front of white stone is crowned by an insipid Madonna in gilded bronze. The original front, modest and harmonious in comparison, lies behind the baroque extravagance, its bricks bare, with a stone balcony over very tall central doors of wood. In the years following the 1832 earthquake the church was rebuilt in exactly its previous form, and some harrowing new frescoes were the result.

Our first impression of the inside is influenced by the numberless over-ornate side-chapels whose walls bulge with every kind of monstrous decoration and statue and gilded column. Under the dome lies St Francis's little oratory, with an intimate glow of lights

164

inside. Tradition says that it was built in the fourth century by four pilgrims who came from Jerusalem. All we know is that by the beginning of the thirteenth century it was as good as abandoned in the middle of the woods, and belonged to the Benedictine friars whose monastery was on the slopes of Monte Subasio. In 1210 St Francis asked to have it, and got it. With the help of his companions he built cells and an infirmary.

These huts were all he ever wanted. The townspeople once had a chapter-house built for him, but he tore it down. Apart from journeys, he lived all his adult life here. During Pentecost of 1219 he held his famous chapter or meeting here, known as *'delle stuoie'* or 'of the mats' (a reference to what they sat on), in which more than five thousand friars took part.

The little chapel is like any other that stands in open country, roughly built in white Subasian stone. But the closer we go the brighter it is—with an ornately carved tabernacle of stone added to the apex of the roof, and a fresco on the front, *St Francis implores Jesus and Mary for the concession of the Pardon*, painted by Johann Friedrich Overbeck (1789-1869), of which Hippolyte Taine said in his book on Italy that 'its Jesus looks as if he has just had a bad lunch'. But, given the date, it could be worse. On the right outside wall of this chapel there are two other frescoes from the fifteenth century, or rather their remains: a last shadow of sweetness lingers in them—*Madonna and Child with SS. Francis and Bernardine*. In this wall there is a wide Romanesque arch through which we can see the glowing altar: on the left of it, low in the wall, an old inscription tells us that the Blessed Pietro Cattani, St Francis's second companion, was buried here: he died in 1221 (five years before the Saint).

We should now go behind the back wall of the chapel, where we see a fresco of the *Calvary* which shows only the lower part, with the base of the cross: the movements and style have suggested Perugino to some people, but others say Andrea d'Assisi (died 1516). At the apex of the roof, to match the stone tabernacle at the other end, a terracotta statue of St Francis has been added (1828). At eye-level and on either side of the archway cut into the apse we see an *Annunciation* in two panels, where everything that the new art offers has been perfected, without the slightest falsification of feeling: the robes and the angel's wings, one hand delicately holding a lily while the other points, are all done with the most devout care and even with what we

165

might call realism, while in the other panel Mary is at prayer, a simpler creature, her hair loose. This is attributed to the school of Perugino: it has been completely restored, which accounts for a certain roughness in the Madonna, and in both faces.

Inside the chapel the walls are black from constantly burning oil-lamps; they form a simple, light Gothic arch as a ceiling, without supporting beams. If we look up we shall see a hole in the roof said to have led in Francis's time to another storey above, where the friars could hear Mass without being present. The intimacy here is really centred on the gold and russet colours of the fresco behind the altar which fills the whole wall and is worth a long and loving look: there is an *Annunciation*, a splendid lower panel fervent with decorative detail, where not one element is at variance with the feeling. All round it other panels close in on one another to make a mass of glittering colour, *the stories of the Pardon*, which are crowned by a larger panel depicting *St Francis imploring Jesus and Mary enthroned* (that is, he is asking them for the Pardon). This is the work of Ilario da Viterbo, 1393. It is reminiscent in its shuddering golden richness and warmth of the later Gozzoli. The movement of a head and not the individual cast of face is important here: the angel in the *Annunciation* captures a gentleness, in his person, that radiates to the whole wall.

Leaving the chapel we go to the presbytery behind it and see on the right as we face the main altar the **Cappella del Transito,** or infirmary. The walls have been frescoed badly and there is a vulgar enamelled statue of St Francis (Andrea della Robbia). The frescoes are by Lo Spagna (1450-1528): his saints have a look of sublime insincerity, beaten only by the frescoes on the outside of this chapel (left), *death and funeral of the Saint* (1886).

The presbytery is vast, and the apse has a tall wooden choir with a gallery on top, baroque, intricately carved, the work of friars in the seventeenth century. Everywhere there is vastness for its own sake: but it is just this side of the offensive, and the craftsmanship mitigates the lack of art. The wooden pulpit on the left of the high altar is amazingly carved. And in the left arm of the transept della Robbia acquits himself better with bas-reliefs of white figures in terra-cotta against a blue background, representing six scenes— *St Francis receiving the stigmata, coronation of the Virgin, St Jerome penitent, Annunciation* (bottom left), *Nativity* and *Epiphany*, which have a touch of grace apart from their craftsmanship.

If we now cross to the right arm of the transept we shall find a tall padded door leading to the sacristy. On entering we should go first to the *Roseto* or rose-bush, which has a story behind it: on a January night St Francis was advised by the Devil to spare his own body more, and in reply he left his cell naked and threw himself into a rose-bush and rolled in it. This wild rose at once transformed itself into a rose-bush without thorns. Now, obedient to the story, the leaves annually show reddish marks on them as if to remind us of the blood spilled by the Saint. We see the short thin stems of this rose beyond a window on the left of the corridor marked 'Roseto', past the souvenir shop. And a little farther on there is the **Cappella del Roseto,** or chapel of the rose itself: as we at once perceive from the noise of traffic, it has its back wall on the road. Not all of this existed in St Francis's time. On the right as we enter we see an iron grille, and behind this, raised above floor level, the little oratory of St Bonaventure, who edited a biography of the Saint, with his own additions, in 1261. Underneath this raised oratory there is St Francis's grotto where, according to another story, he lived and slept (he was praying here when the Devil tempted him): in this cave-like space we see two beams which are the remains of the pulpit from which he and seven Umbrian bishops promulgated the Indulgence of the Pardon. The rest of the chapel, that is the main part, was added by St Bernardine of Siena. As to the frescoes, they are all by Tiberio d'Assisi (1470-1524) but they do not all belong to the same period, with the result that they are uneven in performance. Those beyond the grille, in the oratory of St Bonaventure, are to no great effect, showing (behind the altar) *St Francis and his first companions*, an awkward panel out of tune with the rest, with *SS. Clare and Elizabeth* on the right and *SS. Bonaventure, Bernardine of Siena, Louis of Toulouse, Anthony of Padua* on the left. In the ceiling there is *the Eternal Father*. This was all done in 1506.

The part of the chapel in which we stand was frescoed by the same hand twelve years later, and we see the difference. On the right wall as we face the altar, the panel nearest it, is *St Francis throwing himself in the rose-bush*: the panel next to it (that is, towards the street), *two angels lead him to Porziuncola*. On the other wall, in the panel closest to the street, *St Francis asks Jesus and Mary for the Pardon*, and next to it *the Pardon is confirmed by Honorius III*; and in the last panel, before a great crowd, *the Indulgence of the Pardon is published*. The colours here are sober and delicate, while the faces have a stillness that is almost stiff, but without losing a certain rapt quality reminiscent of art four hundred years before this artist's birth.

We should now see the *museum,* which is not an easy thing to do if we visit the church out of season, as it is unheated and opened only for parties. The friars explain that they are short of staff (there are over two hundred of them). We cross part of an old cloister of St Bernardine, with archaeological fragments on the walls and a well which some say goes back to the time of St Francis. A door on the left takes us to a room (Sala dei Parati) with ecclesiastical vestments and massive Gregorian chant books of parchment standing open on lecterns. There are some lovely altar-cloths, one with a magnificent bas-relief of gold thread. The next room is the Sala delle Pitture, where we find on the right wall a *Crucifixion* on wood by Giunta Pisano, the earliest artist we hear of in Assisi, said to have come to the town in 1236 to paint at the St Francis Basilica. On its left there is a fresco of St Francis which tradition says was painted on the strip of wood on which he died: this also was once attributed to Giunta Pisano but now to the so-called Maestro di S. Francesco; in fact, this panel is the origin of the term, not the Basilica. The expression of the Saint here is sad, closed, mute. On the end-wall is a *Madonna with Child and angels,* the loveliest and most delicate work I have seen by Pier Antonio Mezzastris, though it is only attributed to him: the Madonna has a sweetly reflective expression, and the tones fall in well with the design. On the right of the Pisano crucifix we see *two angels* painted on wood carved out to their shape, by Lattanzio, son of Nicolò Alunno, who died in 1523. The *Madonna and Child* on the left of the door is by Sano di Pietro (from Siena), 1405-81, and is warm and dark and mellow.

We now climb the stairs (inside the museum still) to the former convent, this part deriving from the fourteenth century. We see a kitchen with pots and irons, and cells, the one at the end being that of St Bernardine (in a cupboard, a book of his sermons). And at the other end of the corridor there is the cell of St Charles Borromeo (he did much of the work of the Council of Trent, and was the first major figure of the Counter-Reformation): a letter of his is framed on the wall.

On our way out we are usually shown, immediately on the left of the museum entrance, a room behind an iron grille where, high on the left wall, we see a pulpit from which St Bernardine preached.

Eremo delle Carceri

The Franciscan retreat in the hills called **Eremo delle Carceri** has a steep and excellent road to it from Assisi, and by car is reached in very few minutes. There are frequent buses. But you can also walk, and the footpath is found just outside the Porta Cappuccini (the *cappuccini* were a late Franciscan Order started in the sixteenth century as a branch of the original Order, the term being derived from their hat or *cappuccio*). We are in open country at once, between olive groves and plain green fields, getting a more stupendous view of the valley below with every yard. Soon we look down on the Rocca Maggiore, and the town begins to seem tiny behind it. If we do take the footpath, we should equip ourselves with a stick and heavy shoes or boots: we shall walk uphill for six or seven kilometres. At the entrance-gate of the hermitage there is a tiny refreshment bar.

The name Eremo delle Carceri means literally 'hermitage of the prisons', but its origin is doubtful. However it is, the hermitage was at the beginning a very small oratory, probably Benedictine (though most Franciscan friars will deny this): the likelihood is that the Benedictines of Monte Subasio gave it to St Francis, as they did the little chapel of Porziuncola. The Franciscans were never a hermit order, but the Saint and his companions withdrew here to pray and reflect, between journeys and local preaching. In the fifteenth century St Bernardine of Siena built a small monastery here, and there have been additions to it ever since. It lies snugly in the woods and on a fine day glitters like a jewel, with dark trees all round and birds singing: but when in the clouds it is lonely and sombre, and mist drifts between the trees.

We enter by a small arch above which there is a clean fresco of the *Madonna and SS. Francis and Clare* and follow a narrow lane (pedestrians only) which will accustom us to the silence and the rare sound (for Italy) of birds singing: 'hunting'—the Italian name for a massacre of wild life that goes on from September to May every year —is forbidden up here (cynics say that the friars like to keep it as their own game reserve). At the end of the lane a staircase leads us down to the entrance proper of the monastery, with its tiny courtyard and a parapet looking over a ravine straight to the plain.

169

As the friars conduct us personally round their monastery, and have their own short cuts, as well as keys to places we would otherwise not see, we should read this account before going in, rather than try to follow it while the guide is talking.

It all looks neat and new, which mostly it is. There are two wells in this little courtyard and, as we should expect by now, the story goes that the water flowed in answer to St Francis's prayer. Half the building is tunnelled into the rock: the closed doorway on our left as we walk into the church, by the way, is that of the refectory, while the dormitory or cells are above; we shall leave the monastery by this door at the end of our tour.

The 'church' is really no more than a chapel, or series of tiny chapels: the first one has an awkward fresco behind the altar (*Crucifixion*), where we see angels drawing the blood from Christ's wrists into chalices; and under the altar another fresco shows one of the arms or emblems of the Franciscans (now that of the Monte di Pietà, a bank started here in the fifteenth century for lending money on security). Christ has his arms crossed in front of him and is standing in what seems to be a tomb. There is also a cupboard which we should open (the light comes on automatically) for the usual display of relics: a piece of wood said to have been St Francis's pillow, a belt belonging to one of his followers, St Clare's veil and other unsightly objects.

The second room is actually the original grotto of the place, where hermits used to come for at least three hundred years before St Francis. This is called the **Oratorio Primitivo** or the Chapel of St Mary, and it has a fresco of *the Madonna and Child* at its altar which is also called 'Madonna delle Carceri', a work of the sixteenth century which unfortunately was painted over an earlier fresco from perhaps St Francis's time. On the left there are four steps leading up to a tiny room with a semi-circular wooden choir, which is from the time of St Bernardine. Leaving this we take the doorway opposite (still in the Oratorio Primitivo) marked 'Grotto S. Francesco'; we go down a stone staircase and squeeze and bend ourselves through tiny doorways, which at one time were open grottoes of the kind we shall see outside the monastery. In the first tiny room on the right we see the naked stone on which St Francis slept—yet for all its simplicity it manages to look snug and safe, perhaps because St Francis's disposition has endowed it with permanent happiness. In the next room, at a lower level, he used to pray: the altar is a small wooden crucifix which tradition says he took with him whenever he preached.

And from here we reach the open air again, noting the red stone of the threshold across which we tread. We climb the path and cross a bridge, after hearing that the torrent underneath, now a dry bed, was silenced by the Saint because the noise of the waters disturbed his prayers (an unlikely act for the author of the *Canticle of the Sun*). The tree supported by iron stakes is the holm oak called 'the tree of the birds': they flocked round St Francis and were said to come to him for his blessing. We pass on the left a quarry often used for open-air Mass, and if we climb to the top of its first embankment we shall see a shallow square hole where the cross is placed. The grotto of Fra' Silvestro, a companion of St Francis, will be pointed out to us in the ravine below. There are eight grottoes in all.

For the last part of the tour the friar will take us upstairs to the cells which look out across the plain, and then to the refectory below where the place of St Bernardine of Siena is marked by a bowl of flowers.

Rocca S. Angelo or Rocchicciola

We take the road from Assisi leading to Petrignano: just short of Petrignano we find a signpost to the right, along a track road, and a second signpost takes us to a tiny village perched on its own hill overlooking the river Chiascio. The **Rocca S. Angelo,** or Rocchicciola, as it is known locally, has a castle and one of the oldest Franciscan monasteries in existence; its church of S. Francesco has over forty votive frescoes of the greatest interest, dating from 1393 to 1559.

We shall have to look for the custodian: S. Francesco is a small one-nave church. Starting at the entrance, on the right, we find on the back wall a drowsily tender *Madonna and Child between SS. Bonaventure and Anthony of Padua* (a heart in his hand) by Bartolomeo Caporali (late fifteenth-century), where the Virgin is blonde. Then, going down the church on the right, we find half-ruined votive frescoes from the fourteenth and fifteenth centuries, including a *Mary Magdalen* and the legs (being bitten by fish) of *St Christopher*. On the pilaster there are two figures of *St Roch*, again fifteenth-century. Farther down we find a large panel in the Giottoesque style of a *Madonna and Child*, unfortunately much ruined, with *SS. Clare and*

Francis and angels behind: there are signs of its first beauty—fourteenth-century. In the panels on either side of this there are two figures of *St Catherine of Alexandria*. Then, in the same vault, there is a *Crucifixion* by a local rustic hand, from the sixteenth century. Farther down on an otherwise unfrescoed wall we see a faint trace of *St Francis receiving the stigmata*: it seems fairly late, but some say Giottoesque. Behind the main altar there is a suave and vivid *Madonna and Child* by Lo Spagna, with *SS. Anthony of Padua and Francis*, and *the Eternal Father* above: these saints were given white habits (which spoil them entirely) this century.

In the apse we have a fascinating cycle of three frescoes in the Giottoesque style—obviously the pupil was superb: beginning on the left, *Jesus in the Temple among the doctors, the flight into Egypt* (in the middle), and *the presentation in the Temple* (the baby is in the arms of St Simeon, whose eyes are raised to the sky). On the wall left of the high altar there is a *St Michael the Archangel* (1521), said to be also by Lo Spagna.

Going down the other side of the little church we find a *saint-bishop*, much ruined, by an Umbrian artist. In the next vault, on the right side of it, there is a rough Umbrian *Madonna and Child between SS. Sebastian and Lucy*, from the sixteenth century. On the main wall, dated 1393, there are panels side by side in a grave and stiff style that recalls the Byzantine, on the left *St Francis* and perhaps *St Louis of Toulouse*, next come *St Anthony the Abbot*, a *Madonna and Child*, and *St Lucy*. The two panels above are of *St Anthony the Abbot* again and a *saint-bishop* of unknown name, from perhaps 1502. Some say Nelli had a hand here, but the date makes this impossible. In the last vault there is a magnificent large panel from the fifteenth century, *Madonna and Child with St James the Apostle and St Catherine of Alexandria*, and then *Mary Magdalen* and *St Anthony the Abbot*. Here we have the full decorative ease of the Renascence. Under this picture there is *St Bonaventure* on one side and *St Joseph* on the other, from the seventeenth century. The Madonna and Child here has beautifully mellow and warm suggestions under its pallor of damp. On one side of it there is a *St Roch*, from the sixteenth century, much touched up later, and on the right another *Madonna and Child* of the seventeenth century which has the tiny kneeling figure of the man who commissioned it underneath (his name was Menecarello, if we look hard).

The custodian will open another door here into a separate chapel of sixteenth-century construction for the villagers (the main part of the church was used by the monks). Here we have some rustic, awkward and sincere frescoes of the same period. Behind the altar there is a *Crucifixion between SS. Peter and Paul*, sketched nearly to the point of caricature, with the names of the male confraternity which commissioned it at the bottom of the panel, and figures of its members kneeling at the foot of the cross. There are two panels of the *Madonna and Child* on the side wall: the first has written on it '*Questa hopera*', which is the same as saying 'This work of hart'—the artists here (1559) were villagers, perhaps. A statue is painted on the left of it which seems pagan—it could be Pan: his genitals have been scrubbed out by the faithful of a later epoch. The women had their turn in the fresco (opposite the entrance) of the Madonna holding her cloak round kneeling figures, women on one side and men on the other. It says underneath, '*La fata fare le donne per loro devotione*', which again isn't very exact Italian but it sounds nice. In this fresco there are figures in the background haymaking (1556).

CHAPTER 7

Towns near Assisi

Spello – Bevagna – Montefalco

Spello—the Consular Gate—Pintoricchio—the Edict of Constantine

The town of **Spello,** compact on its hillside yet seeming to slide off, has fallen heavily from its first glories in ancient times. Its people have a reputation for communism nowadays: which in Italy means largely the lack of local industries. Yet the town is neat and pretty, with many silent and winding walks up and down staircases, and closed bridges over the streets, and sudden distant views; other towns—Bastìa, Perugia and Foligno—have drawn its young away to their factories, and it is mostly this, the desertion, that makes for sadness, a touch of squalor where it doesn't belong.

It was first settled by the Umbrians and then became a Roman town called Hispellum. Augustus gave it a great deal of land, including the Baths of Clitumnus at least twenty kilometres away: and he constructed its walls and gates. Constantine the Great honoured it with a temple for religious celebrations which had hitherto taken place at Bolsena, near Orvieto. In fact, Spello achieved a peak of importance as a religious centre nearly comparable to Gubbio, and only in the barbarian invasions did she begin to decline. She became part of the dukedom of Spoleto, and with it passed under the Church. After being Ghibelline she was devastated by Frederick II's troops (having rebelled against his rule), and then internal quarrels began aggravating her external ones. There was a series of tyrannies and family-governments, beginning with Giacomo Bartolocci in 1373. During all this time Spello showed an enormous fighting spirit, which was slowly broken until in 1535 its walls were demolished, in a final act of castration. It remains within the area of these walls as if it had never really dared to stir again.

174

The gate we shall come to first is the **Porta Consolare,** which dates back to the time of the Roman republic: the stout central arch has original blocks of stone, intact though beginning to crumble, with two other arches on either side (for pedestrians) now filled in because the level at which they were first built has sunk. Above the central arch three ancient statues have been mounted on the wall, two figures in togas with a *matrona* (a woman highly placed by marriage) between them.

On the right of the gateway there is a mediaeval tower built in red Subasian stone, with olive bushes growing out of its top. We enter the uphill Via Consolare (best to keep a car out of these narrow lanes), but to avoid the grinding one-way traffic we should take the staircase-lane called Via Tempio di Diana that goes off left after a few yards. At the top we come to a widening of the road, now the Via Cavour, but a few yards before this road actually begins we see on our left, hanging from the wall about ten or twelve feet up, a chain which used to be drawn across the street at night to divide the quarter of Porta Chiusa from that of Mezota: the town has three mediaeval quarters or *contrade*, the third being S. Martino— an indication, this, of the inner rivalries which more than anything broke the town.

The widening of the road at this point is called Piazza Giacomo Matteotti: immediately on the right, tucked into the corner, we find **S. Maria Maggiore,** a twelfth-century church which strikes us at once with its splendidly ornate door and a stout tower now surmounted by an ugly cement pyramid roof. The façade was demolished and rebuilt in 1644, which accounts for the elaborate doorway: the Church was by this date completely in control of the town and therefore the vehicle of its glories, which are many, considering its size. Old materials were used for this new façade, so we have a Romanesque frieze and a design of acanthus leaves—these were perhaps done by Binello and Rodolfo, thirteenth-century architects who worked together (notably on the magnificent side-entrance of the duomo in Foligno). The wooden door is in eight carved panels. Before we go in we should notice the two Roman columns similar to those of the Temple of Minerva in Assisi, and presumably taken from a former temple here.

The church is particularly serene and harmonious inside, though baroque. We shall notice at once the holy water font, its delicate top polished by thousands of hands through the ages; this was once a funerary urn in Roman times, with its bas-relief remarkably intact. And on the other side of the church there is a font made out of the capital of a Roman column.

And then, on the left, is a deep chapel without windows, the pride of the church: the **Cappella Baglioni,** its walls frescoed by Il Pintoricchio in the first year of the sixteenth century. (The name Pintoricchio was given to Bernardino di Betto, born in Perugia in 1454, by derivation from the old Italian word *pintore,* meaning painter.) On the left wall there is the *Annunciation* which will already be known to us from reproductions, where every trace of the Byzantine is gone, and even the roots of the new painting in Giotto and Cimabue are hardly recognizable any more: the buildings are now rendered in full realistic ornateness, with not a cornice or window-frame spared, in a most intricate and thorough design and the subtlest and most varied colours, from the paving-stones in the foreground to the green hills that roll beyond the archway, showing a closer attention than ever before to the actual beauty of the human figures, yet without losing that sweetness of feeling for the religious theme that marked the earlier, particularly the Sienese, painting. At the same time we are on the borderline of that realism which did away with the religious subject, turning everything into the divinely created world but with such care and emphasis that the divine is lost and only the world, that is to say elegance, remains. But in Pintoricchio the border has not been crossed. In the right-hand lower corner of this vast panel there is a self-portrait of the artist and his signature. In the middle wall there is *the adoration of the shepherds and the arrival of the Magi,* where the gold of the haloes shines in the light from a window on the other side of the church, and where we see a reminiscence of the same artist's famous *Nativity* in S. Maria del Popolo in Rome. Here the faces of the shepherds are observed with something like Breughel's attention: splendour spreads itself over the whole panel in trees, cloaks, a camel, a distant church. On the right wall we have *the dispute in the Temple,* the most stylized of the three and that closest to what we call High Renascence, where we no longer see beyond the painted splendour and the perfect form (an ensemble of standing figures, backed by a dignified cupola behind) to the religious subject itself. Here the Madonna has a beauty from which all the interest of the panel springs, in her shy and proud movement as she holds the cloak of St James: one of the figures near him has a scroll in his hands which

176

bears the name of Pintoricchio. In the ceiling there are four figures
—the sibyls (the prophetesses to whom various parts of the world
were apportioned, ten of them in all) who in this case are the
Tiburtine, Erythraean, European and Samian. All but the Erythraean are damaged by damp. The floor of this chapel is in Deruta
tiles from 1506—faded greens and yellows and blues.

The high altar we shall have noticed for the harmony of its stone
canopy in the form of a cupola, supported by four finely carved
columns; its richness is not at variance with its simplicity, a rare
enough thing in art. It is by Rocco da Vicenza (1515). The eight
heads of the *prophets* at its corners look out of place, and indeed
they were added fifty years afterwards. On the left of the altar, at the
edge of the wooden choir, a picture hangs alone, its tones delicate—
a *Pietà*, with *St John* and *Mary Magdalen* (1521) by Perugino in his
old age, with a strange faded grace and no strong projection, so that
the subject seems to lie behind a veil of detachment, Christ sitting
shy and exhausted in the lap of the very day-to-day Virgin. On the
right of the altar, in the same position, there is a similar picture by
the same hand, *Madonna and Child enthroned with two saints*. These are
said to be the last paintings signed by Perugino. The wooden choir
was carved by Pier Nicola da Spoleto at about the same time.

On the left of the apse we find the **Cappella del Sacramento**
which was built in 1478, with a sixteenth-century tabernacle at the
altar: on the walls there is a deep mellow design not usually seen in
churches. If we walk left of this chapel-altar we shall find a stone
washbasin with two taps which has an angel painted by Pintoricchio above it. A doorway on the right of this admits us to a tiny
ex-chapel where the same artist has painted a pleasant and cheerful
Madonna and Child over the altar.

In the right arm of the transept we find the **Cappella del Crocifisso,** where there are two frescoes that have been detached from the
walls; on the left, the *Madonna and Child and SS. Jerome and Bernardine*, attributed to Pintoricchio (1503). The one on the right is an
awkward *Madonna and Child with SS. Jerome and Sebastian.*

We continue uphill until we come to the thirteenth-century
church of **S. Andrea** on the right, about a hundred yards farther on,
with its narrow Romanesque entrance. Inside, there is one nave
again, of a striking simplicity, but spoiled at an overall glance by the
frescoes round the back of the apse. In the right arm of the transept
there is another Pintoricchio, behind the side-altar, *Madonna and*

Child with the infant St John, SS. Louis of Toulouse, Andrew, Francis and Laurence. The artist had the help of Eusebio da S. Giorgio here, another Perugian, and the work was done in 1508. A light can be switched on.

The high altar-table is supported by six little twirling stone pillars forming Gothic arches, a fourteenth-century piece. Returning down the church along the other side we pass a wooden pulpit with inset panels attributed to Pintoricchio (*Christ risen*), and farther on a tall wooden crucifix of the thirteenth century which is dim with dirt.

Opposite this church a little street, Via Torri di Properzio (Spello is often claimed as the birthplace of the Latin poet Propertius, but so are Assisi and Bevagna), will lead us down, after about a hundred yards, to the restored Roman gate, **Porta Venere,** from the Augustan epoch. It was so named because of the Temple of Venus which lay just beyond it. Originally there were two gates enclosing a courtyard, and what we see is the external of the two; the other one remains only as mere foundations on the other side of the road. The ancient roads that passed under the arches are still visible (one of these was subterranean and went along the inner wall of the town). The three arches of the intact gate are set between massive polygonal towers (the 'towers of Propertius' from which the road gets its name), which rest on vast square blocks under the level of the road.

We return to the Piazza Giacomo Matteotti and continue our walk uphill, that is to say, left. We come to a square with trees and a fountain in a floral bed, called Piazza della Repubblica, where there are no delights. The **Palazzo Comunale** that faces us is an ugly building with an original thirteenth-century porch: in one of the rooms upstairs there is the so-called *Edict of Constantine*, in which the emperor gave the town the privilege of putting up a temple in his honour, an act which endowed Spello with its importance as a religious centre.

We now continue uphill until we come to the little Piazza Giuseppe Mazzini, where the church of **S. Lorenzo,** with its enormous façade, dominates everything. It was built in 1120 to replace an earlier church of the sixth century, but the façade was restored in the sixteenth century and has a neo-classical doorway—and more rose windows than we shall ever see in one church. The central one is filled in but three are open, with an ugly effect.

Inside, we realize the use of the many rose windows when we see the flood of light from them, especially on a sunny day. The church has three baroque naves, from the last restoration in the seventeenth century. At the first pillar on the right there is an interesting baptismal font of inlaid marble (1607) with floral designs of yellow and Siena red, blue and green. The main altar has one of the vastest and most sumptuous baroque canopies in Umbria, with twirling, gold-threaded columns, an imitation of the one at St Peter's in Rome, and based on a drawing by Teodosio Quintavalle in 1631. The wooden choir round the apse is a sixteenth-century work, with inlaid pictures behind the seats which represent views of the town, saints (including St Lucy, the saint of light, holding, as always, two human eyes), a bishop, and church façades.

A fresco of the Perugino school is attached to the first pillar on the right as we leave the church—*St Anthony the Abbot*, which has no particular life; then a vast and magnificently carved wooden pulpit, clinging to one of the pillars under a canopy, with carved figures in bas-relief which represent *the martyrdom of St Laurence*, by Francesco Constantini (1600).

Still uphill, we take the Via della Torre Belvedere under an archway that was once clearly twice as large; we are now in the oldest part of town, the S. Martino quarter. Near the crest of the hill we pass a tiny church with a tall Romanesque entrance, S. Martino, of the twelfth or thirteenth century. And at the crest we bear left with the road (passing an immense villa, still in private hands) and come out on to a balcony from which we have a view of the country towards Assisi and Perugia—the **Belvedere,** or **Spiazzo dei Cappuccini,** as it is called locally.

We should leave Spello by taking the road towards Assisi; or we can take a pleasant walk down, in order to see the splendid Villa Costanzo more closely. Farther on by about half a mile we see the so-called *chiesa tonda* or 'round church' with its octagonal cupola, a pleasantly shaped building of 1517. Inside, neglect and damp have won but there is a Mezzastris fresco, *Madonna and Child* (1533), much vandalized. A not ugly fresco on the same subject at the altar is in a better state.

The **Roman amphitheatre** on this road is no more than an oval cluster of stones grown over with grass and weeds, where sheep graze. It had a circuit of over three hundred yards. Almost opposite these remains we have the small Romanesque church of **S. Claudio,** where we should notice the rustic lack of symmetry: the rose window

179

is not flush with the doorway underneath or the belfry above. If it should happen to be open we shall notice a similar asymmetry inside, as the side-naves are of unequal height; also the arches get lower towards the altar, but this is to give the illusion of greater length than the church has.

Bevagna and Montefalco

Drivers can combine Bevagna and Montefalco in a day-trip, as they both lie beyond Foligno, taking Bevagna first and lunching perhaps at its excellent Ristorante da Nina in the Piazza Garibaldi (genuine wine served from the family's own vineyards). Montefalco has a splendid collection of frescoes and paintings and needs a long afternoon at least.

Bevagna is one of the few Umbrian towns which lie comfortably and serenely in a plain; it has remained in its ancient position without flying to the hills for protection against armies or floods. In fact, Bevagna still contains herself inside the old town gates, hidden and peaceful at the side of the road that winds from Foligno to Terni. In Roman times it was called Mevania and was noted for its cattle-breeding—Pliny, Livy and Tacitus all wrote about it, praising the town for its prize bulls. But Bevagna owed its importance most to the fact that the Flaminian Way ran through it, bringing trade and travellers (as well as marauding armies). It suffered during the Punic Wars, and Livy describes the battle of Mevania in 308 B.C. That was the first Flaminian Way: an alternative branch was made in the third century A.D. which passed through Spoleto, and Mevania began its long process of decline. This also accounts for the absence of late Roman monuments in the town. But it has kept that sense of being a traveller's stopping-place, hugging its river modestly, a backwater stirred daily into life by visitors.

Barbarian assaults on the town in the sixth century put paid to what importance it still had as a commercial and agricultural centre, and from that time on it slumbered. It was burned down rather thoroughly by Barbarossa in 1152 and again in 1249 by one of Frederick II's imperial captains. The Trinci family from Foligno sacked it a hundred years later in a struggle for the governorship of the town. And in 1439 it passed into the hands of the Church, whose sleepy administration seemed to suit it, since there were only two brief occasions when its power was broken, in the sixteenth century when the Baglioni family took over.

It is a pleasant, rustic little town where the chickens stroll over the road and dogs take the sun in the lazy, uncobbled squares. We enter the city wall from the Foligno road at Porta Flaminia or Folignate (or even S. Vincenzo). The wall is partly Roman but it belongs mainly to the period between 1249 and 1377 (between two major plunders), though its general form is of Roman origin. It has fascinating polygonal, square and cylindrical towers set into it at intervals, and there are five gates to the town.

A few yards after we have entered the town along the Via Matteotti there is the little ex-church of S. Vincenzo (the town's patron saint), now a cinema: we see Roman remains in its front. A turning right called Via G. Crescimbeni reveals after a few yards four semi-columns from a Roman temple on this spot, mounted on high foundations. Going down the Via Porta Guelfa from here we find in a house on the right (we shall have to do some enquiring, and perhaps get the key from the town hall), what remains of a splendid and precious **Roman mosaic** that once belonged to one of the ancient town's baths: it has survived time well, but recent neglect has taken the edge off its splendour. It shows a sea-horse six feet long, driven on reins by a Triton, then three dolphins, two lobsters, two cuttlefish and other divine sea-animals. A horned bull is the owner of the tail which we see near the entrance. The mosaic belongs to the second century A.D. (before the town's decline). There is an eighteenth-century drawing based on this mosaic by Mattassei in the Royal Library at Windsor Castle.

We take the main Via Matteotti again. If we turn left down the Via S. Margherita we shall find a church of that name with a graceful neo-classical doorway (now a convent) and a cosy baroque interior, with a Cammassei (local artist, 1602-49) behind the altar for those who like the period, and splendid green whirling pillars on either side of it. These look marble but are plaster painted. We should have a peep at the wooden Christ behind a curtain on the left side of the chancel: we must pull the cord. And we shouldn't forget the inscription on the floor-tomb near the entrance as we leave, which says that having lived with an empty head, the deceased takes pleasure in being trodden on.

In the Via Matteotti again we come to the long yellow front of the **Palazzo Comunale** or town hall on the right: we mount its staircase and see on either side of us, set into the walls, remains from the local Roman amphitheatre; there is part of a colossal stone leg; next to it, set into the wall, are its enormous toes. There are professional plaques for the gates of houses—'*valetudin magister*' denotes a doctor. We also see the cover of an Etruscan tomb with a leaning figure and what looks like a wreath of flowers round his neck. The Pinacoteca is not worth a visit: it has little but a few nude busts by Cammassei, pleasant but neglected, a Dono Doni and some Roman coins.

We have almost reached the heart of the town, which is one of the loveliest little squares in Umbria: the first Flaminian Way would have passed through it, approaching it by the route we have just taken. But before we enter the square, on the left, there is the fourteenth-century church of **SS. Domenico e Giacomo,** its tall entrance original, with a slightly Gothic arch, and its façade unfinished. If the church is closed we shall have to enquire in the shops near by for a key: and if a solution is found we shall see a one-naved church heavily restored in 1737. At the left of the entrance, in the church's back wall, there is a tomb in carved stone, with the arms of a local Bevagna man (1302). There are three panels on either side of the church made up of bright stones in a flowery mosaic, a mixture of painting on plaster and pieces of marble. Behind the altar we see fragments of fresco that remind us of Giotto. There is an *Annunciation* and *stories from the life of St Dominic*, which have a certain sweetness. The coffin at the altar belongs to a disciple of Albertus Magnus (a Dominican scholar and saint from Swabia, 1193-1280), the Blessed Giacomo Bianconi, a friar who incited the town to revolt and brought down the vengeance of the Trinci family on it (1375). In a chapel left of the apse we see behind glass a wooden *Madonna and Child* from the early fourteenth century, a reminder of the German school, nicely carved. The chapel on the other side of the apse has a *Crucifixion* in wood of an earlier date, a simple, felt work where the arms hang from the cross almost vertically, in a vivid suggestion of agony, while the head sinks down: tradition has it that this cross spurted blood during one of Friar Bianconi's ecstasies.

There is a cloister behind the left wall of the church where we see a well: Friar Bianconi is said to have made wine from its water just before his death. The Sala Capitolare here contains perhaps the best fresco in Bevagna (*Christ on the cross with the Virgin and saints*), a fourteenth-century work which some people say is reminiscent of the ceiling of St Clare's Basilica in Assisi. But it is under restoration at the moment.

We now enter the gracious and sombrely intimate little Piazza Filippo Silvestri which is more or less intact in its mediaeval form, its fountain set to one side, which adds to the ancient appearance though it was only put there in 1889 (composed partly of earlier material). Immediately on our right, standing quite alone, for no apparent reason other than that it has never been moved from its first position in Roman times, there is a single Corinthian column, called by the inhabitants *Colonna della Rocca*, or 'castle-column'. If we stand with this on our left we shall find ourselves looking at the front of the *Palazzo dei Consoli*, with its wide flight of steps over an open gallery of stout arches reminiscent of the Palazzo dei Capitani in Todi (1270). It is now a theatre, with one of the gayest interiors we shall see in Umbria, imitating the grandness of an opera house without losing that sense of intimate thrill necessary to provincial life.

On the right of this we see the squat church of *S. Silvestro*, which gives us a greater sense of austerity and importance than all the taller buildings close by, with its three windows close to the roof, each with slender columns forming narrow Romanesque arches. A jewel of the Romanesque, it has been called. Binello designed it (1195) and left his name and the date on an inscription at the entrance: '*Anno Domine MCXCV Enrico Imperatore Regnate Deustesalvet Prior et Frates Eius et Binellus Magister Vivant in Cristo Amen*—In the year 1195, during the reign of the Emperor Henry VI, may the prior Diotisalvi and his fellow monks and also maestro Binello live in Christ. Amen.' The portal has carved reliefs round it and the cornice running along the top of the façade consists of pieces taken from Roman remains. The two obtruding squares of wall at the top are what survives of a bid to build a tower, which came to nothing. Inside, there are three naves with a complicated system of arches based on very stout pillars and rough capitals, a sombre and over-bearing place, with the presbytery raised up majestically at the top of thirteen steps, under which there is a crypt. There are various fragments of frescoes by local artists from the thirteenth and fourteenth centuries.

Opposite us as we come out is another church of the same period called *S. Michele* with a pleasantly decorated façade and an ornate doorway, also by Binello. Again we have the Romanesque form untouched by anything soaring or Gothic: a still and fixed world, as if the sun had never ceased shining on it. It is only broken by an inexplicable plain-glass rose window, much too big for the façade, put there in the eighteenth century. Clearly a former rose window of the right proportions was set lower down, as the stones in that place show. The doorway is worth a closer look and has similarities to that of the duomo in Foligno, with elaborately carved decorations and a mosaic of stones round the arch, and two complete figures of angels with inscriptions in Latin (again the one on the left refers to the builders). Above the narrow doors on either side arches are set into the wall under jutting cornices, with the heads of men and animals. On the right a tower actually rises out of the façade, of later construction and not an improvement.

Inside we see massive pillars looking Roman in origin: only the bare form of the church, with twelve steps rising to the chancel, is original. A wide Romanesque arch forms a kind of triumphal curtain before the chancel. It was all restored in 1741 and then in 1834. We can leave by a side-door in the left wall, which will take us round to an outside view of the apse, almost as it originally was, with Corinthian columns set in the wall.

Montefalco—eight saints and a rich collection of art (Benozzo Gozzoli, Melanzio, Tiberio d'Assisi, Nicolò Alunno)—St Clare of Montefalco

What agricultural importance Bevagna had was taken over by **Montefalco,** sometimes called the 'balcony of Umbria' (also 'a strip of sky fallen on to the earth') because of its views commanding most of the province from a height of nearly fifteen hundred feet. To reach it from Bevagna we can take the track road marked Montepennino that goes left from the Foligno-Terni road, between silent, green fields, with mountains far to our left (snow-capped in late autumn and winter). This is a marvellous uninterrupted walk for the brave—seven kilometres or more: after passing the first h 1 we see Montefalco straight ahead, silhouetted against the sky. For motorists the track is navigable but not good: there are alternative routes on asphalted roads from both Bevagna (we have to continue along the Foligno-Terni road for a later turning left) and Foligno.

In the Middle Ages this town was called Concurione and was

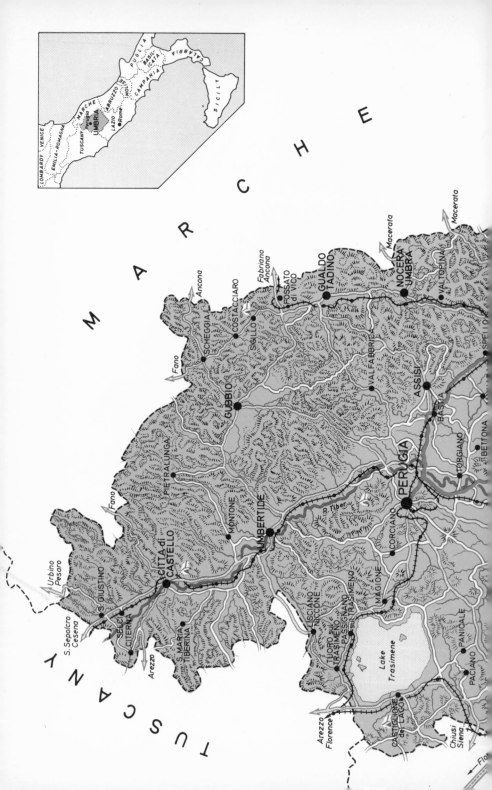

Macerata

Ascoli P.

NORCIA
PRECI
CERRETO di SPOLETO
CASCIA
SELLANO
MONTELEONE di SPOLETO
VALLO di NERA
POGGIODOMO
R. Nera
ANATOLIA di NARCO
TREVI
CAMPELLO sul CLITUNNO
SCHEGGINO
MONTEFRANCO
POLINO
SPOLETO
FERENTILLO
ARRONE
Rieti

BEVAGNA
MONTEFALCO
GUALDO CATTANEO
CASTEL RITALDO
ACQUASPARTA
CARSULAE
TERNI
STRONCONE
Rome

COLLAZZONE
GIANO dell'UMBRIA
MASSA MARTANA
MONTECASTRILLI
SANGEMINI
NARNI
CALVI dell'UMBRIA

MARSCIANO
FRATTA TODINA
TODI
MONTECCHIO
GUARDEA
AMELIA
OTRICOLI
Rome

S. VENANZO
MONTECASTELLO di VIBIO
BASCHI
ALVIANO
LUGNANO in TEVERINA
GIOVE
PENNA in TEVERINA
ATTIGLIANO
Viterbo

MONTEGABBIONE
PARRANO
R. Tib.
PRANO
Rome

MONTELEONE d'ORVIETO
FICULLE
Viterbo

FABRO
ALLERONA
CASTEL VISCARDO
ORVIETO
CASTEL GIORGIO

Orbetello

L   A   Z   I   O

(ROME)

Autostrada del Sole
Superstrada
State roads
Provincial roads
Railways
Rivers
Mountains
Archeological sites
Camping grounds

MILES
5   0   5   10

CHARLES GREEN.

divided into four parts named after SS. Augustine, Francis, Bartholomew and Fortunatus. Its present name derives from after 1244. It became part of the Lombardian dukedom of Spoleto and was destroyed by one of Frederick II's captains (though not the one who destroyed Bevagna). Pope John XXII built a fortress here (1327) which Maitani (the architect of Orvieto cathedral) was asked to advise on. It was sacked again in the fifteenth century and then passed to the Trinci family, succumbing to the Church much later than Bevagna. The town was the birthplace of eight saints: hence the description of 'a strip of sky fallen on to the earth'. Francesco Melanzio, the pupil of both Nicolò Alunno and Perugino, was born here, and for a town of its size it has the richest collection of art in Umbria. One of its specialities, by the way, is a sherry-like drink called *sagrantino*, which we should try at one of the *cantine* before leaving: it is a heavily sweet apéritif, but can be drunk as a dessert wine too. On an empty stomach it will make an angry liver angrier.

Our tour of the town should begin at the lower gate, the Porta S. Agostino, with its graceful little tower and Ghibelline crenellations. This was all part of the fourteenth-century wall: it takes us into the Via Umberto I, which rises steeply to the principal square. Immediately on the right as we enter the gate, at the corner of Via Pompilio de Cuppis (he was a doctor and philosopher of the sixteenth century), we see a house called the Casa Mattioli with fragments of Roman urns and arms embedded in its wall, a relic of a scholarly interest in the ancient world. On the left about fifty yards farther on we come to the Gothic church of *S. Agostino* (1275), with its simple front and a portal with pillars. The church was enlarged in 1327 and again at the end of the same century. We enter (usually) by a side-door and find one nave, skirted by a side-nave that was opened during restorations in 1921. The church was attached to a cemetery for two centuries. On the right of the entrance, on the back wall, there is a *Madonna with Child taking milk* which has a sleepy charm, by a painter of the Umbrian school at the beginning of the fifteenth century (under Sienese influence, as we see from the faces). On the left of the entrance another fresco (also on the back wall), a *Madonna della Misericordia*, is by an artist from Gubbio, also fifteenth-century. On the left wall of the church, at the very back and close to this Madonna, almost at floor level, we find a much-damaged *Nativity with a praying figure* which shows the influence of Ottaviano Nelli.

Farther down the church, in a niche high in the wall, *Christ in glory among seraphim* is by a follower of Mezzastris; his fineness of touch is apparent. Then comes a large fresco of *the coronation of the Virgin among angels and two saints*, also much damaged, where the figure in the foreground (face just visible) represents Eve: the piece is said to resemble the work of Cola Petruccioli from Orvieto (died 1394). Farther on there is a clearly later *Madonna and Child with two saints* (1522) by an unknown, heavy hand but with something pleasing about it. Then comes a vividly decorated piece where the figures fit like a jig-saw puzzle, a *Madonna and Child between SS. Augustine and Nicholas of Tolentino*, from the second half of the fifteenth century, a sincere and sweet piece perhaps by Ugolino di Gisberto, the Foligno artist. Above this a niche contains a *Madonna and Child and St Catherine of Alexandria*, which has a quiet dignity recalling the Byzantine artists, also from the fifteenth century.

The rest of the church's frescoes, including those of the whole area above the triumphal arch, once rich and dazzling, have been lost to damp and wear. The right wall has lost frescoes by Mezzastris and perhaps Melanzio. On this side of the church, going back towards the entrance, we find at the next alcove a ceiling that still bears the heavily coloured traces of *doctors of the Church* and—on the wall—a *Crucifixion* with a *Madonna and Child and saints* below it: there is just a shadow of the former golden richness. On the right of these there is *the story of SS. Fortunatus and Severus*, and in the archway leading to the main nave *Christ carrying the cross*, with *St John the Baptist* opposite, by a pupil of Benozzo Gozzoli (fifteenth-century).

The sacristy is reached by a door on the left of—and behind—the altar, that is, through the choir: in the ceiling we find an *Eternal Father and four doctors of the Church* which shows an amazing richness of design and sobriety. In the lower corners of the doctor panels the saints include *Catherine, John the Baptist, Anthony the Abbot and Paul the Hermit*. These frescoes are by a local painter of the fifteenth century, whose consciousness is still Byzantine, though he has learned the new manner. On the right-hand wall there is a rustic *Crucifixion* from the end of the fourteenth century which has a quiet elegance. And on the entrance wall a late fourteenth-century *view of a city*, probably the artist's idea of Jerusalem, makes it a very inviting place, behind a wall and sprinkled with trees, ordered like a suburb, and quite unlike Italy.

We continue our walk uphill until we reach the heart of the town and its highest point, the Piazza della Repubblica, in fact not a square at all but almost circular. On our right as we come in there is the Palazzo Comunale, with a fifteenth-century porch before it, though the building was started in 1270. Here we shall have to look for Signora Clarice Servili, who is usually knitting under the shade of a tree opposite the Palazzo Comunale: otherwise the shop behind this tree will know where she is, and if this fails we can telephone her from a bar, at 79146. In Umbria we learn the sound lesson that greatness begins in the personal: this lady has the key to the ex-church of **S. Francesco** just down the road, where we shall find one of the biggest art collections in the province. If we would like to see Umbria from the highest point of her 'balcony' we should ask Signora Servili to take us up to the top of the town hall's tower, which she will not be at all happy to do.

It is best to deal with S. Francesco vault by vault, as its side-naves are divided into chapels. The entrance takes us straight into the right nave, with a great barn of a church before us, gleaming with frescoes but otherwise quite bare. In the first vault, the ceiling shows well-preserved *evangelists* by Benozzo Gozzoli: in the archway leading into the centre nave a vivid and striking *Eternal Father among angels*, with *St Bernardine and two angels* on one side and a defiant *St Catherine* on the other, also by Gozzoli. On the wall (that is, right of the entrance) we see a *polittico* with a delicate and fine *Madonna and Child* where the colour has gone from the Virgin's robes, and, above, a *Crucifixion*: on each side of this *polittico* there are *episodes from the life of St Jerome*, also by Gozzoli (1452). At the second vault down we see in one section of the ceiling *St Jerome* again, and on the wall a much damaged *Crucifixion* with, underneath, *St Bernardine and two scenes from his life*, on either side, a rough fresco: the two detached pictures on either side are attributed to Melanzio—*St John the Baptist* and *St Jerome*.

The third vault has two Madonnas by the same hand, one a copy of the other, by Melanzio (1510), where the fact that she holds a scourge to beat off a black demon (his belt is a snake) takes nothing away from the compassion and sweetness of her face—a marvellous combination. The left of the two is beautifully designed, while the face of the Madonna on the right is more thoughtful and suave. The ceiling of the fourth vault has excellently preserved *doctors* and *evangelists* and *prophets*, and in the archway leading to the centre nave, in little medallions, *Christ and the apostles* with another *Madonna and Child*, all by an Umbrian hand close to Ottaviano Nelli in style (1440). Opposite this last fresco there is another from a near-by church which shows Sienese elements, delicate and faint, by an unknown hand. On the wall there is a wooden crucifix (tempera) by an Umbrian painter which is reminiscent of the famous cross at St Clare's in Assisi: this is from the fourteenth century, though in the old style. On the left of it we see a *coronation of the Virgin* by an artist of the Perugian school in the sixteenth century, much damaged. And on the right of the crucifix we see a *Madonna and Child and angels*, another detached fresco, attributed to Tiberio d'Assisi, as is also the fresco on the pillar to the right of this (*St Stephen*) and on the left pillar (*St Peter*), which have a graceful touch.

The fifth vault shows the *story of St Anthony the Abbot* in the ceiling, a literal piece which tells a full and crowded tale, with touches of the so-called 'international' style of the fifteenth century: partly damaged. In the archway leading to the main nave there is *Christ among the seraphim* (centre medallion) and *three temptations of St Anthony*. The archway frescoes are attributed to the Gubbio school of the fourteenth century. The last traces of a *Crucifixion* on the wall show a Sienese touch, from the end of the fourteenth century. Below this there is a *St Messalina in prison*, of the same period, a rather heavy work. A panel of tempera farther below still shows a *Madonna and Child and saints* by Melanzio (1488).

The sixth vault has a *Christ blessing* in the centre of the ceiling, and in the other sections *four evangelists*, from the beginning of the fifteenth century, by a retarded artist showing strong Gothic influences. On the wall there is a wooden *Christ* attached to a painting (saints and the Madonna are painted behind it) by Nicolò Alunno, which is of no great distinction. On the wall left of this a detached painting of the *Crucifixion* with the two Marys and St John, of the fourteenth century, has certain tender Lorenzetti characteristics. As we leave this vault we pass under an archway which has a *Madonna and Child* behind glass, tempera on silk, a copy, by Melanzio or perhaps a pupil, of the same picture at the altar of S. Maria del Popolo in Rome.

We are now in the right-hand part of the presbytery: on the wall facing us as we look inside we see, below, *St John the Baptist* (right) and *St Francis* (left), with an *Annunciation* above. In the arch between them there is a remaining figure of *St Lucy*, with her usual plate bearing two eyes. On the right wall there is an *Entombment* below and a *Madonna and Child between SS. Peter and Paul* above. On the left wall: a damaged *Crucifixion* above, and *the martyrdom of St Catherine of Alexandria* below. In the entrance archway we have *St Bartholomew* on the right, and *St Anthony the Abbot* on the left: all work by an Umbrian artist in the fourteenth century, showing influences from Florence.

In the apse we come to a complete Gozzoli cycle—*the life of St Francis*—which still recalls Fra' Angelico (whose pupil he was) but with its own personality. At sundown this is wonderfully illuminated. It is the crown of the church and was commissioned by Fra' Iacopo da Montefalco (1452), who also suggested the themes. In the triumphal arch the medallions show busts of *St Francis and his first companions* (thirteen figures). In the ceiling (we must face the back of the church to see this section) there is *St Francis in glory*: the rest is in five sections, with leafy decorations along the ribs of the vault between them, showing *SS. Anthony of Padua, Catherine of Alexandria, Bernardine, Elizabeth of Hungary and Louis of Toulouse*. We must begin the actual narrative panels below on the left and go round clockwise (they sometimes hold two stories): first there is the very unlikely *birth of St Francis in a stable*, and then *a simple man holding a cloak for him* (recalling Giotto's St Francis, except that now we have passed into the full detail of Renascence work); secondly, *Francis gives his coat to a beggar*, and *has a vision in bed of the Church Triumphant* (and here the differences between Gozzoli's house spread with banners and Giotto's economical and almost symbolical version strike us); thirdly, *Francis renounces his inheritance in front of the bishop*. The father's very movement seems to be threatening here, as if to strike Francis —there is an altogether greater reliance on movement than in Giotto, while St Francis is much less convincing in his praying attitude than in the Giotto series: and Giotto has a much more realistic bishop—covering Francis's nudity for the sake of reputation, a veneer of careful hypocrisy on his face—while Gozzoli's bishop seems actually to be protecting Francis, which could hardly have been the case. In fact, it begins to dawn on us that the Church is now in charge of the artist's work, whereas Giotto's work was free, ungoverned by policy. Everything is safe in this Gozzoli series: there is no direct conversation with simple people, but more an exposition of history, slightly slanted for official purposes. Fourthly, there is *the meeting of St Francis and St Dominic*, with, above, *Mary placating Jesus* (the church we see here is St Peter's in the Vatican, with the obelisk to one side).

We now start again above the first panel with (5) *Francis holds up the Church and the pope approves his Rule*; (6) *the demons are chased away from Arezzo*; (7) *he preaches to the birds and blesses Montefalco and refuses bishopric*; (8) *at dinner with Orlando da Celano and predicts his death*; (9) *he institutes the Christmas crib at Greccio*; (10) *he preaches before the Sultan and undergoes the test of fire*; (11) *the stigmata*; (12) *his death, and the patrician Girolamo ascertains the truth of the stigmata.*

Underneath the lowest panels a set of medallions show various Franciscans who became illustrious; under the window there are *Petrarch, Dante* and *Giotto.* In the actual arch of the window we see *SS. Clare of Montefalco* (we shall see her convent here later), *Agnes of Assisi, Fortunatus, Severus, Elzear* and *Louis.*

In the chapel left of the apse there are more medallions in the archway itself containing lifesize figures of *saints and prophets*: in the right pillar of this archway a little cupboard contains a *Madonna and Child* of the thirteenth century, in an early pre-Giotto style. The right-hand wall of the chapel has a *Noli me tangere* below, which is simple, awkward and tender all in one, especially in the faces that watch Christ turn to forbid contact. Above, we see a *descent into Limbo* with the same slight heaviness of hand. On the left wall the *Crucifixion* has a clear Giottoesque face on the right. The ceiling is much ruined, with *evangelists*, and an *Annunciation* facing us on the wall on either side of a blocked-in window: in the actual arch of the window there is an *Agnus Dei*, with *St Onuphrius* and *St John the Baptist* at the sides. All this is by the same hand as the right transept, an Umbrian artist who has seen Florentine work.

Coming down the left side of the church the first niche we reach has, in its lunette above, a *Madonna and Child with SS. Louis of Toulouse, Raphael and Tobias* (fish in hand). On the right column of this niche, inside the arch, there is *St Sebastian*, a little crude. All this is by Francesco Melanzio (1506). The framed picture in this niche is also by him, an elaborate *Madonna and Child and four saints* against a gilt background, with a very ornate throne (1487), which shows less assurance than the fresco above it painted later. Next, under a gilded arch with fluted pillars of the sixteenth century, there is a wooden *tavola* attributed to Antoniazzo the Roman (1460-1508), showing *SS. Vincent, Illuminata and Nicholas* with no particular purpose about it. We then come to a large canvas on an easel: a *Madonna and*

Child and five saints (St Severus here is a self-portrait—the figure holding a city in his hand) by Melanzio in 1498: the mother and Child are set in a nice design of dignified blue, with a green throne behind.

We now come to a baroque chapel with a fresco by a Bevagna artist behind the altar where false piety and insentience hinder the design and the tones. Farther on there is another niche with a *Crucifixion* above, and *St Anthony of Padua* and *two stories of the Saint* below, where a devil jumps out of a man's mouth at his admonition, and the Saint replaces someone's leg miraculously. These frescoes have been attributed to Mezzastris but I am sure wrongly. In the next niche we return to more graceful styles in a *Madonna and Child and SS. Bonaventure and Andrew* by Tiberio d'Assisi (1510), where design and delicacy of feeling unite in a modest picture. Next to this, on the back wall of the church close to the entrance, there is another niche with a *Nativity* and *Eternal Father* above it (probably 1515), where we can see the ease and clarity and Umbrian spaces of Perugino (the work perhaps of his pupils).

If we now go back down the church towards the altar, on the right, we shall be able to see the pictures hanging between the arches which were not included in the vaults: first a *tavola* from the second half of the fifteenth century with the gilt background clear and excellently designed, by someone perhaps associated with Nicolò Alunno, a *coronation of the Virgin*. Next, two leaves of a door have nine panels showing *stories from the life of Christ*: the lowest panel on the right is in two parts, the *Crucifixion* and the *Virgin giving milk*, a work where the Byzantine has reached a climax of observation and design under Florentine influences. Next there is a *Madonna enthroned* and two medallions above showing an *Annunciation*, which are not very interesting. The next pilaster has another *Madonna and Child*, a framed fresco, which some people attribute to Gozzoli: underneath a further *Madonna and Child* of a later date and by an unknown hand. And the last pilaster we reach has a third one which is more generally attributed to Gozzoli.

St Clare of Montefalco and stones in the liver

If we have time we should leave the square by a downhill lane, Vicolo degli Operai, on the left as we face the town hall, and at the bottom if we bear right we shall come to the **Porta di S. Bartolomeo** or Federico II, which was put there in 1244. Walking through this arch we shall see on its outside, above the apex of the arch, a stone showing two imperial eagles and the Swabian Cross (Frederick being Swabian). On the left, actually attached to the gate, is the back of the church of **S. Bartolomeo** from the eleventh century, with a tiny window in arches and one square column remaining from the original construction, with little carved designs round it. We continue outside the town wall, turning right from the gate: and after about a hundred yards we come to a massive cylindrical tower issuing from the wall. A little beyond this on the left we find the church of **S. Chiara**—the St Clare of Montefalco, an Augustinian nun (1268-1308). It came into being during the thirteenth century but manifestly underwent complete overhauling in the seventeenth century to make the present sad brick mausoleum. Inside, at the right of the chancel, we find a door with a bell: we ring this and a nun answers, to show us the saint's body. She speaks to us from behind a hidden grille, and goes away for a little time. There is suddenly a frightening crash in the right transept, and little doors are flung open, revealing a glass case in which the 'uncorrupted' Saint lies. The nun will tell us, hidden still, that St Clare was a great enthusiast for the image and meaning of the Cross: legend says that she met Christ in a dream and he told her that he had always been looking for someone to take the cross from his shoulders, and she replied, 'I shall carry it in my heart.' So when she died the nuns, in the frightened and pagan state of mind that festered in these convents, cut out her heart to see if this was the case. And it was. There was a little cross made up of muscular tissue, which the nun will show us if we step to the right, by flinging open, after an unnerving silence and another crash, a second door. There we see the heart, in a tiny glass case, together with a container of her congealed blood, the knife and scissors she was cut open with, and— presumably—the cross she was blessed with. We look closely at the heart but cannot find the cross in it. And in fact we have made a mistake: the cross itself comes after a third crash: for this we have to step over to the left and a third cupboard is flung open (we are in quite a state by now) and we see another little glass case containing the actual tissue in a cross shape; the little stones at the arms and top of the cross were taken from the Saint's liver of all places, and these, the nun will tell us, are miraculous. She then explains why:

one of these tiny stones weighs the same as two, two of them the same as three, and three the same as one again. That is the miracle. You ask her to repeat this and she does: one weighs the same as two, two as three, and three as one. It has been tried again and again through the centuries, she goes on, and never failed: it is the miracle of the Trinity, and you can take it or leave it. This little show is played out perhaps a dozen times a day in the summer, with the greatest warmth and care.

Then we ask her to conduct us to the Chapel of S. Croce: and the frescoes there reassure us. They were done in 1333 (restored 1932): we must ask the nun for the strong light to be switched on. Above in the ceiling are the *evangelists* with the symbolic heads of beasts: in the wall behind the altar, *Calvary*, and on the side wall *scenes from the lives of St Clare, St Catherine and S. Biagio*: and next to them again *St Catherine*. On the right wall, middle, *Jesus is helped by St Clare*, and on the left of the arch we see Clare's sister, the Blessed Giovanna, with St Clare on the right as a child, in the company of the child Jesus; underneath, she brings food to S. Biagio (he is the saint of the throat, by the way). This was the work of a local artist, rather heavy, rustic and slow, an Umbrian working in the post-Giotto idiom but with the old really Byzantine consciousness, where observation did not count. The nun will also take us behind the Enclosure, if we ask her, to the closed cloister of the fifteenth century, and then to the nuns' private chapel, where, on the right of the entrance, we see a very Giottoesque *St Lucy* and the first coffin of the saint, painted, and a tall wooden crucifix in the Byzantine manner. We shall be shown into the little garden too, after we have been modestly offered little trinkets—key-holders, rosaries. This garden has a tree planted by the saint, which botanical authorities say does not exist anywhere else in Europe: but we have stopped believing these sweet, hesitant, kindly nuns by now.

CHAPTER 8

Gubbio

The 'mediaeval jewel'—the Pennine Jove—strategic importance in ancient times

Gubbio is mediaeval, exclusively and completely. Nothing has been added, little has been taken away of importance: it was built at such a time of fortune and wealth that its houses are always solid and often magnificent; it has suited people's needs until today. But its importance stretches back into pre-Roman times, despite its apparent isolation in the hills north of Perugia, where there are no neighbours. Its first role seems to have been a religious one, as a sacred town with temples and seminaries: the Eugubine Tables which we shall see later, with their Umbrian and Etruscan texts, point to that. Somewhere in the mountainous regions behind the town, perhaps on Monte Catria (over five thousand feet high), there was the so-called Pennine Jove, the god of light to whom pilgrimages were made from all over Italy. He was first known as the Giove Grabovio (*graba* meaning stone or rock), that is, Jove of the mountains, or Jove adored on the mountain, just as in Greece there was the Jove Olympus. And some people think that this was how the name Gubbio started, or Agubbio as it used to be: in Roman times it was named simply Iguvium.

If we have no car we should arrange to spend the night there, as the bus journey from Assisi or Perugia is complicated and long. By car we take the Cesena road and half an hour will find us there, after a drive over the top of the world, with hills on either side that grow steeper and more wooded, less cultivated as we go higher, until quite suddenly, after about ten kilometres, the hills divide and reveal a plain immediately before us, where Gubbio glitters. As we come closer we see how much its quiet, grey stone has settled into the countryside, like a splendidly designed plant. Its resources in the Middle Ages were much greater than ever afterwards, so that its intactness is a result of necessity, too: comparable buildings could never be afforded now. It is detached from the rest of Umbria in every way, alone in its own hills. Gubbio's strategic strength in ancient times (a stout military post guarding the Flaminian Way) ceased with the Romans and it remains alone with its memorial walls, regarded a little strangely by its neighbours on the other side of the bare hills. In fact, you get the impression that people think the Gubbians odd: their annual festival of the Ceri, as it is called, is certainly that.

Though at the foot of a hill, the town is fifteen hundred feet above sea-level, tucked compactly into the lower reaches of the Monte Ingino, without outskirts to speak of, much less factories. D'Annunzio called Umbrian towns 'cities of silence', but Gubbio ought to be called the city of noise: not only are its streets and staircase-lanes narrow and free to traffic but they rise, too, so that low gears are required nearly all the time. We should choose a hotel off the main roads—the Cappuccini if we can afford it (first category), though we shall eat remarkably well at the Hotel S. Marco (third category), at the entrance to the town. Gubbio is a favourite resort among Italians for its coolness in the summer: the fact that Italians pay more attention to their food than to sleeping conditions makes hotel accommodation rather poor. But foreign tourists have increased since the war, which brought the Hotel Cappuccini into being last year.

In Caesar's time the town was responsible for the defence of the whole Metauro valley down as far as the Tiber—more important strategically than Perugia. He found the Gubbians remarkably loyal soldiers, and today you can still see a certain barely quenched ferocity in their eyes. In the Middle Ages travellers had to pass through Gubbio and, as in ancient times, every communication between Rome and Ravenna depended on it, so that its importance continued. We have the feeling of a backwater which is nevertheless at the centre of things: the detachment is tempered with a certain confidence and ease, and the visitor is never fussed over. There are about nine thousand inhabitants.

Gubbio flourished most in the early years of the Roman empire, and this was when its great amphitheatre (still partly there today, and used for performances) was built: it stands a little below the present town, outside the mediaeval walls, showing that after the barbarian invasions the population moved a little farther up the hill,

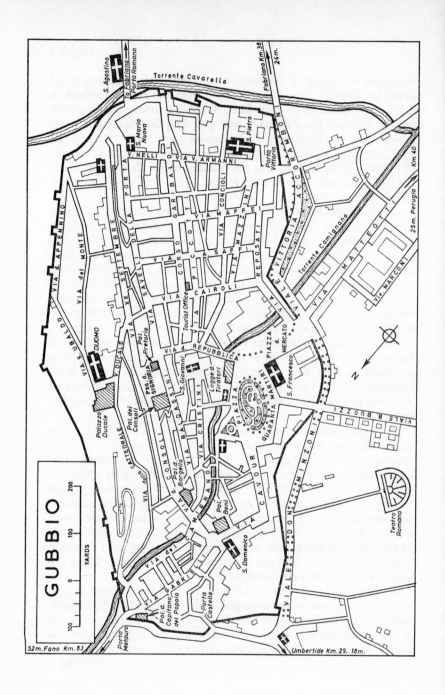

presumably for better defence. The town suffered badly from barbarian attacks, of course: Totila sacked it and after a short period of
revival it was sacked again in 917. Barbarossa gave the town its
freedom in 1163, after a bitter struggle, and put the executive power
in the hands of the so-called Consuls. And the Palace of the Consuls,
as it is called, dominates all Gubbio: it is the first building that
strikes us, with its stout crenellations, half-way up the hill as we
look from the square. Gubbio began Ghibelline but ended Guelf,
perhaps out of necessity.

It was now, when it had got its independence, that Gubbio's
second period of prosperity began. There were fifty thousand inhabitants at that time, over five times the present number. In the
thirteenth century the consuls were replaced by a mayor, who was
joined by a Captain of the People, a sort of chief policeman. After
that it was under the rule of private families like all other Umbrian
towns, notably the Gabrielli (one of these had taken a thousand
knights with him on a Crusade) and the first Montefeltro of Urbino,
who introduced a short period of real civilization, though his suc-
cessors were hard. These families were sometimes more and sometimes less under the influence of the Vatican. There were inter-
mittent revolutions in this period when popular leaders took over:
but finally in 1624 Gubbio was entirely handed over (by the last
Montefeltro) to the Church, that sad and slow but peace-bringing
parent: it became part of the province of the Marche; its re-in-
clusion in Umbria came about only in 1860.

As we stand facing the town from below in the Piazza dei
Quaranta Martiri (forty hostages were shot here by the Nazis in the
last war) we see layer after layer of mediaeval roof and wall, from
which the Palace of the Consuls protrudes on the left, its single
tower and massive crenellated bulk, its hanging arches and slender
columns making a picture of power and wealth that dwarfs nearly
everything else. Higher up on the right there is the simple tower of
the duomo with two bells showing—next to the palace it looks
rustic. Near by there are traces of the mediaeval wall. And beyond
rises Monte Ingino with its *funivia*, or ski-lift, though there is no
skiing at the top—only a hostel for summer visitors and the monastery of S. Ubaldo (Gubbio's patron saint). On either side of Monte
Ingino there are neighbour hills of about the same size, the Monte di
S. Girolamo (on the right) and Monte Calvo (it means 'bald')
with its peak of smooth green lawn. Monte Ingino is sometimes

called (and signposted as such) the Colle Eletto, because of Dante's line *'il colle eletto del beato Ubaldo*—the chosen hill of blessed Ubaldo.'

S. Francesco—Tiratoio dell' Arte della Lana—the 'doors of death'—Palazzo dei Consoli—the Eugubine Tables—Palmerucci

On the left side of the square there is the tall Gothic church of **S. Francesco,** grey and yellowing, with the curves of its apse and not its front facing the square. We shall have to walk round it to the other end for its façade, but for all practical purposes this side-wall is the front, with its rather magnificent portal and rose window above. The façade proper is simpler (in its own courtyard, opposite the hospital), just a door and a rose window, and unfinished.

The building is attributed to Fra' Bevignate of Perugia (1259-92). Inside, we find a spacious church divided into three naves with tall pillars (twelve of them): the whole form is much altered from the original, a transformation that took place in the seventeenth century. Some restoration is still going on and more of the original form will be brought to light, so that there may be a less bleak and bare church in a few years' time. In the chapel on the right of the high altar there are some fragments of fourteenth-century frescoes (a light-switch on the right wall): *saints,* and *Christ blessing among the four evangelists* in the roof. The vault overhead (above the ceiling of this little chapel, but opened to our view, like a loft) has more frescoes but these are invisible to us: a pity, as they are probably from an earlier epoch.

But the chapel on the left side of the chancel is what people come to see, and its frescoes are the best preserved, a series by Ottaviano Nelli who was Gubbio's own painter (died 1444). But they also are damaged, and three panels are entirely missing. They show *stories of the Virgin,* and were brought to light only in 1942. There is a light-switch in the left wall a few yards in front of the chapel, but even with this it is difficult to see. In the lunette high above there is a *coronation of the Virgin among angels.* Some people consider this his best work, and certainly its narration is less baldly matter of fact than his other more famous series in S. Agostino which we shall see later.

In the cloister next to the church (at present we reach it through a door facing the Piazza dei Quaranta Martiri, marked *Raccolta d'Arte*) we shall see a ruined fresco of the *Crucifixion*, and a large fragment of Roman mosaic showing a sea-horse with Cupid on his back, and Neptune, in faded reds and greens and yellows. In a hall giving off this cloister there are various fragments of frescoes which have been detached from the walls of a country church, including another *Crucifixion* and a *Last Supper* and *the washing of feet*, in an awkward rustic style that shows a surprising eye for design. Facing the doorway there are other pieces of probably later date, with a neo-classical frieze in a design of incense-bearers. A part of the wall has been stripped to reveal *sinopie* underneath (a large Crucifixion).

The founder of all painting in Gubbio—and hence of all the Umbrian schools—is said to have been Oderisi or Oderigo da Gubbio, who died in 1299, one of those shadowy figures like Giunta Pisano: their work is rarely seen, and then only in fragments, a cross here, a dubious collaboration there. Dante speaks to Oderisi in Purgatory: '*O, diss' io lui, non se' tu Oderisi?*' For Dante he was 'the honour of Gubbio'. None of his work survives here. But perhaps it does survive in the work of others, such as the marvellous Guido Palmerucci, who died half a century later and in whose work there is all the lingering tenderness of the Sienese school combined with Umbrian mysticism, with its root in Byzantine stillness. In fact, Meo da Siena was Palmerucci's teacher. And Palmerucci (we shall see his work later) was the teacher of Martino Nelli, the father of Ottaviano.

Outside again, looking across the square towards the town, we face the long **Tiratoio dell'Arte della Lana** (or simply the Loggia dei Tiratoi), a kind of weaver's gallery where wool and also skins used to be spread out (*tirati*) in the shade. This is a most pleasant building, humble and low and leisurely, giving the square its atmosphere far more than the tall S. Francesco opposite. Under its porch there are shops and vegetable stalls. It was built when the town's wool production was at its height in the fourteenth century. The upper storey is open to the air, to allow the skins to weather: today it stands empty, no longer used. There used to be frescoes between the shops underneath: these have faded with time, but there is a sleepy fifteenth-century work, the *Virgin between SS. Peter and Paul*, and a nice fragment on the extreme left said to be by Palmerucci, close to the church of S. Maria dei Laici or dei Bianchi, the entrance of which is just round the left corner of the Loggia. This church was annexed to a hospital at the time of its building in 1313 and belonged to an organization called the Lay Confraternity: the old entrance to their rooms can still be seen under the porch, two Romanesque doors, close to the faded Palmerucci fresco (which may by the time this book appears have been rescued from the light and air to prevent further fading). The crypt of the church used to have some fourteenth-century frescoes but these have been ruined, due to their nearness to the Torrente Camignano, which tends to flood in winter. Twenty-seven canvases by Damiano da Gubbio (1530-1608), sometimes called the Veronese of Gubbio, used to be here but they were removed from danger to a room in the Franciscan monastery opposite: devotees of the period will find them on enquiry, and with patience. The old front of this little church was removed, by the way, in the seventeenth century, which gives it a contradictory look.

From this point, outside the little church, we should walk up into the town: the roughly cobbled lane is called Via Ambrogio Piccardi, and we have the square Guelf crenellations of the Palazzo dei Consoli, or Palace of the Consuls, immediately above us. We are in the S. Giuliano quarter: Gubbio is divided into *contrade* like most Italian towns that have retained their mediaeval character. Behind the Palazzo above we see the pines of the Ingino hill. And we cross a little bridge over the Torrente Camignano, active only in winter unless there is one of those increasingly frequent summer downpours. Just before we reach the deep archway which leads up to the Palazzo dei Consoli we turn right along an unnamed lane and after about fifty yards find at the end the light-grey side of the church of *S. Giovanni Battista.* We walk round to the right (Via Beni) for its façade and the Piazza S. Giovanni. The church has an enormous portal at the top of steps and a single rose window: a thirteenth-century building restored to its first simple lines, after baroque depredations. There is a stout tower attached to the façade on the right, which has survived from the time of construction, with single open arches in its wall. Inside the church we have one nave, the triumphal arch tall and Gothic, closing the chancel off in such a way that the transepts are missing. Four great brick arches support the roof. At the back of the church on the right wall high up there is a fragment of a fourteenth-century fresco, where we see the last faint shadows of a *Madonna and Child with saints.* There is a Gothic chapel farther down which is of later date than the rest of the church, with a Renascence font in its middle, and if we step round this we shall see behind the altar a fresco by one of Perugino's pupils, *the baptism of Jesus.*

We turn left outside the church and then first left again along Gubbio's narrow main thoroughfare, the cheerful, uphill Via Repubblica. We take the wide and gently graded staircase immediately before us and at the top turn left along the Via Baldassini. After a few yards we pass the four immense open arches supporting the square of the Palazzo dei Consoli above, while further arches higher in the wall support the actual palace. On both sides of the road there are houses with their so-called *'doors of death'* intact: we shall see this type of doorway more in Gubbio than anywhere else in Umbria and therefore in the world, as they are an Umbrian characteristic (the only other place where they are found is the Provence): a palazzo usually has two of them, one on each side of the main entrance, and most of the bigger houses have them, too. They are tall, narrow, arched doorways raised about four feet above street level with a stone staircase behind them, equally narrow, leading up to the first floor. They are barely wide enough for two people to squeeze through side by side. Mostly they have been converted into ordinary doorways, but here and there they have simply been filled in, together with their staircase behind. The theories about them differ. Some say they were used for funerals, hence their name: only the dead passed through, on their last journey from the house. That is the usual story and the least convincing. Others say they were there for troubled times, when horsemen and armed bands marauded through the streets: the other entrances were barricaded from behind and only these were used, defence from the top of a narrow staircase being easy. As times were often troubled in Umbria it seems the likelier tale. A third theory is that they were simply convenient entrances for the owners and their families, taking them straight up to the *piano nobile*, or reception rooms on the first floor, without their having to walk through the courytard first: the raised level of the door made it possible to step straight from the carriage into the house without getting muddy. In fact, the truth may be the last two theories combined: they served both purposes, according to whether times were troubled or not.

Among the houses on the left there is one said to have been the birthplace of Ubaldo Baldassini, the patron saint born in 1084 and canonized in 1192: but no one is quite certain which one.

The houses we see on either side are in a perfect state of preservation, some with their own separate strips of forecourt as they were in the thirteenth and fourteenth centuries. Just beyond the foundations of the Palazzo dei Consoli there is a gravelled ramp on the right which bends round steeply to take us into the square (Piazza della Signoria) where the palace itself stands. We turn right at the top into Via dei Consoli and emerge into the 'government square', as we might call it, with the external staircase of the palace on our immediate right and then a wide parapet looking across the roofs of Gubbio to the plain beyond.

Opposite the Palazzo dei Consoli is the Palazzo Comunale and along the remaining fourth side of the square we see the long and fascinating front of the Palazzo Ranghiasci-Brancaleoni, with its many shuttered windows and nine little iron balconies, and bright fluted pillars designed on the ancient model, set into the wall at first-floor level. Here again is a door of death, on the left corner of the palace front.

The **Palazzo dei Consoli** dominates this square arrogantly: it clearly means to be the tallest object in the plain and always within sight of the citizens below, not to say the people outside the gates. It was the work of Gattaponi, though Angelo da Orvieto was responsible for the entrance, the steps leading up to it and the double windows on either side. The six windows high above in sets of two with their decorated cornices are typically Gubbian (or Eugubine) and we see them repeated again and again in the town's best palazzi. High up on the far right of these windows, under the gable, a hole shows us where the *gogna* or pillory used to be placed—a cage in which the guilty were hung out for public view. The palace tower has its original bell which weighs forty or fifty hundredweight and is rung at festivals. A single arch holds up the front staircase, and this is cleverly coupled with another arch supporting the balcony. Over the main entrance we see a fresco, *Madonna and Child with SS. John and Ubaldus*, a work by Bernardino di Nanni (1495). And round the lintel there is an inscription: 'A.D. 1332 *chomencata quest' opera, e quando fu posta questa pietra* 1335 *mese d' Ottobre.*—This work was begun in 1332 and when this stone was placed here it was October 1335.' It isn't a pretty or warm building: there is an atmosphere of power, a trace of brooding historical sureness, not civilization.

We enter a great hall (*Salone dell' Arengo*—'hall of haranguing', literally) where audiences were held between the consuls and the chief families of the town. It looks like a banqueting hall of a mediaeval castle, and a narrow staircase leads not to a sort of minstrel's gallery, as we would expect, but to what used to be the consuls' rooms. Above this staircase there is a small window, shaped in such a way as to amplify their voices, from which the consuls addressed everybody below. It was also a good way of protecting themselves if the discussion got too hot. On the right there is a fascinating chimney bored straight up the wall to the roof, but it looks little used. In this hall there are various Roman inscriptions and memorial stones and tombs. No. 82 is a coat of arms belonging to the local smiths' guild. The marble is from Gubbio's Roman theatre. The two inlaid doors belong to the palace, and there are eighth-century sarcophagi of barbarian origin. In one of the window embrasures there is a bell dated 1236. No. 12 of the exhibits is an inscription by Gnaeus Satrius Rufus, governor of Gubbio at the time of Augustus; it states how much he spent on beautifying the city—nearly ten thousand sesterces. On the wall of the staircase there is a tall fresco, a *Madonna and Child and saints*, attributed to Ottaviano Nelli's school.

There are twenty-six lavatories in the palace and seven water-pipes—a fillip for those who think puritanism and commercial enterprise go together.

The palace contains a museum and the Pinacoteca, at the top of the wooden stairs. The first room (called the sacristy) contains mediaeval measuring pots and a cupboard of local coins dating from the ducal period to the time of the French revolution. In the second room (the chapel) we find the exhibits for which Gubbio is famous —at least among historians and archaeologists: the so-called **Eugubine Tables**. The moment we enter our attention is divided between these tall strips of bronze and a marvellous Palmerucci fresco said to have started the local schools of painting, a large *Virgin enthroned presenting Jesus to the adoration of the standard-bearers (gonfalonieri) of the city*. On the other wall there is a fresco taken from a church near by, the work perhaps of Ottaviano Nelli's father, Martino. And on the left wall an inscription in Latin recalls how the Council of the Consuls and the Captain of the People used to meet here: 'O Citizens, remain faithful to your laws. Reach agreement with each other if you want the well-being of all citizens. Whatever you want let it always be for the good of the country, remembering all the evils your predecessors brought on it.'

And now the seven tables of bronze: they stand behind glass along the whole of one wall. Considering that they are historically the town's most important possession, it is amazing how little we know about them. Even if they were fully translated they would probably yield little new knowledge: like most Etruscan inscriptions they are repetitive. It seems that they refer to religious rites, and consist of a long prayer divided into stanzas or verses. Their importance really lies in the fact that they are in two languages, probably a translation. Three are written in Etruscan characters, one of them half in Etruscan and half in Latin, and the other three in Latin characters only. But the Latin characters do not make up a Latin text: they are Umbrian; that is to say, the Latin characters make the sounds of the vernacular Umbrian tongue, which is lost (though not wholly—what knowledge we have of it has helped in deciphering the Etruscan).

But the historical importance of these Tables lies in the fact that they are together at all: they point to a far deeper Etruscan penetration east of the Tiber than seems to have been the rule, or at least a deeper penetration of Etruscan culture; they make a clear link between Etruscan and Roman life, which helps to dispel the idea that a distinct people called the Romans destroyed a distinct enemy people called the Etruscans, and to show that the Etruscan culture, and therefore people, were absorbed by the Romans.

The Umbrian dialect probably had no written counterpart, making the use of Etruscan and Latin characters necessary. The sounds had to be rendered by visiting Etruscans, and later visiting Romans, for the religious festivals, so that the ordinary people, through their priests, would understand them. The Tables therefore describe rites and ceremonies for the benefit of the priests, in the local tongue, using the characters of the only shared written language of the time, Latin. Processions, sacrifices and prayers are cited for the use of a priestly fraternity called the *Attiedii*, who were divided into twelve religious corporations and ministered to the people of Gubbio. One of the cults involved seems to be that of Jove: and the likeliest explanation of the existence here of the Tables is that Gubbio was a great centre of Jove pilgrimage. The Tables belong to the period from the fourth to the second century B.C., that is, during the decadence of the Etruscan civilization and the flowering of Rome, as we would expect. They were found in 1444—it is said in an underground passage near the Roman amphitheatre. Since then one Table has been lost. They have been interpreted many times: two

good books on the subject are *Le Tavole di Gubbio* by Professor
Devoto (published in Florence in 1948), and *Les Tables Eugubines*
by Michel Bréal (published in Paris in 1875).

The *picture gallery* is at the top of another flight of stairs. On
the left side of its first hall there is a banner showing the *Madonna
della Misericordia* on one side and *St Ubaldus* on the other (1503):
it draws discreet lessons from the Renascence without great spirit,
but achieves a certain mischievous beauty.

But the next rooms contain the treasures we shall want to see.
In Room 2, immediately on the left of the doorway, there is a *Noli
me tangere* by Raphael's first teacher, Timoteo Viti (1469-1523),
which is of historical interest. Then we see a *SS. Augustine and
Monica* with rich colours and crude, awkward lines, from the fifteenth
century, by a local school. By the window there is a triptych by the
Perugino workshop which is much cruder on close inspection than it
seems at a distance, so much so that it throws doubt on the authorship. And on the left wall, waiting for us without any fuss, there is
the lovely and blonde and vivid *Madonna del Melograno* or Madonna
of the Pomegranate, perhaps by Caporali, perhaps by Fiorenzo di
Lorenzo, perhaps by Pier Francesco Fiorentino. It is a superb and
tenderly fresh piece: we see the pomegranate in the lower left
corner of the picture. There is also a tall crucifix in the Byzantine
tradition, of the kind we have seen a good many times in Umbria
(the saints at the edge of Christ's hands have been removed). In
Room 3 our attention is taken by a terra-cotta Gothic *Pietà* on the
right, like the one we shall see in the church of S. Domenico, with
one arm of the Madonna broken off. It is fifteenth-century and may
be of German origin.

The tickets under these pictures are scribbled on by people who
deny what the museum claims: the authorship of half of them is
guesswork, and people get worked up about guesswork. This room
has some small canvases which remind us of Palmerucci and are
attributed to his school or an imitator: the eyes are narrow and
long, their whites contrasting with the sallowness of the face, in a
lingering gaze, sharpened with black pupils, which is characteristic.

Room 4 (opposite) has *politticos* and a thirteenth-century painted
wooden *Madonna* in a niche (the right wall) with the same simplicity
and directness as the German Gothic piece we have just seen. On the
left wall as we go in there is another tall crucifix, this time from the
fourteenth century, where Sienese influences with their sweetness

and delicacy combine with the drowsy Umbrian compassion and reflectiveness, Christ with long red hair, his body bent in the original Byzantine manner. There are tiny cruder pieces round it. And at last, at its side, we have an authentic Palmerucci: a *Madonna and Child with saints*, where again Siena blends with Umbria in a sleepy, tender, thoughtful world, the eyes dreaming distantly, the faces with their classical Umbrian features—a nose straight down from the forehead and wide, large eyes. You see that face everywhere in Umbria today, quite unchanged. The genealogical tenacity of the Italian people is marvellous. The rest of us are what they themselves call polyglots in comparison. But then, they began as polyglots themselves.

At the end-wall there is an over-enamelled *polittico* of the fourteenth century, again Umbro-Sienese, where a rich drowsiness lurks behind a thick sheen, making Palmerucci look simple and mystical at its side. And then comes a picture that is comparable to the little blonde Madonna we saw next door—another Palmerucci *Madonna and Child*, against a gold background that summarizes his perfect touch, in a clean, still, tender, neat and compact design, everything clear-cut but leading to the soft large eyes of both faces that seem to dream far beyond the picture, so that precision is artfully arranged to serve a soft end, in exactly the right consummation.

In the middle of this room there is a small thirteenth- or fourteenth-century reliquary composed of tiny Byzantine pictures against a gilt background, a *Crucifixion* and a *Madonna and Child* among them.

If on the way out we pass through the entrance hall again we shall find on the other side, beyond a further room of late paintings, the loggia with its precipitous command of the roofs below, hugged in green fields. A staircase leads to the tower, but this is temporarily closed, after someone fell down it.

In the square again, the **Palazzo Pretorio,** or town hall, facing us, was conceived together with the Palazzo dei Consoli as part of the same architectural plan, also on a design by Gattaponi (1349). It contains the town's library and archives, with manuscripts dating back to the thirteenth century; some of the miniatures in these may be the work of Oderisi or pupils.

S. Domenico—the Duomo—Nelli's Madonna del Belvedere—a ski-lift—
S. Agostino

We turn back into the Via dei Consoli by which we came. This goes downhill, with a view of green hills beyond the town's lowest roofs. Its mediaeval houses on either side are remarkably intact. At lunchtime when there is no one about we could think ourselves in another epoch. About half-way down on the left a tower sprouts out of a house. At the first opening in the road we find a tiny square called Largo del Bargello, with its own fountain. The squat church of S. Giuliano is dark with age, though it is re-designed inside. And before us there is one of the earliest—and loveliest—houses we shall see in Gubbio, the **Palazzo Bargello,** with Gothic arched windows, from the thirteenth century. It is restored, of course, but faithfully; its roof slopes three feet or so beyond the wall, in the style of that period. At the end of the Via dei Consoli, after crossing the Camignano torrent again, we come into the Piazza Giordano Bruno, and facing us is the church of **S. Domenico** with its massive, untidy, bare, grey front, untouched by anything fanciful. When it was built in 1186 it was dedicated to St Martin, whose district or *contrada* this is.

The inside is baroque though simple enough, without sidenaves. Its bare wooden ceiling has tiny floral designs, unpainted (we shall find nearly all the Dominican churches unadorned in this way). A pleasant fresco of the *Epiphany* can be seen in the second side-chapel down on the right. And in the last side-chapel before the main altar there is a *Last Supper* which some people say is the work of Giovanni Bellini. But neither of these will say much to us after the simple mysticism of the other pictures we have seen. Perhaps the most interesting thing in the church is a tiny terra-cotta *Pietà* in the S. Maria Maddalena side-chapel on the opposite side as we walk away from the high altar. It is almost quite hidden in the shadows, a German piece reminiscent of the one we saw in the picture gallery: its proportions seem exactly chosen for the subject, a perfect unassuming smallness. There is real compassion in the Madonna's face—it makes you stop with surprise; Christ lies in her arms with complete repose, his mouth open like hers; he is broken and yet in the strangest way undefeated. In her left hand there is a handkerchief, the pleats of which fall over her wrist.

Behind the main altar the choir-stalls are from the fifteenth century, and the tall lectern is skilfully carved and inlaid, by a local artist. Near the entrance of the church, in the first side-chapel on the left as we look back towards the high altar again, there are the faded traces of more work by Ottaviano Nelli showing *scenes from the life of St Peter Martyr* (a light-switch on the wall). At one time the whole church was painted with similar frescoes, but they were lost in the seventeenth-century rebuilding. Gubbio never became an artistic town like many in Tuscany. What art it had at the beginning was never repeated. That died with the prosperity: less and less respect was shown to art; today there is virtually none.

If we stand on the steps of this church we shall see in the Via Cavour before us the dark and malevolent front of the Palazzo Beni (No. 1). Much power must have been exercised badly here: two popes stayed here—Martin V in 1420 and Julius II in 1506. It has a curved front and many small arched windows. The courtyard is now in ruins and the palace is divided into flats. Other interesting houses in Via Cavour are the Palazzo Benamati at No. 16, in a clear Renascence style, and No. 28, with its doors of death, though changes were made to it in the sixteenth century.

We should return up the Via dei Consoli and take the lane going left from the tiny Largo del Bargello, which leads us to thick trees swelling beyond a wall; at the Via della Cattedrale we turn right, with a stiff climb before us—but we shall be free of cars. The lane goes between rough walls, with the crenellations of the Palazzo dei Consoli, that everlasting landmark, always reluctant to let itself out of our sight, away on our right. At the top we pass under the supporting arches of the ducal palace, with its garden-balcony overlooking the town, higher this time than the Palazzo dei Consoli. And at the end of the archway we turn left, a short uphill lane leading straight to the duomo, which has no parallel in all Umbria for its detachment from its own town, out of access to traffic, perched at nearly the highest point, as if Gubbio's first Ghibelline affiliations had frightened it off for good. Its forecourt is no more than ten or fifteen yards wide, with the ducal palace (called La Corte) immediately opposite, perhaps for the better protection of both parties. The palace (started in 1476 by Federico di Montefeltro) is closed for restoration, which looks like going on indefinitely.

Right: Assisi's Piazza del Comune lies on the original Roman forum, largely intact beneath it. The Temple of Minerva with its six Corinthian columns nestles beside the Torre del Popolo.

Below: The Piazza seen from the opposite direction, looking towards the hills round Eremo degli Carceri. The duomo's tower and façade are in the background.

Above: Ruined look-out posts and sentry-walks add to the fascination of Assisi's Rocca Maggiore, whose walls date from the fourteenth century. *Below:* This measure at the foot of the Torre del Popolo shows the standard mediaeval sizes for roof-slates, bricks, paving stones and tiles.

The **Duomo** is of thirteenth-century origin but its façade was restored in the sixteenth century, although the only clear evidence of this is the ugly stone stairway leading up to the entrance. Round the large rose window there are symbols of the evangelists, and a figure of the mystical lamb above. These are all from the original building. The inside is a vast open nave, its roof supported by ten Gothic arches, with three strips of vivid stained-glass window behind the altar. There is a lot of bad painting, but close to the entrance on the right wall we see remains of fourteenth-century frescoes which give us a taste of what the church could look like. There is a stupendously rich seventeenth-century chapel on the right, with a dome and much gilded stucco: the richness is entirely visual—even the marble isn't genuine. On either side of the church's chancel we see two magnificent organ-lofts, local work of 1550. The altar is on an ancient sarcophagus, where we see the remains of bas-relief figures. If we now go down the other side of the church the first side-altar we come to has another Roman sarcophagus in a better state of preservation, showing masks and a bust in a medallion. The figure of St Ubaldus above it is by Benedetto Nucci, whose work we have seen in the picture gallery. At the next altar there are the remains of fourteenth-century frescoes on the side walls, one of them part of a *Crucifixion*. Behind the next altar the serene and spacious *Madonna and Child and SS. Ubaldus and Sebastian* against a gold background is by Sinibaldo Ibi (1507), showing a marked Perugino tendency. The next altar has a *Mary Magdalen* by Raphael's first teacher, Viti, which shows how fast painting declined in Perugino's time. And at the last altar the *Nativity* by the Pintoricchio school has all the master's narrative splendour, though here it is at the expense of the feeling. At the last two arches before the entrance we see, high up, more remains of early frescoes, one of them a fading *Entombment*.

Returning down the slope from the duomo again we turn left along the Via Ducale, and reach a crossing road: on the other side of this a staircase-lane called Via Mastro Giorgio takes us to the Via Savelli della Porta and the church called *dei Muratori* (bricklayers) on our immediate left, a seventeenth-century building, neat with restoration and nearly always closed; it is said that St Francis tamed the wolf at this spot, and there is a fresco to this effect above the church door. Inside—should we find it open—we shall see a stone on which he is supposed to have preached too.

We now turn left along this road, passing No. 16 on the right, the Palazzo della Porta, with its Renascence stone-framed portal decorated attractively with bas-relief flower themes. At the end of the road we find the little church of **S. Maria Nuova,** its façade facing us, the portal so placed as to look down the street towards us as we approach; it is fitted into the extreme left corner of the façade instead of the centre. We find the custodian at No. 66 Via Dante, a little farther on; this is no longer a church but contains the marvellously preserved *Madonna del Belvedere* by Ottaviano Nelli (1403). It stands on the right as we enter, in its own blue tabernacle, behind glass, a rich and sadly reflective *Madonna and Child with SS. Emilian and Anthony the Abbot* with (left) two praying figures of the Pinoli family who probably commissioned the piece. It is like a tapestry and only when we have looked at it for some time do we see that it is not so well preserved after all, especially along the edges, which show signs of damp: only its magnificence of design and colour made us think it a perfectly kept jewel.

As to the rest of this one-time church, there are frescoes on the end-wall, including a *Crucifixion* attributed to Giovanni Pintali, a local painter who lived in the middle of the fifteenth century. The panel underneath, the *Madonna giving milk to the Child with saints* is by Bernardino di Nanni (died 1495). The *Annunciation* on the left of the *Crucifixion* is said by some people to be by Palmerucci, but this seems a very tall story: the most elementary draughtsmanship is lacking. On the left of the entrance there is a fourteenth-century fresco of *St Anthony the Abbot*. The two immense coffins are those used for the patron saint Ubaldus; the one on the left has seven locks, which didn't prevent robbers from trying to break it open for the jewels inside—as we see from the holes the size of a hand bored in the wood. The coffin opposite (once bitten, twice shy) is completely encased in metal.

We continue to the Via Dante and turn right there: at the bottom of the little hill we find the Porta Romana on our left and pass through it; immediately before us there is the church of **S. Agostino** behind its own forecourt, its front quite hideous—the work of this century. The morning before noon and the afternoon later than four will find it open. On our left, by the way, there is the *funivia*, or ski-lift station: its little cages will take us up to the Monte Ingino, where we shall find a café beside the monastery, if we need a break and some good air as well as silence.

The inside of S. Agostino is restful, one nave with baroque side-altars: seven arches support the wooden roof, like those of the duomo. At the second side-altar down on the right we shall find another Ottaviano Nelli, *Madonna and Child and saints* in a gilt frame, a slumbering, delicate, pale piece with some awkward painting outside the central group of figures, as if pupils have been at work. At the fifth side-altar down on the same side a fresco has been uncovered of neat and quiet sobriety: there are three panels together, only slightly damaged. The presbytery is entirely frescoed by Nelli and his school: round the triumphal arch we see *the Eternal Father* and *the Last Judgment*, with their patches of damp neatly repaired. Inside the rim of the arch there are medallions containing figures of Christ and the apostles. If it is dark we should look for a priest or custodian in the sacristy on the left, where the light-switches are. In the ceiling of the apse we find the maximum state of preservation, with *symbols of the evangelists* in the centre and *doctors of the Church* filling the rest in four sections. On the walls below, partly damaged, there are the twenty-one panels of *the life of St Augustine*, in a matter-of-fact narrative form, showing his travels and embarkations.

If we now go back into town through the Roman gate and turn left along Via Dante we shall find ourselves in the Corso Garibaldi: as we turn into Gubbio's main street we pass a statue of St Ubaldus that actually closes the street off, between pillars set above eye-level; from the other end of town it makes a pleasing effect—more than it does at close quarters. After about a hundred yards we take a turning left, the Via Vincenzo Armanni, and at the bottom of this, in a corner that comes as a surprise for its air of seclusion while being in the middle of town, we see the entrance of **S. Pietro,** its five Romanesque arches (thirteenth-century) now set in the wall and filled in. The inside was all re-done in the sixteenth century and again two hundred years later, but it has a certain neo-classical harmony. The only work that will interest us is the wooden crucifix at the side-altar on the left nearest the chancel: Christ's arms have left the cross and are inclined forward as if in embrace; so, strictly speaking, this is a *Deposition*. It is from the fourteenth century. If we go to the left corner of this chapel by the altar we shall find an inscription, *Vestigia Pedum Christi* ('a trace of Christ's foot') with a quotation from Job underneath; and if we then walk to the other side of the same altar we shall see what this inscription refers to— the imprint of a foot on a piece of stone. It was found during one of the church's restorations. At least, it is supposed to look like the imprint of a foot. But you have to limit your intelligence to make it seem so—and perhaps this is exactly what the priests want you to do. People's faith has been squandered away on this sort of nonsense.

Outside the church again we turn right, crossing the square before us and taking the first road left out of it, with another town-gate below us, the Porta Vittoria. We pass through this and turn right along the Viale Vittoria Accoramboni until we reach the lower part of town again where we started: the Piazza dei Quaranta Martiri.

CHAPTER 9

Foligno

Foligno is an apparently untidy but in fact the most neatly planned town of any we shall see in Umbria: its rambling outskirts account for this first mistaken impression. Among Umbrians it is not a favourite spot, and few tourists stay here, nor are there striking facilities for the visitor, but it has all the bustling and crowded intimacy of the old Italy, and prosperity with its new coats of paint and tourist signs hardly seems to have touched it. In the days when they were allowed, brothels flourished here, and the town had a kind of gaudy appeal for young men which it has since lost. In the last war it was more bombed than most Umbrian towns, and unlike the others it still bears the mark in crumbling walls and unrepaired corners. But this is mostly in the centre: the narrow, straight roads radiating from it on all sides are clean, glittering and intact. Foligno lies in a plain, hills cupping it all round; its bustling centre and narrow lanes have the appearance of a town in the Veneto, close to the Alps. It is a good alternative to Perugia and Assisi as a place to stay.

To start with, it was an Umbrian centre, and under the Romans it became known as Fulginiae. The town was made the seat of a Roman prefect and inscribed to the tribe of Cornelia, and during the period of the Empire it had some importance. And to this importance we must ascribe the neatness of the town with its straight, parallel streets which give long views from one end to the other: we have, in fact, as exact a replica of the form of an ancient Roman town as we shall see anywhere in Italy. The streets are connected with four Roman bridges on the former course of the river Topino, which at one time crossed the city—a sufficient reason for its modest commercial importance (the Flaminian Way that passed through it being another).

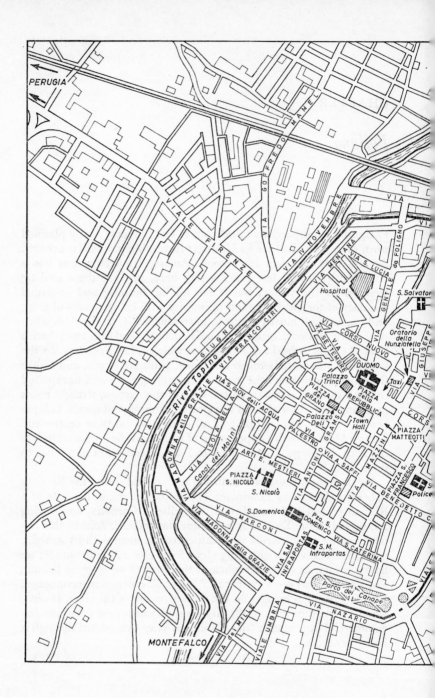

As to the Christian origins of the present town, legend says that a bishop Feliciano who was martyred about the year A.D. 251 was buried here, and his tomb became a place of pilgrimage, until finally a town grew up, called Castellum S. Feliciani, later Civitas S. Feliciani, then Civitas Nova Fulginii—the 'new Fulginiae', since the original Roman site had declined. The new town attracted the inhabitants of the neighbouring Forum Flaminii, three kilometres to the north-east, and was again called Fulginium in mediaeval times. The Saracens and the Hungarians devastated Foligno, but afterwards it became a free commune and the town we see at present was built (presumably on the skeleton of the Roman town).

In 1227 it was occupied by one of Frederick II's captains and the Guelfs were chased away, so that the town became for a time a bulwark of imperial interests and of course, the enemy of Guelf Perugia. But there were continual internal struggles too, until the Guelf captain, Rinaldo Trinci, beat the Ghibellines (Trinci was the pontifical vicar) and started his signoria (1310 until 1439): its length was a tribute to those suave powers of administration which were passed on from one generation of this gifted family to the next. The town flowered into its present bustling and intimate form at the time of Nicolò Trinci, who came to power in 1420, with dominion also over Spello, Assisi, Bevagna, Montefalco, Trevi and Nocera. And it achieved its greatest prosperity and beauty under him. But like all signoria this one too fell, and the last Trinci to rule, Corrado, was taken prisoner by the soldiers of Eugenius IV when they entered the town in 1439: from that time Foligno had no further history of its own.

The Duomo—first Italian edition of the Divine Comedy—the Palazzo Trinci—Pinacoteca (Nelli, Nicolò Alunno, Mezzastris)—S. Maria Infraportas—S. Nicolò

Taking the Piazza della Repubblica (the centre of town) as our starting-point we should walk to where the square opens into the Largo Carducci, and if we turn sharp left into this we shall find the front of the **Duomo** (we have therefore passed its flank). The church is called S. Feliciano—the saint of the town's legend—and was built in 1133, then enlarged a century later to include the arena on the left of the façade. But the original face has been hidden by transformations in the sixteenth and eighteenth centuries, and what we see before us is a restoration of the early Romanesque front done in 1904, resulting in the rather Victorian staircase of red and white stone on one side.

Over the duomo's main door there is an inscription which mentions Maestro Atto as the architect of the original building, together with the date of 1133. Above, there is a closed gallery with over-restored pillars (the church suffered further in the last war), and two closed archway-windows on either side. Over a great double rose window with symbols of the evangelists at the four corners there is a vivid mosaic which, considering its date (1904) offers little immediate offence: this comes if you look harder. It represents *Christ enthroned between SS. Felician and Messalina, with Pope Leo XIII.* Messalina was another Foligno martyr, said to have been murdered when bringing food to St Felician.

Inside the church we find a rather frigid baroque form, the fruit of Foligno's prosperity in earlier days and the work of Cola da Caprarola in the sixteenth century, on a drawing by Sangallo of Florence; the baroque contents have been altered since then, mercifully. But there are some of the most horrific statues to be found in Umbria, in niches: very large, and ten of them. We walk down the right side of the church to the sacristy (an open doorway) and inside we find a *Crucifixion* in the form of a relief on a painted background, the work of Nicolò Alunno, with the Virgin and St John on either side: a light-switch on the right wall will help us here. The simple and awkward wooden Christ will interest us. Returning to the main church again we shall notice the vast gilt *baldacchino* or canopy over the altar with twirling columns and imitation tassels hanging from its roof, surmounted by figures, an imitation (there is another in Spello) of Bernini's canopy in St Peter's in Rome: the imitation is so complete that there is the same opening with an iron gateway to a crypt below. To enter the thirteenth-century crypt we must ask an attendant to take us down: after showing us some relics of little interest he will lead us to the catacombs, which suffered from bombing in the last war but retain the original shape and some wall paintings, together with an old altar in the form of a simple stone pile like that used for pagan sacrifices, said to have belonged to St Felician in the eighth century.

In the upper church again we shan't need to spend time in the presbytery: its baroque extravagance is cold. There is an insipid statue of the Saint on the left of the main altar as we face it—his silver toe is kissed. In the left arm of the transept, at the altar, we see a small *Annunciation* that needs cleaning but is the only restfully pleasant thing to look at in the church.

We can leave by this left transept and find ourselves again in the main square (Piazza della Repubblica); our exit is the main doorway of the duomo's *secondary façade,* which is less restored and much easier on the eye than its main one. It is the work of two artists from Bevagna, dated 1201: an ornate and precisely carved Romanesque arch takes up nearly the whole space (it managed to survive the bombardments of the last war) and in its lunette we see protruding figures which symbolize the evangelists, while round the arch on the outside there are little bas-relief panels of the signs of the zodiac. Above is a tiny sun-dial and a crescent moon, continuing the theme of the zodiac. The two statues are the *Emperor Frederick* (Barbarossa) and a local bishop, *Anselm.* The mosaic work outside the arch gives the whole front its faintly gleaming presence, quietly mastering the long square, without vastness. The wooden door with its carved bas-relief figures is from 1620: overhead, gargoyles of men and beasts hold up a cornice, with a tiny open gallery of twining pillars above it and windows behind. The double archways high up in the wall were added by the Trinci family in the fifteenth century. The rose window and the roof were restored in 1905.

The palazzo on the right of this façade as we face it is the *Palazzo della Canonica* (presbytery or clergy house), which came into being in the fourteenth century in the Gothic style but has been heavily restored since. Behind us, and opposite this building, there is the town hall of thirteenth-century origin. It was partly restored in the sixteenth century and given its present overbearing but not quite ugly neo-classical front, with tall bare-bricked half-columns set in the wall: the tower, with the letters SPQF underneath (*Senatus Populusque Folignus*), is from the century before and has a Ghibelline crenellation. On the right of the town hall as we face it— and joined to it by a bridge—is the more interesting but ruined *Palazzo Orfini,* its doorway and window-frames the delicate work of the sixteenth century: this belonged once to the printer Emiliano Orfini who, together with a German printer, produced the first edition of the *Divine Comedy* (publication day was April 11th, 1472): this first edition consisted of three hundred copies and was incidentally the first book ever to be printed in the Italian language inside Italy.

Farther still to the right there are the ragged remains of the Palazzo Pretorio (the town magistrature) with its bare brick gaping through a front that was once lavishly painted (we can see the last faded traces high up in the right-hand corner) at the order of the powerful Trinci family. To the right farther still, and forming a whole side of the square, we see the cheerful and intimate seat of this great local family (there are no survivors), the *Palazzo Trinci,* which was begun in 1389 and finished eighteen years later. The present neo-classical façade came afterwards, more successful than that of the town hall and smaller, with nice windows; but it was badly damaged in the last war and rebuilt, with the result that a bleak edge has been put on its gaiety. It is now the seat of the town's Biblioteca or library, and the picture gallery. We enter it by a deep arch and find a large courtyard (again restored) with an external staircase on our right. This was once the courtyard of the most active palace in the town, like a miniature Versailles: there are triple windows all round, inside Romanesque arches with three-lobed tops, that make an appealing arrangement. Under tall arches at ground level there are Roman remains lying about haphazardly, brought in from near-by churches. Some guidebooks call this the town's archaeological museum, but in that case there never was a museum so neglected: a precious ancient mosaic lies open to the wind and the feet of tourists. It is awaiting what the Italians call systematization, and has been waiting for fifteen years. There is a complete Roman statue with a toga, only its right arm and left hand missing: we see here how the Greek beyondness has been swallowed up in monumental art, and the first shadow of the baroque has fallen, well over a thousand years before it happened: it is from the first century A.D. The mosaic on the ground has been taken from the church S. Maria in Campis and is deteriorating fast. There are several memorial stones: on one—perhaps a sacrificial altar—we see the words *Deo Romulo.* And here and there we see some traces of Etruscan writing.

The external staircase will take us up to the **Pinacoteca:** if the door is closed we ring a bell for the attendant. Again there is a lack of system, which is not typical of modern Italy but is half of Foligno's lazy charm. The entrance or vestibule is a long, curving room decorated in the fifteenth and sixteenth centuries, bright and airy,

The Companion Guide to Umbria

its ceiling in wooden compartments, some of which still bear the
original inlaid designs: in the middle of the ceiling we see the arms
of Pope Sixtus IV. All this has suffered in the last war and been
restored since. By a door close to the stairway, at the edge of this
vestibule, we enter a room which gives us a better idea of the palazzo
as living quarters with its baronial atmosphere: fifteen figures are
painted on the walls, *heroes of Roman history,* now rather fragmentary
—the work of Ottaviano Nelli's school, and restored at the time of
Sixtus IV. This too suffered bomb damage in the last war. We pass
through a second door and turn left into a loggia (through the arches
we see the vestibule we left a few moments ago), and here we have
frescoes showing *the story of Romulus and Remus*: from the left, *the
vestals of the temple* and *Rea Silvia with Mars*; then, *birth of the twins*
and *the kidnapping of the twins*; then, *Rea Silvia is condemned by Amulius* (almost quite faded, showing the *sinopie* underneath); *Faustolus
takes the twins to his wife, Acca Larentia*; *the siege of Alba* and *the
dispossession of Amulius*—both very faint. We can go up a few steps
from the loggia to a tiny chapel if we ask: there are more frescoes
by Ottaviano Nelli but they are covered with scaffolding and have
been for the last two years; only one wall of these frescoes remains—
the others were removed to Rome. We catch a glimpse of rich,
glowing, rather stiff scenes: they were painted in the artist's last
period and consist mostly of *scenes from the life of Mary* (1424).

The next room (which we already passed through to reach the
Romulus and Remus room) has an intricate wooden roof, and some
Nicolò Alunno pictures: this is the city's most important painter,
sometimes called Nicolò Liberatore and more often Nicolò Alunno
or 'pupil' (1430-1502). We see a *Crucifixion, angels and saints,* a rich
but not very placid triptych. And there is a sweet and gaudy original
St Michael the Archangel by Lattanzio di Nicolò, one of Alunno's
followers. The predella of *four major prophets* by the master (1492) is of
little interest. But *St Francis receiving the stigmata* is a pleasant and
graceful canvas on Lorenzetti's theme, showing the St Francis
Basilica in the background. The *Annunciation* over the doorway bears
the date 1523 on the back, showing that it is probably by Lattanzio.

The next room on is the Sala delle Arti Liberali e dei Pianeti (Hall
of the Liberal Arts and Planets) and contains the best-preserved
frescoes in the house. The splendidly dressed women seated in
tabernacles represent *Grammar, Dialectic, Music, Geometry, Philosophy,
Astrology, Arithmetic* and *Rhetoric*. In parts we can see the *sinopie*

220

underneath. The rest of the room shows *the Moon, Mars, Mercury, Jove, Venus, Saturn* and *the Sun*—badly damaged—while the medallions contain the various *Ages of Man,* and *the hours of the day*. This was all done at the beginning of the fifteenth century, perhaps by a local painter, under the influence of Gentile da Fabriano (died 1427) and the French miniatures.

We pass on to the corridor, actually a bridge over a corner of the square. Here we see damaged figures on the walls, with the sketches and *sinopie* of former frescoes showing through underneath (representing the *Ages of Man*). The figures are *Romulus, Scipio, Joshua, David, Judas Maccabeus, Caesar* (the face lost), *Alexander the Great, King Arthur, Charles the Great, Godfrey of Bouillon* (lost). On the other wall the figures carry on the theme of the Ages of Man, and we should notice here how a time-preoccupation—the beginning of time as a cause of anxiety—enters people recognizably during the late Renascence, after the Byzantine stillness which had lain over Christendom was broken for good. At the end of the corridor as we go out, on the left wall, the two old men, perhaps *prophets,* show a greater skill in painting than the rest, and might belong to Ottaviano Nelli's school.

But we have still to reach the picture gallery proper: we must re-cross the first room we came to (after the vestibule) so that we are now in the other wing of the palazzo. Room 1 consists of frescoes cut down from the walls of various churches, by Umbrian painters of the fourteenth and fifteenth centuries. Sienese influences can be seen in the *Betrayal* and the stiff *Deposition* (both on the right wall as we come in). The local Foligno art, on the left wall and the one facing us, has a quite different opaque and rarified quality, something light where observation gives place to dreaming, a certain sad delicacy. Behind us as we come in is the most complete panel, *martyrdom of St Barbara, and St Anthony of Padua,* by Bartolomeo di Tommaso (first half of the fifteenth century), a Foligno artist whose work has a Sienese intimacy of observation: St Barbara's dress is unruffled though she is being pulled by the hair. On the left of this is the faded glory of a *Crucifixion with angels and saints* by Pietro Mazzaforte, another Foligno artist who lived towards the end of the fifteenth century, and the teacher of Nicolò Alunno.

In Room 2 there is the more delicate and intricate work—we approach the High Renaissance here—of Pier Antonio Mezzastris: more or less contemporary with Nicolò Alunno, and like him born in

Foligno. He was the pupil of Benozzo Gozzoli, and his *Madonna with Child, angels and saints* is stylized and delicately designed. But his *coronation of the Virgin* is especially lovely: an angel gently lowers the crown to Mary's head and the expressions of face are very pleasing —damaged at the top left. The *Crucifixion with angels and saints* (1470) behind us is unfeeling and trite, but the *Madonna and Child with saints* next to it has a faded glow reminiscent of Gozzoli. *The Angel of the Annunciation* by the door that leads to the next room is attributed by some people to Gozzoli but the canvas has barely survived.

In Room 3 among some coarse frescoes the *Madonna and saints* facing us as we come in, by Feliciano de' Muti (1473-1518), also a Foligno artist, is distinct, though we are already moving towards the baroque, with its suggestion of melancholy and brooding. Room 4 has a *martyrdom of St Catherine* by Dono Doni in a special niche, and here we have the observation of life as an end in itself, the beginning of the 'picture' in our sense, a photograph. On the left as we enter there is a vivid *Madonna and angels*, in bright blood-reds, by Bernardino di Mariotto, a Perugian artist who lived in the middle of the sixteenth century. We should note the frieze in this room, in the style of the Umbrian mannerist school, from the sixteenth century. Should we be interested in a glimpse of the sculptor's workshop, Room 5 has a plaster model of the seated statue of St Felician which we saw in Foligno's cathedral. Rooms 6 and 7 consist of awkward baroque pieces—the first of these two rooms has the most inept *Annunciation* ever painted: the angel has a drinker's nose and holds his lilies like a rifle; God looks drunk too.

Leaving the courtyard below again we turn right along the Via Antonio Gramsci, a narrow street with palazzi on either side: one of these, No. 22, the **Palazzo Deli** (at one time Nuti) incorporates a mediaeval tower and is said to have been designed by the Florentine Baccio d'Agnolo (1462-1543): it has a carved wooden door whose panels show lions, eagles, tiny lizards and what seem to be fauns' heads with their tongues out. Farther along at No. 53 we shall notice the frieze running under the roof, a splendid decoration that indicates the prosperity of the town at that time: we can also glimpse the rather frigid neo-classical courtyard inside. Narrow lanes lead from this street on either side, with little bridges joining the houses overhead. With such straight clean streets the country is never far away, and this essentially ancient form is quite distinct from the curved, crowded arrangements of the Middle Ages, when people were threatened and insecure, needing the intimate camouflage of poky lanes. In Foligno today, by the way, the horse-carriage and bicycle are still seen, and even the central square is sometimes free of cars.

We continue along the Via Antonio Gramsci until we come to a widening in the road, Via Frezzi, where a long Renascence palazzo on the right with two balconies and great doors now houses some municipal offices. At the end of this palazzo we turn sharp left into the spacious Piazza S. Domenico with trees in the centre, where we shall be struck most by the squat Romanesque church that lies on the farther side, called S. Maria Infraportas, while immediately on our right as we enter the square there is the tall ex-church of S. Domenico (1251), now a gymnasium.

S. Maria Infraportas, sunk under the present level of the square, has four stout pillars forming a small porch at the entrance (eleventh- and twelfth-century, but restored since), and beyond it, above, we see its bell-tower in the local sand-coloured stone. Inside, there is a simple three-naved church with a curved, unbeamed ceiling, and the rectangular columns that divide the naves on either side rise to join each other in vast Romanesque arches, with the exception of one Gothic arch. The ceilings of the side-naves were added in the fifteenth century and are formed in vaults with crossing ribs. On the columns there are a number of frescoes, in faded patches.

In the right nave as we walk down the church we see three niches containing first a *Crucifixion* attributed to Pier Antonio Mezzastris, then a copy of this dated 1525 by a local artist, and thirdly a more relaxed and intimate work of the same subject which shows Sienese influences. On the second column down there is a *Christ bearing the cross*, with something bland about it and perhaps a Gozzoli touch. On the third column there is a bas-relief in brown stone showing a calf or bull dancing on stones, with an inscription underneath, perhaps of pagan origin, perhaps the arms or sign of a local guild. On the wall just to the right of the presbytery as we look towards the high altar there is *St Jerome and two angels* (they are crowning him) by Pier Antonio Mezzastris. On the left of the high altar itself we find a tabernacle for holy oil set in the wall, with fluted columns forming a neo-classical front and a framed doorway in miniature, done in the style of the Lombardian school at the beginning of the sixteenth century. On both sides of the archway in the left nave close to the presbytery there is *St Roch*; the more serious of these is by Mezzastris. On the same column but on the reverse side there is a stone bas-relief to match the one we saw in the right nave, again with a Latin inscription: this time a monk lying on a couch, perhaps a memorial stone. On the wall of this nave we pass a particularly fine and boldly designed *Madonna and Child and St John* by Ugolino di Gisberto (1500), who rarely achieves this standard.

If we now go back to the entrance, remaining in the left nave, we shall pass through a very narrow archway into the Cappella di San Pietro: it is a very dim room but slowly our eyes will accustom themselves to the darkness and find a magnificent decoration frescoed behind the altar in the form of a tapestry with six rampant lions inside medallions, in the Byzantine style, and above this *Christ blessing* (in the Greek manner) *between SS. Peter and Paul*. In the right wall we see two windows: inside the arch of that nearest the entrance there is a fresco, very much damaged, in the Byzantine tradition from the second half of the twelfth century, with the scene of *the Archangel Gabriel and Dismas the good thief*, though this is now indecipherable. This chapel is perhaps the oldest religious construction in Foligno; seventh- or eighth-century, some say earlier.

If we now return to the Via Antonio Gramsci by which we came we shall find at the second turning on the left a narrow lane called Via della Scuola d'Arti e Mestieri: in the first tiny square we come to we find the disused church of S. Tomaso dei Cipischi on the left, built in 1190. Farther on, we come into a larger square with the church of **S. Nicolò** on the left, a fourteenth-century building, though the doorway was put there two hundred years later. The second chapel on the right has a splendidly decorative *polittico* in an elaborate gilt frame showing the *Nativity, Resurrection* and *saints*, by Nicolò Alunno (1492), without much feeling. (Its predella, with *five scenes from the Passion*, is in the Louvre in Paris.) It is impossible to imagine from this stylized mute piece, where every gesture is rehearsed, that it deals with a birth, let alone Christ's. The chapel on the right of the high altar as we face it has a *coronation of the Virgin and SS. Anthony the Abbot and Bernardine* behind its altar, also by Nicolò Alunno: Christ and Mary are inside a wreath formed by little putti, delicate and thorough, but the two saints below are insipid.

The sacristy leads off from this chapel by a doorway in the right

Right: Calendimaggio, Assisi's May Day holiday, divides the town again into its mediaeval 'upper' and 'lower' parts. Here the banner of the upper town leaves the duomo for the main square.

Below: Heralds of the town hall trumpet its approach.

Above: The Refectory of San Damiano, St Clare's convent. The oak tables and benches are original. Clare's place in the right-hand corner is marked by a bowl of flowers. *Below:* The squat, austere front of S. Silvestro (1195) in Bevagna's main square. The fountain is 700 years younger than the church.

wall, and here we shall find an inlaid wooden wardrobe with tiny frescoes painted by one of Alunno's pupils. Above the entrance door there is a *Madonna and Child* by Luca di Tomme (he died in 1381), with a light, Sienese touch.

We leave the square by a lane that goes right of the church, called Via Mezzalancia, still cobbled. The lane narrows to less than two yards at one point. Then we come out into the Piazza XX Settembre, where we see the great Palazzo Barnabò from the seventeenth century. We take the road left of this palazzo without actually entering the square—the Via S. Giovanni dell' Acqua, its name due to the fourteenth-century church almost opposite No. 14. Here on the left there is a bridge of Roman origin over a canal running into the former bed of the river Topino. These are the pleasant, drowsy outskirts of Foligno, from which we can see the surrounding hills.

At the end of this road is the shell of the ex-church of S. Claudio, built about 1240, its façade half broken down, and partly absorbed into a house. Here we turn right into the Via Franco Ciri, and as we walk at the side of the cheerful, swift river we see the *Sasso di Pale* in the distance before us, a hill nearly three thousand feet high. At the bridge (by which traffic from the north enters) we turn right along the Via XX Settembre: where this widens after a few yards into a square (Piazza S. Giacomo) we find on the left the pink and white façade of the church of the same name: this too is only half a façade, the rest brickwork; an unusual feature is the Gothic arch of its doorway, which takes up the entire lower half. This was built in 1402. Inside, we find a frigid neo-classical form from the eighteenth century—apart from the presbytery which has extravagant gilt and fluted pillars and a cupola with a frieze. The pillars are actually carved wood, a massive work of craftsmanship by Giacomo Grampini. At the first side-altar on the left there is a framed banner showing *St Roch* by local artists in the manner of Nicolò Alunno (1460): there is a classical care here which has overshadowed care for the subject, and so there is no feeling.

Il Trivio—Perugino in the church of the Nunziatella—Convent of S. Anna

Taking the central Piazza della Repubblica once more as our starting-point we walk through the Largo Carducci, at the corner of the duomo, and turn left at the cross-roads a little farther on (known locally as *Il Trivio*, the meeting-place of three roads). This brings us into the Via Garibaldi—the shops and cinemas and markets are in this area. If we turn left for a moment opposite No. 34 we shall find ourselves in a web of narrow cobbled side-streets of mediaeval origin, with the **Chiesa della Nunziatella** (1494) on the left corner of a small square. It is a cold Renascence church, more like an oratory, divided into two parts by iron gates, with two altars. The altar on the left has a rich tabernacle by Lattanzio di Nicolò, with a *Madonna* fresco, and in a niche above the other altar there are *the baptism of Jesus* and *the Eternal Father* (in the lunette), both by Perugino (1507).

Continuing along the Via Garibaldi we reach a piazza of the same name where, on the left, in an intimate little corner, the church of **S. Salvatore** stands with its long façade of red and white stone of excellent proportion, from the fourteenth century. The middle door is set into the wall with six slender half-pillars under capitals, in the Gothic form. And there are three small rose windows of very simple design—which have clearly been restored in the light of another mentality (1889). Behind rises the tower, of the same epoch, with a spire. Inside, we find another product of the eighteenth century minus the extravagance: the surfaces are flat and whitewashed— there simply wasn't the money to lavish. To make it gayer red drapes have been hung on the pillars. At the second pillar down on the left there is a glass compartment (a light-switch on the pillar) containing a *Madonna and Child* from the fifteenth century which is worth a glance for the fleeting look on the Virgin's face: the Child is old and ugly. But if we move on we are compensated by a ravishing six- teenth-century tapestry that covers the back of the apse: this is a Flemish work, worn and fading, but its quiet, green splendour still lingers, showing scenes from the Old Testament.

Opposite this church, with two enormous dirty statues in niches, is the church of **S. Agostino,** an even more thorough work of eighteenth-century re-building. But this one has a spectacle—the glittering construction at the back of the altar, and also what must be the biggest picture-frame ever made for the most ineptly vulgar *Madonna and Child* ever painted. The organ balconies on either side are in a quieter and more pleasing baroque: in any case, the baroque rightly belongs to organ-lofts and galleries.

We return down the Via Garibaldi and turn left where it opens into the Via Umberto I, and after two or three hundred yards we reach a narrow lane called Via dei Monasteri: at No. 44 of this lane we find a courtyard with two young trees—a convent school for girls, **S. Anna**—with a delicate, dreaming fresco over the door, a typical work of Pier Antonio Mezzastris, *Madonna with Child, angels and two saints*. In the closed courtyard beyond this door (a ring at the bell will bring a nun) we find frescoes in the same green distemper we have seen in Assisi at S. Francescuccio, as finely traced as a veil. These are *twenty evangelical stories*, attributed to two artists, Lattanzio di Nicolò and Feliciano de' Muti (1518). The scenes are quiet and graceful, and the green is especially suitable for conveying an impression of delicacy.

In the second cloister up the steps there are frescoes showing *St Francis receiving the stigmata*, attributed to Mezzastris but to my mind rough and coarse and not up to his mark. In the Refectory there are four large frescoes (just before the door a *Crucifixion* shows signs of Nicolò Alunno or his school): on the left as we go in *the wedding at Cana*, and along the right wall *the Last Supper* and *Jesus and the apostles at the house of Martha*, and on the end wall *Martha cooking*: they remain in a private setting (children mill round us or sit at table eating) exactly as they have been since they were painted towards the end of the fifteenth century. They are in the manner of Nelli, and a grave and mellow stillness pervades them, with something rustic and unsure in the execution. The nun may also want us to pay our respects to the little chapel of the Beata Angelina, but there is nothing to keep us here. Until 1798 the famous *Madonna of Foligno* by Raphael was here: the French troops of that time stole it, but it was given back in 1816. Then the Vatican stole it and, unlike the French, they never returned it. In 1656 Christina of Sweden tried to buy it on a visit to the convent but the abbess told her, '*Se ad altre simiglianti profferte avessero in addietro aderito le religiose, non avremmo ora noi l'invidiabil fortuna di godere della presenza di V.M.*'; that is, 'If the nuns had accepted similar offers in the past we would not now have the enviable pleasure of Your Majesty's presence'—which must be one of the most flattering refusals ever made.

Near Foligno—S. Giovanni Profiamma

If we leave Foligno by the northern gate (Porta di Firenze) and turn right, an immediate tourist sign will indicate the way to the church of S. Giovanni Profiamma, four kilometres from town. The village is now a few straggling houses and we come to the little church (1239) after we have passed them. It is built in simple Subasian pink stone blocks with one rose window over a portal arch: and the arch has symbolic figures on either side carved by a certain Maestro Filippo. We know his name because the right-hand figure (spiking a dragon and holding a book marked *Pax Vobis*) bears the words '*Filipo me fec*—Philip made me.' In the other little relief the figure is battling with the dragon before the actual kill. Maestro Filippo also left work at Ancona.

S. Giovanni Profiamma derives its name not from anything to do with flames but from the Roman town out of whose materials it is made: Forum Flaminii (founded by the consul Flaminius whom Hannibal routed at Lake Trasimene) became corrupted into Forfiamma, which then became—perhaps in an attempt to make it sound authentic Latin—Profiamma. Inside, we find a tall, slim little church of one nave, with thirteen steps leading up to the chancel where most of the functions take place (the congregation sits in the transepts). On the right wall over a doorway there are the remains of a very early altar screen, with a lightly carved design of knots on either side of a cross, comparable to a screen we may have seen at the church-museum in S. Maria degli Angeli in Assisi and also symbolizing the Eucharist, of eighth- or ninth-century origin.

We walk up the chancel steps, an intimate arched area which is virtually another tiny church. The altar-table is supported by a broken ancient pillar of granite, and the canopy (another reminder of the altar screen at S. Maria degli Angeli) is engraved with the motif of the Eucharist, birds eating from the Tree of Life which issues from the cross. The crypt can be entered below the chancel steps on either side, and is the oldest part of the church, with low vaults and six squat pillars, perhaps a first nucleus of the present church, from the tenth century.

This visit is best made as part of a walk in the lazy hours of the afternoon: little traffic will worry us and the valley is green and leafy, with plenty of shade.

S. Maria in Campis—frescoes recently brought to light (Alunno's first work)

Two kilometres from Foligno, more or less in the middle of an ugly industrial suburb, we shall find some unexpected frescoes at a church called **S. Maria in Campis,** or St Mary's in the Fields. This time we leave by the southern gate—Porta Romana—as if towards Spoleto, and after about two hundred yards a yellow tourist sign points ambiguously in the air but intends us to turn sharp left along a wide gravelled road, then right with this road after a level crossing, so as to travel away from the railway. This will bring us directly to a neat little courtyard with the church facing us. It is probably Foligno's oldest church: some even place its origin in the third century. It dates from at least the eleventh century.

It lies on the site of the original Roman Foligno (Fulginiae), and radiographic pictures of the area show many Roman buildings waiting to be unearthed. The church was partly destroyed in the 1832 earthquake and put together again rather badly: and there was more damage in the last war, making the hideous modernization of its interior possible. But some recent work has brought to light hidden frescoes, apart from those which had survived the restorations.

At the first chapel in the left nave there is a *Crucifixion* on the right wall (behind the altar) and opposite it (above) an *Annunciation* of Pier Antonio Mezzastris: on the other wall *the ship of St Peter*, an imitation of Giotto's *Navicella*, is partly by Mezzastris but mostly by a pupil of Benozzo Gozzoli. There is also a *St Lucy* and a *St Helen* which show Sienese influences. Outside this chapel, on the pilaster between the arches, there is a *St Roch* by Nicolò Alunno, discovered only four years ago. And in the corner by the entrance there is a *St Anthony the Abbot*, again by Alunno, dated 1482. At the next chapel down, on the left wall, we see small panels from the late fourteenth century which show *the story of St Anthony the Abbot*: the large St Anthony on the throne in the middle has two tiny figures close by, said to be portraits of the people who commissioned the frescoes.

The same chapel has a *Crucifixion* in the Giotto manner, and there are faded *evangelists* in the ceiling, in four sections.

At the third chapel down, still in the left nave, there is a small fragment of a fifteenth-century fresco, unrestored, which is all that remains of the past among modern frescoes with their staggering wanton vulgarity and slackness: the priests who uncover the old frescoes (and usually an enterprising priest is responsible) do it more for the history than the art. This chapel, by the way, was originally closed off from the church, perhaps as a cremation room: the fragment of fifteenth-century fresco here is stained black with smoke (Chapel of St Anthony of Padua). Nothing old is hidden under the new frescoes, by the way. The chapel on the left of the presbytery has a heavily restored ceiling showing *doctors of the Church in dispute*. These and a fragment (*Ascension?*) on the right wall are certainly by Ottaviano Nelli, but it is difficult to see this because of the restoration which has even changed details. The ugly seventeenth-century *Last Supper* on the left wall hides intact Ottaviano Nelli frescoes which will be worth uncovering one day. The *two saints* behind the altar were also by Ottaviano Nelli. Farther left in a chapel under the tower (it used to be the sacristy) more frescoes were brought to light in 1959: they were an important discovery because the *Crucifixion* (1458) is the first undoubted work of Nicolò Alunno. Most of the other frescoes by the same hand treat *the life of St Thomas*. The *Annunciation* on the left wall above (cited by Berenson) seems different from the other panels but this is put down to the artist being only eighteen years old. The chapel was painted earlier with the story of St Martha, and perhaps Alunno was taken by certain of its pieces and included one in his *Annunciation*. A little piece showing a child, between this chapel and the organ pipes on the left wall, is sometimes attributed to Perugino and at other times to Pintoricchio.

On the wall of the right-hand nave there are fragments of a *Crucifixion*, also by Ottaviano Nelli: a little farther down another fresco, much fainter, was discovered in recent months, perhaps by the teacher of both Nicolò Alunno and Mezzastris—Caporali. The cloister has further careless sketch-work by a contemporary which makes it an eyesore: they say that to get a commission from the Church nowadays you have to be pretty bad; an exception to this is the new door of the Orvieto cathedral by Emilio Greco (see p. 310): but then they haven't dared to install it yet.

The Benedictine Abbey of Sassovivo

A short trip by car or a longish walk will bring us to the **Abbey of Sassovivo,** founded about the year 1070 and always open to the public: the silence alone makes it worth a visit. We should take the road to Macerata and after a kilometre or so turn right (a yellow tourist sign) and continue for another four kilometres until we find a bridge and a second tourist sign. The abbey was a famous centre of scholarship in the Middle Ages but went into decadence in the late fifteenth century: it is now a holiday place for ordinands and priests, known among them as 'Villa del Seminario'. Its position is quite isolated, locked among wooded hills: we may have to look for the custodian, and the most likely place is the adjacent farmhouse. She will point out to us the fossil of a gigantic snail embedded in the stone leading up to the abbey entrance. An air of scholarship—a memory—lingers round the place. And we enter the most elegant little cloister we shall see in Umbria, with slender pillars all round in sets of two. It is the work of Pietro de Maria, a Roman (1229). On the left wall as we enter the inner court we see an inscription with the name of the abbot and the architect at the time of the building, together with the date. The cloister has one hundred and twenty-eight little pillars, supporting fifty-eight arches. There is a classical cornice above with two strips of mosaic, mostly ruined: and each piece of mosaic has a distinct design different from its neighbour. The orange-brick building overlooking the side by which we entered contains rooms for the priests and has tiny Gothic arches and pillars set in its wall, a miniature terra-cotta colonnade put there in 1314. The well in the middle of the cloister is from 1340 (restored 1623).

CHAPTER 10

The Road to Tuscany

Città di Castello

The valley between Assisi and Città di Castello—the road to Tuscany—is winding and intimate, with low hills on either side and
secluded, wooded corners, vineyards, olive groves and single farm-
houses tucked cosily among trees. In fact, the nearer we approach
Tuscany the more Tuscan the landscape becomes, and the spacious
Umbrian country with its yawning sky is left behind us. We shall
find a difference in the accents, too: the Umbrian is rather sung,
questions have an upward lilt, with the words run together in a way
suggesting real family concern; the Tuscan is distinct and lighter,
perhaps gayer, but cutting, clear-sighted, declaimed. Especially in
Città di Castello, our farewell to Umbria, we shall hear them
mixed.

*Città di Castello—a Pintoricchio and the Byzantine treasures of Canóscio—
Pinacoteca (Sienese and Florentine artists, and more Signorelli)*

Città di Castello lies in the plains of the Tiberina valley, flat and
harmonious and bright, with wide streets on the outskirts and many
trees lining them. Buses drop us at the Piazza Garibaldi, and if we
are driving from Perugia or Assisi we arrive at the same point: the
piazza lies left of the road we enter by, beyond a lawned roundabout.

The town was the Umbrian settlement of Tifernum, later called
Tiberinum by the Romans. Pliny the Younger had a villa on the
outskirts: he was made a patron of the city and ordered a temple to
be built. It was therefore quite a prominent town. Its conversion to
Christianity came about early, through the Roman legionary
Crescentius, later made a saint. Tradition says that after being
destroyed by Totila and flourishing again under a bishop Florido,

232

the town was named Castrum Felicitatis, the 'castle of happiness', but this may be a piece of Church romanticism (or plain fiddling with the facts). After the tenth century the name Civitas Castelli prevailed, and that is virtually the name we have today. It was alternately under Perugia and Florence, as we would expect from its tenuous position on the border between the two provinces, but in 1422 Braccio Fortebraccio took it. Then it went from one family to another in the usual way until it fell into the permanent—or for those days permanent—embrace of the Vitelli family at the end of the fifteenth century: their grand but not pretty houses are dotted all over the town. Even when it was under Church rule they continued to exercise the real authority—a rare example of inherited skill and tolerance, and administrative care: perhaps this accounts for the town's happy aspect.

For those travelling from the north it is an excellent introduction to Umbria: not yet the mystical Umbria we come to know, but with the lightness of Tuscany, a relic perhaps of Florentine rule. We frequently hear the Tuscan *diamine!* (usually translated as 'the deuce!'). But there is the Umbrian sweetness and reflectiveness as well.

As we enter the long Piazza Garibaldi we have the biggest of the Vitelli mansions on our right (1540), a rather plain affair. The last private owner was the Princess Buoncompagni, who then gave it to the Church. Walking into the town we take the left of the two narrow streets offered us, the Via Mazzini, and come in to the grand central square, Piazza Giacomo Matteotti, which has all the echoing bustle of the old Italy, hugged round with shops and bars and kiosks. Farther down on the right we find another palazzo belonging to the Vitelli family, as undistinguished as the first, with the Palazzo del Governo (now the Prefecture and formerly the Palazzo del Podestà) facing us at the lower end of the square, its baroque façade capped by a little open bell-tower (minus its bell), dated 1686. We walk across to the right side of this façade (Via Cavour) and see that in fact it is a much older building, a vast one, perhaps the work of Angelo da Orvieto (he died in 1352); the top windows of its side-wall are set together in pairs under Romanesque arches, and slim pillars divide them; at street level the tall Gothic arches are mostly filled with shop-windows now. The wall is in a bad state but where it has been repaired we see how clean and glittering the original must have been.

233

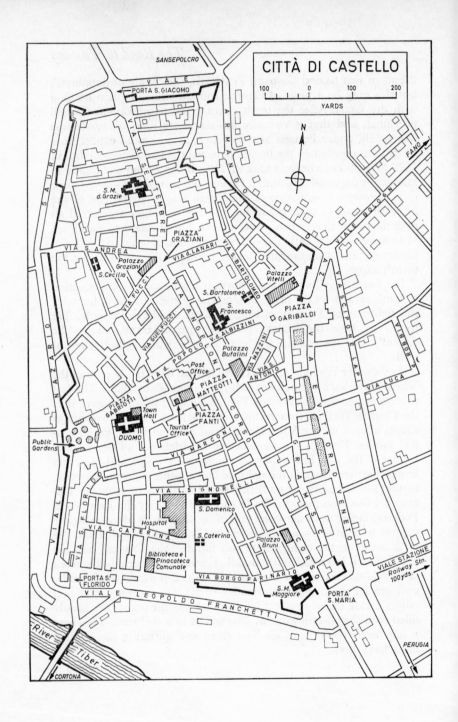

This little street, Via Cavour, has a certain excitement, with its tall shop-fronts and new cobbles and the long indoor market. If we continue to its end we shall find (with a glimpse of country beyond) an irregular square with large paving stones, Piazza Venanzio Gabriotti (he was a partisan in the last war, shot by the Nazis), with the massive **Palazzo Comunale** immediately on our left, the work again of Angelo da Orvieto, who incidentally took twenty years over it. From where we stand we should look back to the Via Cavour and notice the bridge crossing it overhead, from the fourteenth century; it unites the town hall with the houses opposite. The vestibule of the town hall is rather striking, with two great pillars supporting Gothic vaults and a wide staircase. If we are interested in Roman inscriptions we shall find many upstairs on the first floor (Sala Maggiore). There is also a set of iron measures once used for local markets—a *piede* or foot, *braccio* or arm's length.

Opposite the town hall there is perhaps the tallest and slimmest tower we shall ever see in Umbria, the *torre comunale*, really part of the town hall though physically separate. It sits on a side of the bishop's palace, which is of much later origin. There is a dilapidated iron sunshade running along this palace over the shop-fronts, another reminder of the old Italy.

If we walk along the left side of the square we shall find, just beyond the town hall but drawn back behind its own balustrade formed by two stone staircases, the **Duomo,** with its sombre and unadorned front. The portal is its last remaining glory. This is actually the side, the only survival of a fourteenth-century reconstruction: the subtle carvings at the borders of the doorway show *the life of Mary* in two or three scenes, framed with vine branches and clusters of grapes, and figures of *Justice, Charity* and various putti. When we walk round to the actual front we see a very heavy, unfinished affair of 1632: the exposed brickwork above—the unfinished part—looks pleasanter than the wasted grandeur below.

Inside, we have one vast nave, a Renascence mausoleum, completely open in the Latin cross form. The roof has massive compartments of painted wood with rosettes in the centre, from the eighteenth century. Its saving grace is simplicity, with imitated Corinthian columns set in the wall on each side to form great arches. The cupola was redone in 1789. The presbytery has a splendid openness and calm, with its rectangular form.

We should go to the **museum** in the sacristy, in the right transept (a curtained doorway): we may have to look for the attendant.
He will show us to the end room where there is a Pintoricchio, a
Madonna and Child and infant St John on the right wall, dirty but tender
and even clear in its darkness. On the left of the doorway here we
find a Francesco da Castello, imitating Raphael. And then we come
to one of the most precious collections in Italy: this **treasure of
Canóscio**, a collection of silver chalices, with a sixteenth-century
cross of agate, was found in 1934 and taken first to Perugia and then
to Rome, but in 1938 it was returned to Città di Castello by the
personal order of Mussolini, to whom the bishop had applied. It
is one of the most precious Byzantine treasures in existence: most of
it was made in the sixth century in Constantinople. The pieces were
found by accident near the sanctuary of Canóscio, a local centre of
pilgrimage. Also in this room there is a rare fourteenth-century
bishop's pastoral staff, in the Tuscan style. There is a famous *paliotto*,
or altar frontal, made of gilded silver, a great tablet worked in
bas-relief showing *Christ blessing*, with *symbols of the evangelists*, an
Annunciation, a *Visitation* and a *Nativity*, an *Epiphany* and *presentation
in the Temple, flight into Egypt, Betrayal, Crucifixion*, and *three saints*,
a work of the twelfth century perhaps given to the duomo by Pope
Celestine II who was born here. It is all a dazzling collection and,
because so precious, rather sickening and claustrophobic, like a
jeweller's shop. If we leave the church by the sacristy entrance we
shall be able to look up at the immense round twelfth-century tower,
one hundred and fifty feet high.

Opposite the duomo's façade we see the 'public gardens', which
are no more than a bit of lawn and gravel. They were planted this
century and sit on part of the town's fortifications: the statue is of
King Victor Emmanuel II. Looking from the parapet we see, far to
the right, Mount Averna, where St Francis spent the grand climax
of his life.

We walk with the duomo's façade on our left along the narrow
and cobbled Via Pendinella and cross over to the Via dei Casceri.
At the Via dei Cavalieri we turn left: here is another straight and
narrow street, arguing a town plan conceived on the ancient Roman
model like Foligno, and perhaps for the same reason, that the town
was converted very early, so that ancient civic habits continued
easily into the Christian epoch. We cross a street into Via Luca
Signorelli and continue along it until we come to the vast church of

S. Domenico, built in 1424, with towering plain walls and tall windows. We can enter at the side-door (a dreadful fresco in the lunette), and find an immense bare hall with no naves or transepts and only a shallow presbytery. Various frescoes have been recovered from the stucco. On the right, starting at the back of the church, we find a lovely fragment where a German has scratched a prayer on the Madonna's cheek: '*Sancta Anna hilff selb . . .*' ('St Anne, help me . . .') is all I can read. About half-way down the right wall we come to a large *Crucifixion*, an *Annunciation* and *saints* of an unusually strange and stirring vigour and earnestness, from the early fifteenth century. In the chapel following this there is a Giottoesque *Crucifixion* at the altar. For lovers of carved wood the choir here is the work of a Florentine artist (1435).

On the opposite wall, as we return back down the church, the *Nativity* at the side-door is by a sincere, awkward hand in the Sienese style, followed by a *St Anthony the Abbot* attributed to Antonio da Ferrara (died 1449), with *scenes from his life*. And lastly there is a faint, gentle and loving *saint receiving the stigmata* from a winged-crucified figure in the sky, as in Lorenzetti's picture of the same subject (and many followers since).

We go to the façade of S. Domenico and take the street in which it lies, the Via Mons. Giovanni Muzi, with the town hospital on our right. At the edge of the town a fragment of the old town wall, pierced by a low arch, faces us and here we turn right. The decorated walls (designs of fountains and putti and birds and flowers) of the **Palazzo Vitelli alla Cannoniera** are now before us. This was the house in which the Vitelli family kept their armoury and guard. We pass what clearly used to be the stables, and a quadrangle where the guard was mounted, then come to a low-slung *cavalcavia* joining two wings of the palace (through a hole in which one of the Vitelli women used to throw young men after she had slept with them). Immediately after we have passed under this we turn into the cobbled Via della Cannoniera. A short ramp leads us up to the entrance of the **picture gallery**—a most important one, perhaps the best Umbrian collection outside Perugia—open all day. Thus it is actually in the Vitelli palace: an antiquarian bought the palace in 1912 and restored it from its last previous existence as a granary, then it passed to the town. After ringing the bell for the attendant we enter a dark entrance court with a Roman sarcophagus, its bas-relief showing a Bacchanalia, with a satyr in the middle. Opposite it, in stone, there is another bas-relief from the thirteenth or fourteenth century, in two panels, *the temptation of St Anthony*.

Upstairs in Room I we see a marble bas-relief of Sienese origin by Sano di Giovanni da Siena (1356). Going along the left wall, clockwise, No. 1 is a *Madonna and Child* against a background of gold, a still and calm work, with a northern touch, intricately designed, by Neri di Bicci (1419-91). No. 2 is a Bartolo di Fredi, a sweet and assured *Madonna and Child*, one of his loveliest. Then comes (3) a triptych by Antonio da Ferrara, *Madonna and Child and two saints*, followed by a case (4) that contains a reliquary of gilded silver (temporarily away for restoration). There is then (5) another *Madonna and Child* by Spinello Aretino (1346-1410), which has a Sienese touch. No. 6, a big panel, is a marvellously rapt and grave piece of work where the Virgin sits tall and imposing in a long gold-threaded cloak of blue, with angels on either side of her throne. It is not known who did this but some suppose Duccio di Buoninsegna; others call him '*Maestro di Città di Castello*', which is cheating. No. 7 is a bright, golden and luxurious *Madonna and Child* by Antonio Vivarini and Giovanni d'Alemagna, fifteenth-century. No. 8, a triptych by Pietro Donnini of the Florentine school, fifteenth-century. No. 9, a larger triptych from the Umbrian school (1417), a luscious piece of local, rustic origin.

In Room 2 (Sala di Luca Signorelli) there is an *Eternal Father* of Signorelli's school on our left as we enter, and facing us a *martyrdom of St Sebastian*. These put Signorelli in the best light possible: we are spared numerous posed figures. Again we notice his stupendous éclat and designing power, with something genuinely deliberate in the expressions of the soldiers. Then there is a framed *Baptist*, one of his earliest works, where innocence struggles with his tendency to too hard and successful a design. And opposite this we see the ornate and hotly crowded *coronation of St Cecilia*. The single *saints* on the wall are also by the Signorelli school.

Room 3 has, facing us as we come in, a much ruined Raphael, *Adam and Crucifixion*. And on the right wall there is a Ghirlandaio (Domenico), *coronation of the Virgin*, which has openness and candour: the Virgin is a blonde girl with plaited hair. The *head of Christ* has been attributed to followers of Piero della Francesca, and to the Flemish Giusto di Gand (but this was previous to its restoration). Room 4 has frescoes from the fifteenth century, except for the one over the fireplace which is clearly Giottoesque. The spacious loggia beyond it, which looks across roof-tops to the country, has two large enamelled bas-reliefs by della Robbia (Giovanni and Andrea), a *Nativity* and *adoration of the Virgin*.

Room 5 has a tall *Annunciation* which shows clear signs of Perugino in its summery ease—by Francesco Tifernate, sometimes called Francesco di Città di Castello. Room 6 (Sala delle Armi) has large baroque pieces of no great interest; a frieze runs all round the dado with a design of helmets and spears. Room 7 is a simple sitting-room.

We then come to the bridge over the road from which Laura, a sixteenth-century daughter of the Vitelli family, signalled to young men below: we see the window where it was done. The hole through which she threw them after their last love-affair is said to be under the floor's tiles. Room 8 has mediocre work and Room 9 (Sala di festa) has delicate little frescoes which belong to the building and were done at the time of construction. When we leave this long room and return downstairs we should notice in a lunette over the well of the stairs a fresco in which Laura Vitelli figures—riding a young man on all fours as if he were a horse. The roof over this staircase fell in during the 1790 earthquake, and used to have other frescoes. The lower part of the staircase has the Vitelli arms overhead (a calf, that is *vitello*, sitting on the crescent moon) with figures representing the various arts. The bust at the bottom is that of the antiquarian who bought the palazzo at the beginning of this century.

CHAPTER 11

Lake Trasimene and Città della Pieve

Lake Trasimene and District

Coming from Perugia along the road to Arezzo we first see Lake Trasimene from high above, a vast blue expanse with yellow waves of reeds at its edge, the hills smoky beyond and almost fading into the sky. If we are looking for a meal, we should turn left at the signpost for Monte del Lago: the lakeside hotel serves good food and excellent foreign wines, though its standard was higher some years ago before it hit prosperity (their Alsatian Riesling is worth trying). There is bathing just below.

Should we be approaching the lake from the Autostrada del Sole or Chiusi we pass through some of the grandest country in Umbria. Then the lake appears to us in a great placid, shallow-looking basin, blue at first and a light aquamarine beyond.

Lake Trasimene is also called the Lake of Perugia, being the city's favourite resort. It is the biggest stretch of inland water in the Italian peninsula proper (that is, excluding Alpine Italy), only a little smaller than Lake Como and the fourth largest lake in the whole of Italy. Its origin is a river, though the source may be partly a spring too. There are one hundred and twenty-eight square kilometres of it, but surprisingly it is not much more than twenty feet deep. This makes it no less dangerous than the deeper lakes: the hardiest swimmers fear its currents, which can be treacherous on calm, sunny days as well as on stormy ones.

No approach to the lake is mediocre: we shall always get a stirring first glimpse. But on a dull day Trasimene broods forbiddingly, like its brothers Bracciano and Albano near Rome. The lake has an underground outlet dug by the Romans in the south-east corner and restored by Braccio Fortebraccio in 1421, and again by the pope in 1602. Another outlet was dug in 1896 for irrigation purposes and also to regulate the level of the water. The lake was always a malaria trap—this has helped to keep Italians away since Roman times—but is now of course quite free. The lake can freeze over in parts. The fish are roach, tench, pike, carp and eel.

And of course we know the name from our schooldays, as the scene of an ancient battle that took place in the plain just beyond Passignano, on the northern shore. It was one of the worst defeats the Romans ever had: they were massacred by the Carthaginians, taken completely by surprise in a dawn attack. In the spring of 217 B.C. Hannibal moved his troops out of their winter quarters in the Apennines and camped close to Fiesole, just outside Florence. He then penetrated the Arno valley and passed the Roman camp in such a way as to draw the Romans after him, as if he were making straight for Rome. But instead, after passing Cortona, he sat down on Monte Castelnuovo, before reaching Lake Trasimene: the Roman consul Flaminius followed him carelessly into the plain, watched all the time from above. Before sunrise—it was now towards the end of June—the Romans moved on along the lake's northern shore, though it was very misty: and Hannibal chose this moment to attack from the flank. About sixteen thousand Romans, including the consul himself, were killed. The survivors had no way of escape short of the water and were easily rounded up. A village near by is perhaps called Sanguineto for this reason; and there is an Ossaia (*osso*—'bone').

The lake has three islands. The largest is called **Isola Polvese,** near the southern shore: it was visited by Pope Julius II and in 1643 was sacked by Florentine troops. The so-called Olivetan monks (a Benedictine sect founded in 1313 at Mount Oliveto near Siena) were here until 1832. But few people are left now and it is known chiefly for its hunting possibilities—pheasants and hare and birds.

There are two other islands, **Isola Maggiore** and **Isola Minore.** The Maggiore has the appearance of a prehistoric monster, crowned by the church of S. Michele. Motor-boats leave from Passignano regularly. The island is eight hundred by two hundred yards, and second in size to Polvese. It was the scene of St Francis's long fast: he came in a rowing-boat on February 16th, 1211, and remained on the deserted island until March 20th, in prayer, eating only half a loaf of bread in all that time. He moored up at the Cappella dello Sbarco, as it is called now (the Chapel of Disembarkation). On higher ground a little farther up there is the chapel where he made his hut. A village along the island's west coast is inhabited mostly by fishermen and their families; some of the houses are of fifteenth-century origin. The women work at lace. On the south-east shore is the Villa Isabella, made a Franciscan monastery in 1328 and enlarged in 1480: a pope was one of its guests. The church of S. Michele Arcangelo at the highest point of the island was restored this century, and has various frescoes ranging from the fourteenth to the sixteenth century. A boat leaves this island for Castiglione del Lago quite frequently, so that we can make a complete trip across the lake in half a day or so.

The Minore is private and not visited: it consists mostly of woods, and again is known to hunters.

Boats take about fifteen minutes to reach the Maggiore. There is one round trip a day taking just over two hours. On Sundays and at the height of the season boats leave and return continuously.

Passignano sul Trasimeno is a sweet little resort with several bathing places, beach-cafés and piers. The road that passes through it no longer thunders with trucks as it once did: the Autostrada del Sole absorbs most of the traffic now. From here—we are on the north side of the lake—the islands Maggiore and Minore appear to be one. Passignano almost certainly began life as a fishing village, and was often quarrelled over by Arezzo, Perugia and Florence; when it settled down under Perugia it was quarrelled over by the Oddi and della Corgna families (we shall hear of the latter in Città della Pieve).

Città della Pieve, birthplace of Perugino

For drivers the road from the lake to **Città della Pieve** passes through some luscious countryside: and it is close to the Autostrada del Sole. We find a red-brick town—an unusual sight after so much stone—hugged close together over the wide and steep Chiani valley, at a height of about fifteen hundred feet. Cool breezes sweep through it, and on a fine day it has a clean and sparkling look. We know that it existed in Etruscan times, and in the Middle Ages it was called Castrum, probably little more than a look-out post. Its isolated and unprotected position made it a target for any marauding army that passed by and only when times were more peaceful did it begin to come into history: before, it had to look to its survival. Pope

Clement VII put it under the administration of the Church, and
Clement VIII made it a bishopric and gave it its present name.

The town's unusual red-brick appearance is due to the lack of
stone quarries near by, and the abundance of good clay. The town's
noble families each had their own brick foundry, and what appear
to be blocks of stone on a palace front are usually a stucco design
on brick.

Most people come to Città della Pieve because it was Perugino's
birthplace. And perhaps his most superb work is here. Arriving by
car or bus we come to a little square with trees and a mercifully
simple war-memorial in the middle, called Largo della Vittoria. The
thirteenth-century church of S. Francesco occupies one side of it.
From the railway station we reach the same point by turning left
along a tree-lined avenue before us.

The inside of S. Francesco is of little interest, but on its right,
attached to it, a little door under an archway takes us into an oratory
(we have to ring a bell) where we shall see a large *Crucifixion*: angels
float on either side of the cross, hence the fresco's name, '*Pianto
degli Angeli*—the angels' grief.'

If we walk towards the centre of town—there is no mistaking it—
we shall come into the Piazza Giacomo Matteotti after a few yards,
with the broken brick wall of the fourteenth-century Rocca or
castle on our left, with its three towers. The lane before us is the Via
Vittorio Veneto, which brings us into a third square, Piazza del
Plebiscito. Immediately on our left, occupying the corner nearest
to us as we enter, is Perugino's house, clearly restored, and re-
designed to make way not for any kind of memorial but for new
shops.

At the farthest left corner of the square there is the **Duomo,** its
front a conglomeration of arches, steps and portals, testifying to
many epochs: we enter by the side. The church is twelfth-century in
origin, but as we see in a moment it has been tampered with again
and again, internally and externally, especially in the sixteenth and
seventeenth centuries. But the tower at the church's front with its
simple blocks of stone (the rest of the church is mainly brick) is a
reminder of its first appearance. Inside we find masses of imitation
marble. In the first side-chapel on the right a wooden Christ by a
sixteenth-century German artist gives a weaker impression than it
should, because it is polished. But we are rewarded for our visit by
the Perugino panel behind the main altar, grandly framed, a

243

Madonna and Child and SS. Peter, Paul, Gervase and Protase (1514). There are light-switches left of the altar. The picture has all the spaciousness and untroubled happy light we associate with this painter, an immobility in which objects seem to float and at the same time achieve the utmost movement, but outside ordinary time. The Madonna and Child are contained in a frame of putti, while praying angels float on either side and saints stand below.

On the right of the altar we find a less joyful panel, reflective and sober, with a burdened edge, a *Madonna and Child and SS. John the Baptist and John the Evangelist*. This is less certainly Perugino's work: of course it is by his school and his guiding hand is there, but less proclaimed. At the last chapel on the right as we go out we find another of his works, *the baptism of Jesus*, where the sweet and healthy immobility prevails again, with bare hills along the horizon and a plentiful sky which holds the key to the whole mood of the picture, as always. There are signs of his being helped here, too.

Under the apse of this church, by the way, there are the remains of the church's eleventh-century origins: access to the crypt is outside, at a door in the apse wall.

We may already have noticed, opposite the duomo, the crumbling red-brick front of the Palazzo Mazzuoli, with its stone portal and balcony overhead. It once belonged to the dukes della Corgna, a great family in this town, and was designed by Galeazzo Alessi (1551). If we peep inside the courtyard we shall see a handsome fountain and frescoed ceilings in the archway approaching it, from the seventeenth century: these decorative frescoes continue up the staircase.

We now take the road along the right side of this palace (Via Pietro Vannucci): it curves downhill and one of its surprises is a pavement on either side, perhaps a tribute to Pietro Vannucci or 'Il Perugino'. On the right after about a hundred yards we see the red-brick S. Maria del Bianchi, an oratory where Perugino's resplendent and astonishing *Epiphany* (1504) seems to contain all the virtues of his painting life in one image. In the background we see Lake Trasimene, and among the figures left of the porch (standing close to the pillar) is a portrait of Raphael: next to him (with the bird) is Perugino himself. On the right wall there is a copy in large characters of his letter accepting the commission: '*Caro mio signore, il pittore che io voglio fare nel oratorio dei Disciplinati vorrai al meno due cento cinquanta io come paesano mi contento di 75 fiorini detto contratto mi sto bene me mandi la polizza e quatrini e sara subito fato e la saluto io Pietro pittore dipingo di mano propria questo quadro Feb.* 1504.' There is no more concrete language than Italian: he says that he would like the sum of two hundred and fifty florins but as he is local he will let it go at seventy-five, and to send him the contract and the cash, on which the picture will be done at once, painted with his own hand. On the opposite wall there is a similar, shorter version.

We now go back to the duomo and turn right along the Via Garibaldi. We pass through the Piazza XX Giugno, noting its **Palazzo Farnia** facing us, now the town hall and formerly the property of a branch of the della Corgna family: it holds the town's library and will soon be open to the public. Inside, there are exquisite seventeenth-century door-frames in moulded and painted plaster, and painted bas-relief walls, and decorative frescoes on every inch of the ceiling, and gilded capitals belonging to mock pillars set in the walls, proclaiming the utmost civilization. All this is being restored slowly and carefully by local hands. One of the rooms will contain a copy of Perugino's famous self-portrait, in oil, and a great many of his personal documents.

At the end of the Via Garibaldi, after two or three hundred yards, steps lead us down to a road outside the town wall where we find an undistinguished-looking church called **S. Pietro** (otherwise known as St Anthony the Abbot), where there is another Perugino. The church has its own little balcony giving us a view of the steep and green Chiani valley with its olive groves and sudden wooded rifts, and taller hills behind. The Perugino (behind the altar) appears to be a faded fresco but is actually on canvas, though attached to the wall. Its subject is *St Anthony the Abbot enthroned with SS. Marcellus and Paul the Hermit* (1503). The faded condition gives us little chance to see its spacious qualities, but we realize again the importance of sky and horizon in Perugino's work through its absence here, and there is something awkward about the enthroned figure which suggests a pupil.

When we leave this church we continue along the country road outside the town wall (keeping this on our left as we walk) and after two or three hundred yards we re-enter town and find immediately on our right (next to the hospital) a red-brick church, **S. Maria dei Servi,** usually closed. Should we find it open (it is under very active restoration at the moment) we shall see another Perugino, *Deposition* (1517). The church is a good example of the baroque style, and

sensibly the town has decided to keep it and even restore it, rather
than break it down to reveal bare primitive origins which contain
nothing of great interest. Perugino's picture here is tragically ruined:
the azures and reds have preserved themselves better than in the
town's other Peruginos but much is lost to the damp. Christ's head
as he is lifted down from the cross, just appearing at the edge of a
ruined patch, gives us a glimpse of what we are missing. This road
will lead us back to the square.

CHAPTER 12

Spoleto

On the way—the earliest Christian frescoes—Fonti del Clitunno

On our road from Foligno **Trevi** sits neat and clear-cut on its hill, surrounded by a sea of olive trees (at one time, until the cold snap of 1956, there were over a million of them). A good place for a meal is the 'Cochetto'. If we have time we should see the church of S. Martino, standing in its own grounds just outside the town (frescoes by Lo Spagna, Tiberio d'Assisi and Mezzastris), and the convent of the Madonna delle Lacrime, on the road between Trevi and the superstrada below, for its Perugino frescoes.

We should certainly see the **Tempietto di Clitunno,** about five kilometres beyond Trevi: this 'little temple' looks like a humble version of the Temple of Minerva in Assisi, but though made of Roman materials it was built in the Christian epoch, about five centuries after Christ. It has probably the earliest frescoes to be found in Umbria.

A kilometre beyond this there are the lovely **Fonti del Clitunno** or 'springs', famous in Roman times for their freshness and purity. Here on the banks of the slim river Clitunno the Romans had both a resort and a centre of religious pilgrimage. The god Clitumnus was celebrated for his oracles. The water is less plentiful now, due to an earthquake in the fifth century. (Was the *tempietto* built with the ruins from this?) Propertius, Virgil, Claudius, Pliny the Younger and Byron (*Childe Harold's Pilgrimage*, Canto IV, 66-68) mention it. And Caligula was also there.

Spoleto—a four-legged creature—declining population

If we approach it from the north along the superstrada (or the Flaminian Way) **Spoleto** lies before us like another satisfying picture of the old Italy, compact and unassertive, its clustered brown roofs

247

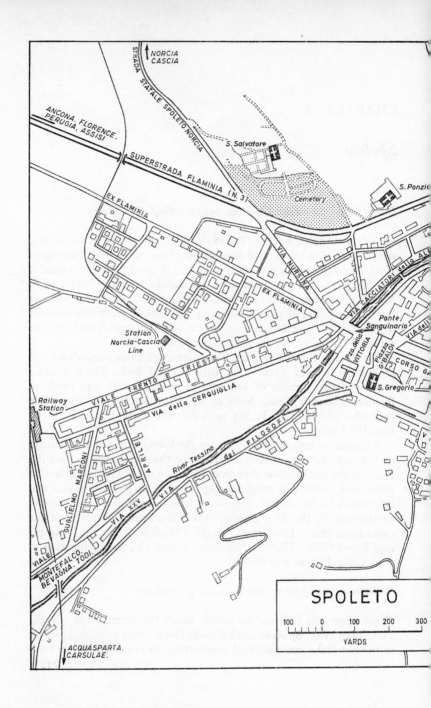

NORCIA
CASCIA

STRADA STATALE SPOLETO NORCIA

ANCONA, FLORENCE,
PERUGIA, ASSISI

SUPERSTRADA FLAMINIA (N.3)

S. Salvatore

Cemetery

S. Ponzic

EX FLAMINIA

VIA NURSINA

EX FLAMINIA

VIA CACCIATORI della ALI

Ponte
Sanguinario

VIA della

Station
Norcia-Cascia
Line

VIALE TRENTO E TRIESTE

VIA della CERQUIGLIA

Pza. della
VITTORIA

Piazza
G. BALDI

CORSO GA

Railway
Station

River Tessino

dei FILOSOFI

S. Gregorio

GUGLIELMO MARCONI

XXV APRILE

VIA XXV

VIA

VIALE

MONTEFALCO,
BEVAGNA, TODI.

ACQUASPARTA,
CARSULAE.

SPOLETO

100   0   100   200   300

YARDS

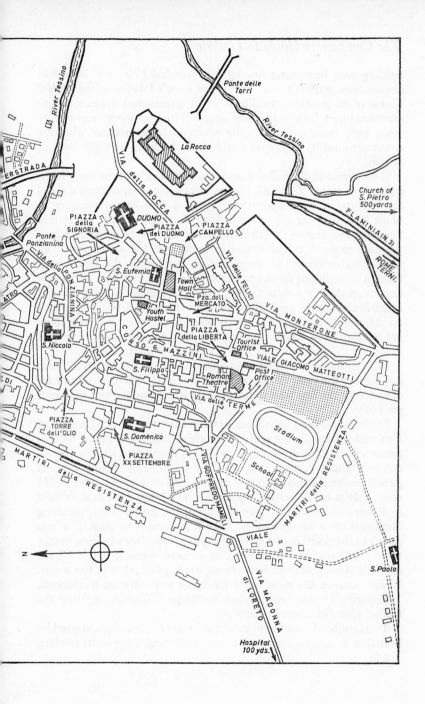

nestling and burrowing among low wooded hills as if they had always been part of them. This is the town's loveliness, the perfect fitness of its position, the fitness of its streets and squares one to another, like a little bland and serene Rome, as Rome was twenty years ago, before it had quite severed its connection with the country round it, when you could smell the fields at night from its centre.

If we arrive at the railway station our first view of the town is the gigantic so-called *Teodelapio* (the name of a sixteenth-century duke of Spoleto) by a contemporary sculptor, a four-legged creature of black iron with an arrow for a head that towers over the station forecourt and frames the whole approach to Spoleto under its legs—the only piece of megalomania to be seen in Umbria, apart from fascist monuments. The megalomania lies less in the figure itself than in its unfitness for the town. It frames our first view of Spoleto and its castle like a dirty factory overhead gallery, a bleak piece of nineteenth-century puritanism plonked down on a site where such an attitude to life has never even been guessed at. Of course there are wild quarrels about it all the time, and this is enough to keep it there, on the grounds that new art creates wild quarrels.

Most of the town lies on one bank of the Tessino torrent, which is dry most of the year, though in the winter of 1965-6 there was a rush of water for the first time in thirty years which endangered the lower part of town.

Spoleto has been inhabited since prehistoric times and was an Umbrian centre, hence perhaps its ideal position, brushed by cool breezes from the surrounding woods: on days when the sky threatens rain round Perugia this town will be in full sunshine. Spoleto passed under Roman influence in the third century B.C. and in 241 was made a colony called Spoletium. It always remained faithful to Rome, and was especially so during the Punic Wars, checking Hannibal after his victory at Lake Trasimene. In 90 B.C. it was raised to the position of a township *optimum jure* (with its own magistrates) and was already known as a 'most splendid city': Cicero called it 'fixed and illustrious among the highest', that is, like a star. It was ravaged like most other Umbrian towns by the barbarians, Theodoric, Totila; Justinian's commander Belisarius, fighting the Goths, also did it much damage.

The Lombards put the town at the head of a dukedom, started by Foroaldo I in A.D. 569, and this was the beginning of its modern importance. Later the dukedom was enlarged far south, nearly to Rome. When the Lombards fell it passed to the Franks and was so prominent that after the Frankish empire broke up the duke of that time (Guido III) won the imperial throne (890). Barbarossa attacked Spoleto on account of its loyalty to the Church, and this defeat broke its long epoch of splendour. From now on it was caught in the bitter struggles between Church and Empire. Not only this, but the same division ravaged it internally in the form of the Guelfs and the Ghibellines, especially while the papacy had its seat at Avignon. In 1354 it was returned to the Church by Cardinal dell' Albornoz and became an important centre of the pontifical state: Lucretia Borgia was among its governors (1499), ruling from the vast castle that still looks down on it. Thus—unlike most of the other towns in Umbria—Spoleto flourished in Roman, mediaeval and Renascence times: another key to the sense of splendour which it gives us.

There was some bad bombing in the last war, with the result that the tourist has much less to see than in other Umbrian towns of the same size. A German ammunition train blew up under a bomb and this caused great devastation in the lower town. Nor does the town seem to care for what it does possess, despite the fact that it runs an international culture festival every year in July (*Festival of the Two Worlds*), under the direction of Gian Carlo Menotti. The chief reason for this is its relative poverty, and the consequent habit of looking on itself as a backwater. From this small area alone three or four thousand workers have emigrated to Germany in the last few years. In a decade the population has gone down from about fifty thousand to thirty-two thousand. The international festival has brought in money, but the ordinary people say that they have yet to feel it: the number of visitors to the town has increased over five times, and the number of hotel beds available has doubled, but there are those who say that by putting the prices up the festival in fact aggravated the situation and forced the emigration rate up too. Three mayors of Spoleto have been communist since the last war. There used to be lignite mines—from the old Lago Tiberino, which in prehistoric times occupied the upper course of the Tiber. The banks of lignite are about nine feet deep and used to be mined a thousand feet underground: these mines started in 1889 and by 1950 were producing about fifteen million tons a year. During the war there were seven thousand workers. But that has collapsed too

(1960). To survive, it needed a subsidy from the State but did not get it.

The upper town—the Ancaiani family—a Roman temple—the Pinacoteca (a twelfth-century crucifix, and Gozzoli's influence)—a Roman house—the Duomo (Pintoricchio chapel)—tomb of Fra' Lippo Lippi—S. Eufemia

The upper part of Spoleto is pleasanter and more intact than the lower and we should therefore begin at the **Piazza della Libertà**, which is easily reached from north and south and contains the Post Office and the tourist information office. Those driving from Perugia have a mostly one-way route to it from the Porta Garibaldi, but if they wish to avoid the narrow lanes of the town they should continue along the superstrada to the second entrance (after the tunnel), and this will bring them straight to the square. Buses and trains deposit us in the lower town, and this means a short walk up.

On the southern side of the square there is the Palazzo degli Ancaiani, partly built on the supporting arches of a Roman theatre. The ruins of this theatre—probably built during the first years of the empire, with a diameter of over a hundred yards (nearly twice that of the theatre at Carsulae)—can be seen from two specially constructed balconies. In 1319 it was the scene of a massacre: four hundred Guelfs had their throats cut and were then burned alive.

The Piazza della Libertà only became an important public thoroughfare two centuries ago: before that it was the private courtyard of the Palazzo Ancaiani. The present palazzo was built in the seventeenth century, and the other buildings in the square were simply extensions of the house. It became public property at the beginning of the last century and now houses the Italian Centre for Mediaeval Studies and the committee for the Two Worlds Festival. Where Viale Matteotti leaves the square on the left of the palazzo there used to be the family chapel: it was demolished to make way for this road in 1865. And another Ancaiani property was demolished in 1954 when the Roman theatre was excavated thoroughly: the terrace of the former Ancaiani stables is now the pavement from which we look down on the theatre ruins. The Ancaiani family, prominent in local government for some generations, had big properties in southern Umbria. Goldoni dedicated his *Gli Innamorati* to them.

We take the uphill Via Brignone from the other corner of the square, and after passing under an archway notice the Roman origins of the walls on our left, with their massive blocks. Then there is a cheerful, modest little square with a fountain in the middle, Piazza Pietro Fontana. On our right we see the Palazzo Mauri, forbidding and austere, from the beginning of the seventeenth century: it houses the town archives, the town library, and the Academy of Spoleto. Continuing, we come to a low arch over the road—the Arco di Monterone—which is really an open gate in the town wall from the third century B.C., as we see from its neatly placed blocks of stone that required no cement. If we pass under this arch we find, embedded in the wall on our left, another taller and thinner arch, called the Arco delle Felici, a name perhaps derived from a temple devoted to happy Venus or Venere Felice. And this belonged to the earliest wall of the town. Going through this arch too, we walk along a rough track with the apse of the church of SS. Simone e Giuda facing us at the end. If we look down into the valley towards the right we shall see a broken tower and a primitive sloping wall in ruins, the remains of the Tower of Fortebraccio, the *condottiere* whose name we have heard in connection with Perugia: he tried to occupy the castle above Spoleto and attacked it from this tower, but the attempt failed (1419).

We return to the little square by the Monterone arch and take the Via dell' Arco di Druso which passes by a baroque church (S. Ansano, of eleventh- or twelfth-century origin) and brings us to a third arch, the **Arco di Druso,** made of travertine and put there by the senate of Spoletium in honour of Tiberius's son, Drusus. At first it was thirty feet high, as we can see from the right side under the level of the road (we can walk down steps to the lower level if we pass under the arch) but the level of the town has risen since then. There were shops here until twelve years ago: they were demolished to reveal the Roman temple which we see—the work took three years. The temple is also in part of the crypt of the church of S. Ansano (turned to Christian purposes in the seventh century A.D.).

The entrance to the temple is at the foot of the steps, and there is an attendant. Above the entrance a fluted Roman pillar is set into a niche: originally this continued to twice its present height (the continuation is signified by stucco for us), and another stood next to it (this one crumbled during an earthquake). Farther above still,

253

we see a cement imitation of the frieze that once surrounded the temple close to the roof. On the right of the Roman column set in the wall there is a Roman inscription which no one can decipher but which seems to refer to a family. This wall is the only one that remains: and part of the original pavement is intact too. If we walk right of the entrance we shall find a niche in the wall which is actually a well, twelve feet deep, of Roman origin: perhaps a fountain once stood here. At the end of this wall, at the corner, there is a single block of stone about eleven feet long and nine feet deep, still unblemished. Visiting hours are 9.0 a.m.-12.0 p.m. and 3.0-6.30 p.m.

The first door on the left after the entrance leads us into the crypt of S. Ansano, dedicated to SS. Isaac and Martial, who fled to Spoleto to avoid persecution, taking refuge on the hill of Monteluco (which we shall see later). This room was once perhaps a public oratory but the raising of the road outside suffocated it, and from then on it was a crypt, annexed to the church above in the eleventh or twelfth centuries. The tiny room has three naves with an apse formed out of short fluted columns, probably of Christian origin. There used to be frescoes here, said to derive from as early as the tenth century, but two years ago they were removed for restoration to Rome, where works of art tend to remain once they have settled there.

We return to the corridor and at the end find the actual Roman temple, built probably in the first century A.D. There is a massive stylobate or foundation-block for the columns, sixty feet by thirty feet. The temple, clearly very large, had Corinthian columns and looked out on the forum of that time. The two corridors we have access to here are carefully constructed, and understandably several earthquakes since Roman times have made little difference. On the right the wall opens into what were presumably shops: the holes where the doors swivelled are there; the sills, for a window or serving bar, have the same form as others we shall see in one of Spoleto's streets. The attendant will show us a room full of fragments, including what came down during the earthquakes. The corridor here was of course a road, wider than it is now, with the temple-wall along one side. The temple thus lay between two roads. This back part was excavated only twelve years ago: a semi-circular apse was brought to light, showing that there was an even earlier church, belonging perhaps to the first years of Christianity; the church was orientated in the same direction as the temple. The god or goddess to whom the temple was dedicated is unknown.

We continue along the Via dell' Arco di Druso until we come to the Piazza del Mercato or market-place, a wide, bustling, friendly square closer to Roman life than any other part of town, with a vegetable market and a trattoria where it is pleasant to sit under the awning. The square is actually built over the ancient forum of the town (it lies six feet below). Before us as we walk to the other side of the square we see the **Fontana Grande,** rebuilt in honour of Pope Urban VIII in the seventeenth century, with its semi-circular bowl and horse-posts, and a complete wall forming its background like the façade of a church, with a clock and two shuttered windows above. On the left of the fountain (Via del Palazzo dei Duchi) there are traces of Gothic arches in the right wall, the remains of a porch from an early twelfth-century church called S. Donato, also erected above a Roman temple, perhaps the Capitol. The shops here will remind us of those we have just seen in the temple; the sills have the same form; these too may be of ancient origin. If we go to the end of this little road we shall find facing us a pretty mediaeval house reminiscent of those in Gubbio, intact, restored only in its arched windows and complete with its original torch-holders. At one time this was the seat of the Compagnia dei Comacini (the '*maestri Comacini*' were a group of architects who worked all over Italy during the Middle Ages, their name deriving from their place of origin, Lake Como).

Returning to the Piazza del Mercato we take the uphill lane of the Via del Municipio on the left, where after a few yards, in the piazza of that name, steps lead us up to the wide and grand balustrade of the **Palazzo Comunale** or town hall, with its slim tower rising out of a Renascence-style building (1782). The left wing is especially delicate and pleasing, and this, surprise of all surprises, was added in 1913 in the Venetian style, with a pattern of clovers on the wall. The town hall actually goes back to the thirteenth century, but signs of that epoch are hidden. In front of us as we go up the steps is another insipidly 'modern' piece of iron sculpture, like a twisted girder from a bombed site: it is called 'Iron and Steel', and that is about all it conveys. The Italian fear of criticizing contemporary work for fear of being considered backward may be the reason for its position here, bang in front of the town hall.

At the top of the steps we find the entrance to the **Pinacoteca**

255

Comunale, on the first floor. If we ring the bell an attendant will come at almost any time of the day. The room we are shown first is actually the one we should see last, so that we must begin our tour by going first to the end room, Room 1. On the right of the door as we enter there is a panel, *Madonna and Child*, which is dark and dirty but has a wonderful happiness, something restful and tender, with an *Eternal Father* in the lunette above. The work is dated 1502 and is by Bernardino Campilli, a follower of Pintoricchio. Left of this on a sort of cyclorama there is a copy of *the dormition of the Virgin* by Fra' Filippo Lippi which we shall see later in the duomo. Under it there is a recumbent figure in wood from the fifteenth century, evidently part of a tomb. Then there is part of a big *polittico* from the sixteenth century, showing *SS. John the Baptist and Peter*, and *the Angel of the Annunciation*. Farther along, above, about half-way down the right wall (for every picture isn't worth looking at) we see a *Madonna with Child and two angels* which has a mellow, damaged splendour, by an Umbrian follower of Gozzoli, on the lines of Mezzastris's design. Next there is a complete *polittico* in a gilded wooden frame showing *four saints*, from the Umbrian school of the fifteenth century, with a sleepy Tuscan touch. In the corner a pale painted crucifix of wood is said by the connoisseurs to be an important document in the history of Umbrian painting, being similar to the work of the so-called '*maestro di Cesi*', from the fourteenth century. It shows the Madonna on one side of Christ, St John on the other: by Christ's feet are St Francis and St Dominic; by his hands St Stephen and St Thomas; above his head we see the *Ascension*. The next *Madonna and Child* shows Gozzoli's influence again, with the same lined faces and a sweet, relaxed Virgin.

In the middle of the end wall there are frescoes detached from the church of S. Nicolò, Umbrian work of the fifteenth century, faded, delicate in feeling except for the lower *Annunciation*. St Cosmas on the right in these frescoes is believed to be a portrait of the famous Spoletan doctor Pierleone Leoni who committed suicide after failing to cure Lorenzo de' Medici: it once decorated his tomb. There is a painted crucifix in the manner of the thirteenth century, with the Madonna fainting on the left and the centurion on the right, and once more an *Ascension* above. Now we come to the oldest piece in the gallery, another large crucifix of wood (we can just see the Madonna at the side of Christ's body, and the faint outline of St John on the other side), with a stark and bold assurance, from the

A view from the top of Gubbio to the ruins of the Roman theatre which dates from the time of Augustus. Summer performances are still held here.

Above: Gubbio, at the foot of Monte Ingino, is almost unaltered since the Middle Ages. To the left, the crenellated bulk of the Palazzo dei Consoli dominates the town, as it was meant to. *Left:* The thirteenth-century Palazzo Bargello, one of the earliest and loveliest houses.

twelfth century, probably by Alberto 'Sotio' (or 'Sozio', a local painter of the twelfth century). Then there is a warm and rosy *Madonna and Child with saint*. By the door again we find a fifteenth-century inlaid chest. The *Madonna delle Grazie* by Nicolò Alunno which is usually at this point is under restoration. Before leaving this room we should notice on a cushion the town's splendid silver mace with gilded relief, by the Roman silver-worker Bartolotti (eighteenth-century).

As we walk into Room 2 we see between the windows on the right a *Madonna and Child and SS. Augustine and Stephen*, dated 1530. Going round the room anti-clockwise we come to a large framed picture behind glass by Lo Spagna, a *Madonna and Child with saints*, showing the arms of the Ridolfi family above (Ridolfi was Spoleto's governor in 1514). It is only just sincere, on the edge of the worst posed baroque, and the picture is considered his closest to Raphael. Most of this wall is taken up by other frescoes of his (1512): they show the *Virtues* (*Charity* has the babies, and there are also *Clemency* and *Justice*), and were originally painted to glorify Pope Julius II, though they were converted to the glorification of another pope (Leo XII) in 1824. *The adoration of the Child* on the next wall is actually a copy of the Lo Spagna picture now in the Vatican museum (1515). The *Madonna and Child* above the door is an imitation of the altar-piece by Raphael, on a drawing of Perugino (1507), which is now in London at the National Gallery.

Between the windows of the right wall in Room 3 *the Trinity* is an eighteenth-century piece where only the face of Christ shows a trace of the old religion: otherwise it is a document of detached reminiscence. Again going round anti-clockwise we find a large canvas, *Mary Magdalen*, by 'Il Guercino' as he was called, an artist from Ferrara, dated 1636. Immediately to the left of this, below, there is a *Madonna and Child and saint* (all without haloes) of the same Ferrarese school, oil on wood, pockmarked with stains but one of the nicest things in the room. Above it, at the top of the wall, there is a fine and sophisticated *Madonna and Child between SS. Peter and Paul* by a Roman painter of the sixteenth century. The two portraits on the left of this are women from the local Palettoni family. We pass an over-sweet *Immaculate Conception* where the child Jesus delicately pierces the serpent at his mother's feet with a long spear, and reach a vast canvas, *the calling of St Matthew*, which shows clear signs of Caravaggio's influence in the shining whites of the robes.

Room 4 (the one we came in by) has another Lo Spagna, set in the wall in an arched niche, a *Crucifixion with the Madonna and St John*, but it colud conceivably be by Jacopo Siciliano, from the same period. Under it we see a strange *Iconographic Table* of local origin (1755) showing the arms of the various saints. In Room 5, or the ante-room, we return to the lay world, where ambition, elegance and comfort reign: the nineteenth-century canvases show French influences. All these dazzling fineries are by one artist, called Detti, except the portrait on the right of the entrance which is by an eighteen-year-old boy, a self-portrait, of the same epoch.

We now enter the Sala del Consiglio, or council chamber, whose walls bear a once-glorious damask wall-paper and four tapestries of the seventeenth century with blue-toned landscapes; they used to belong to the Collicola family and before them to Queen Christina of Sweden.

The attendant will now take us outside to the **Roman house** which lies in the foundations of the town hall. An inscription found here mentioning a certain 'Polla' has led people to think that the house may have belonged to Polla Vespasian from Norcia, the mother of the Emperor Vespasian: the family is known to have had possessions in this area. The signs are that it was a splendid house. It was built in the first century A.D. and restored a hundred years after that; and it was inhabited until late in the Middle Ages, when it was probably destroyed by fire. The first excavation, in the last century, was undertaken at the expense of the English ambassador of that time, Savile Lumley.

It is a Pompeii-type house: that is, the *peristilium* or outer court-yard, surrounded by pillars, opens not at the back but the side. We enter the *atrium* or central court by means of a corridor, with the centre *impluvium* or basin which received rain-water through the open space above. There is also a deep well, but the well-head we see was not found in the excavations: originally there might have been a fountain here. Leading left and right from the atrium are two rooms and two recesses called *alae* or wings with mosaic pavements: the ones on the left lead to what was probably the peristilium, with the garden beyond (we see the remains of its columns). Beyond the atrium lies the *tablinum* or reception room (where the family archives were also kept). And this has a room on each side of it, their pavements probably of later origin than the others. The room on the right here is the *triclinium* or dining-room (on a slightly higher level), with two smaller rooms, a corridor and perhaps a bath-place. The fresco here—a trace of it is left—is an imitation marble skirting-board or dado.

In glass cases on the right of the entrance there are fragments found during excavation—tiny figures that once decorated the furniture, household utensils, needles, oil-lamps of terra-cotta. We see the inscription with the name Polla. There are long nails, what looks like a key, a spearhead, a fragment of the house's cornice.

We leave the square outside along the Via del Municipio: a dark, narrow lane takes us between mediaeval houses until we emerge into a little treasure of a square called Piazza Bernardino Campello (he was a local playwright of the seventeenth century, when Spoleto's theatre was very much alive). Its little park has various types of pine-tree, and flower-beds. On our right as we enter is the Palazzo Campello, of mediaeval origin: in the entrance we see a Roman sarcophagus with bas-relief figures in what seems to be a Bacchic scene. At an angle from this palazzo there is the ex-church of SS. Simone e Giuda (thirteenth-century), whose apse we have already seen from the edge of the town (now part of the orphans' school next door). If we walk past this church we shall see a fountain—at the side of the school entrance—where the water, when flowing, emerges from the tusked mouth of a great stone mask. Standing here and looking down the sloping square, we again glimpse the greatness of Italian life as it was inherited from the Romans. Everything is sane and harmonious at this spot. This is perhaps Spoleto's best square, detached from the rest of the town and almost in the fields, with the Rocca or castle frowning down on it much closer than we expect.

The hill on which the castle stands is the Monte Elia (over twelve hundred feet high), and the rather bleak fortress was started by Ugolino di Montemarte and finished by Matteo di Giovannello, an architect from Gubbio better known to us as Gattaponi, on a commission of Cardinal dell' Albornoz (1355-67). The idea was to make one of the strongest defence points in the papal kingdom, on the pope's return from residence at Avignon. The castle is now a prison. It has six towers and is divided into two wings, the one overlooking us designed for defence, the other the Governor's residence. A number of popes have stayed there—Nicholas V, Pius II, Sixtus IV, Julius II—and both Valentino and Lucretia Borgia. Numberless coats of arms are displayed on the towers and walls, belonging to the

Borgia family, the Piccolomini, the Medici, the Visconti, the Aldo-brandini, the della Rovere, the Colonna; these commanding names tell the story of Spoleto's immense power and prestige in the past.

We leave the Piazza Campello by its lowest corner, under an archway (Via Aurelio Saffi), and after a few yards we see at the foot of a wide, sweeping, serene staircase a great flat courtyard, then the façade and porch of the duomo. The staircase is called Via dell' Arringo, because it led to the *arringo*, meaning in this case the people's assembly, which from the earliest Christian times was in this square. As we walk down the gradual slope we have the fascinating, many-windowed **Palazzo Arroni** from the sixteenth century on our right, its doorway framed in carved stone, the designs on its wall faded (they once showed *the triumph of Neptune*), its cornices broken. We should have a peep into its strange and lovely little courtyard where the fountain takes up the whole of one wall, decorated with three figures, the centre one, Artemis, like an ancient Egyptian, with fertility breasts hanging round her waist, and a lion whose mane forms the whole shell above the fountain, with the effect of a grotto, obelisks on either side. The palazzo has been sold by the Anderson family (descendants of the Arroni) to Perugia university, and its *graffiti* on the wall outside will be restored.

On the opposite side of the square—left as we face the duomo—there is the one modern bronze figure in Spoleto which looks as if it means to stay, and has found the right place (by Kenneth Armitage). The **Piazza del Duomo** is a silent and restful square, big enough to be used as a garage but difficult of access: and then, no business is done in this part of town.

On the right there is another Roman sarcophagus, apparently a companion to the one we saw in the courtyard of the Palazzo Campello, with striking relief figures that seem to comprise a hunting scene. On the left side of the square again the house farthest from the duomo's porch is the Opera del Duomo (1419), with alternate pink and white stones. Next to it is the modest and elegant front of the **Caio Melisso theatre,** the town's oldest theatre (though the building owes its present design to the year 1880 and was restored in 1958): it began life in this spot in the seventeenth century. Then there is the little church of S. Maria della Manna d'Oro with its octagonal cupola and simple classical front (1527), now the baptistery of the duomo.

To reach the Opera del Duomo, or the **Civic Museum** as it is now known, we should ring at No. 3 and the attendant will show us into the foyer of the little theatre, where a staircase under the auditorium takes us down to the damp and chilly crypt (visiting hours, 9.0 a.m.-12 noon and 3.0-6.0 p.m.). We shall be allowed a glimpse of the delicious little theatre with the lights up, if we ask: the stage is tiny, the boxes tinier still, and there are the original gas-globes from the last century. These marvellous little theatres dotted all over Italy are falling into neglect, there being almost no theatrical life to speak of in the provinces, even if there is in the great cities. An alternative—and the official—entrance to the museum is in the side-street running by the Opera del Duomo, depending on the season we choose and the mood of the attendant.

The museum downstairs is actually on the ground floor of a big fourteenth-century palazzo, said by some to have been built by the *gonfaloniere*, or town standard-bearer, Pinciani (1330-40). But it has always been known as the Palazzo della Signoria, and more probably it originated in the fourteenth century (on the former Piazza della Signoria) as the seat of town government, but was gradually abandoned, with only one storey complete. It may have been designed by Gattaponi, and built at the order of Cardinal dell' Albornoz. There remained a space between this unfinished palazzo and the church of Manna d'Oro on the right, and the little theatre came about in that space. As for the unfinished house, that became part of the cathedral and was called Opera del Duomo: the museum we visit is actually in this building.

The large hall into which we descend is actually the former guard-house, in two naves with pillars supporting heavy arched vaults. Going round it clockwise, we see a fine chimney-piece from the beginning of the sixteenth century, from the Palazzo Arroni; two oil tabernacles from Renascence times, and bells; fragments of tombs and a striking and important twelfth-century bas-relief showing five scenes from *the martyrdom of S. Biagio*. The saint's head has been cut off and a column of blood is sprouting from his neck in the form of a tree. Then we pass two church screens, again of the twelfth century, the upper one showing *two apostles* inside ornamental arches of carved stone. A tiny arched doorway reveals a collection of hefty cannon-balls. There are carved friezes, and in the corner the side of a sarcophagus with a figure of *the Saviour* and *the Constantine monogram*, and *the Book of Law*, with an inscription and *two figures*, one male and the other female, on either side.

In the middle of the hall there are other early Christian sarcophagi, including, on the left of the staircase as we face it, that of St Isaac the Syrian, showing a bas-relief (*Christ blessing*) inside a medallion, and *symbols of the evangelists*, with monks and the Madonna on either side. St Isaac was one of the hermits who lived on Monteluco in the sixth century, but the tomb was carved in the twelfth. Farther along to the left there is the tomb of the Blessed Gregory: the fifteenth-century relief shows the hermit (also from Monteluco) kneeling before his own cell.

In the next and last room (under the church of Manna d'Oro) we find in the right-hand far corner the so-called *Lex Spoletana* of the third century B.C., written in archaic Latin to remind the people of Spoleto that the sacred woods (*luci*) near the town were not to be used for firewood and that there were penalties for those who broke the law. There are actually two tablets and they come from the same period, and were brought to light in 1913. One fragment has been translated into Italian for our benefit: it mentions the penalties (an ox, three hundred coins) for offering 'offence to Jove' by cutting down the trees.

And now for the **Duomo**. It was built at the end of the twelfth century and is dedicated to S. Maria Assunta, or Mary of the Assumption, and stands on the site of a previous cathedral destroyed by Barbarossa in 1155. And it was restored (as we shall see at once when we go inside later) during the seventeenth century. But the façade remains from the earlier epoch, on the whole giving the square its harmony and focal point, especially in its quaint little marriage with the green hill rising intimately on its flank, towards the Rocca. The front is typically Umbrian, divided horizontally into three parts, the lowest forming an elegantly decorated Romanesque porch, with five arches and a balcony that were clearly a Renascence addition, started in 1491. At either end of this porch, set narrowly into the wall between pillars, are two pulpits of carved stone, and in the middle of the three horizontal parts we see a small 'blind' or closed gallery with three slender pillars and two caryatids forming the outer pillars; above this there is a series of rose windows, five in all, the central one with symbols of the evangelists at each corner. The top part of the façade has a triangular crown and three more rose windows, in a crescendo of magnificence; and there are three Gothic arches set in the wall here side by side, with a mosaic in the Byzantine style occupying the middle one, against a gilt background,

Christ blessing between the Virgin and St John, dated 1207, and signed by one Solsterno. The tower we see on the left was built in the eleventh or twelfth century, partly out of ancient Roman materials. If we walk under the porch we shall find a middle portal surrounded by a luxurious carved stone frame from the same period as the porch, imitating the classical.

The façade might lead us to expect a harmonious or at least magnificent interior, but this is not so: the damp church is in a bleakly baroque form of the kind we have seen in all the once-wealthy towns of Umbria, and Pope Urban VIII's architect was responsible for it. This pope's bronze bust is behind us (the work of Bernini) as we enter, above the main door. The flooring is nice, from various epochs: it has little pieces of green and red stone, in an intriguing design, much of it from the twelfth century.

There is at least one very good reason for coming inside: the first chapel on the right has some frescoes by Pintoricchio. It is called the Chapel of Eroli (Bishop Eroli and his brother built it during their period of office, 1449-1540) or the Sacred Heart. Pintoricchio worked here in 1497. The attendant will unlock the door for us, and expects a tip. Facing us in a niche behind the altar we see a calm and touching *Madonna and Child with SS. John the Baptist and Stephen* (some say St Leonard) with Lake Trasimene behind them and a city which probably represents Jerusalem: the little figures on the right are Mary and the Child with Joseph, on their flight into Egypt. The whole subject is dominated by the episode of the Dominican monk preaching the rosary before a crowd in a corner of the picture. Above, there is *the Eternal Father and angels*. Under the altar-table we see a *Pietà* with Christ only, his arms lowered from the cross. And set into the wall there is a fifteenth-century carved marble piece, *Christ blessing among the angels*.

A door on the right leads us through to the actual Chapel Eroli, where the bishops' tombs are. The *Crucifixion with angels*, on the left wall above, is the only fresco here with any feeling, by Iacopo Siculo (sometimes called Siciliano—he came from Palermo at the beginning of the sixteenth century). The other frescoes are by two artists from Verona—except for the ceiling, the authorship of which is unknown. Before leaving we should notice the stone bench on squat, slender pillars round the wall.

In the right arm of the transept, on the left wall as we face the side-altar, there is a monument with a gilded decoration, the tomb of

The Companion Guide to Umbria

Fra' Lippo Lippi, showing a head of the painter, on one of his own drawings: the tomb was ordered by Lorenzo the Magnificent of Florence. The body of the painter is no longer here: it was lost during the seventeenth-century restorations, when the monument was put into its present position.

Fra' Lippo Lippi frescoed the presbytery (1467-9), with the help of two other artists. On the left, below, there is a vast *Annunciation*, where the modesty of feeling survives the size. In the middle there is an even bigger *dormition of the Virgin*, where the small group on the right represents, it is said, Fra' Lippo Lippi himself (in a monk's habit) with the two artists who collaborated with him, and his own son. On the right we see a *Nativity*: above, forming the roof of the apse, a rich and splendid *coronation of the Virgin*.

Going down the left nave we come to the first chapel—the door is usually closed (though not locked) and for this reason is almost always missed by tourists—called the *Coro d'Inverno*, or Winter Choir, with a lovely inlaid wooden choir skirting the walls, and tiny frescoes in the panels. This was all done by local artists during the sixteenth century. And here we find, on the right, perhaps the church's oldest possession, a *Crucifixion* by Alberto Sozio (1187), a parchment on wood in the Byzantine style. And on the left wall as we enter there is a *Madonna and Child* in painted wood by Tiberio Fidi di Cerreto (1660) which is grave and sincere.

Leaving the Piazza del Duomo by the steps of the Via dell' Arringo, as we came, we turn right at the top and enter the first doorway on the right, No. 13, which is the archbishop's palace, and may once have been the ducal palace of Spoleto in its earliest Lombardian times. In the pleasant courtyard we see, nestling there peacefully, the little church of **S. Eufemia,** of perhaps tenth-century construction, though it has been restored since. It has a fascinating interior of three naves, with the unusual feature of galleries above, over the side-naves: at least, this is unusual for such a tiny church. We see elements of the ancient building—a fluted pillar, an intriguing square column carved with intricate designs. On one of the right-hand pillars there is a fifteenth-century fresco, and behind the altar on the apse wall a delicate triptych (*Madonna and saints*), with a crude *Eternal Father* overhead. Originally the church belonged to a Benedictine monastery founded by a man of perhaps German origin, Gunderada, who rescued the body of the local bishop and saint, Giovanni, martyred by the Goths, and laid it in this

264

church (980). The church has sometimes been called S. Giovanni for this reason. In 1017 the monastery was given by Emperor Henry II to Count Acodo, which meant that it was disbanded: and the site became the bishops' palace towards the end of the twelfth century, while the duomo was being enlarged. The galleries above the side-naves came into existence in the sixteenth century, and belonged to the bishops. The church gradually fell into decay and was restored only this century.

This whole area is wonderful for quiet walks where there is hardly one visible reminder of the age we live in: we see traces here and there of the primitive walls of the ducal palace, though its exact site is not known.

The Lower Town—Ponte Sanguinario—S. Gregorio Maggiore—the 'tower of oil' and the 'gate of flight'—one church on top of another—S. Domenico—SS. Giovanni e Paolo (twelfth-century Sozio frescoes)—S. Filippo

To cover the rest of Spoleto we shall do best to begin in the lower town, that is to say at the Piazza Garibaldi, as if we were coming in from the north or Perugia. The actual Porta Garibaldi (previously Leonina) is unusual for being a modern structure on the ancient model, with small arches on either side under which the pavements run. Our starting-point should actually be outside the town in the Piazza della Vittoria with its fountain among trees and its bridge over a dry torrent bed. Here are the ruins of the Roman bridge or **Ponte Sanguinario** ('bloody bridge'); it lies under the square, close to an absurd monument dedicated to Garibaldi; steps lead down to what looks like a lavatory. We may have to return to the Porta Garibaldi, under the right-hand arch, to find a door marked 'Ufficio Imposte di Consumo', for the hand-sized key. Down below we see two massive arches of travertine which probably derive from the time of Augustus. The name '*sanguinario*' comes from the tradition that many Christian martyrs were sacrificed in the near-by amphitheatre and their blood flowed under this bridge. More likely is the fact that it is a corruption of the name 'Sandapilarius', there having been a 'Sandapilarian Gate' in the amphitheatre near by. Others say that the name refers to the town's bloody resistance to Hannibal at this point. The bridge was discovered in 1817 but only made accessible this century. A side-road of the Flaminian Way passed over it in Roman times but the bridge fell into disuse when the Torrente Tessino was re-routed, during the building of the new town wall in the fourteenth century.

And now we enter the town by the Porta Garibaldi: this was built in 1825 at the order of Pope Leo XII, but destroyed in the last war, hence the modern neatness. On the right side of the square before us —the only part of Spoleto that bustles with commercial life—lies the squat church of **S. Gregorio Maggiore:** it was started in 1079 and consecrated in 1146, but damaged both by fire and floods from the Tessino torrent; and it suffered bombardment in the last war. Its last restoration was in 1949. The façade is simple and elegantly small, hugging the tower at its side. Most of it is from the original church, including the attractive pillared arches set in the wall above, with statues of saints on either side in niches, worn with time and trouble. The front was raised to its present height only in the fourteenth century, in imitation of the duomo up the hill. The porch with its three arches was added in the sixteenth century, clearly with Roman remains, making a harmonious entrance that looks older than it is. Along its top there is an inscription referring to the ten thousand martyrs said to have been buried at this spot. We shall also recognize ancient Roman blocks at the base of the tower, dating from the first years of the church (it was raised higher in the fifteenth century). On the left as we enter the porch we see the wide arch of the fourteenth-century Chapel of the Innocents, now the baptistery, with bad frescoes showing *the life of St Abundatius*, who was buried in this church.

Inside, we have a simple church of mostly bare stone, including the pillars with their roughly carved capitals: this is all a result of the recent restoration (in the proper sense of the word) back to the first Romanesque form. On the walls there are frescoes dating from the twelfth to the fourteenth centuries. On the left the Cappella del Sacramento has behind its altar an attractive carved stone tabernacle with angels and flowery designs, attributed to a Pistoian artist (sixteenth-century).

The chancel is raised up eleven steps and here the columns have classical capitals taken from ancient ruins. On the wall left of the altar (we mount the steps) we see fifteenth-century frescoes by various Umbrian artists. In the left part of the apse, behind a small altar, there is a graceful *Madonna and Child* by a local, rustic hand perhaps under Gozzoli's influence, where a genuine sense of the countryside seems to come intact from ancient times, while the Church is personified in the warm person of the Madonna. We should always remember that the Church was first and foremost the protector of family-life—elevating it to a sacred role—and that this was the key to its survival through endless troubles, as it is the key to life in Italy still today.

The crypt lies left of the chancel steps as we walk down them again: it has square fluted columns, and capitals of ancient or at least 'barbaric' origin (one with a leafy capital of the sixth-century Byzantine type). On the left of the altar we see the tomb of St Abundatius; or at least local tradition says it is.

We now climb into the town by a cobbled lane that leaves the square opposite the Garibaldi gate, the Via di Porta Fuga, and we are at the beginning of a curious, leisurely, winding walk that will bring us back to the Piazza della Libertà. At the summit of the narrow street we see the massive Palazzo Vigili, now known as Pompili (but some people call it Palazzo Cecili). Fabio Vigili was a Latin poet of the sixteenth century, and secretary to Pope Paul III, also bishop of Spoleto, so that of the three tenants his name has tended to dominate. The building is a mass of different epochs, from the thirteenth to the sixteenth centuries, and it frowns over the little street with its great tower called the *Torre dell' Olio* or 'tower of oil', because of the favoured mediaeval habit of pouring boiling oil down on attackers. We pass by the palazzo's stupendous supporting wall and under the arch called *Porta Fuga,* or 'the gate of flight'. This name too has a mixed background: the gate was known in the thirteenth century as Porta Furia ('the gate of hurry') and also Porta Fuja; it was probably in the sixteenth century, when classical memories began to revive, that its present name came into being, as a deliberate reference to Hannibal's defeat here in 217 B.C. There is an inscription above the arch which records this— a sixteenth-century addition.

At the top of the hill we come into the tiny Piazza Torre dell' Olio, a meeting-place of five lanes. Here we turn left downhill along a Via Cecili and pass a row of splendid trees and then, after a widening of the pavement into a gravelled area with seats and hedges, we see the original wall of the town, parts of it from the third century B.C., others from the Etruscan epoch three or four hundred years before that.

At the end of the row of trees is the tall apse of *S. Nicolò*. This is really two churches, one on top of the other: we see the thirteenth-century portal of the lower church (*della Misericordia*) at the foot of the upper apse, chipped and wrecked: if we pass round to the other side we come to a second stone portal of much the same design, which takes us into the lower church. Inside, the frescoes are in a bad state: one of these (on our left if we face the back) is a so-called 'clothed crucifixion' in the style of the '*Santo Volto*' festival at Lucca, where Christ is crowned and robed on the cross. Continuing downhill we reach after a few yards a staircase-lane on the right called Via Misericordia, which brings us to the side of the upper of the two churches (S. Nicolò). We walk round to the façade which has perhaps the biggest portal arch we shall ever see on a simple church-front, with carved fluted and twirling pillars of stone: it was built in 1304 and burned down in 1849. In the lunette of the portal arch we see the *Madonna and SS. Augustine and Nicholas* (1402), where some of the original mellow and russet splendour survives. The rose window lacks glass and, as we shall already have recognized, the church is no longer used.

We pass along with the wall of this monastery on our right and find ourselves back in the tiny Piazza della Torre dell' Olio: and now we take the continuation of the road from which we have come, the Via Pierleoni (Pierleone Leoni was one of the humanists who frequented the S. Nicolò monastery). Immediately on the right there is a square fourteenth-century tower, cut off at the top, with blocks at the base which derive from the Bronze and Copper Age. We come to a narrow square with trees and benches, and flanking it on the right the long, peaceful, pink-and-white side of the church of *S. Domenico,* built in the thirteenth century. We find a one-naved church, strange and dismal, with an open-beamed roof, now restored to its original form after baroque ravages but without recapturing the first intimacy. If we look back at the entrance we shall see above it a *Transfiguration* which is a copy of the original picture by Raphael. On the walls there are various rescued fragments of votive frescoes from the fourteenth and fifteenth centuries. At the first altar on the right, inside a niche, there is *the triumph of St Thomas Aquinas* in which the saint sits *in cathedra*, showing an open book to his disciples, bishops and cardinals among them: all inside a nice design of medallions containing *prophets and the four evangelists*. It was painted at the beginning of the fifteenth century. In the left transept a reliquary at the altar contains, they say, a nail of the Cross brought here by the Blessed Gregory. By the door leading to the sacristy behind us there is a sweet and delicately sad *Madonna and Child* by an imitator of Fra' Angelico.

Almost opposite the church's side-door a short staircase-lane leads us up into the Via Vaita S. Andrea, where we turn left, uphill. After a bend we pass the entrance-porch of the Teatro Nuovo (or 'Massimo' as it is sometimes called), two tiers of arches built in the neo-classical style of 1864, with a rather flat effect: but it makes a pleasant site for a theatre—a church was once here, and, in Roman times, baths. Continuing uphill we pass deserted lanes sensibly protected against cars by stone posts.

After a few yards we come to a cobbled yard on the right called the Vicolo Valerio Corvino where we see the side of the tiny church of **SS. Giovanni e Paolo** (twelfth-century), hardly bigger than a chapel. It has a fresco outside, very faded, of the *Madonna and saints*, from the thirteenth century. If the church is closed we must go to a café near by, the Bar Tebro, reached by walking past the little church front, turning right and then right again: there we shall be given the key (with more pleasure if we take a drink as well). The light, once we are inside the little church, is on the left wall. There are votive frescoes everywhere, from the twelfth century onwards. We should notice *the martyrdom of St Thomas of Canterbury* on the left wall as we come in, a fresco perhaps by Alberto Sozio: the soldiers cut off St Thomas's hands. There is a fragment by the same author, on the left, from *the banquet of Herod*, a sequence that has mostly disappeared, and *the dance of Salome* (she is the tiny figure in the right-hand lower corner not proportioned to Herod's banqueting table). Above, there is the *Madonna della Cintola* (the Madonna of the Girdle) and *St Francis*, very much damaged: this is one of the first iconographic documents we have of St Francis, by the way. On the right wall there is the *Madonna del Latte* (the Virgin giving milk) and, underneath, *St Catherine* and *St Peter Martyr*, which are fourteenth-century pieces of little interest. There are then *three saints*, said to have been painted by a follower of Alberto Sozio. In the little presbytery on the right, there is a semi-circular fresco taken from the crypt five or six years ago, *stories of SS. John and Paul*: on the left, *the Emperor orders their execution*, and on the right we see *the two Saints beheaded*, with their *being received in heaven* in the middle, while *the Redeemer blesses* in the space above, from the last years of

269

the twelfth century and also associated with Alberto Sozio, though this name really denotes a style rather than an actual known artist.

We continue uphill along the Via Filitteria past a restaurant in the bowels of a palazzo (the Paint-brush Club, or Taverna del Pennello), and bear right round this palazzo, so as to take the Via Mazzini. This ends in a little square dominated by the baroque façade and attractive wide steps of S. Filippo, which has only one interesting feature inside—the pillars at the altar in the left transept which come from the Temple of Clitunno (see p. 247). Just before we reach this church we see on the left another square, the narrow and fascinating Piazza Luigi Pianciani, with its pretty winged staircase forming a balustrade which also is the arched-over entrance of the tiny Via di Fonte Secca. On the left side of the square is the Palazzo Pianciani, with its shuttered windows on two levels re-calling a French country house. If we continue up the Corso Mazzini, considered Spoleto's main street, we shall find ourselves back in the Piazza della Libertà; and this will be our starting-point for walks just outside the town, where some of Spoleto's most precious sights are. The bar in this square serves good coffee.

The outskirts of Spoleto—the public gardens—St Paul-among-the-Vines—some of the earliest frescoes in Umbria

The road running along the left side of the Palazzo Ancaiani as we face it, is the Viale Giacomo Matteotti. The **public gardens** farther on are a splendid corner of the town from which we have a command of the hills that hug it towards the south, fertile, smooth with olive trees (the Val del Tessino). No town in Umbria caters for the pedestrian better than Spoleto: it has an almost suburban order, though nothing could be a less Italian concept than suburbia.

If we turn right along the Viale Martiri della Resistenza we shall find ourselves in peaceful country: the first track going left takes us downhill towards the little church of **S. Paolo inter Vineas** (St Paul-among-the-Vines) which we can already see with its mellow nucleus of walls and shady trees. We walk with vineyards on our left and the beginnings of a residential district on our right: on a fine day it is one of the lovelist spots in Umbria, rich and green and varied. And where we turn left for S. Paolo (a little wayside shrine blocks our path by a roughly stuccoed garden wall) we again have a glimpse of the old Italy, which prevailed even ten years ago, but collapsed precisely when the country's agriculture collapsed.

The church nestles at the side of a tiny clinic with a rough fore-court. A large rose window occupies an upper section of the façade, while the lower part is divided by two columns set in the wall, a simple portal between them and a graceful cornice above. The fresco in the lunette is almost quite faded, a *Madonna and Child with angels and saints*, said to be the work of Mezzastris. If we ring at the hospital door the attendant will unlock the church for us: we shall find it bare of ornament—even an altar—due to the recent restoration back to its primitive appearance, but it is more restful than anything we have so far seen in Spoleto, reminiscent of those earliest Christian churches where an element of pagan wonder is still alive. In fact this church goes back to the sixth century and was rebuilt in the twelfth and thirteenth centuries, then transformed again later on. It has the sober and utterly serious form, complete and still, of a first religious statement: no ambition or sophistication, just a new attitude that engulfs life and gives it a true explanation for the first time in centuries. There are frescoes from the beginning of the thirteenth century, which means that (together with the work we have seen in the tiny church of SS. Giovanni e Paolo) Spoleto has some of the earliest painting in Umbria. These frescoes bear the sure Byzantine design, with rough and rustic decorative strips, along the back and right-hand walls of the presbytery. There are two damaged panels, primitive and tentative, with small childishly drawn animals and birds of all kinds—*Adam gives names to the animals*; *God* (in the left lower corner) *raises his hand in blessing*, and the two figures in the same panel we recognize as *the birth of Eve*. Closer to the back wall another panel shows *God admonishing Adam*: we see him gesturing him away. The other subjects are *the creation of Man* and *the Saviour among the angels*. The church was consecrated in 1234, and these frescoes were probably painted before then. The *patriarchs and prophets* are said to be the work of a different hand.

Ponte delle Torri—bombs and earthquakes failed to shake it

For our next walk we should take the Piazza Campello as our starting-point and go uphill, beyond the town gate, as if towards the Rocca above us. We shall find ourselves in a narrow, tree-lined avenue with a stretch of Roman wall on our left (part of the primitive Acropolis), while the valley stretches deep below us on the right.

If we walk or drive round the corner we shall see, astride the valley, the **Ponte delle Torri,** or 'bridge of towers', an aqueduct which still bears water to the city from the hill of Monteluco. It is a series of steep arches made of fine bricks, bearing a narrow bridge from one side of the valley to the other (we can walk but not drive across). Behind us if we look back there is the omnipresent Rocca: always close, watching.

The aqueduct is as clean and straight now as it was on its day of birth. There are ten arches and the bridge is approximately two hundred and forty feet high and two hundred and fifty yards long. Such is the sturdiness of the thing that it seems to shrink the width of the valley to quite half its real size. In its present form the bridge came into being in the fourteenth century and was probably another work of Gattaponi, with his genius for supports: and again it was ordered by Cardinal dell' Albornoz, the idea being to convey water to the higher part of the town and above all to the Rocca (in case of siege); and it provided a quick road across the valley to Monteluco. Probably the builders used a smaller Roman aqueduct in the same place as their model: our first impression is of an ancient construction, but intact as we never otherwise see it. Goethe when he saw this bridge described it as a work of the ancients, so convincingly on Roman lines is it built: he said that Roman architecture was like 'a second nature'.

He also said how well the arches had stood up to the centuries: but they were to suffer more after his death. They were bombed in the last war, though barely scratched; the water supply was cut off for a little time. They have survived earthquakes too. If we are on foot we should walk across the aqueduct and turn right along a road that will bring us down to the church of S. Pietro under the slopes of Monteluco. If we are driving we can continue on the same road, which skirts the Rocca and gives us a view across Spoleto's roofs towards Assisi: the road will then bring us back to the Piazza Campello from which we started.

Right: The Temple of Clitumnus, near Trevi, looks Roman, is Christian, and contains some of the oldest frescoes in Umbria.

Left: The near-by Fonti del Clitunno, where the little river begins. Caligula, Propertius, Virgil came here. Corot painted it and Byron wrote about it.

Right: The twelfth-century façade of Spoleto's duomo, a typical Umbrian church front, apart from the portico and balustrade added later. The great stones in the lower half of the tower are of Roman workmanship.

Below: S. Pietro has the most crowded façade in Umbria. The Tree of Life twines around the central doorway flanked by stone animals. The panels symbolize the soul sheltering from sin at the Redemption.

S. Pietro—the most crowded mediaeval façade in Umbria

We shall already have noticed from a distance the crowded façade of **S. Pietro,** since it directly faces the southern outskirts of the town, a stone's throw from them. It is perhaps the strangest church-front in Umbria, though a typical one in its design. There is a flight of steps leading up to its courtyard, from which we have our fullest view so far of the bleak and functional Rocca. The church derives from the fifth century, on the site of a cemetery in continuous use from the Iron Age to Christian times. S. Pietro was built at the order of Bishop Achillus, who had a relic (St Peter's chain) brought to this spot from Rome, but we have no trace of this today. It was enlarged in the thirteenth century and burned down before the century was out, then rebuilt, and altered even further in that dangerously meddlesome epoch, the eighteenth century (Etruscomania started in that century but there was no feeling for earlier Christian work). But this façade, as a glance will tell us, belongs thankfully to the first rebuilding five centuries before.

It is decorated with many reliefs, especially in the lowest of its three horizontal sections: these are by various thirteenth-century artists; nowhere else shall we find so much mediaeval stone carving, so minute and elaborate. The panels always have a meaning and serve an end. The very top of the façade is crowned by a tiny stone statue of *St Peter*, almost worn to nothing now: the pediment just below this has an empty framed space which should have taken a mosaic but never did; on each side there is an angel, the *turiferario* (a rather literary word for censer-bearer) with a bull, its head jutting, below each of them. The middle section of the façade has three 'eyes', round windows of plain segmented glass, the large central one framed in a mosaic, with the four symbols of the evangelists.

In the lowest section we have most of the bas-relief work. There are three doorways, with stone animals flanking each one. The lunettes above the side-doors have eagles on each side, and above them too are bas-relief figures, the one on the right *S. Vescovo* (a bishop-saint) and on the left *St Michael slaying the dragon*. In the lunette over the centre door, in a horseshoe, its frame an intricate mosaic, there is an inscription with an eagle on either side. Below it is one of the most cleverly ornate and satisfying door-frames of stone we shall see in Umbria, its small panels enclosing the doorway in a square frame, eight of them consisting of sets of tiny pillars, fluted and twirling, their little arches against a background of minute carved rosettes, like seals set into the wall, with a sheaf of wheat or a rampant lion here and there. There are fourteen of these panels in all, and the remaining six are taken up by symbolical bas-relief figures and animals—the lowest of these on each side show *men driving oxen at the plough* (with a dog), the middle ones show *the hind giving milk to her young* and *devouring a serpent* (the young are missing from the left panel), and those at the top show *the peacock eating grapes*. Now all these have a meaning, individually and collectively. They show the symbolic sheltering of the soul from sin through the redemption —the peasant with his plough means human labour, a result of sin, the hinds devouring serpents are a complicated theological reference to redemption through Christ, while the peacocks are symbols of immortality. The flowery designs immediately round the doorway represent the tree of life, springing from the cross, and also paradise.

Framing these are more bas-relief panels twice or three times the size. Beginning at the top right-hand corner we see *Christ washing the feet of St Peter*, while below *Christ calms the waters of the Lake of Tiberias for St Peter and St Andrew* (these two panels are probably by the same artist). Underneath this, *the fox feigning dead and the ravens* (the fox is a symbol of the Devil and the ravens mean the soul seduced by the flesh—a fable). Lower still, *Brother Wolf has a hood on his head (cappuccio), and a ram fleeing*: a skit on monastic life, where the wolf is trying to read from a book but his eyes wander greedily to the ram. At the bottom, *a lion chases a griffin or dragon*: the lion symbolizes Christ, the dragon evil. At the top left corner, we see *the death of the just man*, perhaps the most narrative of all these panels: St Peter frees the just man from his fetters, while the just man's soul is in the scales held up by St Michael the Archangel, and a demon, flourishing a scroll (with the words '*Doleo Quia Ante Erat Meus*—I mourn because formerly he was mine'), tries to weight the scales down on one side, but he gets a blow from St Peter's keys. Below this there is *the death of the sinner*: two demons torture and bind him, his body is then thrown into a boiling pot, and St Michael withdraws scandalized. Below this, *the lion and the woodman*—a theme that continues for the last two panels as well, rather obscure in its meaning: here the woodman is cutting wood and the lion's paws are somehow caught in the trunk of the tree, said to refer to a mediaeval fable about man's ability to free himself of demonic influences; the lion here probably represents godly power. In the next panel down *the man kneels to the lion,* and the lion is peaceful, meaning that grace and the forgiveness of God have to be invoked in order to be achieved. The last panel on the left shows the opposite of this: *the soldier has challenged the lion and is being attacked by him.* Before we leave the façade we should have a peep at the wall of the Canonica on its right: the triangular stone above the doorway (now a farmhouse) is decorated with an Etruscan scylla or six-headed monster.

Inside S. Pietro we have nothing but a clean baroque church where not a scrap of the façade's gravity is conveyed, though twice the effort was made.

Monteluco—the sacred woods and the Lex Spoletana—S. Giuliano

Car-drivers will be able to combine their visit to S. Pietro with a journey to the top of **Monteluco,** but walkers will either have to wait for a bus or make the long trek uphill by one of the paths leading from the church. The road takes us round seven kilometres of curves, but the paths are much shorter. The woods at the top were understandably sacred (*monte luco*—'sacred hill of woods') in Roman times: and protected against mutilation by the *Lex Spoletana*, one of whose proclamations we have seen at the museum. Town noises fail to reach us here. We are well over two thousand feet above sea-level.

Ten years ago we could get to the top by hired mule, along the many hidden paths (they started from the Ponte delle Torre then). The top is now an area of hotels (open for the summer season only) and residential compounds for citizens who want to escape the Spoletan heat. There are cafés and benches in the woods. At the terminus of the asphalted road we find a sanctuary of St Francis, rather like the Eremo delle Carceri above Assisi. An opening in the wall takes us into dark woods with a smooth floor: we pass a facsimile of the *Lex Spoletana*. The ancient sense of sacredness in these woods survived well into the Middle Ages, and was probably the reason for the existence of the Franciscan sanctuary here.

St Francis founded it in 1218, and the present building is on its site. The place was given to St Francis by the Benedictines, and here too the Saint is said to have caused a spring of water to come into being, as if the only important thing about him was his hydraulic powers.

On the way down we should have a look at **S. Giuliano**, nearly two thousand feet above sea-level: the curves of the road can easily obscure it for us. From the lawn fronting it we can look down on the city, its ancient nucleus compact and cleverly designed in a semi-circle, as if to take the best of the day's sun every day; and immediately below us are clear green fields. The church belongs to the end of the twelfth century and is on the site of a former sixth-century church in honour of the Syrian martyr, Julian. We have to go to the farmhouse attached to the church for the key. The façade faces not Spoleto, as we would expect, but the woods: here too there is a sweet little lawn, an air of peace. The most striking thing about the façade is its portal, made from fragments left over from the original sixth-century church, but above a three-arched window it suddenly breaks off, unfinished. The frame round the portal has light bas-relief panels of animals, a cross and various symbols, with a flowery design at the edge, in a fleeting reminiscence of the S. Pietro façade six hundred yards down the hill. Inside (the church is no longer used) we see massive, swelling pillars dividing the floor into three narrow naves. The apse-wall is frescoed with a *coronation of the Virgin* (1442) and below her we see *saints* and *beati*, the Blessed of the Monte-luco order of hermits (a group founded by St Isaac). The now almost invisible frescoes above the pillars on either side of the presbytery show *the story of St Isaac* (twelfth-century). The crypt (steps descend beneath the chancel) has a little opening in its left wall which leads to a tiny repetition of the church above, and this may have belonged to the original sixth-century buildings: but we shall be glad to escape its chill air.

Basilica di S. Salvatore—S. Ponziano

The church of **S. Salvatore** hugs Spoleto so closely that it is difficult to find (in Roman times this was the residential quarter). We leave the lower town at Piazza Garibaldi and bear right after we have passed through Piazza della Vittoria, as if going towards Norcia. We then come to a tourist sign which points us right and after a few yards this brings us to a tunnel (it goes under the superstrada), then directly to the town's cemetery: the church is just beyond this.

Its origins go as far back as the fourth century—we know of its being restored in the ninth century: and once again in the twelfth. It has been damaged by earthquakes and fire, but it submitted to the most drastic changes of all in the eighteenth century, and in 1906. We walk into the cemetery entrance at the side of the church and come on the façade, which is in ruins but keeps some of its first character. The door-cornices have a motif of rosettes and flowers, with a cross in the middle, and are one of the earliest examples we have of the marriage between the classical or Roman and the Byzantine. The frame of the portal has a protruding, curling handle of stone, S-shaped, the façade's most unusual feature: the handle that should match it on the other side is missing. Originally the whole front had a marble face: we can see how it was divided into two sections by the stone cornice across its middle. If we look up at the three windows we shall see an unusual design round the arch of the centre one, tiny steeple-like cones, with a cross crowning them.

Inside, the one nave was clearly three before: the arches between the ancient pillars on either side have been roughly filled in—a desperate twelfth-century attempt, perhaps, to keep the building erect after a fire or earthquake. The presbytery is almost an ancient temple in itself, its tall fluted columns seeming to belong to a superb Parthenon, with capitals of Corinthian design at all four corners. It is removed from the main body of the church by two steps. Doric cornices are supported by four pillars irregularly placed on each side. And it has the odd appearance of being the result of two separate plans, there being two shapes here, the rectangular (closed by the triumphal arch) and the semi-circular apse-form, which at one time probably rose to a vault higher up (the present dome is a baroque addition). Restoration has thus unearthed two periods of building, close to each other in time but quite different in concept.

In a niche behind the altar we see a rough and damaged painted cross from the beginning of the ninth century. For five hundred years, from the eleventh to the sixteenth century, the church was called S. Concordio, who tradition says is buried there. It then came to be called 'del Crocifisso' because of the cross, taken from another church in the sixteenth century, which we see at the altar today. Only in our time did the church return to its mediaeval name of S. Salvatore, during the restoration (1906-50) to its first shape. The monastery attached to the church was Benedictine.

Returning down the lane towards Spoleto we take a left fork before we reach the tunnel under the superstrada, and this will lead us to **S. Ponziano.** He was a local martyr, and is the town's patron saint: he was killed (A.D. 175) under the Emperor Antoninus. If the church is closed we should ask at the house on the opposite side of the court-yard. It is Romanesque in form, from the twelfth century, and was built on St Sincleta's catacomb. She and some Syrian monks began a settlement here in veneration of St Pontian, this probably being his burial place, and later it became a Benedictine convent.

The main door has a mosaic frame, and stone lions on either side of the base: the one on the left rests on a Roman urn which bears an inscription. Above the portal tiny medallions enclose bas-relief animals—a lion and an eagle on either side of the mystic lamb, with a propitiatory inscription above. A rose window has large symbols of the evangelists at each corner. The decorated pediment at the top of the façade is a fourteenth-century addition.

The church has a baroque interior, of 1788. The attendant will show us a rather fascinating crypt with two of its columns tapering towards their capitals, which is very rarely seen. There are votive frescoes from the fifteenth and sixteenth centuries, and two sarco-phagi which come from the catacomb of the tenth century on this spot.

CHAPTER 13

A Country Route to Narni

Acquasparta – Carsulae – Amelia

The superstrada is the quickest but not the quietest or even the most interesting avenue of approach to southern Umbria. A good and eventful road will take us all the way from Assisi (or Foligno) to Narni: it makes an excellent—but long—day-trip. Hardy walkers will find many paths and track roads, and some modest heights to scale. If we are coming from Assisi we leave the superstrada before we reach Foligno, where a signpost directs us to Bevagna. Passing Bevagna on our right, with Gualdo Cattaneo on its hill before us, we begin to penetrate serene and fertile countryside, and after several kilometres of winding road we go through an ugly village fitly called Bastardo (the site of a thermo-electric plant) and continue towards the Via Tiberina and Acquasparta. From this point the road is less good for motoring and more attractive for walkers: it is all superb on a sunny day, bright green—and you feel on top of the world as you rise among the flat clear fields (a fog-trap in late autumn and winter) close to Massa Martano, about three thousand three hundred feet up. The whole way is enchanting, fertile with streams and sheep-grazing land and sudden valleys, with here and there clean-limbed cypresses close to the road.

We pass through Collevalenza where on our right what looks like a factory turns out to be a convent: and a little later we reach asphalted road again and the Via Tiberina, or 'road of the Tiber'. This goes straight to Narni, and comes from Todi. Here we are among chalky and woody hills and the road is busier.

After another kilometre we should keep our eyes open for a sharp bend in the road that takes us across the Ponte Fonnaia, an ancient Roman bridge still in use today and showing no signs of surrender despite constant heavy trucks; it has been reinforced rather than rebuilt; the original blocks of stone, placed clean one on another, are still there. It dates from about 200 B.C.

Acquasparta—the house where Galileo stayed

Our next town is **Acquasparta,** a modest spa hardly more than a main street and a major palazzo, surrounded by a crumbling wall and commanding the valley of the river Naia. Bare, wooded hills close all round it, giving it an air of isolation in wildness. It has about five thousand inhabitants and is worth a call for a number of reasons, among them the tiny Trattoria Sacchi which we may be in need of, in the Via Marconi as we enter the town: it offers good food and even—at the moment—genuine wine.

And at the centre of the old nucleus of the town is the *Palazzo Cesi,* a dark and ponderous house in its own square, brooding with memories of power, square and gaunt and pock-marked, with holes in the walls that may be for defence but more likely for a marble face that was never put there: at any rate they now make nice homes for the pigeons. It is a worthwhile experience for those who like carved wooden ceilings; here are some of the finest imaginable, left to the mercy of the rain for the past two, if not three, decades. But Perugia university, the new owner, is doing something about it, and putting the building to ,use as a college for commercial studies. The Cesi family started the Accademia dei Lincei in Rome, and Galileo, together with other scientists, took refuge here from Vatican disapproval. Upstairs in the main salon the vast fireplace has been restored (it had collapsed to the floor). Most of the rooms have fireplaces: and with tapestries on the walls Galileo and his friends must have been quite comfortable. The sounds of the town drift in pleasantly through the windows, with that perfect suggestion of refinement in nature which country houses should give. The superbly carved wooden ceilings are repeated in room after room. Some of the heavy centrepieces have crashed to the floor. The main salon bears the Cesi arms in its centre vault, carved in depth, with its faint reflection—restored exactly as it always was—in the bricks of the floor immediately beneath it.

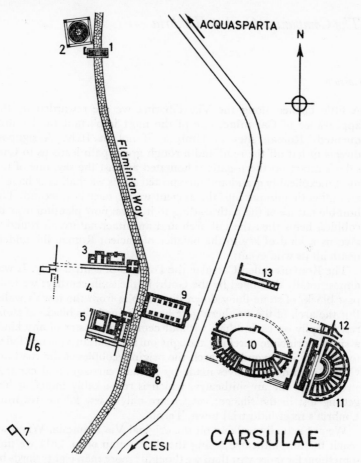

1. Gate of town, originally with three arches
2. A monument or memorial, with a square base
3. Public buildings
4. The Forum
5. The foundations of two identical temples
6. A fountain
7. Baths
8. The church of S. Damiano (built in the Middle Ages out of material
from the Forum)
9. Law Court
10. Amphitheatre (approx. 260 × 190 ft.)
11. Theatre (diameter approx. 190 ft.)
12. Brick columns belonging to an unidentified building
13. Another fountain

281

Carsulae

A little farther along the Via Tiberina we are rewarded by the appearance of **Carsulae,** one of the most important (and unfrequented) Roman sites in Umbria, if not in Italy. A signpost directs us left off the road and a rough green path leads us to Carsulae's intact northern gate, silhouetted against the sky, one of the most inexplicably grand and unexpected sights we shall ever have—an authentic glimpse into the ancient world, over in a second. The humble nature of the path leading to it, grass now plentiful over its cobbles, helps this: the tall arch and an intact nature all round it give us a kind of key to the balance of ancient Roman life underneath all its wild events.

The Romans called Carsulae the Pompeii of central Italy. It was almost totally destroyed by the Goths in the sixth century: we walk past blocks of stone flung down like pebbles from the town's walls. But the arch of the northern gate has remained: its blocks of stone rest happily on each other, without cement or plaster of any kind, a simple principle carefully thought out: barbarian violence failed to dislodge it. Beyond the arch the original cobbles of the road are visible, with deep grooves made by Roman carriages and carts. A stroll round the amphitheatre, which is remarkably intact, is like getting lost in the silence: yet we are only a few kilometres from Umbria's most industrial town, Terni.

We are actually walking on the original Via Flaminia. When we reach the amphitheatre (using the sketch-map on p. 281) we find something far more vast than we thought: more than eighty yards by sixty. The theatre close behind it has its acting area intact, with a slope running down on each side from the wings, presumably for heavy props or carriages. If we look up the hill from this point we shall see unexcavated remains—the trace of an arch here, a wall there: a lot has still to be done. When we see it all in this silence the vastness of the building operation strikes us, the blocks of stone are really huge, sometimes six feet in length and nearly two feet wide; and then there is the fact that none of it disturbs the country all round in its proportions, but gives it all a sudden intimacy. It was the Romans, after all, who first made Europe a garden.

At the back of the theatre a staircase takes us to the top of a hillock from which we can see the rear semi-circular wall, which must be one of the finest ancient remains in the country, so that we really can imagine its first period, instead of having mentally to reconstruct it as we usually do. It looks rather like the corner of an Arab town with sunlight bleaching it and breezes wandering slowly down from the hills as if afraid to interrupt. The permanent backcloth to the theatrical performances here must have been the wall of the amphi-theatre, and, for those sitting high up, the whole of the city beyond it would have been visible too. Here and there we can see the frieze round these walls, reconstructed from fragments. We see the inner staircase of the oval amphitheatre—presumably for the gladiators and performers. Beyond the amphitheatre lies the forum of the city, which we can walk over. An arch before it frames the amphitheatre exactly in its arms. In this area we shall find a fragment of what must have been a gigantic statue—just the knee and part of the toga falling over it, in marble.

The most important monuments of the town were those close to the road and it seems to have been a traveller's city: Vespasian's army stopped here in A.D. 69, according to Tacitus, because of the loveliness and fertility of the spot. And of course there were the baths near by: the whole region here is dotted with them still. Carsulae achieved its greatest importance during the empire and became a Roman colony with its own magistrature. Long before the Goths came on the scene there appears to have been an earthquake, during the last period of the Roman empire, which toppled some of the buildings, and there was a general exodus to safer areas.

Just outside the northern gate, on our way back, we may notice a sarcophagus half sunk in the earth, and a fragment of stonework that may have surrounded a well or fallen from the arch, with flowers and a bull's head.

Amelia—a baroque gate—the town-crier's balcony

Perhaps the most graceful little town in Umbria—in name too—is **Amelia,** sparkling in the sun, cleaned by strong breezes from the valleys all round. An unusual sense of order prevails in its narrow, winding streets—perhaps a survival from the Roman settlement here. And like all towns in this southern part of Umbria (except Terni, which has an industrial life all its own), it seems to belong to Rome and to draw its spirit from the proximity.

The town is said to have been founded over eleven hundred years before Christ. 'Ameria' was a famous Umbrian settlement long before it became a Roman town inscribed to the tribe of Crustumina. In the Middle Ages it was a free commune, then in 1307 it passed to the Church. It has been sacked a good many times, and was much destroyed in the 1832 earthquake. Drivers can get their cars all the way up to the duomo, the highest point, but the narrow lanes and one-way signs make it hardly worth while. In fact, the hill is so steep and fine that the duomo occupies the whole of the peak.

We begin our climb at the so-called Roman gate which will strike us at once by not being very old: it has stone pillars and an ornate baroque frame, and was put there in 1703. The town-wall is unusually intact (about ten feet thick), and again we see great Roman blocks of stone placed together without cement; its upper parts are mediaeval.

We walk uphill into the town by the Via della Repubblica. The first road on the right takes us into a tranquil square with the church of S. Francesco on one side—though this is only an adopted name, the real one being **SS. *Filippo e Giacomo*,** built in 1287. It has a wide, forbidding front of grey stone with pink traces, its rose window containing a tiny stone lamb at the centre. Inside, its baroque has a sort of lower-middle-class order about it, frowsy and pinched and over-respectable. The church is known for its chapel (the first one on the right as we walk down) with its elaborately carved tombs— a splendid reminiscence of more intimate epochs, when trouble was taken over small ends. On the right as we enter the chapel we have the three tombs of the Geraldini family—Camillo and Belisario who were nephews of the couple lying above (Matteo and Elisabetta). Except perhaps for the tomb of Belisario this is all by Agostino di Duccio (1477), whose work we have seen in Perugia. Hieronumo Geraldini lies on the right of this group, and on the opposite side of the chapel there is Angelo's tomb (1548). The latest Count Geraldini restored the chapel in 1929.

The Via della Repubblica winds left after a further rise and we keep left at a fork until we reach the Arco di Piazza, a kind of tunnel through which the road passes briefly, with blocks of ancient stone visible in its walls. And we come out into the Piazza G. Marconi, which still breathes the atmosphere of the past with its tiny cobbles underfoot and low buildings all round, an image of the former intimate provincial life that sometimes sparkled into happiness. Like all of Amelia, it conveys a sense of small-scale splendour. On our left immediately as we enter the square, attached to the archway under which we have just passed, there is a mediaeval *tribuna* or *loggia dei banditori*, which still has an air of minute fuss and gossip, with its clock-tower and bell and slightly jutting pulpit or rostrum from which the town-herald used to shout his news. On our right there is the sixteenth-century Palazzo Petrignani with its excellent sobriety of design, symmetrical and quiet though tall. At its side a staircase-path will lead us up to the ***Duomo***. At the top we come out at a medley of buildings including a gigantic polygonal tower made of huge blocks of stone, with the curve of an apse elbowing it, amid grass and gravel. And opposite these a low and modest building of brown brick balances and tempers it all. The church was all redone after a fire in 1629, and there was a lot of restoration—or rather embellishing—in 1904. The tower, though, dates from 1050, and of course it is based squarely on Roman finds. Inside (we may have to ring at the low rustic building opposite for the priest) we see an ornate presbytery and apse full of gilt, a poor reward for that climb. And the whole place was badly frescoed in the nineteenth century. Immediately on the right after we have entered, surrounded by an iron fence and securely clamped to the wall, is a column to which Amelia's patron saint, S. Fermina, is said to have been tied. The second chapel down on the right has in its wide entrance corridor, behind glass on either side, two Turkish flags captured during one of the Crusades. In the chapel itself we see the tombs of two members of the Farrattini family (1534) carved by Ippolito Scalza, which achieve nothing like the intimacy of the five tombs we saw a little earlier.

The chapels here are deep and splendid in the baroque manner, with twirling gilt-leafed pillars and intricate wood-carvings. The organ-loft is extraordinarily luscious, above the wooden choir. It looks as if people decorated things frantically at that time lest an ugly truth showed through: a nervous activity for activity's sake which has survived in the Italian character. Returning back up the church from the high altar we find at the first chapel a stone tomb belonging to another Geraldini (1476), this time a bishop. It has a bas-relief above of a *Madonna and Child, with Faith,*

Hope, Charity and Strength: Agostino di Duccio had a hand here, too.

If we return to the lower town by the way we came we pass round the façade of the little church of S. Caterina in the Via Aless. Geraldino (1455-1525, the first bishop of Santo Domingo in America), which takes us downhill to the church of S. Agostino. It faces us at the bottom with its one Gothic doorway, elaborately carved, and one rose window above: a fourteenth-century church, though the façade was restored in 1477. We turn left from the façade and then left again, which brings us into the spacious and delightful Piazza Giacomo Matteotti, with its cylindrically clipped tree and round lawn. On the right, with an iron balcony and clock, is the terra-cotta face of the *Palazzo Comunale*. In its little courtyard we find Roman and mediaeval pieces: there is a figure with toga, the head missing; and a sarcophagus, and two sarcophagus lids. Under the square there is a complete ancient Roman reservoir (hidden of course), divided into seven compartments each with arched entrances of stone, and in ancient times the water used to be over twenty feet deep, to serve the whole town. At present it is about six feet deep, and there is a local plan to dry it out and open it to view, with an entrance from the square.

CHAPTER 14

Todi

Todi stands hidden on the peak of a hill at a sharp turn in the Tiber, and this may have given it its important defensive role, with its superb command of the river and all approaches from the sea. In fact, the town's history—even its atmosphere today—is military. Its symbol is a menacing eagle, used on its buildings in every epoch. Todi was particularly known for its worship of the war-god, and in fact one of its alternative names in Roman times was Marzia. The statue of Mars now in the Vatican museum was found here too. There is something austere and detached about the town, with its long, spacious square that bestrides the highest point of the hill, and the steep declines on every side to the sparsely populated countryside all round. The people, too, have that reticent and numbed quality bred by garrison life in which everyone's role is to obey in peace, and in war to do or die. Their voices are subdued in cafés— an unusual thing in Italy: their speech is orderly and sparing. Historical origins are of great importance in Italy, especially in regions like Umbria where town-life has been closely knit for centuries and changes have come slowly, without disrupting it.

The birthplace of Jacopone

You approach the city under its observant but unseen walls: if you come from the south you face its Roman gate, leading straight up into the city, after leaving the Via Tiberina at the foot of the hill. It is a long climb to the central piazza (the Roman gate is barred to incoming drivers), through the town's three walls and three gates. Traffic is directed round to another gate that once guarded the road to Orvieto, and this will be our point of entry from the north. But

287

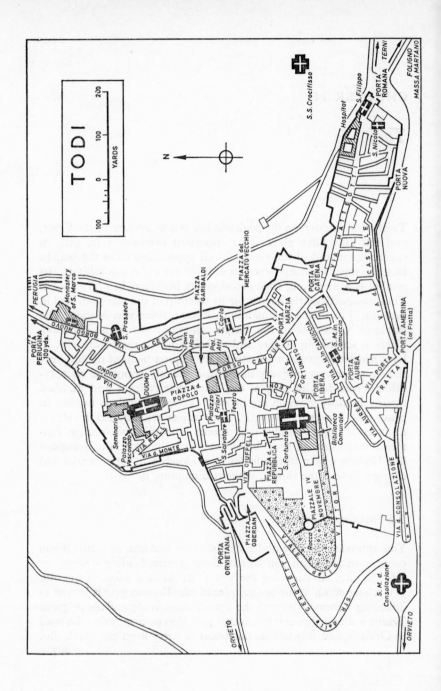

wherever we arrive we should begin our itineraries from the south, or the Roman gate.

Todi was founded by the Umbrians, and between the fifth and third centuries B.C. was taken over by the Etruscans, a fact we hardly expect from the character of its people. It must always have enjoyed marked independence, because pre-Roman money has been found bearing the name Tutere, or 'of Todi'. It was colonized as a military camp by the Romans under the name *Colonia Iulia Fida Tuder*, and its historical reputation is for ferocity in war; it stood up to Totila and was partly preserved against barbarian savaging, just as it defied Frederick II seven hundred years later. It became a free town (SPQT can be seen today on its walls) in the twelfth century, and its quarrels (the external ones—though it had plenty of internal ones too) were with Spoleto, Orvieto and Narni. Its decline as a city began during the fourteenth century, when it passed from one master to another like most other Umbrian towns, finally ending under the Church. It had some bombing in the last war, but none of the monuments suffered: its reputation for jealous independence was revived in the partisan movement, for which the town lost ten citizens in reprisal.

Above all, Todi is famous as the birthplace of Jacopone—**Ser Jacopone**, who became a Franciscan after a wild youth and was the author of many *laudi*, or 'praises', a popular form all over Umbria after St Francis's death. All that later becomes known as humanism and the new learning and the Renascence owes its first stirring to this peaceful and undidactic rebellion against dogma and theology, in praise of life. Jacopo Benedetti (1230-1306) withdrew from town life when he was thirty-two: there is a legend that he was dancing with his wife at a wedding when the floor gave way and she was killed; he found that unknown to himself she had been wearing the rough shirt of penitence under her dress, like one of the *battuti* (beaten ones) who were coming into existence all over Umbria at the time to carry on St Francis's work by self-mortification; the tragedy is said to have brought about his conversion. He became one of the *fraticelli*, the monks in open rebellion against official Franciscanism and the Vatican.

The Umbrian *laude* was written to be sung, on themes like the birth of Christ or the crucifixion, told in the direct and natural way that Francis had conveyed in his own talk. They were ballads really, haunting, with that great primitive vigour of suffering which we find in all ballad-forms. The most famous of them is probably Ser Jacopone's *Pianto della Madonna*, which describes Mary going from one person to another frantically enquiring after her son, until she reaches Pontius Pilate and then the cross itself; people tell her how her son has been taken—'Lady, he was betrayed; Judas sold him; thirty dinars he got for it, he made a bargain!'

S. Nicolò—Porta Marzia—Piazza del Popolo with its three civic palaces —the Museum

Todi has the remains of *three walls*—each distinct from the other: the first Etruscan, then the Roman and the mediaeval, showing how the town grew with each epoch. There are tiny, winding lanes tunnelled under houses, suddenly remote from the traffic, with views of the wide valleys and smooth hills on either side, which make it a fascinating town to walk in. It has so many levels, so many un-expected corners, where a lane suddenly emerges into open country or a piazzetta, that we are always surprised. Mediaeval wells still stand at inconvenient places in the road. And dominating it all, with a great unyielding frown, is the central square, to which most of the winding lanes lead.

The first fragment of wall we see, coming from the Roman Gate up the narrow Via Matteotti, is from the fourteenth century. (The words *prima cerchia* or *seconda cerchia* are constantly seen at various points in the town, and they mean the first, second or third 'circles' of wall.) Immediately on the left after we pass through the Roman Gate is the little church of **S. Nicolò** in its own square. This is worth a visit for its lovely Gothic interior with one wide nave, the roof supported by two high arches in the main body of the church, and by a lower one in the chancel which frames a series of dome-arches behind it delightfully at variance with each other. This is because, when the present church was built in the fourteenth century, a former apse was used (there was an eleventh-century S. Nicolò) which pointed in a slightly different direction. The ceiling is wooden, newly painted blue and decorated with white fleur-de-lys; the beams are inscribed (it was done ten years ago by the unusual resident priest) with fragments of scripture put into rhyme.

Continuing to the top of Via Matteotti we pass under the Porta della Catena ('Chain Gate'), belonging to the second (that is, the Roman) wall, with the town's eagle crowning it. On the left a narrow lane called Via di Mezzo Muro ('half-wall') shows traces of the original Roman wall (usually recognizable by its neatness). Almost at the top of Via Matteotti the Etruscan arch called Porta Marzia is a lovely sight, with its loggia overhead, used as a private terrace now, and reached by french windows. This is the first wall of the city, so that judging by its closeness to the main square the original settlement was no more than a village. A little farther on there is the tiny Piazza di Marte, with a pleasant porch closing it from the valley beyond: an intimate corner which cannot have changed for three hundred years, where a staircase-tunnel burrows under the houses, and a fine little palazzo watches it all gaily, as if the sun had never once ceased shining here.

Via Matteotti emerges at the top of the hill into the small, rectangular Piazza Garibaldi, with its tall, mute Garibaldi standing in the middle and, beyond it, bringing a fresh breeze from the plains far below, a wide balcony from which woods and cropland can be seen, with the church of S. Crocifisso yellow and rather new-looking to the right, just outside the town, near the Roman Gate. Closing one side of this square is the stern and brutal Palazzo Atti, built in 1552, its main door framed with great blocks of stone, everything about it arguing worldly power. The Atti family were for long rulers of the town: it was Raniero Atti who rallied the Ghibelline elements a hundred years after Todi had become a member of the Umbrian league of Guelf towns.

Now we get our first glimpse of the central square beyond, with its thirteenth-century Palazzo dei Priori (its side-wall on our immediate left) and then, remote and bright and calm at the top of wide steps in the distance, the chief enemy of this civic building, the duomo itself.

The **Piazza del Popolo** is spacious, self-assured, ordered: we get the best view of the contradictions and struggles out of which it achieved its order by standing with the duomo far on our left, so that we face the twin, connected buildings of the *Palazzo del Popolo* and the *Palazzo del Capitano*. The *Palazzo dei Priori* on our right now seems to challenge the other two, with its gaunt battlements and a front which has retained its humble mediaeval proportions despite being restored in the sixteenth century. We can see the Aquila Tuderte, or eagle of Todi, high on its wall, intact

and green (1339). This was the home of the town's administration—
the priors, then the rectors, then the vicars and finally the pontifical
governors.

And the Palazzo del Popolo with its Ghibelline battlements turns
an answering hostile side-glance at it, with a sternness of later date:
it is a Lombard building begun in 1213 and restored at the end of
the last century; its base, and thus that of the Palazzo del Capitano
connected to it, is a deep, tall archway, or rather series of archways,
that now shelters the vegetable market; there are two storeys, and
the windows are contained in three slender arches, square-framed,
contrasting with the more ornate windows of the Palazzo del Capitano at its side. These three Gothic windows have a wonderful
elegance, set in so much gaunt power-architecture, and are surmounted by a rose window and spired roof where the two Gothic
curves meet; on the second storey there are four smaller versions of
this. Wide steps, going parallel and not frontally to the square, lead
up between the two buildings, turning sharp left to meet their doorways, which have mock iron portcullises above them.

We stand in this square, with only bare architectural details to
interest us—the types of crenellation, the windows, the vaulted
arches over the vegetable market; there is order here but not
harmony. The square makes a convenient car-park. A cavernous
bar (where you can get good coffee) peers out from a corner of
the Palazzo dei Priori. The truth is that perhaps for the first time
in history the square is as silent, as still, as its stones: in the time of,
say, Rolli, the first Italian translator of *Paradise Lost*, who lived
in an exquisite little villa at the foot of the duomo steps, this square
was full of carriages, rang with the noise of hammers and saws,
had great planks leaning against the houses weathering for use
as beams for coffins or tables, and now the noise and therefore the
life has gone.

At the top of the steps leading into the Piazza del Popolo, we shall
see, facing us before we turn left to the actual doorways, two slim
iron rods set in the wall which were used in mediaeval times as
measures: at each end of them we can make out the tiny Todi eagle.
The right-hand of the two doorways leads us to the *Museum*
upstairs, on the second floor, a higgledy-piggledy show where
nothing is itemized; though for those who know Italian, some of the
exhibits have typewritten descriptions under them, yellowing with
age. Yet there are extraordinary things to see, set in three or four

glass cases of Roman and Etruscan finds. On a table near the entrance we see Roman fragments of stone and marble—a small bust with toga, pieces of an ornate column, a graceful, broken, marked head of Dionysius, the lovely head of a girl with a diadem which looks almost too delicate to be Roman, a head of a satyr, and pots found in fields close to the Via Flaminia not long ago. There is a fragment of a Roman altar from the first century B.C., etched with olive trees. On a sarcophagus you can see Romulus and Remus under the wolf of Rome, or rather one of them, as the other has broken off. There are fragments found in tombs—including the so-called *kylix*, or painted pot, derived from Greek models.

The Etruscan case conveys to us in a tiny space the whole range of Etruscan domestic life in engraved hand-mirrors, colanders, cups for libation, wine goblets, clasps, a cylindrical receptacle with three legs and a circular cover for keeping perfume or sometimes jewellery (the covers are invariably decorated—this one has a griffin). And very common in the Etruscan tombs opened round Todi are the oil-lamps—these too have three legs about eighteen inches high, holding a cup for the oil. There are sets of small, identical, oval stones, used in the children's game which the Romans inherited, the *ludum latrunculum*; we would say knucklestones or—at least in my part of London—dabs. We see little bronze decorative pieces from candelabra and dish covers and pots for the dressing-table, depicting all kinds of savage animals. A candle-holder meant to be carried by hand has seven spikes fanning out from a handle, with two subsidiary ones like the back claws of an eagle. There are bronze door-knockers in the form of curved swan-necks holding rings; and decorative safety-pins, a golden ear-ring representing putti or a child holding a bird—the whole thing hardly bigger than a finger-nail. This glass case, by the way, has one of the only three Etruscan figures of a Celtic soldier that exist in Italy: the Romans called them Gauls, and they were tall and blond, with flowing hair; being a quite fearless people, they terrified the Etruscans at the time of the latter's decline, and worried Rome. Then they settled down in the north of Italy (Milan was founded by them). A bilingual Latin-Celtic inscription was found in Todi and is now in the Vatican museum.

There are four more or less intact Etruscan *buccheri*, grey or black pots made from a mixture of natural clay and charcoal so that they retained a uniform colour throughout, unlike black painted pots which have much the same appearance. These all conform to one style: the lip is curved slightly, never fully rounded. There are also painted pots and plates showing conversations between couples or young men, always in pairs; there is a seated youth playing the flute.

On a side-table there are terra-cotta heads and pieces of cornice said to have decorated the wooden temples of Etruscan towns. On a pedestal we see a bronze pig which could have been cast yesterday for all the wear it has suffered: it is Etruscan, a solid piece of bronze weighing well over sixty pounds; some people think it was used as a weight. There are also tiny bronze soldiers dated at between the fifth and third centuries B.C.; presumably they are ornaments; or perhaps Etruscan children played with them.

The big hall (through which we entered) holds the picture gallery, also uncatalogued. A vast *tavola* stands by the right wall, the work of Lo Spagna, *the coronation of the Virgin* (1507), reminiscent of the Ghirlandaio on the same subject which we shall see later at Narni. In fact, this was painted in imitation of it: Christ's face has a similar delicate solemnity as he leans forward and places the crown on Mary's head. Underneath there are *twenty-five saints*, but the little panels at the bottom are missing (Napoleonic troops took them off to France). In a glass case opposite the Lo Spagna there are some episcopal robes worth looking at, particularly one with a faded motif of angels, the oldest there. But the most interesting things here are the frescoes in a far corner, from the fourteenth century, showing part of a *Crucifixion*, and some saints, with the Byzantine stillness that is now familiar to us. And in a magnificent cupboard there are all sorts of painted bowls and plates and dishes and jugs, mostly from Renascence times.

The Sala del Consiglio, or Council Room, is still used by the town today, and the attendant will take us there on request. It is a tall, domed, square chamber with faint traces of thirteenth-century frescoes—part of a *Crucifixion*; and two stone eagles that date perhaps from the first origins of the building.

The Duomo—an unusual side-chapel and an imitation of Michelangelo

But the Church really has the last word in this square: the **Duomo** sits withdrawn and placid behind its twenty-nine steps, gazing down at the once-feverish arena (now a feverish garage) where arguments have been going on for five or six centuries without impairing the need—if only in the case of baptism and marriage and death—for her suave co-operation.

It was begun in the twelfth century, perhaps on the foundations of a Temple of Apollo, and restored twice in the next two hundred years. The church has a fine, broad face, remarkably tranquil, with three doors and three rose windows, its main door a magnificent Gothic arch among twining acanthus leaves. On the right of the façade the tower rises with Gothic arches to enclose its bells.

Inside, there are three naves divided by alternate columns and pilasters, massive and stark; the saints sculptured at their capitals have the characteristic disproportion that marks mediaeval work, as if the body had been dwindled by a special humility of attitude rather than by the artist's hand. The best—most contemplative—thing in the church is the long chapel on the right with Gothic arches formed out of low, slender columns, running along the west side, narrow and exposed to view, yet more withdrawn than most chapels that are closed. The main altar is a simple block of stone on slender columns, a refusal of baroque grandness: and in fact modern. There is a rather luscious organ-loft of gilded wood, mounted in 1530. And behind the altar, dark and intimate, a marvellous choir of wood can be seen—the work of an artist born in Pesaro in 1530: behind each seat there is a clever inlaid picture—glimpses of doorways, courtyards, a room seen through a window with an open book of music, and the Blessed Sacrament, crucifixes, hour-glasses, musical instruments, a birdcage, building sites, while the central throne itself, taller and deeper than the other seats, bears the theme of the *Annunciation*, and is backed with gold cloth. Such a priceless piece of workmanship in wood is rare even in Italy: you will find no chip or blemish however hard you look.

At the back of the church there is a fresco of *the Last Judgment* over the main door, interesting as an imitation of Michelangelo's work in the Sistine Chapel, by da Faenza (he was called Ferrau and people tacked on 'from Faenza', 1562-1645). On this wall, and easy to miss, there is a *Madonna and Child* on wood, in which her head emerges from the board in bas-relief plaster: it has a primitive grace, mute and retiring, and from a distance looks like the realization of a bad—and late—idea, which it isn't at all (probably late fourteenth century).

295

The crypt can be reached by steps on the left of the chancel— the light-switch takes some looking for. On the way down there are Roman and perhaps Etruscan fragments on either side, and in the lower church itself we find what may be the original form of the pagan temple, or at least part of it.

Two walks—the monastery where Luther stayed—arches from the time of Augustus—S. Maria in Camuccia and a Gothic Madonna and Child

Two interesting walks can be taken from the duomo, one using the little lane on the left of the church steps as we face them, and the other that on the right.

The narrow roadway running by the right wall of the church is called Via del Duomo. This wall, incidentally, is worth looking at for its lofty slender pillars and a 'hanging arcade' formed by arches set into the wall. The Via del Duomo becomes after a time the Via di S. Prassede—we pass another stretch of the first wall (restored by the Romans) and there is a plaque to that effect: after winding our way downhill we reach the little church of S. Prassede, quite a surprise with its pink-and-white stone face, simple and undecorated, its porch repeating the pink-and-white motif in pilasters. In fact this front is unfinished, as we can see from the rough brickwork above. It was started in the fourteenth century. On the right there is a door leading to a balcony from which we can see the cloisters of the previous Augustinian monastery: Luther stayed here on his way to Rome. The church itself has been done up in quite pretty and cosy baroque. We can return to the central piazza by Via Cesia, turning right past the little church of S. Ilario whose bell-tower now stands empty, along the Via del Mercato Vecchio until we reach the piazza of that name with its four vast niches that at once proclaim ancient Rome, with a Doric frieze above. No one knows what these were part of: perhaps a basilica (law-court), or—much more likely perhaps, since things in Italy have an astonishing continuity —exactly what the name of the piazza says, a market-place. They date from Augustan times.

At the end of this road we find Via Matteotti again. If we walk downhill for a moment we shall find on the right Via S. Maria in Camuccia, which will take us to a remarkable little church of that name, standing raised in its own square, quiet and simple, its main door set to the left of the façade in an appealing lack of symmetry; the Corinthian pillars on either side may have come from a Roman building—perhaps a temple—on the same site. In fact there are Roman remnants in the wall—the trace of a marble arch, square ponderous blocks of stone. Inside, the church belongs to the late eighteenth century except in one astonishing respect, of which few people in Todi (or elsewhere) seem aware: a chapel in the left wall —a relic of the original building—has a lovely *Madonna and Child* in wood, almost lifesize, in its first radiance, confounding all the ornateness of the rest of the church; a Gothic piece, firm and un-demonstrative without the slightest rigidity, a marvel of care and devotion, though its little imitation crowns were clearly put there in recent times, and the Madonna's face has been a little too smoothly restored. It is a reminder of the tiny terra-cotta *Pietà* in S. Domenico in Gubbio, and who knows that it isn't the work of the same man, travelling from place to place in Umbria, a German artist, perhaps? Near the entrance, on the left, there is an equally German fresco, Ambrogio's *Madonna* (he was born in Milan and brought northern influences down to Umbria, perhaps as the head of a school).

S. Fortunato—the scrawling of pilgrims—Tempio della Consolazione

And now for Todi's most spectacular piece. We reach it by starting off again from the central piazza, taking the Via Mazzini alongside the Palazzo dei Priori. After passing the Teatro Comunale—one of those pleasant nineteenth-century theatres to be seen all over Umbria—we find our road bending to the right, and there (we could easily have passed it) at the top of a steep ramp composed partly of steps and partly of paths zig-zagging between clipped hedges, perched bright and magnificent on top like the icing on a cake—the church of **S. Fortunato.** This whole square is a miracle (Piazza Umberto I), rising steeply, with marvellous little palazzi on either side, shuttered, arched, balconied, terraced, as if one bene-ficent hand had brought them all suddenly together: and each is different from the next. The church is well called 'fortunate'. I sus-pect that its peculiar ramp was designed to stop a frontal attack, though how anyone could bear to assault this lovely thing is difficult to see. Only half-way up, after the zig-zag bushery, do real steps begin, wide and reflective like those before the duomo.

This church took nearly two hundred years to build—and work on it was more or less continuous. It was begun in 1292 and the façade is actually the latest piece: all that we see shining so brightly, even at night, is the work of Fiorenzuola di Spoleto; but it is unfinished, as we see from the naked brickwork staring from behind and above. At the top of the steps, on either side of the church like sentinels—so old as to be almost indistinguishable now—are two Romanesque lions sitting on their haunches. Then there is the vast arched doorway, between two others of smaller size: only in Orvieto is there anything like it for sheer generous splendour—twirling columns, arches garlanded four times over with leaves and figures of bishops and, most surprising of all, naked figures that seem to be sitting on each other's shoulders, rising to the arch: all so warm and unstinted that we might be in Jerusalem. In niches on either side there are figures of *Gabriel* and *the Virgin*, statues in the style of Iacopo della Quercia, as if they were done in wood, painted. And on the left of the church, withdrawn from the front, is the stout tower: walking under this by the path that runs at its side, we have an impression of fearful vastness.

The church inside is a tall, open basilica with all three naves soaring to the roof by means of high arches set on pilasters—and these pilasters consist, each of them, of eight pillars clustered together in a staggering show of strength. They slope outwards, as we notice if we stand at the back of the church in line with them; this lean is taken up by closed arches (which rather spoil the effect, but without them the whole thing would fall down) set between the pillars and the outer wall. At the foot of the first pilaster on the left there are two fragments from the heads of former columns rescued, probably, from the first church in this place: one of them, decorated with vines, is used as a holy water font, its stone so polished by hands that it must have served the same purpose for centuries. In the fourth chapel down on the right a *Madonna and Child and two angels* is intact and wistful—a moment of dreaming in what seems otherwise a stiff, military town, as if history had fixed its character for always. This is one of Masolino's last works, after he had painted at S. Clemente in Rome. The lower part of the fresco has suffered, but the faces of the Madonna and the two angels remain clear and delicate. It makes us stop—with its sudden gravity.

The last chapel on the right has been the scene of many little pilgrimages, and the signs of these are scrawled all over the walls and marble columns. Pencil has more lasting power than we think: devout messages written in the 'eighties of the last century, in a kind of scrawl we rarely see nowadays (denoting peace of mind) are still perfectly legible. There is a message from someone who couldn't spell, '*Qui pregammo per il nostro bun Jesu per la pace eterna*—here we pray through our good Jesus for eternal peace,' dated almost exactly a year before the last war began.

On the right of the presbytery, facing the church, is a pulpit set higher in the wall than I have seen before: underneath is a steep drop—and the entrance to a chapel. This chancel too has a mar-vellous wooden choir, by Maffei da Gubbio (sixteenth-century): the first three seats are especially lavish. There is an overpowering organ-loft high in the left wall—at the moment stripped of its paint. Everything in this church is on a big scale—self-assertive, on the de-fensive even.

A lane on the right of the church leads through a little square to the cloisters—now a school: the cloister arches are low, in the Romanesque style, with sturdy, angular supporting pillars. If we continue along this path uphill, by the old monastery wall, we shall reach a clearing with parapets, a playground for children, and the last remaining stump of a castle which must have commanded the approaches from the sea; and down below we see the serene cupolas of the Tempio della Consolazione, so finished and ordered that nobody goes near it.

The **Temple of Consolation** stands in its own lawn outside the town-gates, closed for all but one day of the year. It is a prestige work: Italians are proud of this late-Renascence grandeur which states its maxim of order and proportion clearly, and leaves nothing more to be said; but the effect—like the title—is sentimental. The perfect church, it was meant to be—but nobody goes there: the cumbersome wooden altar inside looks like backstage scenery. It pays court to the idea of religion without any real reference at all: only in the serenity of the lines is there feeling—for serenity; so you get a monument.

The attendant lives in a house up the hill, and she brings the key, which is enormous. The door is almost certain to stick because the damp has been eating into all this superb rhetoric for decades. It may remind us of Wren—the Radcliffe Camera, St Paul's Cathe-

dral: but in a country which never experienced the Enlightenment or
Dr Johnson it sticks out like a sore thumb. It was begun in 1508
and finished almost exactly a century later. The lawn is sensibly
used by children for football—it lies on the way home from
school.

CHAPTER 15

Orvieto

Our first view from the Autostrada del Sole is of a town perched high and even perilously on a vast slab of stone (the *tufo* much used by the Etruscans). And every horizontal inch of this steep rock has been used, so that the cliffs are also the natural walls of the town, clean-cut, rising straight up out of the plain. **Orvieto** can have no neighbours in the ordinary sense: however near, they are far below in the plain; even the approaches—the usual corridor of petrol-stations and detached villas now divided into flats—are in the plain, straggling for a little distance up the hill but then seeming to lose heart. Yet Orvieto isn't really high, less than Todi—about nine hundred feet: but no surrounding hills take from its height. There is a straight drop to sea-level on all sides. Of course this gave the town a natural importance which it could never lose, and its history shows no sudden decline after the period of the *comuni*. It watched approaches from the sea, and those from north and south were laid bare to it like a map far below. In fact, the plain is reminiscent of the Liri valley that yawns open to the west of Cassino. On a sunlit day there is nothing more peaceful and cheerfully mysterious, as we look down on it from Orvieto, all sounds muffled, the movements below so slight that it all seems close and touchable: the river Paglia curls round between beaches of grey stone (farther south it flows into the Tiber) and the autostrada travels as straight as a blue cable at its side, with the railway line beside it almost hidden, sunk into the scene like something mediaeval now. If we arrive by train we shall see all this from the funicular railway as we rise.

Tufo is a volcanic stone and Orvieto's rock was thrown up like a little mountain from the sea or perhaps a gulf, so that the water all round turned into a lagoon and finally sank to the present plain, with the river Paglia bearing its only water.

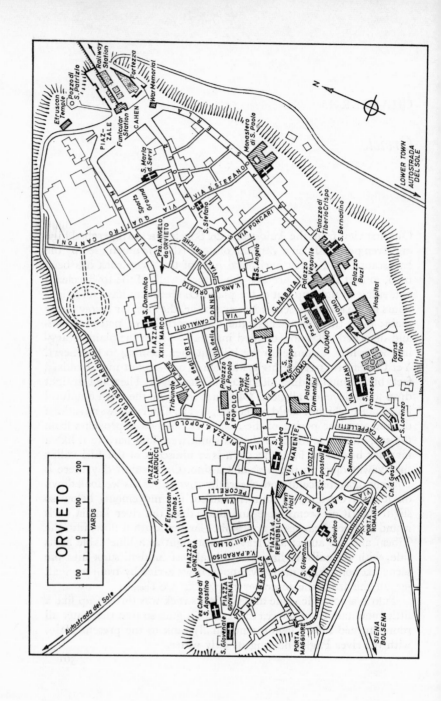

ORVIETO

YARDS

100   0   100   200

The first record of Orvieto—the Duomo, a Gothic jewel—three centuries of building—the façade

Orvieto was settled by the Etruscans but there is a gap between the Etruscan and Roman settlements which worries the historians. It is due to the simple fact that they can't find Roman traces previous to the very late date of the first century A.D. This gap has induced some people to say that there was also a gap in the history; that the town was totally destroyed for a time, or simply evacuated. But neither story seems likely. Perugia too (another town on a steep hill) lacks early Roman remains, for the simple reason that old foundations were absorbed into new work, necessarily because of the lack of space.

The first record of the town, a manuscript by the Byzantine general Belisarius (he chased the Goths out of Orvieto and occupied it himself), gives the name as Ourbibentos, which the Romans called *Urbs Vetus* (that is, 'the old town'), from which the name Orvieto derives. At the end of the sixth century A.D. it was occupied by the Lombards, and later got a bishop of its own. It was during the period of the *comuni*, between the eleventh and twelfth centuries, that the town we see today began, with its towers and mansions for the noble class. It flourished commercially, and attempts were made to find a water-outlet to the sea which would give the town better trading opportunities, but they came to nothing. Its chief enemies were Siena, Viterbo, Todi and Perugia, and it had alliances with Rome and Florence. Its internal quarrels became famous all over the country and were mentioned by Dante—the classical one being between the Monaldeschi (Guelfs) and the Filippeschi (Ghibellines): as usual it was probably their hatred that made them choose different sides, rather than vice versa.

Towards the end of the thirteenth century Pope Martin IV established himself in Orvieto and filled the place with Franciscans—the town rebelled against them, as it had earlier against the pontifical rectors. The Filippeschi family was chased out of town in 1313 and with peace hanging heavy on their hands the Monaldeschi family divided into two and fought each other, so that from this time they have to be denoted by the branch of the family they come from. And then, in 1450, the Church beat the lot. Orvieto put up a stout, lonely resistance to the French Charles VIII, and then became a refuge first for Pope Alexander VI and later Pope Clement VII (during one of the sacks of Rome).

The object of nearly all visits to Orvieto is the **Duomo,** the focus of the town even historically, and clearly—the moment you set your eyes on it—the Gothic jewel of Umbria. Its square (Piazza del Duomo) is narrow and small and busy, with that tea-shoppy atmosphere of a great tourist centre (there really is a tea-shop opposite the cathedral): and the vast church rises up like a great piece of sugar candy. The effect is gay and scrumptious: nothing of the sombre gravity you get in the tiny Romanesque churches that hide in so many Umbrian towns; a deliberately festive piece of embroidery in stone, to commemorate a miracle. We see a rush of colour—red and white stone, bright yellow and blue and gold and red mosaic filling the areas between twirling pillars and arches and slim steeples and lifesize figures. The series of bas-reliefs between the doors, divided into panels each telling a story, twice the height of a man, the steps leading up to the doors, alternately in red and white stone—it is all a huge enterprise, and yet not quite serious. Only the structure, the outline, seems—and actually was—the decision of one man; the rest is the gradual and often interrupted work of about three centuries. How it got built at all no one will know.

In this church the old, carefully solid symmetry of the Romanesque, which was like the unfolding of a system of prayer, is replaced by a sort of hymn of praise and beseeching: not the simple house of God any more but a tribute, where all the same engineering calculations are made but to an end which celebrates and clamours; the Romanesque stillness is lost; this new architecture is more like an exclamation. There is a stunning difference between this cathedral and the tiny S. Maria in Pensole which we shall see in Narni, yet in time the difference is not so great.

The duomo is approached only by narrow lanes, one of which, Via Lorenzo Maitani, looks straight at its front so as to capture it inside its dark walls. If we are lucky enough to be walking towards the *façade* in bright sunlight we shall see it glittering against the blue sky like something at sea, its twirling columns rising to a green bronze *Madonna and Child* under a canopy, an intricate gallery high above with slender pillars, niched figures clustering round the great sculptured rose window; a red and white motif carried to the highest pinnacle, with a simple cross crowning it all, and four subtly

The Ponte delle Torri, or bridge of towers, Spoleto's fourteenth-century aqueduct, still bears water to the town. It has ten arches, is about 250 yards long, and can be crossed by footpath.

Left: Roman fragments lie
jumbled in the tiny courtyard
of Amelia's Palazzo Comunale.
Below: The northern gate of
Carsulae, now called the arch
of S. Damiano, leads to the
amphitheatre and forum.

worked spires, and at ground level seven slim steps in red and white stone rising from the mosaic pavement.

The Miracle of Bolsena happened in 1263, and was reckoned of first-class importance by the pope as a way of discouraging the doubt and scepticism of the time. The result was not only the duomo but the Feast of Corpus Domini. Here is the story: a Bohemian priest on his way from Prague to Rome was afflicted by doubts about the truth of transubstantiation; he happened to be celebrating Mass at the tomb of St Christine in Bolsena when he saw blood coming from the consecrated Host on the altar-cloth. It was carried in procession to Pope Urban IV while he was staying in Orvieto (it was the residence of the popes when Rome was hot and stinking), and in August of the following year (1264) he put out the Bull that started the holiday of Corpus Domini, aware that this town in particular was full of people who doubted the possibility of the Eucharist. And, secondly, he wanted the occasion marked with the building of a stupendous church which would always astound people and remind them of the miracle. At that time, Orvieto was one of the most prosperous towns in central Italy—there was none more powerful between Rome and Florence. It even owned part of the sea-coast, where it had always yearned for an outlet. So it was thought to be the right place for a new cathedral: its people were proud and rich and independent, and sceptical. But as this cathedral went higher and higher and became more splendid over the next two hundred years, the town suffered one disaster after another, and its importance dwindled. What you see of Orvieto today from the plain is mostly the slim outlines of the duomo rising above everything else. The streets round it have remained the same; just as if Pope Urban's decision had put a seal on its fortunes.

The first stone of the new church—chosen to stand at the highest point of the town—was blessed twenty-six years later, in 1290, by Pope Nicholas IV. There is supposed to have been an Etruscan temple on the site which was used as a foundation for two previous churches. The first plan for the duomo was a Romanesque one, a straightforward three-naved church with a semi-circular apse, under the direction of Fra' Bevignate of Perugia; the work was taken over by a local architect who tried to introduce the Gothic form—ribbed vaults with arches crossing each other—but he endangered the walls underneath. Lorenzo Maitani was then called in, and to him the church owes its final form. He strengthened the walls with external arches and made the design thoroughly Gothic, with the apse no longer semi-circular. And he started the façade: all this took until 1330.

Artists came from everywhere, especially Siena, to complete the work on the façade and the chapels: in both arms of the crossing a chapel was designed—one became the Chapel of the Corporale (where the Bolsena corporal is kept), with the Chapel of S. Brizio opposite. Both were, so to speak, excavated out of the church, under the arches built by Maitani to strengthen the walls.

At this point the façade began to give trouble, and there were long discussions as to whether Maitani's design should be followed through. Antonio Federighi, one of the Sienese artists of that time, was called in, and he revised the design to include the twelve niches we see separating the central pediment from the rose window, thus introducing a clear note of the Renascence for the first time: they were completed between 1452 and 1458. If we look at the façade and imagine these absent we find a much soberer note, with the clean lines of the Gothic undisturbed; and these additions begin to seem fussy. About a half century later the middle cusp of the façade was built, taking twenty years, and the right-hand side was completed in 1590, on drawings of Ippolito Scalza. At the beginning of the seventeenth century the left was completed too, thus finishing the façade as we see it today. From the time Lorenzo Maitani started in 1310 it took nearly three centuries, during which period the town suffered the Black Death, the worst tyranny of its history, famine, earthquakes, and attack by the armies of Charles VIII. But this wasn't the end of architectural problems. A few years after the façade was finished two columns began to show signs of collapse, and architects from Florence and Genoa had to be called in to save them. Then on the night of December 10th, 1795, lightning struck it, and restoration—the labour of a decade—was necessary: the top right-hand spire was rebuilt.

The façade is floodlit in the evening: this shows it in better detail than dazzling sunlight. But the best time of day in which to capture its magnificence is the morning. The models for the bas-reliefs were made by the originating architect, Lorenzo Maitani, but who actually did the work is undecided. Perhaps he directed it, with artists from Pisa and Siena under him. The reliefs are unusually lifelike, and represent *stories from the Old Testament* and *scenes from the New Testament*. We should walk across the façade from left to right to get a first summary impression. At the first pilaster we notice that the lowest panels are squeezed as if insufficient room had been left for them after the clearer designs above were finished. In fact, they begin the story—with the *Creation* at the left-bottom corner, so that ideas must have changed after they were done; some people say that this row was completed by other artists before Maitani got to work, and was then incorporated into the grander design where each picture is divided from the next by ivy-branches.

Beginning at the bottom, then, we have *the creation of the fishes, birds and plants, the creation of mammals,* and *the creation of man;* in the second row above, *God gives life to Adam, extracts a rib from his side and creates Eve;* in the third row, *Adam and Eve are shown into the Garden of Eden,* then *commit the original sin of the forbidden fruit,* after which they are fallen from divine grace; in the fourth row, *they are evicted from Eden; Adam hoes and Eve plants;* the fifth, *the offerings of Cain and Abel, Cain murders Abel;* the sixth, *Naomi teaches a child to read, Jubal invents sounds,* and *one of Adam's children uses a compass.*

Second pilaster: here are two vertical series, divided by acanthus leaves—at the bottom, *Adam (or Abraham) sleeping,* and along the middle line *the kings David, Solomon, Rehoboam, Abijah, Asa, Jehoshaphat,* then *Christ and Mary;* at the sides, *the prophets with their tables.* The scenes represent *Balaam; the vocation of Gideon; the miracle of Joshua; David anoints the king; presentation of Samuel to Eli; the Children of Israel in Egypt; bread and wine prepared by Melchisedech for Abraham,* and lastly *the Crucifixion.*

Third pilaster: these are also two vertical sets among acanthus leaves—*the evangelists;* at the bottom *Adam sleeping,* with *angels* at the sides and *prophets* down the middle line; from the bottom left, *Annunciation* and *Visitation; Nativity* and *Epiphany; presentation in the Temple* and *flight into Egypt; massacre of the Innocents* and *the disputation in the Temple; baptism and a miracle of Jesus; entry into Jerusalem* and *the kiss of Judas; Flagellation* and *Crucifixion; Mary at the sepulchre,* and *Noli me tangere.*

Fourth pilaster, that is on the far right, *the Last Judgment* is treated, with five rows of pictures among vine branches; *Christ the judge among angels, prophets, apostles, Mary, the instruments of the Passion,* and *angels summoning the dead to Judgment;* in the second and third row, *the elect led to heavenly bliss;* the fourth row, *division of the elect from the damned;* fifth row, *resurrection of the dead* and *banishment of the damned to hell.*

Above the main door the *Madonna and Child*, in marble, was probably done by Andrea Pisano a year before he died, and the bronze canopy and angels by Maitani about twenty years before. The other bronzes on the same level represent *the evangelists*—all done by Maitani. At the top of the first three pediments the bronzes are, from the left, *St Michael, the Lamb of God* at the centre (both the work of Ugolino da Bologna), and an *angel* in marble of unknown origin.

The rose window, with its slender radial bars (twenty-two of them) has the head of the Redeemer for its centre. The rose is enclosed in a square, and in the four corners there are mosaics done in the first century of the duomo's life by Pietro di Puccio, a local painter, representing *the four doctors of the Church, SS. Augustine, Gregory the Great, Jerome, Ambrose*; these have been heavily restored since. If we look carefully at the frame round the rose window we can see fifty heads in bas-relief: these were put there in the fourteenth century. At the sides we see full-length figures in couples, standing in niches, representing the twelve prophets, marble statues done by various hands including Ippolito Scalza. Above, there are twelve niches each enclosing a marble figure, the apostles, by several artists including again Scalza and Rafaello da Montelupo.

Nearly all those mosaics which fill the spaces not taken by arches and niches were added in the last two or three hundred years; some of the original ones were sent in homage to Pope Pius VI at the time of the French revolution. They are the least attractive part of the façade, an element that takes away from the grave Gothic design, while providing glitter. Taking the lowest mosaic on the left, that is the one over the left door, we have *the baptism of Jesus*, (sixteenth-century), and above it, in two parts, *Gabriel* and *the Virgin Annunciate* (a century later); over the main door, in three parts, are *the Virgin of the Assumption* and *the apostles*, work of Leonardelli, a local artist (1366), but heavily restored in the nineteenth century; over the right door in the centre, is *the birth of Mary* also by Leonardelli and restored in the eighteenth century, with *St Joachim* and *St Anne* on either side, also restored. Thus, most of the lower mosaics date from the first century of the church, but with heavy restoration. At the top, under the left gable, there is *the marriage of the Virgin* entirely re-done in 1612; under the gable, *the presentation of Mary*, done at the end of the eighteenth century, on old drawings; and at the central pediment, *the coronation of the Virgin* done by Roman artists in the nineteenth century, on drawings by a Sienese artist.

On the left side of the square as we face the church there is the Little Clock Tower (Torretta dell' Orologio) with its bronze figure in short kilt and tall pointed hat striking the hour on a great bell—locally he is known as 'Maurizio', and came into being in the middle of the fourteenth century.

Inside the church—the two chapels, a Lippo Memmi on one side and Luca Signorelli, mitigated by Fra' Angelico, on the other

The interior offers such a completely different story that the façade now seems like a false offering, the basilica itself the real one. They say that Italians love everything that glitters—it doesn't even have to be gold. And once inside you begin to feel, in this vast deserted nave with pillars on either side like great elephants' paws, firmly set on the wide floor, that the façade—especially in its later additions—was done with this childish appeal in mind: and the interior with the truth in mind.

After the bustle of the little square, this is a wonderful relief. In fact, the church isn't as vast as all that: it was built to seem so, in an artful design that makes the floor rise imperceptibly from the back towards the chancel, with the pillars getting progressively shorter as they go down (we can verify this by examining both the base and the capital of each pillar and comparing them), so as to provide a stage effect of distance within what is quite a modest space (about one hundred and eighty feet in length and a hundred wide).

The motif of the side-walls outside, that of horizontal black and white stripes, is carried on here not only in the walls but in the ten thick pillars and the two pilasters which divide the church into naves. But we should notice that in the highest regions of the walls, above the arches, the motif is painted on: such a weight of stone at that height would have been unwise. The pillars have richly carved capitals, each of a quite different design. And at the end there is the commanding tallness of the presbytery under its great Romanesque arches nearly the height of the roof itself, dwarfing the tiny cross of the altar below and the wooden choir with its central throne over-hung by a crucifix. A pleasant and mellow light enters by alabaster windows on either side, but these make it necessary for us to see the church in the morning, especially the chapels, which are most of the time in gloom. The main floor is made of blocks of red marble.

309

There are traces of fourteenth- and fifteenth-century frescoes in the tall niches scooped out of the walls on either side.

The presbytery and the chapels on each side of it are raised from the main floor by two steps, nearly a separate entity; we have to pass through a wrought-iron gateway (done by Sienese artists in the fourteenth century) to reach it. At once we see the immensity of the apse with its high crossing arches, divided by one massive triumphal arch from the main body.

When we enter the church, by the way, we shall see tall doors of bronze clearly meant for the façade but not yet on their hinges. They are the work of a contemporary artist, Emilio Greco; their panels follow the intention of the bas-reliefs outside. But nobody dares put them in position. Now and then someone writes in to say they should be abolished. And while the dithering goes on the tall doors remain there, making a year-round exhibition all their own in a subtle revenge.

On the left, above the gates of the Cappella del Corporale, there is what must be one of the most colourful organ-lofts in existence, with painted figures of plaster at the corners of its corniced gilt roof. Access to the apse itself is difficult as the attendant likes to conduct parties only to the chapels: we shall have to return when he is less busy. The choir is in three tiers with arches above as a kind of canopy over the seats, carved by various Sienese artists in the fourteenth century but completely restored since then. Above the bishop's throne there is a marvellous inlaid work of light wood, a *coronation of the Virgin*. The throne is boxed in, so to speak, with panels of the saints, over forty of them; and above each of the choir seats there is one letter of the Ave Maria. At the back of the altar there is a vast arched window from which most of the church's light comes—two tall arches with a rose window held between their shoulders, with an internal gallery curving over it in a mysterious way. The window has forty-eight panels of stained glass and is about fifty feet high and fifteen wide; it has been restored a good many times.

The frescoes here in the presbytery achieve a tenderness and truthfulness which I find absent in much of the Signorelli chapel (see p. 312). They were the work of Ugolino di Prete Ilario (an Orvieto painter) and he worked on them with many assistants, from 1370 until 1384. They are only in a fair state of preservation, with great patches of damp; they were restored by Pintoricchio and Pastura, an artist from Viterbo, in the fifteenth century. They tell *the life of Mary* and begin on the left at the bottom and turn clockwise. Above, there are *doctors and evangelists* in a state of bad repair (parts are entirely by Pintoricchio). There are two unusual rose windows in the presbytery side-walls, dug into the wall at a slant, with seven stained-glass pictures inside.

As most tourists will be busily engaged in the 'new' chapel where the Signorelli frescoes are we shall do well to go first to the left side of the cross formed by the church. Facing us as we look towards the altar is an open marble side-altar (**Chapel of the Visitation**) which is a bas-relief of magnificent compactness by Francesco da Montelupo, in imitation of a similar chapel which we shall see later on the opposite side. The work was done in 1547 but the figures have no bombast.

And now, by turning left, we come to the dark **Cappella del Corporale** (*corporale* means the cloth on which the consecrated elements of the Host or Eucharist are kept during Mass), where the relic of the Miracle of Bolsena lies encased twice-over in precious metals and a tall tabernacle of marble and wood (which is all we see). On either side of the wrought-iron gateway (fourteenth-century) we may notice the marble statues, also by Montelupo— one of *Christ* and the other of *Mary*. But they are not equal to the same artist's altar, and seem posed and sentimental, without the natural stillness we find in Lippo Memmi's lovely picture, *Madonna dei Raccomandati*, which we find on the right-hand side of the chapel, half-hidden in the shadows, in its own niche. This alone would be worth a visit to Orvieto. Memmi was a Sienese artist and died in the second half of the fourteenth century. The painting has a striking innocence and verve, the Madonna in her praying attitude is formal without the slightest stiffness, firm yet sweet, her fingers touching each other delicately in front of her, her face dominating everything—the angelic heads, the praying nuns below her—with an amazing radiance.

The frescoes of this chapel were also painted by Ugolino di Prete Ilario, with the help of Leonardelli and others; but they were restored too heavily in the last century. On the right wall there is *the story of the Miracle of Bolsena*, showing *the Bohemian priest giving the news to the pope, the bishop of Orvieto looking at the blood-stains, the pope showing the relic to the people* after meeting the procession at the gates of the town, and *the pope ordering Thomas Aquinas to write the Office and Mass of the Holy Sacrament*; on the left wall there are *the miracles of the*

311

Sacrament; *St Gregory showing the Host as visible flesh*; *the Host changing into a boy to convince an anchorite*; *a fish restores the Host to a priest three years after a fisherman had given it to the fish to eat*; *St Hugo rejects a Host that is not consecrated*; *the Jewish child who took communion is found alive in an oven where his father had thrown him*; *Christ appears in the form of a child in the Host before Christians and Saracens*. At the altar we see the tall tabernacle that encloses the 'Reliquario del Corporale'; this priceless case, only to be seen by special permission and otherwise put on view only twice a year (the afternoon of Easter Sunday and the Feast of Corpus Domini) was ordered by a member of the terrible Monaldeschi family—he happened to be a bishop; it weighs four hundred pounds and was engraved and enamelled by Sienese artists in 1337; and it cost over a thousand florins, in the currency of the time.

And now for the chapel which attracts most of the tourist parties, the New or S. Brizio chapel, usually known as the *Cappella Signorelli*. Before going inside we may notice an open chapel on the left of its entrance like the one on the opposite side, a bas-relief altarpiece started by Pietro da Como in 1503 and completed by Simone Mosca over thirty years later. This is a rich marble panel showing the three Magi approaching a stable overhung by trees; horses in the distance are lightly etched; all very compact and suave, in the best tradition of that time. Opposite this we should notice a seventeenth-century pulpit which has a splendid sobriety, of inlaid wood, with gilt pillars forming a little temple with doors. On either side of the entrance to the Signorelli chapel there are marble figures of *Adam* and *Eve*, the equivalent of the Christ and Mary figures we saw on the other side. And again we pass through a wrought-iron gate, made by a local hand in 1516.

Instead of allowing ourselves to be ushered quickly in and quickly out again we should slip the attendant a sweetener and take it easy on one of the chairs until our eyes are accustomed to the light. Again and again, in this chapel, I find my eyes leaving the crowded naked figures below with their bulging muscles and going upwards to the *Choir of Prophets* which is wholly by Fra' Angelico, and has the inner radiant stillness that earned him the title *Beato* or 'Blessed'. He started this work in the summer of 1447 with the help of three other artists including Benozzo Gozzoli, but was interrupted after completing two sections to work at the Vatican. Gozzoli undertook to carry on and returned from Rome in the summer of 1449: he got as

far as decorating the ribs of the upper vaults when Arrigo Monaldeschi of the Viper faction was murdered, and the whole enterprise
seemed to be dropped, perhaps because of a special Monaldeschi
interest that had been taken in it. At any rate we hear nothing more
of the idea until thirty years later, when a painter called Pier
Matteo d'Amelia is asked for sketches, but these fail to please. Ten
years after that Perugino was asked to carry on and did so for a few
days only. Another ten years went by and this time Luca Signorelli
agreed to finish the work for one hundred and eighty ducats. He
started by restoring the Fra' Angelico sections, then in 1500 he
started work on the walls and worked almost continuously for four
years. Probably the town was less of a nightmare for artists then.
For the completion of the work Signorelli got a further five hundred
and seventy-five ducats.

The dome above is divided into eight parts: *Christ the judge in
glory among the angels* and the *Prophetarum laudabilis numerus* (or *Choir
of Prophets*) are by Fra' Angelico and remain much as they were
originally. All the others—the *apostles, signs of the Last Judgment,
martyrs, patriarchs, doctors, virgins*—are by Signorelli. The frescoes on
the upper walls begin on the left and work round anti-clockwise,
so that the second panel is behind us over the entrance, the third
and fourth on the right-hand wall, until we come round to the left
wall again, when we reach the seventh panel. (1) Depicts *the doings
of the Anti-Christ*; the man in the second row of the group on the left
with a blond beard, looking towards the right, may be Cesare
Borgia, and some say that the clean-shaven man close to the Anti-
Christ is Christopher Columbus, while Dante, his profile towards
the left, is in the second row of the group; the young man richly
dressed on the left, his hands at his sides, may be a Monaldeschi;
and in the left-hand corner the two men standing together, their
hands clasped in front of them, are the painter himself, Luca
Signorelli, looking vigorous and determined, and Fra' Angelico in
monk's habit. (2) Above the arch four putti hold an inscription on
which there is a signature of the artist, and inside the arch (that is,
over the entrance to the chapel) *the end of the world* is represented.
(3) *The resurrection of the body.* (4) *The damned in hell.* (5) *The angels
chase the damned to hell*—at the bottom there flows the river Acheron.
(6) *The angels conduct the elect to heaven.* (7) *The elect in heaven.*

The lower frescoes turn in exactly the same way, that is anti-
clockwise, beginning on the left wall closest to the entrance. They

comprise pagan subjects: (1) *Homer and scenes from the Iliad*; (2) *Empedocles gazing at the end of the world*; (3) *probably Orpheus*; (4) *Lucan*; (5) *Horace*; (6) *Ovid*; (7) *Various scenes dealing with Orpheus and Andromeda*; *the nuptial banquet of Perseus and Andromeda*; (8) *Hercules*.

The lower frescoes turn in the same way, and again begin on the left wall closest to the entrance. They deal with *scenes from the Iliad*, *Empedocles looking at the damned, Horace, Ovid*, and *scenes from Dante's Purgatory*.

This chapel has one shy and certainly simple work that hides behind a curtain over the altar, and we must ask the attendant to draw this aside. It is called *Maestà della Tavola*, for want of an artist's name, and has survived from the thirteenth century with hardly a blemish, a Madonna and Child facing us with a strange primitive grace, shining with unusual colours, green and purple against black and gold; she is also called the Madonna di S. Brizio and is exposed to public view on the Saint's feast-day (November 13th).

The Etruscan collections—the question of the Etruscan afterlife—Simone Martini in the Museum

Opposite the duomo lies a palazzo which houses **Count Faina's Etruscan and Greek collections** from the last century: he left them to the State with a stipulation that the order in which they stood should not be broken. But some alterations are being made to include recent finds and incorporate a second museum at the side of the Palazzo Faina which houses a similar collection, with the difference that it belongs to the Church. A cold war between the two collections—Church and State—has gone on for some time, but in a few years there will be one building, heated (I hope) for those poor tourists who come in the winter. Thus only a general description of the contents can be given; though the final form of the museum will probably respect the present arrangements.

Not everything in the Faina collection is of local origin even when it is Etruscan. The first room contains prehistoric finds from Perugia, neolithic and palaeolithic tools; a glass case in the middle of the room contains Etruscan ceramic urns for ashes, with clay heads as covers, thought by some to be actual portraits of the people who died: these are from the seventh century B.C. The second room has

314

more cinerary urns, found at Chiusi and Florence, from the time of the Etruscan decadence, small rectangular containers that imitate the bigger and grander ones which had been designed for noblemen and leading people. And in this room we should note the clay masks—among them feminine demons—which were found on the tomb walls; there are few of these in existence, by the way. Because of the prevalence of these horrific masks and vase-drawings people have attributed an unusual terror of death to the Etruscans. Some have found an obsession with death even, but there is evidence for neither; the masks (like the stick borne above the corpse in a vase painting we shall see later) could just as easily be there to exorcize bad spirits who come to taunt the dead or (like ourselves) to rob the tombs.

The third room is entirely devoted to *buccheri* of the late Etruscan type, known as 'heavy' because they lack the fineness of the early work: the difference can be seen if we compare one or two early vases (their rims thinner and subtler). But then the Etruscans were always careless, though their unashamed disorder was never chaos.

The fourth room is occupied by bronze pieces from every period —the Etruscan, the Italic, the Roman. Italic here means ancient but not recognizably Roman or Etruscan. The bronze tools or ornaments were found between Umbria and the Marche, though no one can say what purpose they served. There are tiny wheels remarkably like those found on any piece of modern machinery. The Etruscan objects here are from local tombs—mirrors, curved curry-combs, buckles for belts. We shall also notice the *lacramatoii*, like little glass eye-baths, into which it is said the Etruscans wept at funerals—the tears were then sprinkled over the bier or the tomb. There is a votive carriage (unearthed a century ago) about eighteen inches long on wheels, restored for our benefit, a miniature imitation of the carriage on which the dead were borne to the burial ground. In fact, nearly everything found in the tombs is an imitation of something used in life: we mustn't assume that the Etruscans used ceramic utensils in the kitchen any more than we do; the clay vase we see is invariably a replica on a smaller scale of the metal pot or pan used in the kitchen; the tomb was decorated with a kind of theatrical furniture, meant for use by the soul. There are also small glass jars for holding perfume: some are uneven and intricate, called 'spiked' or 'thorned' jars, thought to be made by pouring liquid glass round a piece of canvas which then burned and disintegrated inside.

In the next room the vases begin, a great variety of Greek and Etruscan ceramic work—Etruscan imitations of Attic art, some original Corinthian pots, nearly all local: even when they are Greek they are from the local tombs, since the Etruscans ran a great ceramic trade with the Greeks, and imported both their work and their artists. The black-figured vases are Greek, with their fine detail and expert glazing. This collection continues in a second room, with perhaps a false vase here and there; 'false' means here not a modern imitation but a later hand on an ancient vase, perhaps Roman, perhaps Christian. The so-called 'erotic' pot here with a figure in a sexual position is almost certainly false. The usual scenes on these vases are drunken youths, falling or slipping or trying to dance.

The next room is mostly taken up by large Greek pots, used for wine and water (the narrow-mouthed ones for wine and the wide-mouthed for water); they stood in the banqueting rooms (Etruscans would naturally use Greek pots for their great occasions) for guests to dip into. Here there is the famous group of three so-called 'Vanth' pots: at least, they are famous among the archaeologists because they each bear the name Vanth on some part of the design —the name of the artist, perhaps. All three depict the afterlife: *Pluto and a goddess* and *a dead person being borne to the burial-ground on a cart*; the goddess carries above her a long stick, thought to be her protection against the demons, though she is in fact not holding the stick herself, it hovers above her; it could be a symbol of spiritual power.

Next door the **Palazzo dell' Opera del Duomo** houses a similar collection, including a large Etruscan sarcophagus of the fourth or third century B.C. which seems to be owned half by the State and half by the Church. (A ticket to this museum by the way entitles us to go later to the cathedral museum on the other side of the square. In 1956 all the paintings were taken over the road to the cathedral museum, while the archaeological exhibits were confined to the Palazzo dell' Opera del Duomo.) The sarcophagus has bas-reliefs on all sides, showing *stories of Achilles*. It was once brightly painted, and smudges of the paint remain here and there. There is *Achilles sacrificing to evoke the shade of Tiresias*, the animal rearing up in front of him; *Trojan prisoners being executed by him*, one already dead, another under his sword, while two soldiers stand by guarding prisoners (hands tied behind their backs); in another panel *Achilles has Circe by the hair* and is exhorting her to change the two animal-figures dressed like men on either side (a pig and a ram) back to human form. Then there is *the death of Polyxena*—she was sacrificed to the ghost of Achilles, who had been in love with her. Charon is on either side.

The rest of this little museum is more or less a repetition of what we have seen in the Palazzo Faina, though there is a large and rare warrior's head made of hard stone (tufo wouldn't have lasted). One other of this type exists, in Florence, a better example, but both were found in the Orvieto area; the stone comes from the south of Italy and is called *nemfro*. The head is much larger than life and has something of the early Etruscan smile. There is an unusual little *bucchero* in this collection, a jar formed partly as a ram and partly as a man's head, with the opening in the man's head. And there are tiny stones thought to have been used as weights in spinning by the women. There are some very well-preserved glazed pots, bright as they rarely are. And in one glass case there are the so-called *antifissi*, end-stones that supported the tiles on Etruscan roofs, with a face or mask, so that a gable would show several of these faces in a row.

As we face the duomo we see on our right a separate little square flanked by a stern tufo palace with battlements and a splendid wide-open external staircase leading up to a balustrade: here is the museum entrance—the *Museo dell' Opera,* belonging to the duomo. The building is called Palazzo dei Papi or sometimes Soliano, perhaps by derivation from the word *sole* or sun, as the ancient cult of Mithra may once have been practised on this site. It was built in three stages between the tenth and the fourteenth centuries, and restored to its present neatness at the end of the last century. Visiting popes lived there, or at least used it for their receptions, and it is connected with the very old bishops' palace, whose broken shadow (under restoration) lurks at the side of the vast duomo.

The museum is one large hall and immediately on the left of the entrance we see part of the duomo roof which preceded the present one, with its painted timbers and beams. Going down the hall along the left wall we find an intimate little *Madonna and Child* in an intricate gilt frame with Gothic spires, attributed to Pastura, who came from near-by Viterbo and whose hand we have seen in the duomo apse: he died at the beginning of the sixteenth century. Standing alone, mounted away from the wall, is Signorelli's *self-portrait,* a fresco taken from the church: he is standing in the picture with a

317

man called Nicolò di Angelo Franchi, the bursar of the whole architectural enterprise of the duomo in his time. On the end wall there are fourteenth-century frescoes which have a light, delicate gravity—at least two of them, the best preserved, are on the subject of the *Annunciation*. Farther along, this same wall has a *Nativity* and an *adoration of the Magi* of the same period but poorly preserved; and under these we should note several designs for the cathedral, which some people attribute to Lorenzo Maitani himself; and there is Scalza's plan for altering the inside of the church to the Renascence style.

Returning along the right wall we find a tall fresco, *St Sebastian and a devout man*, which has a striking sweetness and gentleness, in a light mellow terra-cotta wash. Farther along, there is a rather mediocre head of *the dying Christ* by Scalza, and then a serene *Madonna and Child* by Simone Martini in which all the inner firmness of the old world has remained. There is a collection of rusty spear-heads and one squat, dangerous-looking sword that will kill no more. Close to the entrance there are fragments from the original wooden choir that stood in the duomo (fourteenth-century) with saints in inlaid wood, and then a great *coronation of the Virgin* in a high arch that must have been the centre-piece over the throne. We should also notice the painted and glazed terra-cotta *Angel of the Annunciation*, in the form of a bas-relief, by della Robbia, with that finished grace of Renascence work.

Going down the middle of the hall, among the separate exhibits, we find closest to the entrance, two unfinished models in marble which are interesting as a glimpse into the sculptor's workshop. Farther on, a lifesize seated *Christ blessing*, in wood, has no ponderousness about it; attributed to Lorenzo Maitani, though some say Nicolò Nuti from Siena. There is a tender *Virgin Annunciate* from the fourteenth century. And in the centre of the hall a splendid *polittico* by Simone Martini, *Madonna and Child with saints*, is reticent and devout as we have come to expect. Beyond this there is a fourteenth-century lectern which once stood in the duomo.

In the glass case on our left as we stand with our backs to the entrance there are the vestments of Bishop Vanzi which have embroidered scenes supposed to have been based on drawings by Luca Signorelli. In a smaller case nearer the middle there is an altar-cloth hammered with a silver design round an embroidered *Madonna and Child*; opposite it in another case we see a fine embroidered silk altar-cloth showing *St Ignatius,* delicate and only slightly fading now.

S. Lorenzo in Arari—a walk to the centre of town—S. Andrea with an Etruscan road in its crypt—S. Giovenale—Piazza del Popolo—S. Domenico —St Patrick's well

We should now take the Via Lorenzo Maitani exactly opposite the cathedral front, which leads us past a house called Casa Fontanieri (now a hotel), notable for its little balcony held up by so-called Tuscan pillars, one of which is composed of a demon figure curling round, rather like a sea-nymph. At the end of this narrow street we come into the Piazza dei Febei with the church of S. Francesco on our left, its front a massively thick wall (as we can see from the ugly window cut into it): it was started by Pope Clement IV in the thirteenth century and restored almost completely in the eighteenth century, though the façade (which is all we shall see of it, as the church is closed for alterations) remains from 1240; Boniface VIII canonized King Louis of France here in 1297.

If we continue down the Via Ippolito Scalza we shall come to the little Piazza di S. Chiara where—very easily missed, having so long hidden in these side streets—there is the tiny church of **S. Lorenzo in Arari,** made quite simply, without any frontal decoration, from blocks of tufo. It clearly meant to hide itself: originally it lay near the church of S. Francesco but its bells irritated the truculent Franciscans and they ordered its demolition. So it has a specially Christian look—of detached humility. Again, the outside gives no indication of the superb strength and intactness inside. It was built in the thirteenth century, and restorations since then have been careful not to disturb the original form. Inside, the silence and remoteness strike you at once, even when boys are kicking footballs against its façade. There is something so different from the present world in a church like this: things seem to be made too big for us now, as if our concepts had escaped beyond our needs.

The three naves are separated by squat Romanesque pillars, their arches *scemi* or 'stupid', that is, half-filled (a bottle is 'stupid' in Italy if it isn't full), of the kind to be seen in a church of the same spirit and period in Narni, S. Maria in Pensole. If we look at the left wall as we stand in the middle nave we shall find with surprise

319

frescoes whose intimacy has survived some heavy and gauche restoration. These show *four scenes from the life of St Laurence*: we see him drawing people out of a dark cave, being burned and chastised, being brought before the king, and finally healing. It has a wonderful rustic directness, simple like the Romanesque church itself with a glowing familiar humanity—like looking in a childhood picture-book where magic is not incompatible with hot and hungry flesh; this is especially so in the figure of the crowned king as he stretches his head forward to the Saint; and in the simple form of his crown, like all the painted papier-mâché crowns of childhood theatricals, there is the whole Christian story. Some delicate frescoes have been painted on the pillars: the first on the left shows *St Laurence* and *St Bridget*, the second *St William the Abbot*. These are all from the fourteenth century.

Along the right wall (still as we look towards the altar) is a trace of a *Nativity*; Joseph praying is the best preserved figure, and the Child with his clear, watching eyes. The tiny chapel on the right of the presbytery has a *Madonna and Child and St Laurence* on the left wall, pleasant and warm, though faint. Behind the main altar a tiny window has been cut high into the wall in the shape of Christ crucified, without the cross, and filled in with alabaster, so that in the church's darkness we see this tiny body of the crucifixion shining mellowly. The altar-table is sustained by an Etruscan sacrificial slab, which is what gives the church its name '*in Arari*', that is, 'in the altar'. A canopy, or ciborium, was built over it in the twelfth century, with a stone arched roof, but this was restored badly in 1915 and now has an ugly effect, especially as it hides a fresco in the half-dome behind (*Christ blessing Mary, St Laurence, St John and St Francis*). In the chapel on the left facing the presbytery there is another fourteenth-century panel which has a gentle, easy richness, a *Madonna and Child*, the latter resting his arm carelessly on his mother's shoulder, while his left hand clutches her thumb. The Child's robes are russet against the Madonna's blue, and there is the traditional Byzantine background of gold.

If we continue down the Via Ghibellina until we reach the Via Garibaldi a kind of ramp will take us up the narrow lane of Via Ripa Medici (with the square called Piazzale Cacciatore del Tevere below us, a pleasant little corner of terraces and tiny houses) and this brings us out to a parapet on the western wall of the city, overlooking a shallow valley, with the old Roman Gate (first century B.C.) be-

Orvieto's gaily coloured duomo is approached by narrow lanes and glitters against the blue sky like an extraordinary carved mosaic rock out at sea.

Above: The Cascata delle Marmore, or marble falls, near Terni, came into being at the end of the last century when the waters were harnessed to provide power — the beginning of Terni's industrial importance. Now they are active only on holidays, week-ends and floodlit summer evenings. *Below:* Free fried fish is distributed beside the Lake of Piediluco during Terni's annual Festival of the Waters in June.

striding one of the roads into the city just below us. It has clearly been restored (1822). We walk along this parapet with the valley on our left: we shall see, if we look carefully, the remains of a vast old mediaeval aqueduct, built in 1250, descending the opposite hill and passing over a road.

We then go along the Via Ripa Serancia into the Piazza de' Ranieri, after passing a massive square mediaeval tower on our right. We take a lane called the Via Loggia de' Mercanti which comes out into the Piazza della Repubblica, and we are in the centre of town. In Etruscan and Roman times this was the forum. Along one side, over a series of arches, one of which is open (to traffic as well), there is the **Palazzo Comunale**—not much to look at: started in 1216 and restored by Scalza in the sixteenth century, and after that it remained incomplete, an interesting comment on the contrast between Church and civic power in this town. On the left a compact twelve-sided tower is the Torre Campanaria, built between the ninth and twelfth centuries, and very clearly tidied up this century, though brought back to its original form.

At this corner there is the church of **S. Andrea,** which also has a long history of restoration, its origins lying in the sixth century, and its final restoration, like that of the tower at its side, a few decades ago. Along its side runs a porch with columns of travertine, where flowers are sold and perhaps always were. Under it a plaque in Latin describes the great moments of the church since its origin as a temple dedicated to 'Giunone Erbana' (Juno of Orvieto): in the Middle Ages it was the town hall's own church; in 1216 Pope Innocent III proclaimed the Fourth Crusade from here, in 1217 Pope Honorius III crowned Peter of Courtenay king of Jerusalem; in 1281 Pope Martin IV was crowned in the presence of Charles of Anjou; and Popes Nicholas IV and Boniface VIII were both made cardinals here.

If the main entrance is closed we enter by a side door under this porch, by the flower-stalls. Inside, we find a dignified and sombre church with eight columns of oriental granite on either side, of perhaps second-century origin, while the capitals are additions of 1512. They support wide arches under an open roof with wooden beams—though the roof over the chancel is in Gothic vaults from the fourteenth century, painted deep blue with golden stars. The great filled-in arch we see in the wall of the left nave at the back of the church once led to the church of St Bartholomew, which no longer exists (it thus closed what is at present a road).

There are fragments of various frescoes on this wall—some detached. The first we come to, a figure with bare feet and a staff, is *St Christopher*, a fourteenth-century work, then *St John the Evangelist* a century later. A fragment of a *Madonna and Child* above, showing the steeples of a church (perhaps the town's duomo) is also probably fifteenth-century: there is then a panel showing *St Julian about to murder his parents* of the same date; then *two saints*, painted in the sixteenth century. If we walk into the chancel, we shall see, at the first pillar on the right, a pulpit with a mosaic design all round it, glittering quietly in the dimness, with gilt and red and blue and yellow stones of twelfth- and thirteenth-century origin on a base of earlier date. At the second column, closer to the altar, there is the tall tomb of the Magalotti family, by the school of Arnolfo di Cambio, which has a fresco now much ruined but still giving evidence of Sienese sweetness, a *Madonna and Child and two saints* of the fifteenth century. On the pillar opposite this there are frescoes by a local hand of *St Bernardine of Siena* and the *Madonna delle Grazie* (fifteenth-century).

At the back of the church, in the right nave, an iron grille has steps leading down to the foundations where restoration has brought to light the outer walls of the original sixth-century building, among other even more ancient things. We shall have to look for the attendant here, as the gate will be locked: but we should not miss it. He will show us the sixth-century church floor, and a hole in the ground which was once a tomb, with the bones still there. Both this and the fragments of a sarcophagus are of course under the level of the original floor. We mount two steps where the sixth-century floor ends and pass to the period of the first and second centuries A.D., where the remains seem to indicate a square or road, with the foundations of houses perhaps built on top of Roman ruins. We see Etruscan remains too—the phallic stones of their tombs, a road, wall, water-pipes. There are two stone panels decorated with mosaic from the eleventh century on one side and a ninth-century stone design (birds eating the Tree of the Cross, a Eucharist theme we have often met in Umbria) on the other. And a much larger panel follows the same Eucharist theme. We see an altar of the sixth century (three blocks of stone) and a stretch of pavement from a first- or second-century road, in the central nave. In the left nave (as we face what was once the main altar) we see more tombs, but for cremation (in couples). The attendant will now take us round to the original main entrance of the sixth-century church, in the central nave, and will show us the roots of the massive columns we have seen in the church above: they dig right into the remains of the original church. And we see the eleventh-century church wall—which enlarged the church from its first limits.

From the Piazza della Repubblica, or main square, we take a narrow lane (leading right as we face the town hall) called Via Filippeschi, though its name is not shown: but a tourist arrow to S. Giovenale shows us that we are on the right path. The lane first leads us to a tiny square where five ways meet: we take the one going uphill towards the right, Via Malabranca. We shall notice the tall mediaeval houses at Nos. 14 and 18, with their blocks of dark brown stone, ponderous and towering. The little Via del Paradiso is dug under them, through an arch. No. 22 is the Palazzo Petrangeli, formerly Filippeschi, of fifteenth-century origin, with a curving front but an ugly doorway. Farther down on the left (No. 15) there is the tall Palazzo Caravajal-Simoncelli, built in the sixteenth century, with a vast portal and the words '*Caravajal de Caravajal por Comodidad de Sus Amigos Padron*—host for the convenience of his friends' written under its first-storey windows. We now come into the Piazza S. Giovenale and take the lane on the left called Via Volsinia No. 1, arriving at the little forecourt of **S. Giovenale** itself, with a view across the valley (the Tiber lies towards our right): some say this church came into being in 1004, and it was certainly Orvieto's first cathedral. The façade is simple and squat, made of dark blocks of tufo, without facing of any kind. A stumpy tower rises on its left, its base much bigger than its top: it always looked like that, apparently. Along the side of the church—where we have just come—there is a portal from 1497 with the carved stone figure of *St Juvenal* (bishop of Narni) in the lunette above it. We enter the church by this door.

Inside, we see that half the church is on a much lower level than the rest: this is due to recent restorations which dug down to the first level, quite a depth under even the thirteenth-century level; the six fat pillars have therefore now been uncovered to their bases. Both pillars and walls were frescoed at various times between the thirteenth and sixteenth centuries. At the back of the church there is a *tree of the cross* from the late fourteenth century where the cross

323

sprouts branches with inscriptions on them, and medallions of the saints form a frame all round. The other frescoes are a *Crucifixion*, *Madonna and Child* panels, and various *saints*. On the first left-hand column as we face the high altar from the back of the church we see, above, a *Crucifixion* of Byzantine appearance. At the side-altar on the right of the chancel there is a full, once luscious *Madonna and Child*, now ruined by damp, and just to the right of this, by the side-door, a strange *calendar of funeral anniversaries*, with skeletons painted on a coffin underneath. At the high altar (1170) the altar-table has a primitive design we shall now be familiar with—a trellis-work of curved and straight lines: if we lift the altar-cloth at the corners we shall see bas-relief figures of bishops and priests and the words *Guido Abbas AD MCLXX* (the name of the abbot and the date of carving, 1170).

Returning to the Piazza S. Giovenale we find in the far left corner another ex-church, S. Agostino, which has a truncated tower behind and an ornate carved portal of the fourteenth century. We take the lane at its side (Via Guerrieri Gonzaga) to the long and narrow square of the same name and keep along the left side until we reach a cobbled lane which turns sharp right into the Via dell' Olmo. We then turn left uphill and come out into the Piazza dell' Erba: its ugly fountain was designed by Ippolito Scalza (1597); perhaps being suffocated by parked cars makes it look uglier than it really is.

If we turn left out of this square (Via Pecorelli) and then immediately right along a tiny lane called Vicolo Ascanio Vittozzi we come into a square of the same name with a long and elegantly shuttered sixteenth-century palace called Palazzo Mazzocchi. On the right we take the middle lane and at its end turn left: after a few yards we come to the bustling Piazza del Popolo (crammed, most likely, with vegetable-stalls) and are at once struck by the **Palazzo del Popolo** opposite us with its Ghibelline crenellations and external staircase and supporting arches reminiscent of the same building at Todi. This palace too is in tufo, and came into being at the end of the thirteenth century. It became the seat of the Captain of the People and in 1280 was enlarged: the bell-tower at the back was added too. It was then the seat of the Podestà, and was partly ruined in 1483, but recent restoration has brought it back to more or less its first appearance.

If we walk actually under the Palazzo del Popolo we shall find ourselves in the Piazza Vivaria: we go straight across this square through an unnamed street until we reach the small Piazza Corsica, where we continue along its right side (Via della Pace) between mediaeval houses which have been restored to their first order and harmony; and beyond us are the leafy trees of the Piazza XXIX Marzo (on March 29th, 1944 seven young citizens were shot for military desertion by the Nazis). This is a busy, crowded square: on the left there used to be a Dominican monastery but a barracks of hideous fascist design has replaced it. At the end of the square is the church of *S. Domenico,* a tall yellow-tufo church with square columns set into its walls. It was built in 1233, the first church in Italy to be dedicated to the Spanish St Dominic. The break we see in its left side was made to remove a whole nave, so that the hideous place at its side could be put there. The portal was taken from another church outside the gates: its lunette contains an early fifteenth-century *Madonna and Child* which has a sincere warmth of tone.

Inside, we find one of the strangest churches in the world: it has been chopped in half, or even a quarter, so that it is wider than long, virtually a strip of floor in front of a wide chancel and transepts. On the wall on our left as we enter there is a carved stone monument belonging to Cardinal Guglielmo di Braye, who died in 1282, the work of Arnolfo di Cambio. Above, in the niches, are figures of the *Madonna and Child with SS. Peter* (the Cardinal di Braye kneels before him) *and Dominic.* In the chapel right of the main altar as we face it there are frescoes from the sixteenth century, a modest *Crucifixion* in a niche, a faint *Deposition* in a panel at its side, and then a *St John the Baptist.* The chapel on the other side of the high altar has frescoes dated 1430 but these are very faint: they show from left to right *the martyrdom of St Peter Martyr,* a *Madonna and Child and SS. Dominic, John the Evangelist, Anthony the Abbot and Peter Martyr.* At the side-chapel to the left of this there is a wooden crucifix of the thirteenth century, painted: the cross is shaped like a tree with rising branches for the arms, an unusual feature. This is the cross which legend says talked to St Thomas Aquinas. There is also a tall wooden cupboard or tabernacle, which was once the rostrum from which St Thomas Aquinas taught: it was here in the monastery at the time of the Miracle of Bolsena, and Pope Urban IV ordered that it should contain the corporal.

Turning left outside the church along the Via Arnolfo di Cambio with its squat houses we come into the Piazza Angelo da Orvieto, where there are more trees: and we continue along its left side, with a second fascist building on our left. After a long walk past the barracks, downhill, we come to the wide and open square by which we entered the town, the Piazzale Cahen. On the left of the funicular station there is a narrow tree-lined avenue (with a yellow tourist sign) which will take us down to the *Pozzo di S. Patrizio,* or St Patrick's Well, and where the little road begins we shall find an open-air café in case we are in need.

The round brick shelter of St Patrick's Well at the bottom of the hill sits in the centre of a rounded balcony overlooking the Tiber valley. Visiting times are 9.0 a.m.-12 noon, 2.0-5.0 p.m. The well was dug by Pope Clement VII during his stay in Orvieto in 1528, a year after Rome was sacked by Imperial troops: the city would have needed the water had there been a long siege. It was designed by Antonio da Sangallo, who decided on this particular spot because springs existed at the foot of the hill, showing that there were veins of water inside the rock. While it was being dug, in 1532, an Etruscan tomb was found at a depth of about a hundred feet. The walls of the well are formed out of bricks after a certain depth, not simply excavated out of the rock as the upper part is. It was finished in 1537. Its name derives from the fact that it was thought similar in appearance to St Patrick's Cavern in Ireland.

The outside of the well, at the top, is decorated with the Farnese lilies of Pope Paul III: two doors open at diametrically opposite sides of this brick cover, one for us to enter by and the other for us to leave by when (or rather if) we have been right to the bottom and up again. For inside the well, round the wall, there are two staircases independent of each other, one below the other, the first for use going down and the other for coming up (they spiral in opposite directions). Some people are happy enough just to look down the dizzy well to the water far below (seeing someone cross the tiny bridge at the bottom is an eerie sight).

The well is nearly a hundred feet deep and forty wide, and the two spiralling staircases actually form a corridor round the wall wide enough to allow donkeys and mules to pass for the transporting of water to the surface. The two hundred and forty-eight steps are lighted by seventy-two open windows in the inner wall, which allow light in from the open top of the well. About half-way down, if we look through one of the seventy-two windows, we shall see the trace of a small roof and some tiny apertures: the Etruscan tomb.

From this point brick reinforcement of the walls begins. It is not advisable to go down these stairs if we are sweating, by the way.

We return to the Piazzale Cahen and turning left past the funicular station enter the public gardens, which are actually the battlements of the ruined town fortress, or Rocca: our guess that it was built by Cardinal dell' Albornoz is right; it was also designed by the famous mercenary Ugolino di Montemarte in 1364. It was ruined in 1831 and finally dismantled from the military point of view in 1888 to make way for the funicular railway.

And now we may either take the funicular railway down to the station or wander back to the centre of town by the Corso Cavour opposite the public gardens.

Etruscan tombs—Crocifisso del Tufo and Settecamini

There are two Etruscan sites we should see before leaving the Orvieto area, the first a complete cemetery and the second a single tomb with some of the faint wall-paintings intact (an increasing rarity these days).

The first is not many yards from the town, the tombs of the **Crocifisso del Tufo:** we leave the Piazzale Cahen by the only road that leads down to the valley, and after a short walk or drive find a yellow tourist sign leading us off the road left, along a footpath. As this point in the road is too narrow for safe parking it is better to walk. A dry, warm day is essential. The tombs lie directly under the town so that we look up from them at Orvieto's sheer tufo cliff with the backs of houses rising out of it. A caretaker lives in a small hut at the entrance and he is employed to open the gate: he will expect but does not demand a tip.

The tombs are in two parts—those excavated in the nineteenth century, and those found in the last four or five years. The present excavators claim that the nineteenth-century work was careless and did much damage to the tombs.

At first we enter a narrow alleyway between monumental tombs of the sixth century, two rectangular blocks of them. Above most of the doorways a rough inscription in Etruscan can be seen, meaning something like 'I here am . . .' followed by the name of the deceased or his family. And usually this inscription reads from right to left. Taking the alleyway before us we find an inscription over

327

the first entrance on the right, *I am the tomb of Larth*. After we have seen a few inscriptions we shall recognize the character 'I am', a sort of prolonged *m* with a wavy line.

These so-called monumental tombs belonged of course to the highest citizens—whether high as members of an ecclesiastical hierarchy or as courtiers or politicians or soldiers or simply rich men we do not know; at any rate, they were the leading people, and probably close to the king. They were brought to the burial ground with great ceremony, the women weeping and tearing their hair as we see today in the Arab countries. A massive piece of tufo was placed over the doorway after the ceremony, and earth was thrown in to fill the space to the top of the tomb steps. When this earth is found intact the excavator has a valuable source of information about the date of the tomb, as well as an assurance that no one has been there before.

These tombs certainly had decorated upper storeys, as we see from the other nucleus of later excavations, but the careless work of the nineteenth century toppled them down. The stones that stand at the doorways symbolizing the sex of the occupants were originally on the roofs, but came down in the course of time or during excavation. They crowned the tombs, sometimes many of them together, as if to denote each occupant separately: they also vary in size, which could well denote the different ages of the deceased. The rather rounded stones are said to denote the male, the cylindrical the female: though to my mind it could equally be the other way round. Here in Orvieto the stone symbols are not as clear as in, say, the Cerveteri tombs near Rome where the male is represented by a clear phallic stone and the woman by a tiny model house or ark.

An inscription along this first alleyway mentions the occupant as being a 'Latin', which, with one or two others mentioning foreign names, may mean that Orvieto was a military garrison in Etruscan times: these men would have been 'foreign' mercenaries.

If we now go to the end of this little alleyway and turn left down some improvised steps we come to the later nucleus of tombs, which show much more clearly the original look of the place, and justify the word 'monumental'. Taking a path between the tombs we find immediately on our right the one inscription which reads from left to right: MI AVELES THANARSENAS. Inside we see the two beds normal for all such tombs, lying at right angles to each other, presumably for man and wife. In the first and second tomb on the left there is a difference: they have two rooms instead of one, the first being a kind of ante-chamber. And when we find this we also find that the tomb is detached from the others, as if to give it a separate importance: the space from the other tombs is narrow—about eighteen inches. Perhaps these were the kings or members of the royal family.

This new nucleus of excavations also shows clearly the so-called 'false' arch or vault: it is seen best in the second tomb on the left—a pointed roof inside the tomb made up of two stones on each side, leaning inwards, with a keystone dropped neatly between them at the top. It is the simulation of a house in an especially grand way.

Turning along the first lane on the right we can see, leaning against the outer wall of one of the tombs, the block of tufo which they heaved over the doorway after the burial: it would presumably lie on the steps of the tomb as a sort of ramp, until the moment came for it to be lifted. At the next lane we come to the most recent finds of all, where the decorative walls are intact and the upper storey can be seen with its rounded and pointed blocks of stone. These date from the second half of the sixth century. In the very middle of the path, blocking our way, there is a square stone column cut off abruptly at the height of six feet, meaning that there is a tomb underneath. D. H. Lawrence suggested that the varying heights of these columns might have something to do with the age of the occupant. In this case the inscription is actually on the column.

Taking the last path on the right we find the oldest tomb of all, sheltering between the walls of two others: you can pass it by easily, as there is just a worn stone slab over a hole about eighteen inches from the ground; the tomb lies directly underneath. The interesting thing here is that the tombs adjacent to it have respected its existence and been built round it, so that it occupies a kind of dent in the wall. It probably dates from the beginning of the sixth century. The excavators found a glass vase or bowl there which seems to prove that all the other glass exhibits in the Orvieto museums come from this group of tombs and not from elsewhere, as was thought before.

At the end of this site, in the far left corner, there is a strange and inexplicable discovery, or perhaps not quite inexplicable; it is a tomb no more than three feet high and three feet wide—a perfect miniature replica of a tomb, with two tiny beds. This could be thought simply ornamental were it not for the fact that not only the fragments of vases have been found here but the bones of dead

329

people. Nor were they children: the bones were full grown. Thus, they must have been put on the beds as bones, many years after first burial. And symbols for the male and female were found here too—firedogs for the woman and a spearhead for the man. It could be that in erecting new tombs old ones were disturbed, and these miniature tombs, tiny to denote the great passage of time since their dead had been received into the other world, housed whatever remains were found. This is supported by the fact that only fragments of vases, not whole ones, were left in them.

The tomb of Settecamini

Most of the Etruscan tombs in the area of Settecamini have had their contents removed to Florence long ago, but one remains with its original walls, quite alone in the countryside, in its first setting: before long the walls will be removed to the dry, regulated air of a museum, so we should take this last chance now.

Determined walkers will welcome it: there are about ten kilometres of lovely country to hike through, with paths untroubled by traffic; there are buses, but not frequent ones. Motorists take the old road to Rome and after a few kilometres follow a signpost to Porano: a track road leads us directly to this town. Since the tomb is in open countryside about a mile before we reach the town it is difficult to describe. We are most likely to find it by going to the town and working back from it: after returning along our road for one kilometre we find a track uphill leading to a lone farmhouse just where the road curves. But we shall do best to ask for the peasant on whose land the tomb lies, Giovanni Nibio. Locally everybody calls him 'Ciriaghi' but his family thinks this silly as the word means nothing, though 'Ciriaghi' is more likely to find him than Nibio.

The tomb is called by the name of the deceased, Hescana. An archaeologist, writing in 1893, claimed that he read the words *Laris Hescanas* on one of the wall figures (the driver of the horses). This may be Larte, of the Hescana family: anyway, the interpretation has been accepted. Immediately on our right when we enter the tomb (after a wide downhill avenue where we can feel something of the first dignity of the place) we see the figure of this man, outlined in red, driving a chariot and two horses. The peasant or his practised mother will hold a bunch of candles for us to see by, shielding them with the hand so that we may trace the last faint out-lines of what must have been a vivid and robust fresco. The meaning of the chariot is not clear, since there is no winged fury near by as in other Etruscan tombs, to denote a funeral procession. But we may assume that it does mean a journey to the underworld. On the next wall there are several figures hardly visible any more: twelve in all. They are dancing figures and musicians and a winged demon. A young man holds an open book and pen-like instrument used in ancient times for writing on wax, while the winged demon or genius holds another book on which it is supposed that the deeds of the deceased were written. There are also two youths kissing, dressed in cloaks and with sticks in hand, symbols perhaps of departure for a long journey. The feet of one figure face a direction different from that of his trunk and this may not be an error but a sign of the road he must reluctantly take. There is also a group of three men, two playing instruments, the other holding two staffs—perhaps the leader of the funeral procession. Another group contains two women and a boy, perhaps meant to be members of the dead man's family. On the end wall there is another cloaked youth with a staff, a traveller again. But this time a female winged genius goes before him, which has led some people to suppose that this symbolizes the last journey, under guidance. The genius holds a scroll in her left hand where again the deeds of the deceased are written. On this wall next to a figure almost quite invisible there is the outline of an altar with a sheepskin thrown on it, meaning probably the act of funerary sacrifice. There is also an inscription, *Etenace Hescanas*, thought to refer to a member of the family. On the left wall there are only slight traces of an outline: archaeologists suppose the subject here to be a banquet: the table is said to be shaded by two laurel trees—a frequent usage in Etruscan tombs. And the name inscribed here is *Tetinate Hescanas*. The trees perhaps represent heaven, the Elysian Fields.

Some vases were found in this tomb, indicating the last Etruscan period, when something like a baroque tendency came in, between the end of the fourth and the beginning of the third century B.C., perhaps the last real Etruscan art before the Roman conquests.

CHAPTER 16

Terni

Terni is the capital of the southern province of Umbria, much to the disgust of other important towns like Spoleto and Orvieto. When Italy became a nation for the first time a hundred years ago Umbrian towns lost their strong local authority and came under provincial administration (Perugia in the north and Terni in the south). Terni was an agricultural town like most others of its size, slumbering gently in its plain, until the end of the last century when the near-by Marmore waterfalls (or more exactly the waters of the Nera and its tributary Velino) were exploited for their industrial power. It then became a centre of arms manufacture. And it is now certainly the largest industrial town in Umbria, and therefore the most prosperous, which we at once feel in its bustling cheerful streets, in the restaurants and bars and *pizzerie* and well-stocked shops. In fact, if we want the best for our palates we should always make for an industrial town of modest size—one, namely, which has preserved intimacy with wealth. There is an excellent *pizzeria* in the Piazza della Repubblica immediately as we enter it, on our left as we come from the central but cold Piazza Tacito: and it snuggles close to a bar where good coffee can be had.

Terni is surprisingly ancient, given its present appearance and spirit: the Umbrians founded it about 700 B.C. In Roman times it was a colony called Interamna, meaning 'between two rivers' (the Nera and the Serra—the latter has since changed course). Like most other Umbrian towns it was destroyed by Totila and the Lombards, and was involved in fights with its neighbours, Spoleto, Narni, Rieti. It welcomed Barbarossa out of sheer spite against Spoleto, but was sacked by the emperor fifteen years later just the same. There was a bitter internal class-struggle in the sixteenth century after the town had passed again into the hands of the Church. A middle-class faction called the Banderesi climbed the walls and murdered a lot of noblemen, and the town was punished for this (with more murders) by the Church.

The town (about one hundred thousand inhabitants) specializes in steel and iron and chemical products (carbide, calcium), and its hydro-electric power serves a great part of central Italy down as far as Rome. Yet you get almost no physical sense of this in the town itself. The brutal Anglo-Saxon habit of planting factories in the middle of towns, or rather of allowing houses to spring up round them, never seems to have caught on with the Italians, partly perhaps because the Church was always there with its reminder of tradition. For most of Terni's hydro-electric plants and factories you have to go outside—they stretch more or less all the way from the waterfalls (Cascata delle Marmore), five or six kilometres away, to the edge of the town itself. There are few spots in Terni from which you can't see the country.

The commercial exploitation of its water was not a modern idea. A Roman consul thought of canalizing the stagnant waters of the Velino in about 300 B.C. but the result was the flooding of acres of countryside down as far as Rome. This started, two centuries later, one of the many quarrels between Terni and Rieti. The people of Terni wanted the canal closed, Rieti wanted it dug deeper. And nothing was done about it for one thousand four hundred years, when the people of Rieti once more came up with the idea of deepening the canal. Even for Umbrian time this is slow. Finally it was achieved at the end of the sixteenth century. Anyway, the deepening of that canal, which Terni resisted so much, provided in the end the means to its prosperity and its escape, today, from the usual provincial tedium.

Being industrial, the town was devastated in the last war: about eighty per cent of it was destroyed, so that tourism has little to be drawn by. Much of the church of S. Francesco, the municipal palace, the Giuseppe Verdi theatre were destroyed, apart from many lovely houses. About fifteen hundred people were killed in raids that went on for a year (1943-44). But in the side-streets of Terni there are still some marvellous house-fronts; they give us a glimpse of the order and radiance of the Renascence city.

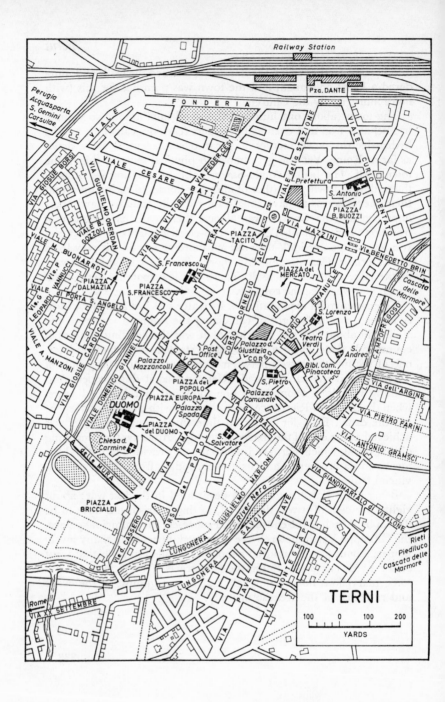

The Duomo—Roman amphitheatre—S. Salvatore—S. Pietro—Pinacoteca
(Gozzoli and Ambrogio)—the mediaeval quarter—S. Francesco (Bosch-
like frescoes)

Coming from south or north we shall probably find ourselves in the
Piazza Cornelio Tacito, which has a tall, strange, solitary flagpole in
its middle, rooted in a basin of post-war mosaic on which—during
the high season—waters play. You can get good coffee at its only
bar before going down the Via Cornelio Tacito to the Piazza del
Popolo. If we continue in the same direction we shall find ourselves
in a great gap (produced by the last war and now called Piazza
Europa) dominated by the dark Palazzo Spada, its brick face pock-
marked with holes for a marble or stone face that was never put
there. To the right of this brooding, rather derelict mass (now improvised post-war flats) we find a narrow street, the Via Roma, of
which the Palazzo Spada is No. 28. If we walk down the Via Roma
we find on our right a small theatre with its own little forecourt, the
Politeama Ternano, Terni's old music hall, but in mediaeval times
a hospital and now a cinema. There are supposed to be frescoes
inside from the thirteenth century. Farther down on the right a little
side-street offers us pleasant reminders of the town three or four
hundred years ago, with its flat, quiet house-fronts that border
straight on to the cobbles of the road, like Turkish houses, bustling
with decorative life and civil care (Via dell' Arringo): and at the end
of this, bright and white and self-assured, there is the **Duomo**
standing in its own Piazza del Duomo. The origins of the church are
Romanesque, but we see at once as we stand in the usually deserted
square that its order and proportions belong to a much later date.
There is a long, pillared porch (seventeenth-century) and the main
door (twelfth-century) shelters from the weather under it, a stone
frame of lions and goats and dragons among twirling acanthus
leaves.

Inside the duomo there are the plain, rational lines of the seventeenth-century neo-classical style, said to be the work of Bernini,
though there are poor grounds for this. Bombing brought to light a
tiny piece of mural at the back of the church, *St Anthony the Abbot,*
holding a bell. Above the main door we can see the outline of the
old rose window, now bricked in. The crypt under the church was

335

the first oratory in Terni, but this is closed except for one day in the year, July 1st, when the church's silver Byzantine cross is on show. Like much else in Terni, what wasn't destroyed in bombardments evokes little local pride.

But almost opposite the duomo there is a corner, between two palazzi, where we can see the graceful pre-war town better than anywhere else. The intimate, compact Palazzo Bianchini-Riccardi has an embossed doorway and a delicate fleur-de-lys design across the whole face, with the retiring delicacy of a French villa.

Turning right down a small lane (the duomo now behind us) we find the remains of a Roman amphitheatre built about A.D. 30, hardly more than a grassy hump of brickwork now: but the base of the outer wall remains, and the size of the whole (about sixty yards by twenty) can be judged if we look at it from the lane outside. It seems too small to have held ten thousand spectators, but it did. If we follow this road down to its end we shall come to the inevitable hideous war memorial, but turning from this into the public gardens we meet the side-wall of the amphitheatre and the remains of the Roman road that curled round it. We see pieces of the original wall-design—porous sandstone and chalk in alternate square bricks, mounted on their corners. Walking along the side of this wall, we shall see the theatre's inscriptive stone where the name of the architect is just visible, *Faustus Titius Liberalis*. Beyond the amphitheatre is a hotchpotch of pleasant and mellow tiled roofs—the real duomo behind its sober seventeenth-century front. At the wide parapet of the public gardens (actually part of the ancient Roman wall) we can look across country towards Collescipoli perched on its hill.

If we return to the bleak Piazza Europa and cross it with the Palazzo Spada on our left, we shall come on the church of *S. Salvatore* raised above the level of the road in its own tiny quadrangle, a fat, round hump of a church that shows at once its Romanesque origins, standing as if the village it once belonged to were still there, clinging round it on the side of the hill. It came into existence in the fifth century A.D. on top of a Roman building which may have been a Temple of the Sun, at least according to people who excavated the bomb-ruins in 1947 and made new findings. On the right wall there are the traces of frescoes which have the ancient look of Roman murals in delicate and hesitant lines, treating secular subjects but probably as symbols of religious ones, during the early persecutions. These are said to be thirteenth-century, but I think them earlier. Behind the main altar there is a rather clumsy painted crucifix of the Umbrian school from the sixteenth century, but at the side-chapel immediately on entering the church we see fourteenth-century murals under Sienese influence, a *Crucifixion* and an *Annunciation*, where the faces are gently and subtly conveyed.

The Corso Vecchio, the old main street of the town, winding and sometimes widening into a little square, offers us a pleasant walk. The first of these little squares is that of the church of *S. Pietro* built in the fourteenth century, another of those simple brick-faced buildings that make the baroque look a little mad, with its strained mixture of the rational and the inspired. If we go to the back of the church we shall find traces of the original oratory on which it was built, its faded pillars no higher than a man, and Gothic arches filled in with stone (probably in the fourteenth century). S. Pietro is perhaps the nicest church in Terni to sit in—plenty of people come to do just that: the bombardments of the last war tore down the whole seventeenth-century superstructure, and the architects decided to restore the church to its first clear proportions, so that it now has one vast nave, without pillars or cavernous side-chapels. There is an open wood ceiling with rafters, quite new of course, and a bright, soaring polygonal apse. Frescoes were found on all the walls, quite clear, though fragments. At once on entering, on the rear wall (right-hand side), we see a fifteenth-century Umbrian fresco of *St Anthony*, with that warm, Byzantine suggestion intact in his wide eyes. In the right wall a niche under a Gothic arch contains a delicate *Madonna and Child* of the Sienese school. A larger niche farther on has one fresco painted over another, divided by a century in time: the earlier fragment, at a depth of an inch under the later one, is a *Madonna and Child* of the same period as that in the first niche; we can therefore compare two styles at close quarters; in the later work, *the story of St Stephen*, by members of the Gozzoli school, some of the earlier stillness has gone and a trace of Renascence restlessness, in the gestures and facial expressions, intrudes. In the last niche going down the church we find another almost quite faded *Madonna and Child* where the haloes are etched out of the wall as in many frescoes of that time, their gilt now fallen or stolen, leaving only the chiselled lines. In the presbytery left of the altar there is a tombstone belonging to the Manassei family (their palazzo is next door). It leans against the wall with an engraving of the knight himself—'*nobilis et respectabilis militis Domini Stephani de Manasseis*', 1480. Going back up the church we see a wonderfully serene piece under a Gothic arch where the fading effect of time seems to have completed the theme perfectly—a *Madonna and Child and saints*, an Umbrian work of the fifteenth century. The last niche of all, close to the entrance, contains *the dormition of the Virgin* with Christ holding a haloed child (that is, her soul) above her, surrounded by angels and saints. The Madonna's soul is always represented in this way, from mediaeval times onward, as a child held by Christ, above the bier where she lies.

If we turn left coming out of S. Pietro, along the wall of the Palazzo Manassei, we shall find at this palazzo's first large doorway the town's **Pinacoteca** or picture gallery (closed on Monday, of course). In the first room there is only baroque exaggeration, tragedy unfelt and lots of flowing robes—but in the next room you see at once, standing alone, small and refined, Benozzo Gozzoli's *Nuptials of SS. Catherine, Lucy, Francis and Bartholomew*, dated 1466. There is extraordinary detail here: it is distemper on wood, rosily gleaming as Gozzoli always seemed to want it. Next to it, much larger, a triptych nearly covers the wall, a fifteenth-century Umbrian *Virgin enthroned among saints*, which has all the delicate form of the Gozzoli at its side except in one basic thing, a certain ease and happy assurance, which it lacks. In the Gozzoli there are almost the same brushstrokes, the same conventions of art, but the touch is never stiff, every formality has gone, the subject commands but never frightens him.

Under glass in the small end room there is a *Madonna and three saints* by Ambrogio; it has a German quality—dramatic and striking, especially in the face of the Madonna; she is thin and blonde. Again we find that stirring informality of something really felt—in the way the Madonna's kerchief is tied round her neck, casually, in complete repose.

Carrying on down the Corso Vecchio in the same direction as before we find the Teatro Giuseppe Verdi on our right, crowding the pavement snugly with its steps, six massive pillars combined with small doorways in a way that makes you think of carriages, the clatter of hoofs in the evening, lighted torches, the cries of coachmen. Farther down on the right there is another church built on Roman foundations, S. Lorenzo; again we see the simple wide front of a mediaeval church, with two sets of slender marble pillars set high in the wall under the gables, but the inside is the result entirely of restoration.

Opposite this church the Arch of S. Lorenzo gives us access to what used to be the mediaeval quarter of the town. The courtyard of No. 10, facing the arch, shows what the rest of the town used to look like; derelict now—a porch with columns and a wide outdoor staircase.

The church of **S. Francesco** is perhaps the largest in Terni, and when you approach it from the direction of Via Cornelio Tacito and Via Goldoni you wonder why it isn't the duomo; it stands there alone behind its cloisters, a Romanesque hump nudging a tower with arches, spacious and tall. It was established in 1265, without the tower, then given three naves two hundred years later, and it has been restored three times, in the seventeenth century, in 1926 and in 1948. In the chapel on the right of the presbytery there are early fifteenth-century frescoes in a better state than most others in Terni, though faded. Here you see strong Gothic influences— you might almost be looking at a Hieronymus Bosch in the *Hell* on the right-hand wall, with its falling and tortured naked bodies, prodded, roped by the neck, under the scourge, threatened by terrible animals, some of whom are winged devils, with one word, unfaded and stark and black—ACCIDIA, like a finger pointing to our century. On the other wall the *Purgatory* is in even better shape, with human creatures in great number walking and praying and standing in water, while above there is *liberation of the soul* and *Jesus in Limbo*, serene and dark, culminating in *Paradise* and *the glory of God* behind the chapel's altar. The subjects were clearly inspired by Dante: some people have suggested Bartolomeo di Tomeso, an artist from Foligno, though this would place the frescoes a century later than they seem. They were painted over earlier work.

La Cascata delle Marmore—the local waterfalls

The sight that tourists are supposed not to miss is the waterfall on which the town's industrial energy is based: **La Cascata delle Marmore.** Most of the town's factories are strung along this road —we pass an electro-chemical works blackened with smoke; a factory-bridge runs high over our road—straight to a broken-down villa where the factory offices are housed, once called Villa Graziani

339

Pressio (the workers call it roughly 'Villa Valle'—the name of the hill behind it). It is nice to imagine the factory and its black closed bridge not here—and Byron riding along the deserted path at the side of the river Nera towards the tall woods and the rocks towering over the water. He stayed at this villa in 1817.

The falls are about five kilometres outside, on the road to Norcia or Rieti or Visso, according to which signpost we find. Before a tunnel, bored under one of the rocky hills that produce the falls, there is a wide parking space where the people of Terni bring their friends and show them—on Sundays and holidays—the cascading waters that have polished the rock to shiny marble. On other days the falls are inactive, only a trickle comes down for the simple reason that local industry is using their power. Once a year, in June, there is a festival of the waters, when they are at full power all day, thundering and sending a misty spray across the bouldery river towards the road. Most evenings, apart from the winter season, they are floodlit too.

The Lake of Piediluco—an echo and a Roman statue

The people of Terni have a lovely summer and week-end resort close at hand, the serene **Lake of Piediluco,** seventeen kilometres away. To reach it by car from the centre of Terni we take the road to Rome and look carefully for a turning left, where there is a signpost. The road takes us high above Terni's hydro-electric plants: the narrow wooded valley stretching down on our left is misted over with industrial smoke. We shall pass the road to Greccio on the way (it is fifteen kilometres farther on)—St Francis began the tradition of the Christmas crib there. And of course there are frequent trains and buses to Piediluco.

The name probably comes from the fact that the tiny town lies at the foot (*piedi*) of a wood (*lucus*). Even this apparently out-of-the-way town failed to escape the ravages of history: it was caught in the persistent bitter fights between Rieti and Terni, and it preferred Rieti (the closer neighbour was nearly always the more hated). The Romans called the lake Lacus Velinus: the name of a river flowing into it.

It is perhaps the loveliest lake of all for its squat tree-crowded hills all round, and tall beeches and firs in rows, and occasional vine-

340

yards, and has a circumference of seventeen kilometres. We can take a boat to the hill called Monte Caperno on the other side: people try out its famous echo, said to have an interval of four seconds.

About a hundred yards after we enter the town we shall find the steep and wide steps (their steepness probably a precaution against flooding) leading to the front of S. Francesco. It was built at the end of the thirteenth century. The left of its two portals (now filled in) dates from 1293 and is carved all round with bas-relief fish, boats, nets, fishing-baskets. A panel above contains the mystic lamb, also in bas-relief.

The inside is a simple whitewashed hall with six wide arches supporting the roof: and there are various traces of mediocre frescoes everywhere. On the right of the entrance we see a holy-water font with a fish carved in its middle—taken from an ancient Roman column. Half-way along the right wall, set in a niche above eye-level, there is a Roman statue of a woman: only half an arm is missing and the rest is in remarkably good condition, though the face shows signs of restoration. It is a reminder of the ancient origins of this resort: the Romans loved their lakes, unlike modern Italians who think them sad and forbidding. The Romans understood the beneficial effects for nerves, high blood-pressure, heart complaints.

CHAPTER 17

The Gateway to Rome

Narni and Otricoli

Narni is perched at the top of a steep valley, the first entrance to Umbria from Rome, where the hills narrow and make the town an obligatory station in or out of the province. It was this position, as the herald and farewell-post of Umbria, that gave Narni its importance as a military post in ancient times, when the Flaminian Way on which it stands was the road from Rome to Florence, Ravenna and the Adriatic coast. Narni was also the starting-point of a road that went to Spoleto and joined up with the Flaminian Way again at Foligno.

Narni achieved its wealth in the twelfth century after rebelling against papal rule (1112), though its later rebellion against Barbarossa (1167) was only temporarily successful: it was sacked by the archbishop of Magonza seven years later. But Frederick II failed to beat it after a long siege; and a claimant to the dukedom of Spoleto was no more successful. Narni then allied itself to Rome (1242) and to Perugia, against the empire. In 1373 it was ruled by the Orsini family. These had been three centuries of continuing importance, but in 1527 it was completely ravished by the so-called Lansquenets (*Landsknechten*, German mercenaries, or literally 'country serfs') on their murderous way from Rome; and after that it declined and slept, so much so that only recently, in 1950, was it given the title of town again (*città*), as opposed to village. A skull supposed to belong to one of the murderous mercenaries is kept in the town library with a sort of loving detestation.

The centre of the town is Piazza Garibaldi, miniature and cosy, dominated on its lower slope by a mediaeval tower and on its upper by the duomo, temporarily closed.

Walking along the Via Garibaldi and turning down the first lane on the right (Via Franceschi Ferrucci), we find the surprising massive front of S. Agostino, devoid of all decoration except for a faded fresco high in the wall, its gilt lost, a *Madonna and Child and two saints*, from the same period as the church (fifteenth-century). On the left as we enter, in the first side-chapel, there are frescoes in quite good condition, the work of Torresani, a local painter (1530-90) though some cynics say he came from Terni.

In 1965 S. Agostino's altar (a tall baroque affair) was dismantled and the present altar was revealed under it, white and tiny, a complete block of stone with five pillars cut into it, standing quite alone, bright and ghostly. The strange thing was that the authorities had designed a new altar that was to be very much the same: they found their work already done for them, five hundred years ago.

Returning to the Via Garibaldi—or we can find our way back through the narrow uphill side-lanes—we walk to the fascinating oblong Piazza Priora. On our right immediately as we enter it there is the Casa Sacripanti, with three bas-reliefs set high in the wall—knights in combat, and winged dragons or griffins, fighting like cocks. Farther along, the deep porch of the Loggia dei Priori houses the vegetable market under its two tall arches: perhaps designed by Gattaponi. Tucked into a corner of the mediaeval tower there is a small pulpit which was used by the town herald.

On the opposite side of the square there is the Palazzo del Podestà, its front formed out of three thirteenth-century houses, with a slight curve; its six windows were added in the sixteenth century, destroying the simplicity but giving the clerks inside some light. To the right of the main door there are tiny columns set in the wall as a false loggetta, and above them, in bas-relief, lions, griffins, mounted knights fighting, and a scene of hunting with falcons.

The Pinacoteca or picture gallery is reached through the bold courtyard of the Palazzo del Podestà with its Roman fragments. Finding the actual room requires tenacity, but once in the council chamber we see facing us an altar-piece by Ghirlandaio—the only work of this Florentine painter in the whole of Umbria, dated 1486. It is a *coronation of the Virgin among angels, prophets, saints and sibyls*, well preserved: the whole piece is concentrated towards Christ's face, in the solemn moment of crowning, as he leans towards Mary. Hanging on the left wall there is the marvellous *Annunciation* of Benozzo Gozzoli, golden and mellow, glowing red, radiant with pleasure, the two surprised faces enclosed in soft light. There, at once, you see

343

religious joy: not the immediate mystical devoutness of Fra' Angelico, Gozzoli's teacher, but the resultant joy.

If we continue through the square past its fourteenth-century bronze fountain we come to the astonishing *S. Maria in Pensole* on the right, tucked serenely into a corner, so old as to seem beyond further disturbance. It has an ancient front quite untouched since 1175. Everything about it is rapt in the first moments of Christianity, before Christ's name was used for power and intimidation.

Going back towards the centre, and turning right immediately after S. Domenico, we shall find ourselves walking along the edge of town, with country on one side: the winding Via S. Bernardo and the Via Aurelio Saffi take us to the church of S. Francesco, its vast wall darkening the narrow lane. There too, you have an utterly simple front, where stones are put together in such true proportion that no decoration or even niche or window is needed. Inside there are four massive pillars with the last traces of frescoes on them. The church has a magnificent wideness: built in the fourteenth century on an oratory founded by St Francis when he was visiting the town in 1213. On the walls of the chapel right of the entrance there are *scenes from the life of SS. Francis and Benedict*, by Mezzastris.

The Bridge of Augustus

When leaving Narni we should not miss seeing the Bridge of Augustus, which once bore the Flaminian Way across the river Nera: it lies close to where the road divides for Terni on the one hand and the Autostrada del Sole on the other. We see one broken arch of what was a bridge of one hundred and twenty-eight yards. It originally had four of these arches but was ruined in the seventh and eighth centuries A.D.; it was restored later—perhaps towers were added—but fell into ruin again in the eleventh century.

Ancient Ocriculum at the side of the Tiber

Otricoli lies on the road from Narni to the Autostrada del Sole, the last Umbrian town on the way to Rome, or the first we see coming northwards: and it couldn't be a better farewell or introduction, as it distils everything we know of Umbria except the

Etruscan element into a tiny space. It is contained almost entirely inside its original mediaeval walls, entered by means of a narrow archway where the gate hinges look as active as they were two centuries ago. At first, when we have climbed the hill towards it from the Flaminian Way, we may think there is no more than one simple street with pleasant porches shadowing the shops. But although mediaeval, this is a later addition, and the nucleus of Otricoli lies on the site of the original Umbrian settlement, enveloping the hilltop like a tiny Orvieto, the backs of its houses sheer on the cliffside, overlooking steep descents to the Tiber valley.

In ancient times the town was called Ocriculum. As we walk through its silent, narrow lanes we see Roman remains everywhere; during the eighteenth century the Vatican undertook excavations and found a lot of material (now in the museum at Rome), including a Greek head from the fourth century B.C., known as the 'Jove of Otricoli'.

And now for **Ocriculum,** the riverside town to which the population moved in ancient times. It has the advantage of being almost entirely hidden, and there is no signpost; we find the ruins in the fields, unfenced and unexplained. The path leading to it goes from the Flaminian Way, directly under the town: in fact, directly under a conspicuous villa in a nest of cypress trees, on its own little hill. If we approach it from the south we must turn left, if from the north right. The path is suitable for cars, but the best plan is to walk down —it is two or three hundred yards at most. The narrow pathway burrows between fields until all sight of the highroad behind us is lost and we draw near the silence of the Tiber.

Among vineyards and little ravines we find the stumps of Roman towers and arches low in the ground, and then all at once, as we look towards the Tiber, the outlines of what must have been the theatre, semi-circular, the ribs of its foundations gaping, its acting-area clear. If we go closer we find a great tunnel bored underneath, turning the whole curved length of the auditorium, with entrances for the spectators. It must be about half the size of the Epidaurus theatre in Greece, it lacks mountains shimmering in the distance, it lacks Greece's vast golden sky: but it has a marvellous intimacy instead, the low green hills all round suggest one step away from the wild gods of Greece, towards a more clement life. We can imagine the afternoon coolness as the sun went down over the Tiber as it does now, and voices ringing out from the stage below; the hills must have seemed the beginning of long journeys, the edge, in fact, of the sky as it lay over the theatre like an intimate spectator. In these theatres the gods were addressed: this is why they seem to lay themselves open to the sky—not hug the stage for concentration like the later Christian theatres; the sky was still the seat of wonder, and of power in the real, not human, sense of the word. These theatres show better than anything what ancient civilization meant, perhaps what all civilization means—that delicate ordering of the earth so that it seems to join in with human wishes. This part of Umbria could be one vast parkland, tilled from bare earth into what we now call countryside: this is the decisive act that marks civilization whether in Egypt in the shadow of the Pyramids or in the Peloponnesus. The earth begins to bear a smile as if it had joined a human intention; it is no longer unpredictable. After all, the Greek and Roman gods were really names for the ancient relation to the sky—they were its parts and powers, in human form. And perhaps civilization is the success of that relationship. It need not mean religion or even complete truth, necessarily. But some successful relationship is struck off. The religious quest, at least, has to be there. The Roman world wasn't all war and hard law and straight roads. We get that impression from history books, and from their vile statues. But there were villas too, and honey, and wine, and an unsuccessful religious quest.

We may believe, as we stand at the top of this theatre, that we no longer have a relationship with things round us, that the earth has gone dead and bleak—something to hide from or protect ourselves against, as unpredictable as it was for the barbarians. The more you go to these first settlements of the Mediterranean world and glimpse that extraordinary order which wasn't a mental one at all but the realization of a great quest, the more you realize how we have lost the touch.

We can get to the tiny church of S. Vittore by a path leading from the theatre, and when we reach it, descending a few stone steps which are clearly ancient in origin, we see immediately beneath us the slow Tiber, as hidden and untroubled as the remotest stretches of the Rhine. An ancient arch and steps once led to the edge of the water for the boats to Rome: the arch before us now may even have been the town's harbour gate. Perhaps a temple stood here originally, the first place to visit on one's way up from the boats.

So we are almost in sight of Rome. At least it feels like that as we stand at the edge of the water without a building near by that could remind us of our epoch, only the sandy banks and swirling currents. Behind us lies the narrow bottleneck into Umbria, a special corridor of introduction to a province unlike any other, a continent to itself, yet always with this connection to Rome, and a flavour of Rome in its best towns. The Tiber comes down to us here (Umbria's possession nearly all the way) from the province's Tuscan edge just north of Città di Castello, a bearer of civilization from the earliest times, a protection against invaders (for the Etruscans against eastern attacks, for the Umbrians against western), a source of fertility in a too-mountainous region, as straight and sure as the Via Flaminia on the other side, two lines of communication that keep the sad, mystical intimate continent in touch with things. Perhaps its closeness to Rome lies here too—in a matter of character: in a sympathetic rejection of the world that washes through it.

Appendices and Indexes

APPENDIX 1

Places to Eat in Umbria

The following selection is based on the idea that what we want when footsore and hungry is a restaurant combining excellence of food, comfort (or intimacy) and cheapness. They are the ones favoured by the local people, on the whole. After that come the restaurants where we pay more and take our chance—in Umbria a good one—that the chef or management hasn't moved since we were told how good it was. I price a restaurant or trattoria 'very cheap' if it offers a three-course meal at between L.700 and L.900, 'cheap' at L.900-1200 and 'economical' at L.1200-1800. Thus we should expect to pay between twelve shillings and one pound a head, and remember that at ten shillings we shall almost certainly not eat well unless we are known there and have made a previous arrangement: this is easy to do, by the way, if we have some command of the language; we can tell the owner that we mean to come for a week or so, and would he make us a price; most of the local people we see eating around us have done that. At the low quota of L.700 we shall be enjoying *prezzo fisso* or the fixed-price menu, where beggars can't be choosers. The service charge is nearly always included in the bill, and in the pricey restaurants about half the tip again is expected. The rule about tipping is the same as for bars: we rarely tip if served by the owner or his wife. Those who, like me, find Italian food mediocre but oddly appetising should avoid the very low-priced places when in a strange town, if they can afford to.

We shall not be wise to reconnoitre the trattorie—that is, the ordinary eating places—for ourselves: we shall have some horrible experiences if we do, in still side-lanes; and we shall often pay just as much. The local tourist office will always help us to a square and clean meal, and tell us the rough price beforehand. A spotless table-cloth is an excellent guide here. A large clientèle is of course an infallible guide. Michelin cannot always say what is happening in a place it recommended a year ago: in my experience it points out the good places but not necessarily the best, which are a matter of knowing the locals. Hotel-restaurants are often excellent and not much dearer, if dearer at all, than the trattorie. The best places are those which show signs of family management and look like home. But one can err more in the line of family-run trattorie than in the big hotel-restaurants.

Pecking is not admired in Umbria: we should never go into a restaurant unless we can work our way through at least three courses; we shall probably be made to pay the same anyway. The more we order, the cheaper it is: I have rarely found an exception to that. Although there is as much diet-consciousness in Italy as elsewhere, fatness still means health at the back of the Italian mind. Nor are people who want to rush their meal appreciated. Only at table, says the Italian, do we not grow old. We are expected to take our snacks at the *tavola calda* or *rosticceria* or *pizzeria*. The cakes at bars, hiding under plastic domes, are nearly always hideous—there are strange stories about where the fat used comes from.

One can eat quite well on either side of the Autostrada del Sole. For my palate the Motta restaurants are the best, but they seem to be more plentiful going down into Italy than coming up. The prices of all are economical: and everything is clearly set out for us on the *carta*; we shall eat cheapest sitting up at the bar, and we can have anything from a couple of fried eggs to a three-course meal, at any time of the day.

Those who find the bleached and stodgy bread-rolls served in most Italian restaurants horrible (especially afterwards) should ask for *pane casareccio* (accent on the third syllable) which means home-baked bread in the dictionary but fresh bread from a shop round the corner in real life.

For people trying to achieve a complete tour of Umbria in a short time wine at lunch is not advisable, unless watered down: there is almost no wine produced today that is purely from the grape; I know of no peasant who does not add boiling sugar to give the wine power, even in the Chianti areas where in good years it doesn't need it. The most ignorant peasant will go to the so-called wine-chemist with a sample of his new wine, to find out what it needs to 'steady' it: these need not be chemicals, but any tampering with wine makes it heavy, at best. More nonsense is written about

Italian wines than about those of any other country: Italian wine is a drink for the table, to be slopped about and drunk in great mouth-fuls. The most superb French wine is not appreciated by most Italian country folk: it is thought dead, flat; they associate good wine with a sparkle, which is to say that they always drink it young. The finest Italian wine I have tasted came from the Barolo area, far to the north and close to France. Otherwise Italians treat their wine roughly: the French would think its preparation crude—a matter of tipping it into a vat and leaving it to 'boil'; much of the acidity characteristic of Italian wine comes not from the type of grape or soil or climate but from the fact that the debris of twigs and pressed grape-skins at the mouth of the vat in the wine's first days is not pressed down frequently enough; once an hour in France will be once or twice a day in Italy. Wine in Italy is ruthlessly mixed, though the wine-corruption of five years ago has been largely scotched by government action: at least one can say that there is now little or no purely chemical wine on the market; it is mostly from grapes, with supposedly harmless additives here and there. The most famous wine in Umbria is the Orvieto white, yet I have had worse and falser wine in Orvieto than anywhere else in the province, the reason being that there is more demand for the wine (especially from the Romans, who make hungry journeys to Orvieto, and drunken journeys back) than there are vineyards. Where I have recommended a trattoria or restaurant in the actual narrative of this book it means nearly always that the wine is genuine, namely from a known vineyard connected with the establishment, and not likely to give you a headache. The rule in Umbria is that the higher we go in the restaurant price-range the less likely we are to find a genuine local wine. In these places we can always choose a wine bottled far away—a Barolo or Greve: Chianti has had some very bad years, due to the collapse of agriculture which followed Italy's industrial expansion, but it is now on the way up again with the development of wine co-operatives.

All the eating places I list below have been recommended locally, and I have usually tried them myself. In the higher price-ranges chefs and managements do change, and a steady flow of foreign tourists keeps the wolf from the door however bad the food.

If we settle down in any part of Umbria for a month or more to do our sight-seeing we will probably do our own shopping too, in which case it will be useful to know the word for 'free-range' when buying chicken—it is *nostrale,* which means 'our own', as opposed to *di allevamento* meaning 'broiler-house' (about half the price of the first). Eggs sell by the pair: the price quoted is therefore double what you expect. To buy wine or oil it is best to contact a peasant: even here the local tourist office may be enterprising. Wine bought retail in this way should cost between ten and fifteen lire a degree of alcohol to the litre: that is, between L.100 and L.150 per litre, according to the alcohol strength and your shrewdness in dealing. Olive oil costs between L.1000 and L.1200 per kilogram and differs year by year according to the harvest and the time you buy it.

Water is a diner's right in Italy and some confusion can be caused if we ask simply for *acqua* as opposed to *acqua semplice* or *acqua naturale.* If we like a less intensely espresso coffee than most Italians take we should ask for a 'long' coffee or *caffè lungo,* in which case the arm of the machine is brought down more slowly and the result is twice as much liquid. A *caffè corretto* is one with a dash of bad brandy, unless you ask for the expensive kind. And *zuppa inglese* in the list of desserts, meaning English soup, is what we would call trifle.

Those places listed below which are also mentioned in the text carry an asterisk.

Acquasparta
Da Sacchi*, Via Marconi. Cheap; home-cooking to order.

Amelia
Anita, (hotel), Via Roma. Cheap.
Centrale, Piazza 21 Settembre. Cheap.

Assisi
La Fortezza* (in the staircase-lane of that name leading from the central square near the fountain): Guglielmo cooks himself, in a real cook's hat; he comes from the Trento, Italy's best cooking area. He has a surprise every day, which his wife serves with unvarying sweetness and charm. No trouble is too great for him: he is one of the very few Italians for whom the kitchen is a passion. Cheap. Wine drinkable but no more.
La Pallotta: if we are in the mood for heavy wine-drinking and don't want a headache afterwards this is the place to go. It is really a *cantina,* though food is served, if not in great comfort. The wine is

the best in Assisi and can be taken away, draught: most of it is *rosciolo*, a rather effervescent rosé of the hilly district above the town, and it can be drunk plentifully as it hardly exceeds ten degrees of alcohol. Rooms very unheated in winter. Very cheap, with a fixed-price menu.

Pozzo della Mensa: at its best the food is good, and cleanly and cheerfully served. The wine should be avoided. We can ask for the fixed-price menu here. Nella, who serves, likes to play pop records throughout, having got them on a tape first. Very cheap.

La Stalla, meaning exactly what it is—a stable. This is for the evenings, until midnight and after, and needs a car as it lies about a mile beyond the Porta Perlici: the local tourist office will give us the exact directions. An atmosphere of wood-fire cooking and dark intimate corners; wine genuine, the thick, bloody type from Cannara below in the valley, and anything up to thirteen degrees of alcohol in strength. Economical, certainly for a sort of night-haunt. Flatlets are available in the garden for renting, should we want the height and the marvellous air, and a silence which even Assisi cannot achieve.

Bevagna
Ristorante da Nina*, Piazza Garibaldi. First-class kitchen, one of the best in Umbria, and thick red wine straight from the vineyards, unless we arrive too late in the year, when the last vintage is exhausted and the new not yet ready. Views across the town's mediaeval wall. Economical.

Cascia
Casa del Pellegrino (next to the Basilica S. Rita). Cheap.
Albergo Ristorante Cursula. Economical.

Città di Castello
Albergo di Roma. Economical.
Albergo Tiferno. Economical.

Foligno
Hotel Umbria, Via Cesare Battisti 1. Economical.
Centrale-Amatillo, Piazza del Duomo 4. Economical.
Poledrini-da Remo, Viale Stazione.

Gualdo Tadino
Gigiotto. Economical.

Gubbio
Albergo San Marco, Viale Accoromboni 4. Excellent food and we are expected to eat a lot of it. We should try their cake as a dessert, and any of their fish dishes. For Italy, a gourmet-kitchen. Considering what it gives, cheap.

Norcia
Albergo della Posta, just off the central square. Economical.
Da Benito, Piazzetta di S. Rita. Economical.
Trattoria da Armando. Cheap.
The Canapine, eighteen kilometres away, can be expensive, but the view—on exceptionally clear days including both of Italy's seas—is worth it. We should sample the truffles of Norcia if they are in season (autumn). Grated over our spaghetti they are excellent. You are forbidden to travel with them in a train, presumably because some people are allergic to the fumes.

Orvieto
Da Peppe. Appetizing and economical.
Ristorante dell' Orso, Piazza Vittozzi. First-class kitchen, genuine wine. Cheap.

Perugia
There are too many excellent restaurants in Perugia for a list to be necessary: our choice will depend on our taste, our needs at the moment, our position in the town and the size of our wallet. But one restaurant is reliable, quiet and, for what it gives, cheap. This is the *Ristorante del Sole** in Via Oberdan. There is no traffic even a stone's throw away, and we have a view across to Assisi.

We should try the restaurants in the Corso Vannucci: a fairly consistent standard is achieved, at economical prices. The Perugians, having been great voluptuaries in their time, like their food too well for there to be many bad eating places. Even the cakes in bars can be good, especially those at *Sandri's**.

San Gemini
Hotel Duomo, at the end of the Via Roma. Economical if we are.

Spello
Il Molino. Cooking good. The fuss and *figura* lead one to expect higher prices than is the case.

Spoleto
Commercio, Piazza della Vittoria. Cheap.
Lello Caro, Piazza Garibaldi 15. Economical.
Taverna Il Tartufo, Piazza Garibaldi 19.

Terni
Our three eating places are in or close to the large Piazza Tacito:
Da Alfio, Via Galilei. Economical.
Zi' Camillo, Via Cassian Don.
Plaza, Piazza Tacito.
The last two are in the L.1600-L.2000 class, and are worth it. But if we are only in need of a snack we should walk down the cosily commercial Corso (Cornelio Tacito) to the Piazza del Popolo, where immediately on our left as we enter we shall find a tiny *pizzeria** with every variety of delicious (and digestible) Neapolitan pizza; and all we have to do when we have eaten it is to slip next door to the café, where we shall have perhaps the finest cup of coffee in town.

Todi
Umbria, Via San Bonaventura 3. Given one star by Michelin, but not always equal to its best. Evenings are better for quiet service and attentive cooking. Laying a copy of Michelin on the table will of course help. Draught wine drinkable.

Lake Trasimene
In Passignano we have *Girarrosto-la Pineta,* Via Roma: overlooking the lake. Economical.
In Monte del Lago* we shall find excellently cooked lake fish, and some foreign wines, at the only hotel there, overlooking a particularly peaceful part of the lake. Economical. We should try their white wine from Alsace-Lorraine, if we don't mind the extra price. This and lake fish go well together. On the other hand this restaurant is not up to its old standard of a few years ago.

Trevi
Cocchetto, Piazza Mazzini. Has dishes out of the common Italian run,

357

and the owner is said to have been Mussolini's cook, though this may be legendary. They also say he can produce any fruit or vegetable, in or out of season.

APPENDIX 2

Tourist Information offices in Umbria

Assisi, Piazza del Comune 12. Tel. 81.2450
Cascia, Piazza Garibaldi. Tel. 71.147
Città di Castello, Piazza Fanti. Tel. 85.23.84
Foligno, Porta Romana. Tel. 2493
Gubbio, Piazza Oderisi. Tel. 493
Nocera Umbra. Tel. 81.273
Orvieto, Piazza del Duomo. Tel. 51.72
Perugia, Corso Vannucci 30. Tel. 3407-08
   Piazza della Libertà. Tel. 50.217
   Piazza Danti 28. Tel. 30.120
Spoleto, Piazza della Libertà. Tel. 23.190
Terni, Via Cesare Battisti. Tel. 26.106

APPENDIX 3

Suggestions for further reading

For those who read Italian, the Touring Club Italiano, Milan, produced in 1950 *Umbria*, a close-packed guide which mentions almost all of what we want to see. The series is written by local residents in each area, often friars specializing in ecclesiastical art history, which results in a tendency to apologism or plain evasion whenever the Church's behaviour is in question (the residence of the popes at Avignon is implacably referred to as 'the imprisonment of the popes'). But we shall be going to this guide for dates and names and not judgments.

After the last war the Touring Club Italiano also published a magazine-type volume on Umbria with over two hundred pages of illustrations and a clever preface giving a bird's eye view of the province and its history, in Italian of course.

As for books on Umbria's frescoes, nothing is more loving than Edward Hutton's *The Cities of Umbria* (Methuen). It could be read as a good corrective to the present volume. Hutton felt that painters like Simone Martini simply didn't care enough about painting itself, which the 'deeper' Giotto did: he called them 'pre-Renaissance'. By 'Renaissance' he meant something very Florentine, and Martini, the pupil of Duccio, remained uninfluenced by Giotto, though he survived him by seven years. Hutton also found Todi's Temple of Consolation 'one of the most lovely if not the loveliest of Renaissance churches in Italy—that is to say, in the world' (and now turn to p. 299 of this book). He has little to say about Palmerucci except that he was the contemporary of Martino Nelli (Ottaviano's father); and he makes the (for me) unbelievable statement that it was Ottaviano Nelli who began Umbrian painting. But nobody knew Italian work like Hutton. In the last war Eisenhower called on him to draw up a list of Italian monuments; so perhaps we owe their survival partly to him.

Many books of course have been written about St Francis. But perhaps the liveliest short introduction in English, which never sentimentalizes the Saint, is G. K. Chesterton's *St Francis* (Hodder & Stoughton). It leaves less impression behind it than we think it will, perhaps because of its sophistication. It is like mediaeval Assisi seen through a London fog and consoled by hot toasted muffins and heaped coal-fires.

D. H. Lawrence's *Etruscan Places* (Heinemann) is still respected even by the Etruscologists for its intuition into the life of this people: and considering what new finds have been made since Lawrence walked round Cerveteri, this is saying something for a book.

For life in the Middle Ages and the theme of chivalry and the troubadours G. G. Coulton's *Mediaeval Panorama* (Cambridge University Press and Fontana Library) is perhaps the soundest guide in English. It has a special chapter on Dante. Professor Coulton also published a study called *From St Francis to Dante* (Duckworth). *Chivalry*, a number of essays in one volume edited by Professor Edgar Prestage (Kegan Paul, 1928), deals with its civilizing influence. And for the connection between chivalry and new (Christian) concepts of love, see C. S. Lewis's *Allegory of Love* (Oxford University Press). As a completion of the picture J. Huizinga's *The Waning of the Middle Ages* (Edward Arnold and Penguin Books) is essential.

For a picture of how Europe in our sense came into being, how its feudal structure began to be broken down by the first appearance of a trading middle class in the eleventh century, nothing is more stimulating than Henri Pirenne's *A History of Europe* (Allen and Unwin), written entirely from memory during his internment in Germany during the First World War.

APPENDIX 4

Dante on Assisi

> Intra Tupino e l'acqua che discende
> del colle eletto dal beato Ubaldo,
> fertile costa d'alto monte pende,
> onde Perugia sente freddo e caldo
> da Porta Sole; e di retro le piange
> per greve giogo Nocera con Gualdo.
> Di questa costa, là dov' ella frange
> più sua rattezza, nacque al mondo un sole,
> come fa questo tal volta di Gange.
> Però che d'esso loco fa parole,
> non dica Ascesi, chè direbbe corto,
> ma Oriente, se proprio dir vole.
>
> *The Divine Comedy*, Paradise, XI

'Between the Topino and the waters that come down from the hill chosen by the Blessed Ubaldus for his retreat [*namely, the hill of Gubbio*] a fertile hillside hangs from a tall mountain [*that is, the hill of Assisi hangs from Monte Subasio, 3,870 feet*] and from there Perugia suffers cold and heat, at its Porta Sole [*that is, winds come from the direction of Assisi on to Perugia through its eastern or "sun" gate*]. On the other side [*of Monte Subasio*] Nocera and Gualdo Tadino suffer from the heavy yoke it imposes on them. But on this side, where the mountain's steepness is broken, [*that is, on the Assisi side*] a sun is born to the world, as it sometimes is from the Ganges. [*Assisi, the sun rising in the east and St Francis—Dante was a member of the third or lay Franciscan order—are all identified here, and compared to the time when the sun rises exactly from the direction of the river Ganges during the spring equinox*]. For this reason, whoever speaks about this place should not say "Assisi", for this would be inadequate, but the "East", if he wants to be exact.'

Dante himself was so exact in metaphor and geography that these

362

few lines give a marvellously clear picture of the valley between Perugia and Assisi, showing the way the sun rises on it, and the bleakness of the hills behind, together with the sharp contrasts of temperature in Perugia.

Index of Places

Index of Places

Index of Places

Index of Persons

Acodo, Count, 265

Agnes of Bohemia (1208-83), 149

Agostino di Duccio (1418-81), 42, 52, 63, 71, 284, 286

Albertus Magnus (1193-1280), 182

Albornoz, Gil Alvarez, Cardinal dell' (*ca* 1310-67), 15, 145, 251, 259, 261, 272, 327

Aldobrandini family, 260

Alessi, Galeazzo (1512-72), 29, 164, 244

Alexander VI, Pope, 304

Alunno, Lattanzio *see* Lattanzio

Alunno, Nicolò (1430-1502), 14, 142, 168, 185, 188, 191, 217, 220, 221, 224, 225, 227, 229, 230, 257

Ambrogio, Monsieur (16th c.), 74

Ambrogio da Milano (active 1473-1520), 297, 338

Amuelle, Charles d' (17th c.), 55

Ancaiani family, 156, 252

Anderson family, 260

Andrea da Bologna (14th c.), 104, 108

Andrea da Firenze (active 1343-77), 36

Andrea d'Assisi (d. 1516), 44, 165

Angelico, Fra' (1387-1455), 37, 39, 40, 41, 65, 117, 127, 189, 269, 312, 313, 344

Angelo da Orvieto (d. 1352), 202, 233, 235

Annunzio, Gabriele d' (1863-1938), 89, 195

Antoniazzo the Roman (1460-1508), 190

Antonio da Ferrara (1390/1400-49), 237, 238

Antoninus, Emperor (86-161), 278

Antony, Mark (*ca* 83-30 B.C.), 22

Aquinas, St Thomas (*ca* 1225-74), 268, 325

Aretino *see* Spinello

Armitage, Kenneth, 260

Arnolfo di Cambio (1240-*ca* 1302), 27, 64, 322

Arrigo Fiammingo *see* van den Broeck, Heinrich

Arroni family, 260

Atti family, 291; Raniero, 291

Atto, Maestro (11th c.), 217

Augustus, Emperor (63 B.C.-A.D. 14), 23, 203, 265

Baccio d'Agnolo (1462-1543), 222

373

Index of Persons

Bach, Johann Sebastian (1685-1750), 114

Baglioni family, 15, 25-6, 56, 62, 167, 181; Giovanni Andrea, 29; Guido, 26; Malatesta, 62; Rodolfo, 26

Baldassini, Udolfo *see* Ubaldus, St

Barbarossa (Emperor Frederick I, 1122-90), 13, 15, 88, 131, 180, 197, 218, 251, 262, 332, 342

Bartolocci, Giacomo, 174

Bartolo di Fredi (*ca* 1330-1410), 38, 127, 238

Bartolomeo di Tommaso (first half of 15th c.), 221, 339

Bartolommeo, Fra' (Baccio della Porta, 1472/5-1517), 49

Bartolotti (18th c.), 257

Beethoven, Ludwig van (1770-1827), 114

Belisarius (505-65), 23, 250, 303

Bellini, Giovanni (1426-1516), 207

Benedetto di Giovanni (16th c.), 72, 74

Benedetto, Jacopo *see* Ser Jacopone

Benedict, St (*ca* 480-*ca* 547), 17

Benedict XI, Pope, 64

Benvenuto da Brescia, (16th c.), 74

Berenson, Bernard (1865-1959), 230

Bernardine of Siena, St (1340-1444), 29, 52, 126, 135, 167, 168, 169, 171

Bernardino Antonibi da Perugia (active 1516-22), 74

Bernardino di Betto *see* Pintoricchio

Bernardino di Mariotto (d. 1566), 42, 222

Bernardino di Nanni (d. 1495), 202, 210

Bernardo di Girolamo (16th c.), 64

Bernardone, Giovanni *see* Francis, St

Bernardone, Pietro, 138

Bernini, Giovanni Lorenzo (1598-1680), 217, 263, 335

Berto di Giovanni (16th c.), 42

Bevignate, Fra' (1259-92), 27, 198, 305

Biancone, Friar Giacomo, 182

Bicci di Lorenzo (1373-1452), 127

Binello (13th c.), 175, 183, 184

Bolognese, Battista (16th c.), 74

Bonaventura, St (1221-74), 124, 162, 167

Bonfigli, Benedetto (active 1445-96), 23, 40, 41, 42, 58, 75

Boniface VIII, Pope, 319, 321

Borgia family, 260; Cesare, 313; Lucretia, 40, 251, 259; Valentino, 259; *see* also Alexander VI, Pope

Borromeo, St Charles (1538-84), 168

Bosch, Hieronymus (*ca* 1460-1518), 339

Brancaleone da Norcia, 14

Braye, Cardinal Guglielmo di, 325

Brunamonte, Alinda Bonnacci, 60

374

375

376

Index of Persons

380

"Few things about S Francis are more fascinating than the speed with which his ideas were accepted." Vernon Bartlett 'Central Italy'

b. 1182.

26 when he founded franciscan order.

Pope's approval within 2 yrs.

1224 (14 yrs later) he received stigmata in the monastery of la Verna

1226   he d—

1228   canonized.

1182
d. 44 yrs old

Giotto b. 40 yrs later.

Crenellated walls.

Horizontal 'merlons' Guelph

Fish tailed merlons Ghibelline

Guelphs tended to support popes.
Ghibellines "   "   "   emperors.
(names taken from 2 rival families in
S. Germany. Their origin had 0 to do with
Italy)   They hired mercenaries to fight
their wars + Rivalled each other in
encouraging artists + writers during the
Renaissance –

   Giotto 13 37 d. ⎞
   ~~Donatello~~ –   ⎞ painting.
   Jacopo della Quercia ⎞ sculpting.
   Brunelleschi –

   according to taste
     Leonardo
     Michelangelo –

  Medici – Florence + large part of Tuscany.
       (1434 – 1494 approx)
  Visconti – later Sforza   based Milan .
  lucky w/c. Genoa, Bologna. Verona. Pisa. Siena

  Scaligeri – Verona.
  Gonzaga Mantua.
  Este Ferrara
  Montefeltro. Urbino Ghibellines
  Malatesta – Rimini. Guelphs